Woodwind Instruments and Their History

Anthony Baines

With a foreword by
Sir Adrian Boult

DOVER PUBLICATIONS, INC.
New York

Copyright © 1967, 1968, 1977, 1991 by Anthony Baines.
All rights reserved under Pan American and International Copyright Conventions.

Published in Canada by General Publishing Company, Ltd., 30 Lesmill Road, Don Mills, Toronto, Ontario.
Published in the United Kingdom by Constable and Company, Ltd., 3 The Lanchesters, 162–164 Fulham Palace Road, London W6 9ER.

This Dover edition, first published in 1991, is an unabridged republication of the third edition, published by Faber & Faber Limited, London, 1967, as reprinted with corrections in 1977. (The first edition was published in 1957.)

Manufactured in the United States of America
Dover Publications, Inc., 31 East 2nd Street, Mineola, N.Y. 11501

Library of Congress Cataloging-in-Publication Data

Baines, Anthony.
    Woodwind instruments and their history / Anthony Baines ; with a foreword by Sir Adrian Boult.
        p.   cm.
    "An unabridged republication of the third edition, published by Faber & Faber Limited, London, 1967, as reprinted with corrections in 1977"—T.p. verso.
    Includes bibliographical references and index.
    ISBN 0-486-26885-3 (pbk.)
    1. Woodwind instruments.   I. Title.
[ML931.B3 1991]
788.2'19—dc20   91-23745
                                                                       CIP
                                                                       MN

To the memory of
JASPER RIDLEY
1943

Foreword

by SIR ADRIAN BOULT

Anyone who pursues an artistic life often comes in contact with enthusiasts, and I always enjoy this when it happens to me. There are, of course, enthusiasts of two kinds: those whose enthusiasm throws their general judgement somewhat out of gear, and those who can keep their sense of proportion with their enthusiasm.

Anthony Baines is emphatically of the latter group. His knowledge—as anyone can see on glancing at this book—is encyclopaedic, but he has been able to do sterling and successful work as a conductor, not only of concerts, but also in the more difficult and responsible field of ballet. He graduated to the conductor's desk by the most thorough and complete route, a seat in the orchestra. As a bassoonist he has occupied a pivotal position (artistically as well as geographically) between the woodwind and brass, and has also often carried a weightier and even more responsible burden in the wind department when in charge of the contrafagotto.

Wind instruments, however, have always been his particular interest, and he has since turned his whole time to their study and practice. He is now occupied at Uppingham with seventy pupils who are learning wind instruments and so qualifying for membership of the many orchestral societies which are stimulating musical experience up and down the country. This book will, I hope, appeal to a much larger public than his own pupils, for orchestral music is becoming an interest for almost everyone, and surely the fascinating story of the different instruments, as told here, will be widely appreciated.

Contents

9

CONTENTS

CONTENTS

CONTENTS

CONTENTS

Illustrations

15

ILLUSTRATIONS

LIST OF FIGURES

ILLUSTRATIONS

ILLUSTRATIONS

Preface

More persons than ever before are now learning to play orchestral instruments. And no wonder, in view of the enormous stimulus given by broadcasting and the gramophone not only to listen to music, but also to perform it. And from this last aspect, the woodwind instruments have perhaps proved an especial attraction, offering a choice of four instruments of the first importance in music, all equally fascinating to play, equally suitable for starting at any time of life and equally quickly mastered up to a certain point by anyone with a reasonably good ear and lively intelligence—though as difficult as any other kind of instrument to play really well. Their parts in orchestral music provide an inexhaustible source of subtle interest and exhilarating excitement, while in solo and chamber music they have a rich share. The present book offers a general, technical and historical background to the study of these instruments, whether practical or appreciative (a non-playing reader will probably prefer to skip certain sections devoted entirely to keywork and fingering). For reasons of space, certain things, including woodwind manufacture and woodwind in orchestration, have been touched upon only very lightly, in order to deal more fully with the nature of the instruments and the playing of them. Nor are lists of solo and chamber music included, since these could only be repetitions of excellent lists already available, as those in F. B. Chapman, *Flute Technique*, Evelyn Rothwell, *Oboe Technique*, and F. G. Rendall, *The Clarinet*. A survey of bassoon music, of which there is plenty, is, at the time of writing, projected by the well-known player William Waterhouse [printed in Camden, 1962; see Bibliography, *Bassoon*].

The book is composed of two Parts. *Part One* deals with the existing woodwind instruments (including many related species found in bands of various kinds but not in orchestras). *Part Two* (*History*) is concerned with early forms of the woodwind instruments and with their precursors, many of these being described in considerable technical detail, though no finality is claimed for the rules and conclusions given; practical musical study in ancient, exotic and primitive wind instruments is still a young branch of musicology in which fresh discoveries are being made every year.

The names of all the friends and colleagues to whom acknowledgement is due for information and kindnesses during the preparation of this book would make too long a list to give here, though to Mr Philip Bate, Mr Thurston Dart, Mr Eric Halfpenny, Mr Bernard Izen, Mr and Mrs J. A. MacGillivray, Mr R. Morley Pegge and Mr Frank Rendell I feel particularly indebted. But I must add this: if any person who loves wind instruments has any query or difficulty in connection with them, let him not hesitate to accost a professional wind-player, no matter how celebrated he may be nor from what part of the world he may come, for there are no more kindly and understanding people in the world.

ANTHONY BAINES

London, 1956

Note to 2nd Edition

Firstly I welcome this opportunity of thanking all the musicians and scholars who have expressed their appreciation of this book since its first appearance. Then I must thank especially those who have drawn my attention to errors, and made expert suggestions for revision or amplification, even if space prevents mention, in this fresh edition, of all the new and interesting things that have happened or come to light during the past few years in this subject of Woodwind, which, with all the work nowadays being done in all its aspects, grows into a larger one every day.

ANTHONY BAINES

Uppingham, 1961

Note to 3rd Edition

Changes from the 2nd edition amount to some minor corrections, additions to the bibliography, and the incorporation in the index of references to instruments shown in the illustrations. An attempt to bring the text consistently up-to-date has not been made; it seems to me better, at any rate for the time being, to let the book rest as a record of the woodwind scene as this appeared when it was written, even though, for instance, some of the musicians named have since retired, died, or moved to different orchestras, and certain historical conclusions could now be amplified in the light of the most recent research.

ANTHONY BAINES

Cheltenham, 1967

PART ONE

The Woodwind Instruments Today

CHAPTER I

General Introduction

The Woodwind Section

As most readers of this book will already know, the woodwind is a small cluster of musicians in whom the greatest virtuosity in the symphony or opera orchestra is concentrated. It is the orchestra's principal solo section, containing, in relation to its small strength in numbers, the highest proportion of star players of all the sections that make up the orchestra. They are stars because composers for over two hundred years have made them so, having entrusted to them those passages and motifs of their music which, by their nature, especially demand utterance by chosen solo voices raised above the orchestra's time-honoured foundation of strings.

Befitting its role, the woodwind section has a unique type of constitution, being basically composed of four unlike-sounding wind instruments—flute, oboe, clarinet and bassoon—with two players of each, and the story of how this amazingly successful and enduring alliance was arrived at makes an interesting subject on its own. Very briefly (for the subject is fully dealt with in Adam Carse's well-known works), it runs as follows. The string section, which forms a homogeneous and logically harmonious group of instruments, was born in the consort days of the sixteenth century, when part-writing held first place in music. The woodwind, by contrast, is a creation of the eighteenth century, when the emphasis had shifted towards pure melody, and it developed primarily as a kind of musical paintbox of contrasted melodic tone-colours; not as a 'consort'. Its actual birth had taken place just earlier, in Lully's time, when the oboe was invented in France. The essence of the section had then been a pair of oboists; a pair was needed in order to accommodate the old predilection for writing melodies in thirds for two identical instruments, and the two players were known as the 'First' (or 'Principal') and the 'Second' respectively, titles which remain in use throughout the section today. When a composer of those early days required a fresh woodwind colour in the course of an opera or oratorio, the oboists laid down their oboes and took flutes, recorders or other instruments for the number in question. Completing this primitive woodwind section were one or, more often, two bassoonists, whose job was at first mainly to supply it with its own independent bass.

With the generation of Handel and Bach, the section began to be expanded to include specialist flute-players (and during this period the oboists and bassoonists were frequently doubled in order to boost their contribution in choruses and tuttis, for woodwind instruments then possessed nothing like the penetrating power they possess now). Next followed a stroke of genius on the part of the eighteenth century, namely, blending into the little woodwind choir the formal supporting harmony of a pair of horns, and the horn-players have ever since remained the woodwind's closest associates under the hand of the composer. Finally, by about 1780, most important orchestras in Europe had come to adopt a pair of clarinets, invented in Germany about eighty years before. With this, the classical woodwind section of eight musicians was completed.

The four main woodwind instruments—flute, oboe, clarinet and bassoon—are so well contrasted in colour, yet so perfectly balanced in their tonal weight and expressive resources, that in the great majority of orchestral compositions composers have asked for no more. For special effects, however, and for richer blends in works of large proportions, a composer can draw upon a range of reserve colours. Four of these are permanently available in a modern full-sized orchestra: piccolo, cor anglais (the deep contralto oboe), bass clarinet and contrabassoon, these often being referred to as the 'extra' instruments, while specialist performers on each of them then bring the woodwind personnel up to twelve. Often it approaches or reaches sixteen, as when a composer has written for more than three of each of the main instruments with 'extras' as well; or when he has also included one or more of the rarely-demanded 'special' instruments, as bass flute, oboe d'amore, heckelphone, small clarinet, basset horn or saxophone.

Fingering charts and diagrams

The characteristic that all these woodwind instruments have in common is that they are all 'pipes', that is to say, wind instruments on which the different notes are made primarily by covering and uncovering holes in the side of the tube with the fingers. Many non-woodwind people will understand this principle through experience with the tin whistle, or with the

Fig. 1. *Designation of notes.*

recorder (which is by rights a genuine woodwind instrument, scored for by Purcell, Bach and Handel in many of their best-known works).

Before discussing woodwind instruments and their technique we therefore need to decide upon some concise method of describing the fingerings of the various notes, and also upon a distinctive symbol for every particular note. For the latter, more and more musical writers today are adopting the ancient German system shown in fig. 1, and we shall do the same. (The older way of this system, with lines above a letter instead of ticks after it, and with double letters for the contrabass octave, may be seen in figs. 57, etc., Chapter X.)

Next, a description of the fingerings. Down the front of any woodwind instrument are the six symmetrically-positioned holes (or sometimes finger-plates) for the application of the three main fingers of each hand. The left hand takes the uppermost three positions and the right hand the lowermost three. We shall number these consecutively from I to VI; I to III for the left hand, and IV to VI for the right hand. In *fingering charts*, a *black spot* indicates that a finger is to close its hole or plate, and a *hollow circle* that it is to be raised from it. As an example, the fingering for *e'* on flute or oboe will appear thus:

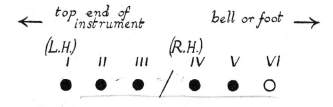

or, for short, . . . / . . o, meaning: put down fingers I to V but not finger VI. With instruments that have a hole or plate for the left thumb, the thumb (*Th*) is generally assumed to be applied unless indication is given to the contrary; but on the bassoon, both thumbs are raised except where it is otherwise indicated.

A *key* is named after the principal note for which it is provided, and this is given in the charts in a position corresponding to that of the finger that actuates the key. For example, . . . G♯ / o o o for flute etc. means: put down the three left hand fingers and press the G♯ key, which, as the mechanism diagrams will show, is for the little finger of the same hand. Again, . . o / B♭ o o o on Boehm clarinet means: put down fingers I and II, and press the B♭ key for finger IV—a 'side key', operated by the middle joint of that finger. Keys provided solely for trills are named after the trill; thus a *b'/c''* *tr* key is for making the semitone trill on B.

The first thing for a beginner is to obtain a clear sound without covering more than one or two of the holes. Next, he will progressively cover the holes in direct order—putting the fingers down smartly, using the muscles well—starting with finger I, then adding finger II (or the thumb, according to the instrument) and so on until all holes are covered. This gives the instrument's basic series of notes. The direct order is, however, departed from in many instances in order to obtain other notes (e.g. putting down fingers I, II and III, and then VI—instead of IV—to make F♯ on the Boehm flute). This is termed *cross-fingering*. The special term *fork-fingering* is used when only the first and third fingers of a hand are put down, as in the 'forked F' on the oboe and simple-system clarinet (. . . / . o .) and the middle E♭ on the bassoon (. o . / o o o). Fingering charts for each of the main current designs are given in Chapters II to VI, though there is no room to include all the alternative fingerings for high notes and trills.

Basic woodwind acoustics

How does a woodwind instrument produce its sound? The foundations of a scientific explanation were laid by Helmholtz in his wave theory of 1862, and although modern research has suggested a number of modifications to this theory, its basic propositions remain in general acceptance today. There is no space to go fully and scientifically into it here (full accounts are given in books on musical acoustics); the following section is intended only as an introduction to the subject and a short explanation of important things like tone-colour and over-blowing.

For a wind instrument to sound a note, the column of air inside its tube must somehow be set and maintained in vibration. Merely blowing into a tube will not, of course, effect this. We need, at the top end of the instrument, some contrivance or 'generator' that will set up a fast, rhythmical beating under the impact of the breath. This beating, the 'generating frequency', then acts upon the head of the air-column, setting the air-particles in oscillation. Each air-particle can (according to the theory) oscillate a minute distance up and down the tube, and the particles at one point pass on their motion to those at the next, which causes waves of pressure to travel down the tube at the speed of sound. (This explains, incidentally, why a wind-instrument may have as many bends or loops in it as we care to make, and yet perform satisfactorily.)

Having traversed the length of the air-column, i.e. having reached the hole or key opened for the note in question, the pressure-waves become reflected back upon themselves. The effect of this is to modify the motion of the air-particles in a characteristic way, building up *nodes* and *antinodes* at definite points along the air-column. A node is formed where interference between opposite waves deprives the particles of their motion while the to-and-fro motion of neighbouring particles subjects the point to a regular pulsation of alternate high and low pressure. At antinodes, on the other hand, the particles move with their maximum swing and the pressure remains constant; there is an antinode, for instance, wherever the air-column is open to the outer air. In this way, a regular, self-contained vibration of the air-column—a 'stationary wave'—is at once built up within the tube, and it is this that produces the note. An analogous thing happens with a violin string: reflection of disturbances builds up a stationary wave in which the string has a maximum side-to-side motion at the middle (antinode) and none at the ends (nodes). In a flute, the phenomena are similar but opposite: there is maximum to-and-fro air-movement at the ends, where the air-column is open to the outer air (antinodes, A, A); and a stationary layer half-way between, where interference reaches its maximum (node, N); thus: A–N–A.

The pitch of the note depends upon the frequency of the stationary wave, i.e. upon the number of pressure-pulsations per second at the node (or of to-and-fro oscillations at an antinode). This in turn depends upon the length of the air-column. When this is increased by closing more holes, the pressure waves have further to travel before reflection, and hence there are fewer reflections per second. This means a slower pulsation-frequency of the resulting stationary wave, i.e. a deeper note. However, the frequency is always pretty fast, as one can sense in the tingling felt at the antinode when a finger is held just above the hole from which a note is sounding, or close by the mouth-hole of a flute. For middle C, the bottom note of the flute, the frequency is over two hundred vibrations per second.

There is, of course, a bodily drift of the air down the tube due to the player's blowing, but this has no acoustical significance, being far too slow in comparison with the sonic speed of pressure-wave transmission to have any bearing on the nature of the stationary wave and the note it gives rise to. Harder blowing does, however, produce more powerful generating impulses, which in turn give a wider swing to the air-particles and a more intense variation of pressure at the nodes, and hence as we know, a louder note.

GENERATION OF THE SOUND. With the reed instruments (i.e. all the main woodwind instruments except the flute) the generating frequency is that of the opening and closing of the reed as it vibrates in the breath stream. With the flute, it is due to the rapid fluttering of the whirlpools or eddies that form in the air in quick succession as the player's breath leaves his lips in a thin stream directed against the far edge of the mouth-hole in the flute. These eddies have been shown to follow one another alternately below and above the direction of the stream, and hence to exert a kind of alternate pushing and sucking effect on the head of the air-column, setting the air-particles in oscillation and so dispatching pressure-waves down the tube.

With any wind instrument, the generating frequency must keep matched to that of the air-column as this changes when one goes from note to note. For the most part, the generating frequency is automatically kept in step through the powerful, regulating back-effect of the air-column pulsation, though the player assists to some extent by sub-conscious lip and breath action. However, the player can also, within small limits, deliberately make the generator drag on the air-column, or hasten it, forcing the frequency of the latter to drop or rise a little below or above its natural value, i.e. flattening or sharpening the note. He does this mainly with his lips, and it provides him with his fine adjustment—the means by which the playing is kept in tune. For it is virtually impossible for a maker to construct an instrument that will be automatically dead in tune on every note whoever plays it and in whatever circumstances, and in woodwind playing, practising included, the ears have to be alert the whole time to detect any note that requires pulling in tune with the lip. When this point is not realized, scales and melodies are likely to be played with intervals that are anything but the tones and semitones they should be.

HARMONICS. If one blows a rich, deep note on an instrument and listens to it long and carefully, one soon begins to hear, besides the note itself, some of its overtones or *harmonics*, sounding at various intervals like octave and twelfth above it. The explanation is that the simple or *fundamental* mode of stationary-wave vibration that we have so far described (and have symbolized as A–N–A for flute) forms only part of the picture while a note is sounding, since numerous *harmonic* vibrations proceed simultaneously with it. With these harmonics, the air column subdivides into smaller sections, introducing two, three or many more fresh nodes, with corresponding fresh antinodes between them.

For a simple picture of harmonics, we may write down their nodes and antinodes in rows of symbols. The fundamental is conventionally numbered as the first harmonic so that the numbers match the sense as we go up the series:

Fundamental (1st harmonic)	A			N			A
2nd harmonic	A		N		A	N		A
3rd harmonic	A	N		A	N	A	N	A
4th harmonic	A	N	A	N	A	N	A	N	A
etc.								

Each harmonic has a definite frequency in relation to the fundamental. The 2nd harmonic pulsates at double the speed of the fundamental (since its wave distance is half), and in musical sound a doubled frequency means an octave higher; i.e. the 2nd harmonic is pitched an octave above the fundamental. Tripled frequency (3rd harmonic) means a twelfth higher in pitch (an octave and a half), and so on. Fig. 2 shows the pitches of the first thirteen harmonics of middle C.

These harmonics are important in two ways. Firstly, they are responsible for an instrument's *tone-colour*. Secondly, they enable an instrument's compass to be extended upwards through several registers (*overblowing*). We will briefly consider tone-colour first.

GENERAL INTRODUCTION

The presence of many superimposed harmonic modes of vibration whilst a note is sounding, naturally modifies the motion of each individual air-particle and gives the sum vibration a complex character. In books on musical acoustics, this complexity is usually pictured by wave diagrams obtained with an oscilloscope: an instrument's pressure-wave vibration is electrically translated into interlooping wave lines visible on a screen. There we see that the wave is full of kinks, indicating the superimposition of harmonics upon the fundamental; and by mathematical analysis of the kinks the harmonics can be identified.

The human ear also sorts out the complex wave. It detects the lowest harmonic present (the fundamental in the cases we

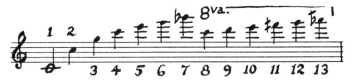

Fig. 2. *The harmonic series of middle C, up to number 13. (The signs before notes 11 and 13 denote sharpness and flatness respectively of about a quarter-tone. The 7th harmonic is also a little flat.)*

are now considering)—however weakly it may be present—and reports it to the brain as the pitch-note, i.e. the actual note we recognize. Simultaneously it reports the total mixture of harmonics as tone-colour. Tone-colour, or tone-quality, is almost entirely due to the proportionate strength and number of the component harmonics, and in fig. 3, adapted in a simple way from specimen 'tonal spectra' published in scientific form by Professor Bernard Hague, we can compare at a glance tone-colour as we hear it with tone-colour as the physicist analyses it. White notes, large and small, indicate harmonics strongly present in the note; black notes, the fainter ones. All are low-register examples (and in some cases we see that the fundamental is only just present) and all of course concern only the sustained tone, leaving out of consideration the various speeds with which different harmonics may attain their peak strength when the note is attacked—a factor that makes the 'attack' of each instrument so characteristic.

Spectrum 1 was obtained from a simple-system conical flute, while 2, from a Boehm flute, shows the more brilliant, reedy tone of a note richer in high harmonics. We see why the tone of the oboe sounds yet more reedy (3), but that of the bassoon (4) less markedly so. If their sounds are recorded and reproduced in such a manner as to cut out their higher frequencies, they become more flute-like. Of course, the above are only single examples; we know well enough how tone-quality can vary with

FIG. 3. *The harmonic composition or tonal spectrum of various woodwind notes, adapted from Hague: 1 and 2, flute; 3, oboe; 4, bassoon; 5, clarinet.*

different players and different designs of instrument. Nevertheless an oboe, say, almost always sounds unmistakably an oboe, and acousticians are now trying to pin down the basic causes behind this—the physical factors that determine an instrument's characteristic type of tonal spectrum. Small finger-holes tend to impede the escape of high harmonics, thus mellowing the sound; narrow bores are said to favour the presence of high harmonics; on reed instruments, harmonics that fall within certain zones of pitch ('formants') tend to dominate the spectrum—as the c'' is doing in the bassoon note in fig. 3. Many such things have been investigated, but a comprehensive explanation has not yet been reached.

STOPPED PIPES AND THE CLARINET. It will be noticed that the tonal spectrum of the clarinet (5) differs from the others in that it is composed principally of odd-numbered harmonics. This is a well-known characteristic of a *stopped pipe*.

Straightforward examples of a stopped pipe are those instruments of the flute class that are stopped at the lower end. as panpipe tubes and stopped organ pipes. The top end is open, with a free antinode there as usual. But at the stopped end, where the air cannot move to and fro, we have a node equivalent to the node half-way along an open-ended pipe like the flute. If we make a stopped pipe by placing a partition half-way down an open pipe, we obtain the same fundamental as we did without the partition; our half-pipe, A–N, really represents A–N–A folded back on itself like a carpenter's rule. The pressure-waves' journey-distance from antinode to antinode remains the same although the *tube-length* is now but half as long. A $12\frac{1}{2}$-inch panpipe tube gives the same note as a 25-inch flute. But the tone-quality is different.

This is because the harmonics are different. A 2nd harmonic, subdividing a stopped pipe into two equal parts and having half the fundamental's A–N distance, would require an antinode at the stopped end (A–N–A), which is impossible. For the same reason, all the other even-numbered harmonics are ruled out. Only the odd-numbered fulfil the conditions, thus:

Fundamental (1st harmonic)	A					N
3rd harmonic	A	N		A		N
5th harmonic	A	N	A	N	A	N
etc.						

Except as organ pipes, stopped flutes have failed to become advanced musical instruments since one cannot employ finger-holes on them. An opened hole would at once un-stop the pipe. Nevertheless, one of the class has appeared in the orchestra: the Swannee whistle, a nineteenth-century bird-whistle now familiar as a toy instrument (fig. 76). Ravel scores for it in *Les Enfants et les Sortilèges* under the name *flûte à coulisse* ('slide flute'), and also Gavin Gordon in his ballet *The Rake's Progress*. It is played by one of the percussion players, like the siren in a theatre orchestra.

But another class of instruments also comes into the stopped pipe category, namely *reed instruments with cylindrical bore*, and this group includes the clarinet.

If the clarinet air-column is excited percussively, by banging the fingers down on the holes without putting the instrument to the mouth, it will give the same pitches, length for length, as a flute, being in this condition an open pipe. If the experiment is repeated, but with the reed pressed closed with the thumb, the tube becomes a stopped pipe. It now gives pitches roughly an octave lower than it did before, since every tube-length that previously represented A–N–A now represents N—A, i.e. the waves' journey-distance has been doubled. (The pitches may in fact be rather less than an octave lower, chiefly on account of 'end-correction': an air-column never terminates exactly at a hole or an open end, but overflows a little beyond it; interfering with one end, as by stopping, therefore gives an air-column with a different total of end-corrections, hence a slightly different pitch.)

Now when the clarinet is being played, we again get these deep fundamental pitches, showing that the top end is, in effect, again stopped. The lips seal it from atmospheric pressure, while the reed (as modern research has suggested) alternately holds itself bent inwards, virtually closing the aperture, and springs open for a brief instant to communicate an energizing stab of breath-pressure. Thus in a reed instrument of this class, we have a stopped pipe in which, since it is excited at the stopped end, finger-holes can be employed freely. The type of reed is immaterial. Clarinet and the old Welsh pibcorn have single-bladed reeds ('single reeds'); bagpipe practice-chanter, sixteenth-century crumhorn, and the ancient Greek aulos have, or had, twin-bladed reeds ('double reeds'). All have only odd-numbered harmonics in their tonal spectrum save for some even-numbered harmonics that may be weakly present since stopped-pipe conditions are not quite perfectly reproduced (e.g. the black notes in 5, fig. 3).

REED INSTRUMENTS WITH CONICAL BORE (or perhaps better, 'expanding bore', to avoid confusion with the contracting conical bore of the recorder and the old conical flute) form a third major class of pipe, and include oboe, bassoon and saxophone, the first two having double reeds and the last a single reed. Their behaviour is acoustically mysterious. Again, when the fingers are banged down with the instrument out of the mouth, we of course get normal open-pipe pitches as with a flute. But when the reed is pressed closed, or when the instrument is being played, we get fundamentals pitched about a third or a fourth deeper, as if the air-column were projected back, in imagination, to the true apex of the cone-bore, which is in most cases several inches beyond the reed (down the player's throat, as it were). Moreover, both sets of harmonics, odd and even, are represented in the tonal spectrum. Mathematicians can explain these things by means of formulae derived from the fact that the wave-front in these bores is not flat, but a segment of the surface of a sphere. An explanation intelligible to the layman seems yet to be worked out.

OVERBLOWING. If the fundamental vibration is completely eliminated, the next-highest harmonic becomes the pitch-note to the ear. It is commonly eliminated, when this is required, by speeding up the generating frequency. This is how a bugler plays his calls—by tightening his lips, making their vibration faster until one by one the lower harmonics of the tube have to drop out, being too slow to respond. He employs thus harmonics numbers two to six. On the flute, the fundamentals provide the notes of the low register. Then, to sound the *upper register*, the player accelerates the generating frequency (by means of his lips and breathing) so that the fundamentals drop out and the second harmonics take over as the pitch-notes and the scale is repeated an octave higher. A bassoonist obtains the same result by slightly increased pressure on the reed. On both the instruments just mentioned, however, the lowest notes of the upper register are helped by opening or half opening hole I, which admits atmospheric pressure to break up the fundamental's mid-way node and strengthen the 2nd harmonic's mid-way antinode. On the other reed instruments the upper register is obtained entirely, or (with the modern oboe) almost entirely, after this second principle, through opening an 'octave key', or with the clarinet 'speaker' or 'register' key. On the clarinet, the harmonic thereby established in command is not the 2nd, but the 3rd—sounding a twelfth above the fundamental—on account of the instrument's stopped-pipe nature already described.

To continue above the upper register into the *high register*, appropriate finger-holes are uncovered to establish higher harmonics as the basis of the notes: the 3rd, 4th and 5th harmonics (on the clarinet, the 5th, 7th and 9th). On the Boehm flute the only 3rd harmonic normally used is that of the low G, giving *d'''* (and made by opening hole I); the succeeding 3rd harmonics are too flat to be employed except in emergencies (e.g. trills), and so 4th harmonics (two octaves above the fundamentals) are used instead. These last are obtained in a way analogous to artificial harmonics on the violin: a hole is uncovered three-quarters of the way down from the cork, i.e. the G♯ key is opened for *e'''♭*, the A hole (finger III) for *e'''* and so on. Above these, high A is made as a 5th harmonic of low F by opening holes at four-fifths of the F tube-length (raising finger III) and at three-fifths (finger I); and high B similarly as a 5th harmonic of low G, lifting finger II and opening the second trill key (fig. 4). Top C is made analogously as 6th harmonic of low F.

In the clarinet high register, 5th harmonics are normally used for six or seven notes, and above these, 7th and 9th harmonics (fig. 4). To obtain most of these notes, hole I is opened as well as the speaker key. The oboe's high register is based mainly on 3rd harmonics, though the fingerings are rendered complex through the need for securing good tuning and stabilizing resonance in the lower parts of the tube. On some models (e.g. the Viennese and the older simple-system designs) one brings in 3rd harmonics earlier, namely from the *a''* or the *b''♭* of the upper register—as one does on the recorder, where *b''♭* of the descant is made as a sharp-sounding 3rd harmonic of low D, and also on the bassoon, where the corresponding note is *e'♭*. The high register of the bassoon is obtained by sharp-sounding harmonics that almost defy analysis. To give two of the less mystifying examples, *a'* and *e''♭* on the German model are made as 3rd and 4th harmonics of low-register *c♯* (theoretically *g'♯* and *c''♯* respectively).

On the flute and occasionally on the oboe, special harmonic

fingerings not ordinarily employed are now and then used for the sake of their ethereal tone-quality. Sometimes this is especially asked for by a composer. For example, in Stravinsky's *Rite of Spring* at figure 87 in the score, three flutes play the chord g'', c''', e''' marked *Flag.*, i.e. 'flageolet tone' and meaning harmonics of low C made with the embouchure alone.

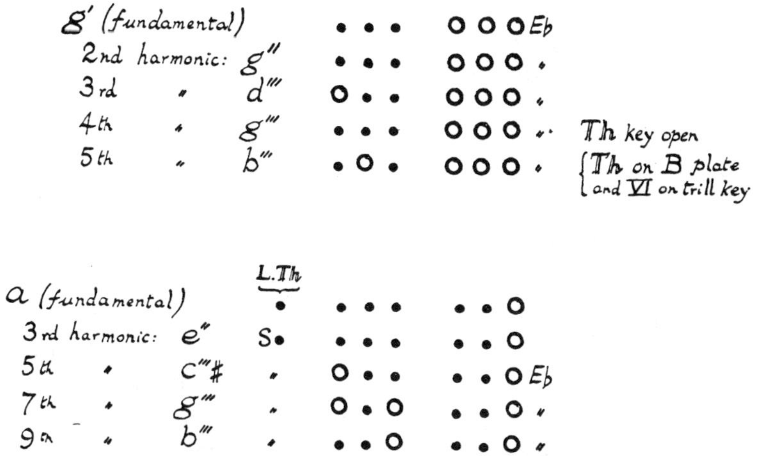

FIG. 4. *Examples illustrating the use of harmonics in normal fingering.* Above, *Boehm flute, notes derived from the low G.* Below, *Boehm-system clarinet, notes derived from the low A.* (*S: open the speaker key; E♭: open the E♭ key.*)

Tonguing and Breathing

The tongue is used in wind-playing to give a note or phrase a clean start (*tonguing,* or *articulation*). The general rule is that every note written in the music is to be tongued unless there is a slur to it from the preceding note—'tongued' meaning a movement of the tongue similar to that made when pronouncing the letter *T*. On the reed instruments it is done by placing the tip of the tongue lightly against the reed, and then drawing it back to release the reed in the breath pressure. It feels, on the whole, more like *N*. On the flute, it is by a *T* against the palate, behind the upper teeth. Besides *T*, some other tongue-movements of speech are made use of in wind-playing; *K* (with the back of the tongue), occasionally *L* (with the sides of the tongue) and trilled *R*, all variously employed in the double and flutter tonguing described further on. The flute can also be sounded with a labial articulation *P* (with the lips alone) and this has sometimes been recommended for beginners first learning to produce the high notes gently. Yet another flute tonguing utilizes a movement not found in speech though it is common in brass playing, namely drawing the tip of the tongue backwards from the upper lip. Many flutists use this as well as, or instead of, the more usual *T* described above.

There are various exceptions to the general rule for tonguing: (1) When a long slur is placed over an entire phrase which includes repeated notes (as for instance over the first six bars of the National Anthem in some band editions); the slur is here intended merely as a general indication of smoothness, and the notes are lightly separated by tonguing. (2) When a slur occurs in combination with dots or lines over the notes. *Dots* over the notes under a slur indicate *semi-staccato*; each note is lightly tongued, and the breath is made to fall away less suddenly on each note than in plain staccato, giving the phrase a subtle forward impetus. *Lines* over notes under a slur indicate *semi-sostenuto*; the notes are tongued and well held, the breath being even pushed a little on each note. Both these last indications are really borrowed from violin writing, and it is of help to the wind beginner to visualize a violinist's method of bowing them, remembering that the true woodwind equivalent to the motion of the fiddle bow, with its fine gradations of speed and pressure, is the breath. The tongue merely releases breath and generator at the right instant, and the 'attack' too is as much a matter of breathing as of tonguing.

Accents (arrow-heads) under a slur ('slurred accents') are, on the other hand, generally intended to be made entirely with the breathing, without tonguing. Thus here the general rule applies, as it also does where two or more notes are slurred together and there is a dot over the last only; the dot in this case shows that the last note is to be cut off short (not tongued).

Important above all in wind-playing is the pure sustained

sound of the instrument, which learners have been taught to develop ever since Mozart's time by practising long-held notes, starting each softly, then swelling it, and finally dying away, all the time watching that the note goes neither flat nor sharp, and listening to its quality. In this simple exercise one can also pay attention to proper intake and control of the breath. Everybody agrees that the correct way to breathe is to sit up naturally, with the shoulders relaxed, and to breathe in and out mainly with the diaphragm and lower ribs. This helps development of an expressive, musical phrasing, like the finest singing—the all-important cantabile manner of playing, in which the model for the instrumentalist is, as the word tells us, singing. In Vienna, the highest praise for a woodwind player is to be likened to a great opera singer. Tight, shallow breathing from the top of the chest, on the other hand, can lead to lifeless playing at a monotonous mezzoforte, and also to poor control; for correct breathing is of great help in overcoming tonguing, slurring and pitching difficulties. The wide expressive range expected from a well-played wind instrument is very well conveyed on paper by Mahler's scores. Mahler, who loved and understood instruments to a monumental degree, left little to chance. He marks in the parts full and precise directions (e.g. fig. 18) where most other composers would have left things to the player's musicianship and experience, contenting themselves with a conventional *p* or *f*, an *espr.*, a *dolce*, or an *en dehors*.

DOUBLE-TONGUING. At fast speeds it may become difficult to keep up the T strokes without flagging or stumbling. This is where double-tonguing comes in. It is normally by T–K–T–K–, using the tip and back of the tongue alternately. In triplets, it is T–K–T—T–K–T-, or (better for dotted triplets) T–T–K—T–T–K-. With the flute, the K stroke is so efficient that double-tonguing in fast passages forms part of everyday technique, and composers sometimes even especially indicate it, e.g. by slur and dots over every pair of notes, or by two dots above one single note. On the reed instruments, the K stroke, deprived of direct contact with the reed, theoretically gives a less positive attack than T, yet with practice the two become perfectly equalized and hundreds of oboists, clarinettists and bassoonists use *T–K–* for fast passages; it may be learnt by practising triplets in a French way, *T–K–T—K–T–K*, which shows up the *K* very clearly.

An older kind of flute double-tonguing, said to be still used by a few players, is that which used to be described in England as *tootle-tootle* (and in Germany as *didd'l-didd'l*). For triplets, *tootle-too*.

When a reed player who does not double-tongue finds his single-tonguing defeated by the speed of a passage, the normal expedient is now and then to slur together a pair of notes the first of which falls upon a strong beat; or to slur the first two in every group of four, known as 'slur two, tongue two'.

FLUTTER-TONGUING, sometimes demanded from flute and clarinet, is generally done by trilling the tip of the tongue (as Italian *R*), but it can also be done by making the uvula vibrate (as French *R*; like a motor-bicycle starting up).

ANTIQUARIAN DOUBLE-TONGUING. Up to the early years of the nineteenth century, double-tonguing was not only an expedient for overcoming speed difficulties, but was introduced on medium-fast notes to bring out the rhythm or lilt of a passage. This makes it a subject that people who specialize in playing early music evidently should study, though it is no simple matter, because the double-tonguing then employed was not our *T–K–*, but a mysterious *T–R–*, which Drouet, the celebrated Beethoven-period flute virtuoso, used to teach his English pupils by means of the word 'territory'. During the earlier centuries, *T–K–* had been barred as too crude and explosive; the only possible reason for using it, wrote the great cornett-virtuoso Della Casa in 1584, could be to scare the audience. Its present vogue appears to date from about the 1820s (when some German flute and clarinet players were using it).

The *T–R–* tonguing, often also described as *di-ri di-ri*, was given for flute, recorder, cornett and trumpet, and even for oboe (in Freillon-Poncein, 1700, and Quantz, 1752). Quantz, describing flute-playing, says that the *R* stroke is made by pronouncing the letter R clearly and distinctly. But since this letter is pronounced differently in every European country, some practical investigation will be needed before we can feel that we really understand how this tonguing was done. Its general intention, however, is clear: to distinguish between a sharper attack T and a weaker one R in order to phrase the notes, most commonly in pairs.

At first, in the sixteenth century, the general rule seems to have been to tongue *every* note. This is, for example, what our earliest informant, Agricola (1528), expressly states; slurring is scarcely mentioned until a century later (by Mersenne) and then as a rather special effect. However, plain single-tonguing was scarcely ever used for shorter notes than crotchets. For quavers, even for an isolated pair of quavers among longer notes, T–R– double-tonguing was advised, and for semiquavers it was insisted upon. This means, to go by the estimated average tempo of sixteenth-century common time at about crotchet$=85$ that double-tonguing was brought in at much slower speeds than nowadays. Agricola stresses its importance in the following lines:

> Wiltu das dein pfeiffen besteh
> Lern wol das diridiride,
> Dans gehört zu den Noten klein
> Drumb las dir nicht ein Spot sein.

> (If a piper you'd live to be
> learn you well your *diridiridee*
> which belongs to the notes small,
> lest you look a fool before all.)

As time went on, instructions became more detailed, and by the eighteenth century we find 'territory' employed in many subtle ways to add to the grace and liveliness of the playing. The following are some of the chief ways:

fast runs of equal notes: T–R–T–R–

medium-fast runs of equal notes; also passages in dotted notes: T–T–R–T– R–T–R–T– (thus reversing the tonguing after the first T). This is interesting since it was in medium-fast runs that each pair of notes was so often played *unevenly*, or 'swung', with a prolongation of the first of each pair.

'slur two, tongue two': *T—R—T—*
syncopated groups like crotchet-minim-crotchet in *alla breve*:
T–R–T–
even triplets: *T–R–T–*
dotted triplets, also even triplets in which the first two notes are
the same: *T–T–R–*.

One can try these out best on the flute, preferably a contemporary conical flute with small mouth-hole. But it is easy to
imagine that in large and noisy ensembles, the subtle impetus of
'territory' might become lost, and this is probably why it went
out during the first part of the last century.

VIBRATO. Vibrato on woodwind instruments forms a tricky
subject. For centuries it appears to have been practised much as
it is today (i.e. some players have used it more than others), yet
it has seldom been introduced into the official curriculum as it is
in string-playing and singing. This is because a wind instrument
sounds well enough without it. Vibrato is therefore a thing that
a wind-player may add at fitting points in the music, after he has
learnt to produce an effective and musical straight sound.

Flutists use it with most freedom, many making it with the
breath (diaphragm, starting to learn it with slow, rhythmical
pulsations) or, less often, with the lower lip. Vibrato suits the
flute best of all, and it is not surprising to find in history that
this is the first instrument for which it is recommended (by
Agricola in the sixteenth century; see Chapter X). On the oboe
and the bassoon, while vibrato *can* have a magnificent effect,
there are dangerously many passages in orchestral works and
opera that are weakened or spoilt by it, so that the important
thing is not to let the vibrato become an unconscious habit (which
it has a tendency to do). It is generally made with the breath,
using either the throat, or better, the diaphragm (like
Ooh-ooh-ooh). In England it is most heard on the oboe, but in
several other countries it is more prominent on the bassoon,
notably Russia, where it is so pronounced that one wonders
whether it has any historical connection with those long vocal
bassoon solos in Tchaikovsky's symphonies and in other
Russian works.

GENERAL INTRODUCTION

The clarinet is traditionally played with no vibrato at all. However, in dance bands a vibrato is made by movement of the lower jaw as on the saxophone, and a few players of recent years have introduced touches of it into the orchestra. But a clarinettist needs to have an underlying tone of outstanding quality for the sound to bear the vibrato successfully.[1]

In former times a vibrato was also obtained on woodwind instruments by trilling a finger on (or just above) some hole further down than the actual note-hole. It has gone entirely out of fashion, and is indeed impossible on many instruments on account of the mechanism. Many folk musicians, however, still use it on bagpipes, etc.

Woodwind transposition

Although woodwind instruments vary so much in size, compass and key, there are three ways only of naming and writing the notes produced by given fingerings on them. Let us take for example the note in the low register for which all six fingers are put down (. . . / . . .):

1. On all *flutes*, of whatever size, all *oboes*, including cor anglais, etc., and all *saxophones*, this note is called and written *d'*, no matter what it actually sounds.

2. On all *clarinets*, small and large, it is *g*.

3. On *bassoons*, including contra, it is G.

As for actual sound, let us consider group 1 first. Only on the ordinary flute and oboe does . . . / . . . actually *sound* a *d'*. On deeper-pitched instruments it obviously sounds a deeper note, as for example on soprano saxophone, *c'*; on oboe d'amore, *b*; G bass flute, *a*; cor anglais, *g*; alto saxophone, *f*; heckelphone, *d*. Consequently a composer or arranger writing a part for one of these latter instruments has to work backwards towards the same end, making whatever *transposition* that is necessary in order

[1] As has Reginald Kell, one of the first orchestral clarinettists to use vibrato in England. This was in the famous woodwind section of the pre-war London Philharmonic Orchestra under Sir Thomas Beecham, with Geoffrey Gilbert, principal flute; Leon Goossens, principal oboe; Kell, principal clarinet; and John Alexandra, principal bassoon. Their instruments were by Lot; Lorée; Boosey & Hawkes; and Heckel, respectively.

that a *d'* written in the part shall always signify to the player: put six fingers down; or an *e'*, put five down; and so on. Thus every note that is to be sounded on a soprano saxophone must be written in the part a tone higher; on an oboe d'amore, a minor third higher, etc., etc. Thanks to this system (which dates from the eighteenth century) a flutist can change quickly to piccolo (written an octave lower than it sounds), an oboist to cor anglais, a variety-orchestra saxophonist to flute or oboe, without the written notes signifying entirely different fingerings and holding up sight-reading.

To *specify* the pitch and transposition of an instrument (except in flute bands; see Chapter II) the old German method is used. This is based on an instrument's C (which, in the low register of these 'group 1' instruments, is made with six fingers plus the C key for right little finger). The instrument is described as being 'in' whatever note this C actually sounds. On the cor anglais, for instance, it sounds F, and the cor anglais may therefore be described as being 'in F', though since every one knows this anyway, nobody bothers to say 'in F' when dealing with this instrument. But with a rarer instrument like the orchestral bass flute, it is customary to jog the memory and to avoid chance of misunderstanding by labelling the part 'Bass flute in G'.

Clarinets receive their pitch-names from their upper register, where, thanks to their overblow at the twelfth, they come into line with flutes and oboes. The non-transposer among clarinets is the now little-used C clarinet. This is of such a length that . . . / . . . C in the upper register actually sounds C (*c''*). On the three-inches-longer B♭ clarinet, the ordinary clarinet of today, it sounds a tone lower, B♭; on the little E♭ clarinet, a third higher than the C, it sounds E♭. On the bass clarinet (today assumed to be in B♭) it sounds a tone *plus* an octave lower, though some composers, as Wagner and Stravinsky, have written its part in the bass clef, to sound only a tone below the written note. By doing so, they certainly make the part look more 'bass' on paper, but they oblige the player to learn an octave transposition as well as a foreign clef, and the whole object of woodwind transposed notation is to avoid such things.

The following excerpt (fig. 5) will enable a reader who is totally unacquainted with wind transposition to see how all this works out. It is a few bars from the wind parts of Stravinsky's *Rite of Spring* just after figure 82 in the score. For the present purpose the bass clarinet parts have been rewritten in conformity with normal practice, and the two horns may be imagined

FIG. 5. *Transpositions. Excerpt from the wind parts of Stravinsky's* Rite of Spring (*quoted by courtesy of Messrs Boosey & Hawkes Ltd.*).

to be two basset horns (large clarinets in F, with the same transposition as the horn in F, i.e. sounding a fifth lower than written).

A small drawback of woodwind transposition is met when it is desired to play untransposed music on a transposing instrument, e.g. C clarinet or oboe parts on the ordinary B♭ clarinet, or from vocal or piano copies on clarinet or saxophone. Every learner of a transposing instrument should teach himself to be able to do this. Some players manage it by thinking all the time of the relevant interval, i.e. reading every note a tone higher, or a third lower, as the case may be. Eventually this can be done without continuous effort. Another method, which some will find quicker to master, is to acquire two distinct ways of reading music. First, the normal way as for a transposed part (written *d″* for a clarinettist or saxophonist means put six fingers down), and second, the way of reading the notes as they actually sound (written *d″* means putting *five* fingers down on a B♭ clarinet, or *one* finger down on an alto saxophone). When reading from untransposed music, one will put oneself in gear, as it were, for the second way.

Pitch

The question of pitch bears importantly upon the purchase of a woodwind instrument in the open second-hand market. The safest way of obtaining a second-hand instrument is to keep enquiring privately of professional or experienced amateur players in the hopes of tracking down a well-tried old instrument of known individual history. Failing this, there remain the instrument-dealers, from whom one may also make an excellent purchase, so long as every precaution is taken against acquiring an instrument built to the wrong pitch.

Playing pitch, usually referred to simply as *pitch*, signifies the standard to which woodwind instruments are built and stringed instruments tuned so that agreement reigns in performance. It is defined in terms of the frequency, in vibrations per second, of the note *a′*, known as 'the A'. Piano tuners carry the A about with them in the form of a tuning-fork. In orchestras, the A is normally given out by the principal oboist, who often keeps a fork in his case to forestall any argument. But unfortunately, the standard pitch has always fluctuated over periods of time, with the result that several different pitches may be met in woodwind instruments today.

FLAT PITCH or LOW PITCH. These expressions cover the following three pitches:

i. The present *International Standard Pitch* of *a′* = 440. This is the A that the B.B.C. has been relaying nightly just before the Third Programme begins. It was agreed at a conference in London in 1939, and woodwind instruments are today supposed to be built to it. In point of fact, however, orchestras in general keep tending to creep sharper in actual performance, with the result that some makers (e.g. some of the French oboe-makers) are now said to be building to around $a' = 444$, which is not going to help matters.

ii. New Philharmonic Pitch, $a' = 439$, is the pre-1939 standard British pitch. For practical purposes it is identical with the preceding. The only important thing to know here, is that the abbreviated expression '*Philharmonic Pitch*' is dangerously ambiguous, since it can also denote sharp pitch, the main bugbear, described later on.

iii. Continental Pitch or *French Pitch, $a' = 435$,* officially prevailed on the Continent before 1939, and large numbers of instruments built to it have found their way into England. It is nearly a quarter of a semitone below the present standard, which is enough to make an instrument built strictly to it sound desperately flat. Many Continental makers during the 1930s were, however, building a little sharp to it; pitch was even then tending to rise, and the Berlin conservatoire, the Hochschule, had already come to recognize $a' = 437 \cdot 5$ as standard. Consequently, pre-war Continental-built instruments *may* go perfectly well to modern pitch, and many British players use them so unaltered. But should an instrument prove incorrigibly flat (assuming that one's embouchure, mouthpiece, reed, etc., are all correct), the odds are that it was built strictly to $a' = 435$, in which case a woodwind repairer must be asked to attend to it. He may shorten the head-joint of a flute, the barrel of a clarinet, the crook of a bassoon, or advise the use of shorter reed-staples with an oboe. Then, if advisable, he will retune the instrument. Tuning, in this sense, mainly entails such things as undercutting a hole or chambering the bore to sharpen a note (a local expansion of the bore will sharpen the note which has an antinode at that point); or lining a hole with shellac to flatten a note.

In every case of doubt concerning an instrument, the first person to consult is an expert woodwind repairer. Sometimes these little publicized but indispensable members of the woodwind profession have their own premises, while others work for a big music store on the latter's premises. There is one of these craftsmen in every large city, and on taking up a woodwind instrument, one should at once ascertain, by asking other players, where he works, and then go round and make friends with him.

SHARP PITCH or HIGH PITCH. This, approximately $a' = 452$, is officially described as *Old Philharmonic Pitch*, but is sometimes loosely referred to as '*Philharmonic Pitch*' (cf. *ii* above). It is about half a semitone above modern pitch, and the psychological effect of this is to make a sharp-pitch instrument feel sharper still. It was the standard pitch of Victorian England. Today it remains standard in brass bands and is occasionally met in local orchestras and territorial bands. But up into the 1920s it was still in wide use. A woodwind player had to possess two instruments, one sharp-pitch, the other flat-pitch, and when engaged for a concert he was notified which to bring. Consequently, among the instruments in second-hand shops today, a very large number are sharp-pitch and these are to be avoided like the plague.

Reputable dealers understand this, and generally a second-hand instrument is clearly labelled 'sharp-pitch' or 'flat-pitch' as the case may be, but a casual dealer may have been misinformed. It is not safe for a beginner to test the pitch himself, because he may sound the instrument flat through faulty or undeveloped embouchure; he may feel perfectly convinced in the shop that a desirable-looking instrument is flat-pitch, only to discover his mistake when it is too late. Measuring too is unreliable, for though the three smaller woodwind measure from a half to one inch shorter in sharp pitch than in flat (the middle flute in Plate III is sharp-pitch), an instrument may have been badly 'converted' to flat pitch by some crude lengthening, or by mixture of sharp- and flat-pitch joints. The judgement of an experienced player or repairer is the only safe guide.

Other countries too have had their sharp pitches in the past, though these had largely gone out of use by 1900 and now survive only locally. However, Continental manufacturers have built sharp-pitch instruments for the British market, so that one must never relax one's vigilance against sharp pitch just because an instrument bears the stamp of a foreign maker.

GENERAL INTRODUCTION

Should one for any reason be obliged to use a sharp-pitch instrument in a modern orchestra, the following desperate procedures must be resorted to:

Flute: pull out the head-joint some three-quarters of an inch and bring the notes in tune with the embouchure. Much can be done with practice and a good ear.

Oboe: the only thing is conversion, an operation in which some repairers have been notably successful. Pieces are expertly spliced into the instrument in one or two places and then the whole is retuned. It is a long job, however, and expensive.

Clarinet: a method adopted by theatre clarinettists in the old mixed-pitch days, in the lack of a flat-pitch instrument, was to hang a length of thick string down inside the bore, having first frayed the end so that it will catch in the mouthpiece socket. This lowers the pitch uniformly by the requisite amount (apparently because in effect it narrows the bore and increases 'end-correction' under the holes, etc.), but it makes the instrument rather tiring to blow and much of its brilliance is lost.

Bassoon: have the crook lengthened at the narrow end by an inch or more, pull out the joints a little, and do the rest with the lip, assisted by flat-sounding reeds.

'OLD PITCH'. An approximate eighteenth-century pitch of *a'* = 415 (conveniently a semitone below modern pitch; but see also p. 274) is often used today in performances with original instruments or reproductions. Most makers supply instruments built to this 'Baroque pitch', or to some other 'historical' pitch up to half a semitone above or below this.

CHAPTER II

The Flute

The flute, the first instrument of the woodwind in the order of ceremonies, has a nature somewhat distinct from that of the other instruments of the section. It has inherited from the ancient panpipe something faun-like, bearing its solitude as the orchestra's sole representative of the edge-vibrated or Flute Class of instruments with an easy unconcern. A flute player in the orchestra, leaning back comfortably in his chair, often forcibly brings to mind the god Pan resting against his forest tree and fluting magic spells; and still more so when the image is confirmed in sound as in *L'Après-midi d'un Faune*, and in the dance in *Daphnis and Chloë*. Undoubtedly the French have become the great flute orchestrators (and this is closely connected with the special qualities of the modern French school of flute-playing), but in German orchestration too, when the principal flute soars above the orchestra in a solo passage the instrument seems, like that other instrument of forest ancestry, the horn, to carry one with it out into clear space, away above the play of striving human passions expressed by the strings and the reed instruments.

General construction

A flute is normally built in three sections: the head joint, with the mouth-hole in the side; the body or middle joint, with the main keywork; and the foot joint, with the keys for the right little finger. The last two joints are sometimes made in one piece, but the head joint is always separate, since its junction with the body is constructed as a *tuning slide*, in order that it can be pulled out to counteract the instrument's rise in pitch through heat. During performance, a flute-player carefully adjusts the tuning of the flute through this means.

When the head joint is of metal or thinned wood, the surround of the mouth-hole (or 'embouchure hole') is raised, to give the hole its proper depth. Just to the left of the mouth-hole, the bore is terminated by the *stopper*, which is of cork, or some hard material lapped with cork, faced with a metal disc. The stopper is placed in its correct position by the maker, but it can be shifted by moving the cap at the top end, which carries a thread. In an old flute, the stopper may have become displaced, in which case the octaves will not be in tune. Its correct position is usually given thus: distance of stopper from centre of mouth-hole = diameter of bore at the mouth-hole. To check it, the D's are sounded. If d''' is sharp in relation to the lowest D, the stopper is too far in, and vice versa; but this test can only be done by an experienced player certain of the correct method of blowing these notes. Some makers put a mark on the cleaning rod, showing the correct distance of the stopper from the lower end of the head joint.

BORE. There are two kinds of flute bore today: 'conical' and 'cylindrical', though in neither case does the word describe the bore completely. *Conical bore*—a heritage from the eighteenth century—is practically the same as the ordinary recorder bore: head, cylindrical; body and foot, contracting conically towards the lower end. Conical bore is retained today mainly for piccolos and band flutes.

Cylindrical bore denotes the bore introduced by Boehm of Munich in 1847. In it, as he said, the preceding proportions are roughly reversed: the head narrows towards the stopper in a gradual curve described as parabolic; body and foot are cylindrical, with the same bore-diameter as the head of a conical flute (about 19 millimetres). The cylindrical bore is standard for the flute itself today, and is used everywhere with Boehm's basic system of mechanism and fingering (Boehm flute) save for certain alternative systems still found in England (Rudall Carte 1867 system, Radcliff system, etc., described later).

THE WOODWIND TODAY

Wood versus metal

The flute is held horizontally to the player's right, supported at three points: by the lowest joint of finger I (against the flute about an inch above plate I); by the lower jaw; and by the right hand. The near edge of the mouth-hole is set against the edge of the red part of the lower lip, and it must be central, not to one side. The lips are partially closed, the tongue is moved as described in Chapter I and the breath is aimed towards the far edge of the hole. To reach the higher notes, the principle is to narrow the lip aperture (by tightening the lips or compressing them at the sides) while directing the air-stream more upwards, i.e. more directly on to the edge of the hole (through a movement of the lower lip or chin; not by turning the hole inwards). No two players do exactly the same, either for playing the different registers, or for guarding the intonation. Methods of teaching vary accordingly, altogether making flute-embouchure a very difficult thing to lay down the law about in a few words. Players do, however, acknowledge a broad distinction between 'tight embouchure' and 'relaxed embouchure', and these, very generally speaking, are associated with the wooden and the metal flute respectively.

WOOD is traditional in England, Germany and Eastern Europe. The wood is cocus—a wood obtained from various species of West Indian and South American tree, and varying from light brown to black in colour. Most instruments have the head joint lined with silver as a precaution against cracking. Among leading makers of the wooden flute—they make metal ones too— are Rudall Carte (now amalgamated with Boosey & Hawkes), renowned as the finest British flute-makers ever since they produced the first English-made Boehm flutes over a century ago; and in Germany, Mönnig and Hammig are among the chief specialists, while most of the general woodwind makers also make flutes.

The wooden flute naturally gives a denser, more powerful sound than the metal and requires rather more forceful blowing and attack; lightness and delicacy of control being secured with skill and practice. Hence the use of a muscular *tight embouchure*, keeping the lips somewhat braced sideways, though not turned inwards. The flute is pressed well in against the lower lip, and the corners of the mouth are often pulled up, producing the well-known 'flute-player's smile'. With this approach, the tone can be made wonderfully rich, and on the low notes a long, muscular lip-aperture makes possible a full, reedy fortissimo. These are characteristics of the traditional English school, so well exemplified by the playing of the late Robert Murchie and of his pupil and successor, Gareth Morris, principal flute in the Philharmonia Orchestra. In Germany and Russia, traditional flute tone is equally full, but of thicker, often duller quality, produced almost entirely without vibrato, and, as in England, with considerable muscular exertion of the lips.

For players in these countries who prefer a lighter-blowing instrument that yet preserves much of the wooden-flute quality, makers supply compromise models, as the wooden flute with metal head, or with thinned wooden head; or a wooden flute with the wall thinned the whole way along. But today many English and German players have changed over to the metal flute, while many beginners also use it, since it is now obtainable in mass-produced cheap models costing about £25 new (as against up to £160 for a superior instrument).

METAL may now be considered the world-favourite. In France, Italy and America it is used almost exclusively, and it is now also used in Vienna (for instance by Reznicek, principal flute in the Vienna Philharmonic). The metal is commonly nickel silver (German silver); stainless steel may be used for lower-priced models. The acknowledged favourite, however, is silver, unless the more costly denser metals, platinum or eighteen-carat gold, be chosen. The great French maker of recent times was Louis Lot of Paris, whose flutes have perforated finger-plates (described further on). Flutes are now made in Paris by Couesnon, Marigaux, etc., while the American flute-makers—notably Haynes, and Powell, both of Boston, and Selmer (U.S.A.)—have won world-wide recognition, and their metal flutes, some reproducing the Lot model

(Plate III), have become greatly prized in Europe through their perfected workmanship.

A metal flute *can* be played with a tight embouchure and to sound very much like a wooden flute. But it naturally yields a lighter, more limpid tone, and it responds well to a lighter attack and to a looser or *relaxed embouchure*. The modern French school, founded by Taffanel in the latter part of the last century, devotes itself especially to cultivation of these properties, caring less about power and sheer sonority, but concentrating rather on super-sensitive control and subtle modulations of tone-colour (which *can* also be obtained with wood) that almost bring to mind Segovia and his guitar.

For a relaxed embouchure, the lips are turned more or less loosely outwards—especially the upper lip—making a rounder aperture, controlled by compression of the lips towards their sides and in-and-out movements of the jaw. The resulting tone-quality is most distinctive. On the lower notes it is rather hollow and overtone-less, and apt to get lost in an ensemble, though the French players' lavish use of vibrato helps to make it tell. But on the higher notes it can be made very penetrating when desired, while the style brings certain technical advantages, e.g. facilitation of diminuendo to pianissimo in the high register, and soft slurring over very wide intervals.

The style has long been known about outside France through the concert tours of Moyse, Le Roy and others, and before them of Fleury, who, it is said, used to make great effect with the French school's ethereal character by performing Debussy's unaccompanied solo *Syrinx* with the house lights turned out. The style now has many devotees in England and Germany, sometimes retaining the wooden flute; and also in America, where one of its chief rivals is an Italian metal-flute style, very musical and expressive, though less sensational than the French.

Piccolo

The piccolo (Ital. *ottavino*) is the half-size flute, fingered in exactly the same way as the flute, but sounding an octave higher. Every professional flutist possesses a piccolo, for although in a full-sized orchestra the piccolo parts are normally played by the third member of the flute team, who is regarded as a specialist on the piccolo (a tricky instrument to handle, especially in very quiet passages), many works demand two piccolos, and some even three, e.g. No. IV of Kodály's *Háry János* Suite. Moreover, in a small or light orchestra carrying only one flute, the player may be required to change instruments constantly.

The standard piccolo has no foot joint; its bottom note is D. It has, however, sometimes been made with a foot, and Verdi, for one, writes down to the low C.

With the piccolo, fashions of design have tended to be conservative. In England up to the 1920s it was quite common for a professional player to use a Boehm flute, but a conical six-keyed piccolo (of which Whitaker was a favourite maker, his instruments largely sold by Hawkes). Today, all orchestral piccolos are Boehm-system, but as a rule they retain the conical bore ('conical Boehm'), which gives smooth tonal results over the whole compass. Wood, metal, or wood with metal head joint are all used. Some players, however, both in Europe and in America, use the metal cylindrical Boehm piccolo, matching their flute. Of this, Haynes wrote in his 1940 catalogue: 'Many players find the cylindrical-bore silver piccolo gives better results than any other piccolo because it is more nearly like the flute in tone-quality and because the high tones may be produced with comparative ease.'

Two of the finest orchestral writers for the piccolo both played the instrument themselves in its simple-system days: Berlioz (notably in the *Menuet des Follets* in *Faust*), and still more, Tchaikovsky (above all in his three great ballets, e.g. in the canary Variation in *The Sleeping Princess*). Tchaikovsky may indeed be said to have revealed the piccolo, just as Wagner revealed the bass clarinet.

Bass Flute and Alto Flute

The bass flute is a very old idea, going back to the sixteenth century. The modern type is Boehm's *G bass flute* (*alto flute*; French, *flûte contralto en sol*). This is a 34-inches-long, 26-millimetres-bore, straight metal Boehm flute pitched a fourth below the ordinary flute, so that its bottom C sounds *g* (Plate II).

The left hand finger-positions are brought higher up the instrument by means of axles, to keep the hand in a comfortable position. It has the full flute range in compass and sonority, though the large bore, necessary for the low notes, reduces the strength of high harmonics in the tonal spectrum, and the upper register in particular possesses a haunting, languid quality quite of its own.

After its initial trials in the orchestra at the end of the last century, the two best-known G bass flute works both followed in 1911: Stravinsky's *Rite of Spring*, and Ravel's *Daphnis and Chloë* (though in French performances of the latter work, the bass flute part has often been played on clarinet or alto saxophone—even in one of the published recordings). In British orchestration it appears in Holst's *The Planets*, and in many of Britten's works (*Spring Symphony*, several of the operas, etc.). But today, at any rate in England, the bass flute is becoming a far better known instrument than hitherto through its great effectiveness when scoring for the microphone, as with the small broadcasting and recording combinations that provide incidental music, song accompaniments, etc. Indeed one may say that the bass flute is now being played every day in the studios, and the number of players who possess the instrument has greatly increased.

It is also worth possessing for recitals and demonstrations. One can read a piece of flute music as it is written, the accompaniment being transposed a fourth lower; or transpose a flute or violin solo a fourth higher, so that it will sound at its original pitch, but, of course, with the novelty of the bass flute's tone-quality. Some of Boehm's own arrangements are listed in Dayton Miller's translation of *The Flute and Flute-playing*. John Amadio, the famous New Zealand virtuoso, also regularly used the bass flute at recitals, especially in slow popular airs like 'Drink to me only', while for another change of colour he had constructed a 'B♭ flute', standing a tone below the ordinary flute.

When contemplating purchase of a second-hand bass flute, it is as well to make sure that the offered instrument really is a G bass flute, and not one of the flute-band bass flutes or a *flûte d'amour* in A. The latter, on which the bottom C sounds *a*, is virtually extinct, but has occasionally been made in the modern Boehm system, presumably for recital work.

Many people prefer to follow the logical Continental practice of terming the G bass flute an 'alto flute'. This releases the term 'bass flute' for the rare but imposing size built an octave below the ordinary flute—the *C bass flute*. In the Bate Collection in London there is one of these by Boehm himself—of metal, perfectly straight, 51 inches long, 32 millimetres in bore, with a tone of formidable power right down to its bottom C. But it is excessively awkward to hold, and in later models the head joint is bent round with a coil in it, so that the player may hold the instrument at a slant in bassoon fashion. In England, Rudall Carte had for some time been supplying large bass flutes to flute bands when, about 1930, they produced a fine C bass flute of this type, with 28 millimetres bore (Plate II). Several amateur flute societies have found this a splendid adjunct to concerted flute pieces, and it has also been used a little in film music. The bracket, for resting the instrument on the thigh, can be detached if desired.

Flute bands and Band flutes

A flute band is a wind band consisting only of flutes and drums. The flutes employed are of various sizes and pitches, and are customarily named according to an old way of reckoning that has long been ousted from English and French orchestral circles by the German nomenclature described in Chapter I and observed with the bass flutes in the preceding section. The band flutes are all transposing instruments conforming with the general rule for woodwind transposition, the six-finger note being written as D in every case. But they are named after the actual sound of this D, instead of after that of their C. The ordinary flute (though not employed in these bands) is then described as a 'concert flute in D'. By 'F flute' is meant a flute pitched a third higher, its D sounding F; in orchestral nomenclature it would be 'in E♭', because its C sounds E♭. Similarly, 'B♭ flute' denotes a still smaller instrument pitched a sixth above the ordinary flute (a third below the piccolo); orchestrally it is 'in A♭'. Its part is written a minor sixth lower than it actually sounds. Popularly, it is often called a fife, though the true fife—a barrack duty instrument (fig. 76)—is today rarely heard save on the Continent.

This difference in nomenclature has always caused some confusion, even in band circles, and every orchestration pundit from Berlioz to Cecil Forsyth has urged the abolition of the old system. Nevertheless flute bandsmen on the whole prefer to stick to it, and therefore so shall we in the pages that follow. The orchestral (German style) description will usually be added in brackets to keep the matter clear.

TABLE OF FLUTES

Orchestral and other non-band flutes are shown in italics.

	Six fingers	Lowest note if provided with foot joint	Approx. total length (inches)
F piccolo (E♭)	*f″*		10·5
E♭ piccolo (D♭)	*e″♭*		11·8
Orchestral piccolo	*d″*		12·5
B♭ flute ('fife') (A♭)	*b′♭*		15·5
F flute (E♭)	*f′*		21·5
E♭ flute (D♭)	*e′♭*	*d′♭ **	23·5; 25·5
FLUTE ('concert flute')	*d′*	*c′*	26·5
Flûte d'amour in A	*b*	*a*	31
B♭ bass flute (A♭)	*b♭*		29·5 (or with bent head)
Orchestral G bass flute	*a*	*g*	34
F bass flute (E♭)	*f*		(Coiled head)
E♭ bass flute (D♭)	*e♭*		„
C bass flute	*d*	*c*	„

* With a foot joint, this is the 'D♭ flute' formerly used in military bands to keep the flute part in sharp keys, suiting the old eight-keyed flute.

Except in some of the largest bands, the instruments are six-keyed conical flutes without foot joints (Plate IV), sometimes with covered holes (fig. 76). They are designed for outdoor use and require stronger blowing than orchestral flutes. Nearly all the civilian bands play at sharp pitch.

The principal melody instrument of a band is the B♭ flute (A♭) (the fourth from the top in the table), and an elementary boys' band may be composed of nothing but a number of these played in unison with occasional thirds, supported by bass drum and side drums. A military 'corps of drums' includes six or more

THE FLUTE

B♭ flutes playing in three parts, one E♭ piccolo (D♭) or occasionally the old F piccolo (E♭; 10·2 inches long), and F flutes (E♭) for the bass. A larger corps will have one or two B♭ bass flutes (A♭; usually with bent heads, as shown in the Plate), in which case the roles of the various sizes are best described in brass-band terms: the B♭ flutes are the cornets; the F flutes, the euphoniums; the bass flutes, the basses. When two E♭ flutes (D♭) are also included, either they double the bass, or they play low harmony parts, like the brass-band baritones. Arrangements are published by Potter and others.

For civilian flute bands, the present great centre is Northern Ireland, especially Belfast. Altogether, a visit to Belfast on a summer weekend is a thing not to be missed by anybody interested in bands. Dispersed at the closest intervals along the long processions of the Orange Lodges, march bands of every description: brass bands, military bands, accordion bands, Highland bagpipe bands, Irish war-pipe and Brian Boru pipe bands, and the various kinds of flute band described below. At every instant the sounds of at least two bands are heard, each playing its own tune in its own key—which is just as it should be in a grand procession. The overlap of the bands' tunes obliterates those dreary moments when nothing is heard but the tramp of boots, adds vastly to the general atmosphere of excitement, and makes the occasion in every way more memorable.

The Belfast flute bands range from unison boys' bands to large contesting bands organized on full brass-band scale, utilizing the complete range of band flutes shown in the table. Some of these large bands are equipped throughout with Rudall Carte 'Guards' model' instruments (1867 model with closed G♯) of wood with metal heads (Plate IV), the first set having been purchased over forty years ago on the initiative of John Murdie, conductor of the Argyll Temperance Flute Band. The composition of these full bands is as follows:

1 E♭ piccolo
1 solo B♭ flute
2 1st B♭ flutes
3 2nd B♭ flutes
3 3rd B♭ flutes

3 F flutes (1st, 2nd and 3rd)
3 E♭ flutes
3 B♭ bass flutes (straight model)
2 F bass flutes (E♭; coiled head)
1 E♭ bass flute (D♭; coiled head)
4 percussion

The arrangements, mostly by the conductors themselves, are fully scored in the brass-band style, and the whole music sounds with celestial brilliance some two octaves higher than that of other kinds of band, while the drums, handled with great

FIG. 6. *A page from a large flute-band score of a waltz. The actual key of the piece is* D♭ (*e.g. the chords in the last bar*). *The melody line begins on* F.

skill and restraint, give a suggestion of the missing low register. The Ravenhill Band recently won a contest with a fine arrangement of the *Thieving Magpie* overture by its conductor, George Hawthorn; a far cry from the fife-and-drum band of old. A few bars from a waltz (fig. 6) will show the lay-out in a straightforward conventional passage.

Flute mechanisms

BOEHM FLUTE. The mechanism of the Boehm flute is standard save in one important particular—the G♯ key—and several minor ones.

G♯ key. Boehm intended this to be an 'open G♯ key', sprung to stay open, and closed by the little finger from G natural downwards (fig. 7, *left*). This arrangement has been widely retained in England, but the French would never have it. Instead, they rearranged the key as a *closed* key (sprung to keep closed) as it had been on the old flute before, so that the little finger presses it only for the G♯'s and for those notes in the high register that require it to be open. Most countries have followed the French practice, and the 'closed G♯' (fig. 7, *centre*) is the general world standard; and it has latterly become the commoner arrangement in England. Conversion from 'open' to 'closed' is possible.

Left thumb. In Boehm's original design there was only one thumb lever, closed to give B. For B♭, finger IV was put down in addition (. o o / . o o). Today, this fingering for B♭ remains available, while a second thumb lever ('Briccialdi key'—the upper plate of the present two) provides an alternative B♭, made without the right hand, and this has become the most usual fingering for the note, especially in passages in flat keys. When B♭ and B both occur in a passage, either the thumb is switched from one plate to the other—if possible during an instant when the thumb must anyhow be taken off for a C or C♯—or the thumb is kept on the lower plate (B) and B♭ is made with finger IV as Boehm intended.

Side key (for finger IV). In England this has usually been a B/C trill key (fig. 7, *centre*), fitted to avoid trilling with the thumb. But on most closed-G♯ flutes it is often a B♭ key, duplicating the B♭ action of plate IV, giving a better-vented note and facilitating passages like G–A♯–B–A♯ repeated, since it may be held down while fingering the G (fig. 7, *right*).

Extra F♯ devices. Certain complications arise from the Boehm F♯ arrangements. Fingered . . . / o . o (with the E♭ key held open of course, as it is for almost every note on the flute, to secure the maximum venting that Boehm demanded) the note is too dull for use except next to E when absolutely necessary. With the proper fingering, however (. . . / o o .), the note is still imperfectly vented and the fingering proves awkward next to E when the smoothest possible legato is required. As a remedy, many flutes carry some gadget through which finger VI can make F$\sharp$ without closing its own hole. The commonest is the 'Brossa key' (fig. 7, *m*), a small touch that independently duplicates the F$\sharp$ action of plate VI (thus: **. . . / o o** *m*). On moving to E, finger VI may be kept on *m*, and this also gives a perfect E/F$\sharp$ trill.

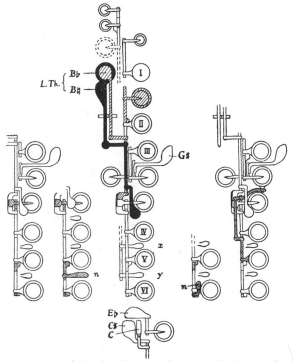

FIG. 7. *Diagram of Boehm flute mechanisms.* Left: *with open G$\sharp$;* centre: *with closed G$\sharp$;* right: *the same, with 'split E'.* n *and* m *Rockstro and Brossa F$\sharp$ keys.*

Fig. 7, *n*, shows the corresponding arrangement on the Rockstro model flute, which is a Boehm flute with open G$\sharp$, vented D (see below) and this lever, and has been the choice of several celebrated players of the English school, including Murchie and Morris. On this model, the position selected for the independent F$\sharp$ touch necessitates moving one of the two trill keys to be actuated by finger IV instead of VI.

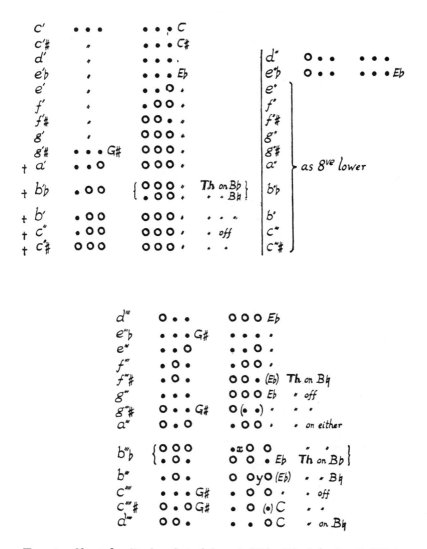

FIG. 8. *Chart for Boehm flute* (closed G♯). *The left thumb* (Th) *is applied to either plate except where indicated otherwise. For flute with* open G♯, *this key is kept closed except where G♯ is given in the chart and for the notes marked* †.

On flutes with *perforated plates* there is less need for an F♯ key, since nearly the same effect can be obtained by putting down finger VI on the edge of the plate, leaving the perforation uncovered. Beyond this, advantages claimed for perforated plates include: (1) the ability to modify the quality or tuning of certain notes through 'shading' them by pressing down a plate by its edge; and (2) the enforcement of correct placing of the fingers, i.e. properly on the plates,—not spread across them like a bagpiper, which makes accurate finger-control in fast scales almost impossible.

Vented D. This is a full-sized key-plate (shown dotted in fig. 7, *centre*) on the near side of the instrument just above the thumb-plates. It is normally opened by trill touch *x* together with the lower of the two small trill keys, which it vents, giving a good 'open D' useful in rapid tremolos and so on with the notes below (down to, say, B). But its greatest value lies in providing a really good C/D trill above the stave, and also, on some flutes, a good G/A trill above that.

Improved top E ('*split E*'). On ordinary closed-G♯ flutes, the G♯ arrangement interferes with the note *e'''*. This note is made as a 4th harmonic of the low E, and its proper harmonic vent is the hole covered by finger III. But when this finger is raised, the next hole below automatically becomes uncovered too, which makes *e'''* a more difficult note than it should be. With the split E (fig. 7, *right*), the two plates can move separately, and the lower one is closed not only by III, but also by V (leaving plate III free to remain open), and so ..o / ..o gives *e'''* properly. On the other hand the device spoils the ordinary high G/A trill (o.. / o.. trilling with III), and so flutes fitted with it often also have the vented D described above.

The preceding are the best-known optional additions to the plain Boehm. Other gadgets (vent for low D, etc.) are mainly confined to Germany.

Low B. Many Italian and German players use a flute with an extended foot joint giving a low B (actuated by one of the little fingers, usually the right). Several composers (e.g. Tchaikovsky, Strauss, Bartók) have put this note in their scores, and Mahler—

characteristically—has even written B♭. In England, should these notes be indispensable to the music they are discreetly slipped in on bassoon or clarinet.

OTHER CYLINDRICAL SYSTEMS. In England, though nowhere else, several alternative designs of cylindrical flute have enjoyed wide popularity in the past and are still used by some players. They include:

1. Rudall Carte 1867 model
2. Radcliff model
3. Pratten model

The 1867 *model* (fig. 9, *left*, and Plate III) invented by Carte and produced by the firm in that year, is by far the best-known of these, and its present devotees in England must run into several hundreds, both amateur and professional, and Rudall Carte will still supply the instrument, normally in wood, though also in metal if desired. It is an excellent design, in some ways technically superior to the Boehm, and the mechanism, though it is complex, is positive in action throughout and never goes wrong.

It combines Boehm with simple-system (pre-Boehm) fingerings and has some extra fingerings as well, so that once these are understood and mastered, a player commands a wide range of alternatives for getting round awkward passages, particularly in the high register. The true 1867 model has open G♯. The 'Guards' model', with closed G♯, has already been alluded to in connection with flute bands. The differences from the Boehm in the lower two octaves are as follows, given in terms of the lowest octave:

all fingers off gives an open *d"*;

c"♯ is either (1) by thumb on upper plate and all fingers off; (since this closes the C hole at the back, there is an extra C hole on the front, to vent the *c"♯*; it is closed by plate II); or (2) by o o . / o o o (thumb off);

c" is (1) as on the Boehm (finger I only); or (2) next to the second fingering for *c♯*, o o . / o o o with thumb on upper plate;

b' is (1) as Boehm (but thumb on *upper* plate); or (2) by the first fingering for *c''* plus IV on top plate;

b♭': the B♭ hole is brought round to the back of the instrument and is covered by the lower thumb-plate. For *b'♭* the thumb closes *both* plates; or the thumb remains on the upper plate and the B♭ is made in Boehm fashion by IV on its bottom plate (or with the F key, *e.g.* in B–A♯–F♯);

Thence as Boehm, down to:

f' and *f'♯*. With IV on its bottom plate, these notes are made in Boehm fashion. With IV on its top plate, they are made in simple-system fashion (*f'♯* . . . / . o o and *f'* . . . / . . F o). The top plate also closes the open G♯ key for a F♯/G♯ trill with IV alone.

The high-register fingerings may be seen in the Otto Langey tutor and in Rockstro's *Treatise*. The following are those that normally differ from the Boehm:

high F and F♯: the same alternatives as in the lower registers; top A: again the choice of fingerings for the right hand; top B♭: . o o / . o o with lower trill touch and IV on bottom plate; top B: thumb to be on upper plate.

Radcliff model (1870). A simplification of Carte's earlier system of 1851. It is based upon simple-system fingering, and includes: full venting; the two thumb-plates of the 1867 model; and an ingenious alternative F arrangement (fig. 9, *right*). John Amadio is one who has always used this model.

The left-hand mechanism is like that of the 1867 model but without the open D. The open note is C♯ as on the Boehm, and for this the thumb may be kept down if desired (e.g. after B). The flute has closed G♯ with a device equivalent to the 'split E' of the Boehm. In the right hand, F♯ is . . . / . o o and F is made with the cross F key, or with the fork-fingering, or with the F♯ fingering *plus* the long F key (left little finger). This last fingering is arranged for by moving the note-hole for F♯ to the far side of the instrument (*l*, fig. 9), there being no hole under finger-plate IV. The long F key closes this F♯ hole to make F, and plates V and VI close it too, for the lower notes. The key need not be released for E and below, and movements and trills between F and E♭ or D are perfectly easy. An excellent design on which nothing is impossible while some high passages are simpler than on the Boehm.

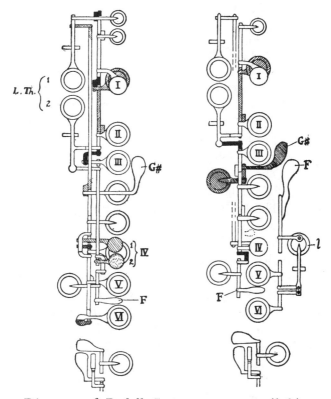

FIG. 9. *Diagrams of Rudall Carte 1867 system* (left), *and of Radcliff system* (right).

Pratten model. This is the old eight-keyed flute redesigned with cylindrical bore and finger-plates. The plates actuate mechanism for bringing $c''\sharp$ and $f'\sharp$ up to pitch without interference with the cross-fingered c'' and forked f'. The arrangement gives a good free tone and is used to some extent by flute bands.

CONICAL FLUTES. Though obsolete as professional orchestral instruments, conical flutes have not long been so—as in Germany, for instance, where all types are still manufactured and are used by some of the amateurs. The principal types include:

1. Simple system:
    (a) eight-keyed flute
    (b) Continental twelve- or thirteen-keyed flutes
    (c) German 'Reform Flutes'
2. Conical Boehm flute

Simple system flutes. These have the full compass, and a tone of remarkable homogeneity from top to bottom, subtle and interesting in character, though less telling than that of the cylindrical Boehm. The fingering differs in many respects from that of the Boehm. Fundamentally, it is that shown in fig. 69. Four fingers (. . . / . o o) give F♯; F is with five fingers plus either of the two F keys (fig. 75; the 'long F' key is used next to D, etc.). The *b'♭* is by two fingers plus the thumb B♭ key, but the upper B♭ is better fingered . . o / . . . E♭. There is no thumb-hole. The left thumb rests normally against the wood, and both C's are usually best fingered o . o / . . . E♭ (the side key for C—finger IV—being mainly for the B/C trill and for passages confined to the lower register). The *c'''♯* is by o . . / . o o E♭, and choices for higher notes will be found in figs. 69 and 75. Altogether the fingering is more cumbersome than Boehm's, yet it serves well enough in the classics, to which the simple-system flute belongs by birthright.

The *eight-keyed flute* (see also Chapter XII) is the orchestral equivalent of the six-keyed band flutes already mentioned, the two extra keys being for the low C♯ and C. The typical English model, now a common object in junk-shops, is characterized by the extra-large holes for fingers II and V, which strengthen the sound on many notes; the difficulty with this model, for the orchestral player, was said to be production of a soft sound firmly and up to pitch. This flute is still regularly to be seen in use in Irish country-dance bands—usually a family heirloom, played left-handed with the keys plugged up.

More advanced are the *Continental models* (Tulou, Schwedler, etc.) fitted with superior keywork and extra keys for improving certain important trills. The classical small holes are retained, yet the instruments blow remarkably freely, especially in the lower register. The German ones usually go down to low B, and often have metal or ivory heads (fig. 76). The keywork varies a little in detail. Shown in Plate III is a modern example of the Schwedler model (1885) with the foot keys arranged in Boehm fashion. Apart from this small modification, it represents the staple design of the 'old school' of German flutists who scorned the Boehm throughout the period of Wagner and Brahms; indeed, Wagner is said to have preferred its sound to that of the Boehm.

The side trill key acting high up by the head is principally for d'''/e''' (giving the latter note as a 2nd harmonic), but it can also be used for certain higher trills. The next key below it, actuated by the cross touch for finger V, is usually for $c''\sharp/d''$, and the lowest of the three is the C side key, already mentioned (Schwedler also prescribes it for venting the $c''\sharp$, which tends to be flat). The 'pimples' carved in the wood above and below the mouth-hole constitute Schwedler's 'reform mouth-hole', an eddy-concentrating device.

The *Reform Flute* (Mönnig, 1912, etc.) represents the last word in simple-system conical flutes—the flute equivalent to other elaborate non-Boehm woodwind designs like the modern oboe and the Oehler clarinet. Again, it varies in detail, but the Heckel mechanism shown in Plate III is typical and includes: plates or rings throughout; an F$\sharp$ correcting device (to save having to sharpen this note with the F key) which can be cancelled for $c'''\sharp$ (its harmonic, which would become too sharp) with the roller on the far side of plate IV; a 'brille' for improving c'' and $c''\sharp$; an A$\flat$/B$\flat$ trill (thumb); and the usual extra trill keys. The head shows the later cusped form of 'reform mouth-hole' (Mönnig's) which enjoys considerable popularity in Germany today on the Boehm as well.

The *Conical Boehm* has such particular historical interest that its description will be deferred to Chapter XII.

Recorders

The recorder is the classic Western instrument of the flageolet family. This is the sub-class of flutes in which the sound-generating apparatus (slit and edge) is rigid, not flexible, so that recorder-playing needs to be approached in quite a different manner from flute-playing. As on the flute, a note sharpens when the instrument is blown hard and flattens if blown gently. Therefore, deprived of control through embouchure, a recorder player is obliged to find other methods of keeping the notes steady in pitch through the rise and fall of loudness demanded by musical expression. Adjustments with the fingering play a large part in this. The finest virtuosi think ahead all the time to employ the fingering that will best bear the crescendo or diminuendo as the case may be. Helping this, it may be that the throat comes into play, being more relaxed in the *forte* to allow a full stream of air to pass into the instrument; and more tightened in the *piano*, to send forward a thinner stream of air at the same speed, so that the note keeps its pitch but has less volume (corresponding to narrowing the lip aperture in flute-playing).

After its last great days in the orchestras of Bach and Handel, the recorder became a folk instrument, played by few other than Italian shepherd boys. Then came its revival at the hands of that great musician and pioneer, Arnold Dolmetsch, who began recorder-making in 1919. He took for his model an English eighteenth-century instrument, and this so-called 'Baroque' model has been followed by most other makers. It represents the recorder as it was remodelled by Hotteterre of Paris in Lully's day from the sixteenth-century design which was bored all in one piece, conical from top to bottom. The Hotteterre model introduced the three-jointed construction, having a cylindrical head joint followed by a contracting body in which the angle of taper is approximately double that of the earlier design. The latter gives a fuller, less reedy sound, ideal for consort polyphony, but possibly less interesting in the expressive sonatas, concertos and arias of the eighteenth century. Also the old type takes considerably more breath and even the tenor can be quite an exhausting instrument to blow. Some modern makers, among them Hans Stieber of Tübingen-am-Neckar, Germany, have gone some way towards reproducing this as well as the eighteenth-century type.

The chart below (fig. 10) is for the ordinary fingering, sometimes referred to as 'English fingering' though it is the fingering of all old recorders, English, French, German, even Chinese. The so-called 'German fingering' arose in modern times through a misconceived notion that since the fingering . . . / . o o is generally too flat for F♯, it might as well be made into a good F by lowering the position of hole V. For a fair

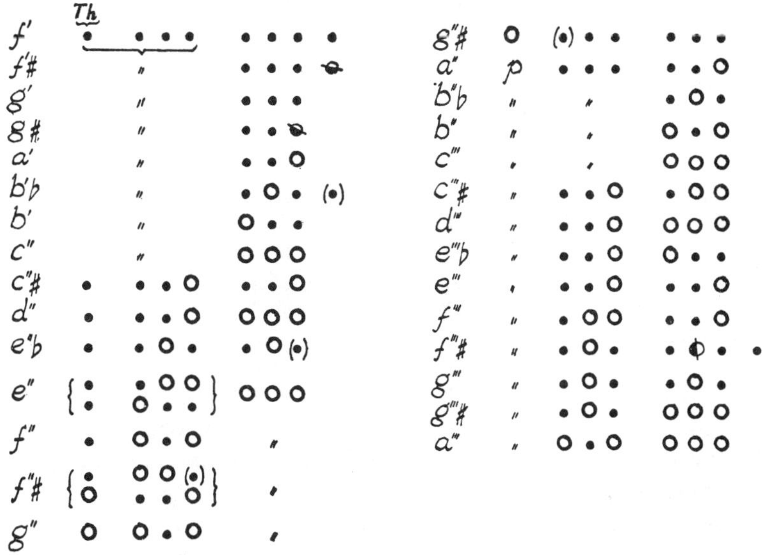

	Th											Th							
f′	●	●	● ●	●	● ●	●	g″♯	O	(●)	● ●		●	● ●
f♯	″		● ●	●	●	⊶	a′	p	●	● ●		● ●	O
g′	″		● ●	●			b″♭	″	,	● O	●
g♯	″		● ●	◐			b′	″	,	O ●	O
a′	″		● ●	O			c‴	,	,	O O	O
b♭	″		● O ●	(●)			c″♯	,	● ●	O	● O	O
b′	″		O ● ●				d″	″	● ●	O	O O	O
c″	″		O O O				e″♭	,	● ●	O	O ● ●
c″♯	●	● ●	O	● ●	O		e‴	,	● ●	O	● ●	O
d″	●	● ●	O	O O O			f″	″	● O	O	● ●	O
e″♭	●	● O ●	● O (●)				f″♯	″	● O ●	● ◐ ●	●
e″	{ ● :	● O O : ● ● }	O O O				g‴	″	● O ●	● O ●
							g‴♯	″	● O ●	O O O
f″	●	O ● O	″				a″	,	O ● O	O O O
f″♯	{ ● : O	O O (●) : ● O }	,							
g″	O	O ● O	,							

Fig. 10. *Chart for treble recorder.* p: '*pinch*' *thumb-hole; half-filled circle: half uncover hole (or uncover twin hole if this is provided). A black spot in brackets indicates an optional covering in aid of tuning a note. N.B. Further fingerings are possible on many notes.*

criticism of the formidable complications that result on the upper F♯ from this distortion, see Giesbert's recorder tutor.

The octave, on the recorder, is overblown by 'pinching', i.e. by flexing the left thumb to reduce the aperture of the rear hole cleanly with the thumb-nail. Half-uncovering with the fleshy part of the thumb is not efficient enough.

Several recorder soloists have fitted an 'echo' device. This makes use of the fact that a small hole pierced an inch or so below the voicing (i.e. the slot and sharp edge) will sharpen every note on the instrument. In some old flageolets, a rather large hole in this position was covered by a key, to provide a semitone trill on every note. For a recorder 'echo', the hole is smaller, and is opened by an ingenious mechanism when the player bites harder on the mouthpiece. The sharpening effect of opening the hole is designed to compensate for the flattening that otherwise results from blowing very softly, and hence passages can be softly echoed without losing pitch.

The present consort of recorders is as follows (in America, the descant is 'soprano' and the treble is 'alto'):

	Lowest note	Approximate length (inches)	Notation
Octave or sopranino	f''	9·5	}Sound an octave higher than written
Descant	c''	13	
Treble	f'	19	}Sound as written
Tenor	c'	26	
Bass	f	38, less crook	Usually written in bass clef, and then sounds an octave higher

In addition to these, some German makers have recently revived a sixteenth-century size that is a most useful instrument if well built—the *quart-bass*, a large bass recorder pitched a fourth below the ordinary bass.

The *descant* recorder is being used today a great deal more than it musically deserves on account of its low price and suitability for very young children. The classic recorder is the *treble*. 'Flutes' and '*Flauti*' in the works of Bach, Handel and their contemporaries do not mean just 'recorders'; they mean 'treble recorders', and it is this size that now cries out for re-admission to the woodwind. It is astonishing that after all the trouble people go to to procure harpsichords, gambas, oboi d'amore, etc., etc., for Bach performances, the treble recorder, equally necessary and so easily available, is never invited except in amateur circles and the most advanced professional circles. Its parts are played on flutes, just as though Bach and Handel had made no distinction between the two instruments, and never carefully introduced arias appropriate for each of them in the same work.

Professional woodwind men, among whom doublers on recorders would eventually have to be found, are obsessed by the vision of myriads of infants learning the descant recorder in schools. In current orchestral opinion the recorder is seen mainly as an instrument of basic musical education. But this is not as it should be, and we should speak less proudly of the revival of the recorder until Dolmetsch's work has been completed by dispelling this professional snobbery, for which conductors are as much to blame as players. Should the treble recorder prove too soft for a modern festival orchestra, then let somebody remodel it to be louder, as has been done with every other woodwind instrument in the course of the last one hundred and fifty years. Already one sound-strengthening device has been introduced by Carl Dolmetsch, and is effectively used by himself, Edgar Hunt and other recorder soloists when playing with a largish orchestra. It is a small baffle-cum-megaphone, of wood or cardboard in the shape of a wheelbarrow top, clipped over the voicing of the recorder with its sloping end pointing downwards. It enables the player to blow much harder without going sharp, and at the same time projects the sound outwards into the hall.

CHAPTER III

Reeds and Reed-Making

Flutists and brass players, with all their worries, at least have the advantage over players of reed instruments in that their sounds are generated with the help of the solid, unchangeable material of the instrument. Oboists, clarinettists and bassoonists are entirely dependent upon a short-lived vegetable matter of merciless capriciousness, with which, however, when it behaves, are wrought perhaps the most tender and expressive sounds in all wind music.

Reed Cane

No string player has one-tenth the trouble with his sheep's guts that the reed player has with his bits of a Mediterranean weed. For in terms of plant economy, this is all that reed cane is. Travellers to the South of France and to the Spanish and Italian coasts—or indeed almost anywhere round the Mediterranean—will remember those tall clumps of green cane that grow in marshes, and in the gullies of streams along the shore. Bundles of it lean against farmyard walls, cut for roofing and gardening purposes, while much more is cut down to waste to clear the ground. This is reed cane growing in the wild state, and for an instrument in which the reed is kept dry—as a bellow-blown bagpipe—such cane can be used for reed-making. For the chanter reed of the Northumbrian small-pipe, W. A. Cocks recommends as handy raw material the split cane of those shallow flower-baskets that florists receive from Italy and Spain. But for a woodwind instrument the cane should not only be of the finest growth, but it must also be hardened by long and careful drying (maturing) from the moment it is cut. Hence it is obtained from plantations where it is cultivated especially for reed-making.

The most important of these plantations are around Fréjus, fifteen miles west of Cannes (Plate V). Cane is also obtained from the east coast of Spain, and formerly (as far back as the sixteenth century) an important source was southern Italy. In America the supply from France is augmented by cane from Mexican plantations. On the plantation, the cane is cut after two years' growth, stacked in tall bundles and left to mature in the sun over three summers, the bundles being turned regularly. Latterly, however, with the swollen demand for reeds, the drying may be hastened by the artificial heat of ovens.

After maturing, the cane is graded in diameter, sawn into short sticks between the knots, and sent off in sacks to reed-makers all over the world. Colour matters little, except that too deep a brown or orange may indicate spongy cane which is of little use. Hardness is an important thing, and the quick test of this is to run the thumbnail along the bark; if it leaves a mark, the cane is insufficiently matured for making good reeds, though it may improve if stored in a warm dry place for several years. The exterior diameter of cane for various instruments is approximately:

oboe, 10 to 11 mm.	bassoon, 23 to 25 mm.
cor anglais, about 12 mm.	clarinet, 20 to 26 mm.

Double reeds

Mass-production of oboe and bassoon reeds, using high-precision tools including rotary cutters for scraping down the cane, is at present more or less in its infancy. The great majority of reed-makers work by hand and as a rule have far too many customers to advertise their addresses at large. If a beginner has not been put on to one by his teacher, he should find one by asking other players. The reeds cost roughly from five shillings each upwards, and re-caning oboe staples about 3s. 6d. Meanwhile, reed-making for oneself remains very much to the fore. Certainly it brings a marvellous feeling of self-reliance to be *able* to make one's reeds, even should one prefer to play on bought reeds as a general rule. Naturally, learning the art takes much time and patience, and one should not be discouraged if (as often happens) the first reed turns out to be a winner, but after that every attempt seems to go wrong for weeks.

The principal stages in making a double reed are as follows, beginning with the plain stick of cane:

1. *Splitting* the stick into three strips, followed by cutting a strip to length (which is a fraction over twice the length of a finished reed), and trimming its sides.
2. *Gouging* the strip thin on the inside.
3. Marking and nicking the centre of the strip and then *bending over*, bringing its two ends together, bark outwards. The joined end of the bent-over cane will eventually become the tip of the reed.
4. *Shaping* the sides of the bent-over cane to the desired outline of the reed.

From this point, oboe and bassoon differ:

OBOE	BASSOON
5. *Tying on*, to the metal staple.	5. Putting on the *wires* and working in the *mandrel* to form the stem and throat of the reed.
6. *Separating the tip* (the joined end of the cane) and *scraping* the blades.	6. *Binding* the stem.
	7. *Separating the tip*, and *scraping*.

SPLITTING AND GOUGING. Most of the tools may be seen in Plate I. The stick of cane is split into three by driving down it a special three-bladed cutter, the *flèche*. For cutting the strip to length, a *guillotine* is generally mounted on the base-plate of the gouging machine. Trimming the sides of the strip may be done with a special trimmer, or in the bed of the gouging machine. Up to a century ago, *gouging* was done with a hand-gouge, the strip being held in a wooden jig. The *gouging machine* now does the work more quickly. It has an adjustable runway for the blade, by which the depth of the gouging can be set. Oboe cane is generally gouged to about 22 thousandths of an inch down the middle, thinning to almost nothing along the edges. Bassoon cane is gouged to about 45 thousandths along the middle, also thinning at the edges.

Many of the players who make their own reeds possess these tools for splitting and gouging. But for those who do not, ready-split and gouged cane—'gouged cane'—is procurable from reed-makers and woodwind suppliers (though in England, not every supplier takes the trouble that, for example, Mr Milner of Sheffield takes, namely, to stock all the materials an instrumentalist could possibly need), and in the brief notes that follow, it will be sufficient to begin with cane already brought to this stage. One can also buy cane that has been brought to more advanced stages as 'shaped cane', in which the sides have been shaped, in some cases before bending over.

OBOE REED FROM GOUGED CANE. With the cane held on the wooden holder, put a deep nick across the exact centre with a file or knife (fig. 11, *iii*). Thoroughly soak in water (e.g. overnight) before *bending over*. This last can be done over a knifeblade, but usually bending over and *shaping* are done together on a metal *shape* (Plate I, 9) obtainable from oboe manufacturers. This tool is generally provided with clips for holding the cane steady after it has been bent over the top edge of the tool. The sides of the cane are then cut along the sides of the shape with a knife. Replacing the cane on the holder, a slither is now taken off the outside at each end (*iv*).

Tying on. The staple (fig. 11, *s*) is a conical, soldered metal tube about 47 millimetres long (though less with some Continental oboes) and slightly flattened to an oval at the tip. The upper part is scored with a file for better grip on the cane, and the wide end is lapped with cork for insertion into the instrument. Some older forms of staple have a collar at the top, with a recess under it to hold the thinned extremities of the cane while tying on. When a reed is discarded, its staple is used for a fresh one, though new staples can be bought from suppliers if

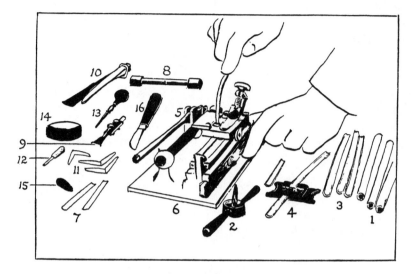

Key to Plate I. Oboe reed-making.

1. *Sticks of cane.*
2. Flèche (*two-handled type*).
3. *Strips of cane, after splitting stick with* flèche.
4. *Trimmer.*
5. *Guillotine, mounted on base-plate of 6.*
6. *Gouging machine in operation.*
7. *Gouged cane.*
8. *Holder.*
9. *Shape.*
10. (*A German bassoon-shape.*)
11. *Shaped and folded cane.*
12. *Staple.*
13. *Mandrel.*
14. *Hardwood block, for cutting tip on.*
15. *Tongue or* plaque, *for scraping on.*
16. *Scraping knife.*

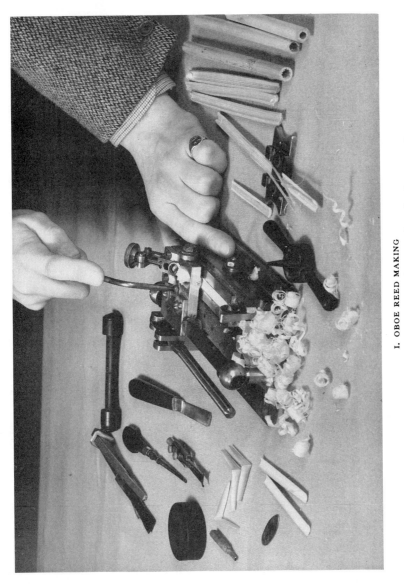

I. OBOE REED MAKING

(Michael Dobson); gouging machine in operation. See key opposite

II. FLUTE

Orchestral set of modern Boehm flutes; *left to right:* G bass or 'alto' flute, *Haynes*; flute, *Haynes*; piccolo, *Marigaux*. *On right:* C bass flute, *Rudall Carte* (with bracket for supporting instrument on thigh)

III. FLUTE, OTHER MODELS

Left to right: 1, Boehm, French (Louis Lot) model, with perforated plates, *Haynes*; 2, Boehm with open G♯, *Rudall Carte*; 3, Rudall Carte 1867 model, *Rudall Carte*. Conical flutes: 4, Schwedler model, 12 keys, *Alexander*; 5, a 'Reform-flute', *Heckel*

IV. Set of band flutes, *H. Potter. On right:* F ('E♭') bass flute for flute band,
'Guards' model', *Rudall Carte*

V. REED CANE

One of the plantations near Cannes, supplying cane to reed-makers all over the world. View shows clarinet cane in final sun-drying

VI. DOUBLE REEDS

Top row, left to right: 1, 2, two English oboe reeds, *c.* 1780–1820; 3, French oboe reed *c.* 1870 (*Triébert*), showing a French V-scrape; 4, modern English oboe reed, total length 2.85 inches (*Morgan*); 5, 19th-century cor anglais reed, made without staple; 6, modern cor anglais reed; 7, modern shawm reed (Catalan *tenora*; *Pardo, La Bisbal*)

Bottom row, left to right: 8, an English bassoon reed *c.* 1810; 9, ditto *c.* 1890 (*Morton*); 10, modern bassoon reed, length 2.2 inches (*Ludwig*); 11, contrabassoon reed (*Ludwig*); 12, contrabass sarrusophone reed (*Couesnon*)

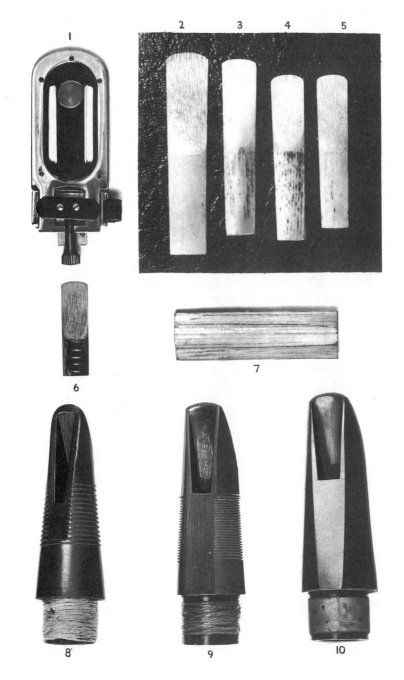

VII. CLARINET REEDS AND MOUTHPIECES

Top row, left to right: 1, reed-cutter; 2, tenor saxophone reed (bass clarinet); 3, a German bass clarinet reed; 4. standard clarinet reed (*Vandoren*); 5, German type of clarinet reed (*L. Wlach*). *Centre:* 6, an English reed, *c.* 1810 (for the small F clarinet?); 7, strip of cane from which clarinet reed is made. *Bottom row:* mouthpieces: 8, French *c.* 1780; 9, modern German; 10, modern French or English type

VIII. OBOE

Orchestral set of modern Gillet-Conservatoire instruments; *left to right:* oboe, *Howarth*;
oboe d'amore, *Marigaux*; cor anglais, *Marigaux*. (The oboe and the cor anglais are
with semi-automatic octave keys, and the d'amore is with full automatic.)

IX. OBOE, OTHER DESIGNS

Left to right: simplified thumb-plate model, *Selmer*; full thumb-plate model, with simple octave keys, *Cabart*; former German model as today used in Russia, *unmarked*; Vienna *Akademie-model* as used in Vienna Philharmonic Orchestra, retaining the profile of the classical oboe, *Zuleger*

X. WIDE-BORE CONICAL REED INSTRUMENTS

1, Catalan treble shawm (*tiple*); 2, Catalan tenor shawm (*tenora*; these two examples from the Ricart Matas collection, Conservatorio municipal, Barcelona); 3, heckelphone, *Heckel*; 4, piccolo heckelphone, *Heckel*; 5, tarogato, *Schunda*; 6, 'Brian Boru' (Irish) bagpipe: chromatic chanter by *Boosey & Hawkes*; 7, alto saxophone in pre-jazz days, *Mahillon*; 8, modern saxophone (showing the rare 'mezzosoprano' size in F), *Conn*

XI. CLARINET

Orchestral set of modern Boehm-system clarinets; *left to right:* bass clarinet
(to low E♭), *Boosey & Hawkes*; basset horn, *Buffet-Crampon*; A and B♭
clarinets, *Boosey & Hawkes*: C clarinet. *Besson*; E♭ clarinet, *Buffet-Crampon*

XII. CLARINET, OTHER MODELS

Left to right: 1, A♭ clarinet, *Rampone*, showing adaptation of semi-full Boehm system to the smallest clarinet; 2 ,full Boehm, *Orsi*; 3, Schmidt *Reform-Boehm* clarinet (A), *Schmidt, Mannheim* (the vent hole in the bell is brought out in the print by a white spot); 4, simple system (Albert model) with patent C♯, *Boosey*

XIII. CLARINET, OTHER MODELS (CONTINUED)

1, Clinton model (A), *Boosey*; 2, Vienna *Akademie-model* (L. Wlach, Vienna Philharmonic Orchestra), *Koktan*; 3, Oehler system, *Heckel* (showing characteristic German method of tying on reed with string); 4, a metal Boehm

XIV. OTHER DEEP CLARINETS

Left to right: B♭ contrabass, simple system, to low E, *Huller*; bass, Oehler system, descending to the low C, *Schmidt*; E♭ alto, Boehm system, *Selmer*

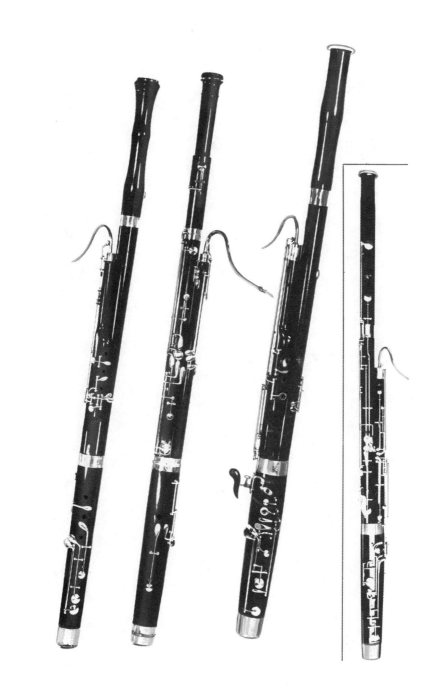

XV. BASSOON

On left, French type: 1, *Mahillon* (front view); 2, *Buffet-Crampon* (back). *On right*, German type: 3, *Heckel* (front); *inset: Heckel*, model descending to low A (back)

XVI

Left to right: Contrabassoon, usual short model descending to low Bb , *Heckel*; tenor sarrusophone, *Gautrot;* Bb contrabass sarrusophone, *Gautrot. Inset above: contrebasse à anche, Rampone* necessary. The *mandrel* (fig. 11, *m*) is a brass or steel rod in a wooden handle, tapered so that the staple fits neatly over it. The original purpose of the oboe mandrel was for making staples oneself out of sheet brass. Now it is retained to provide a better grip while tying on.

Soak the cane again. Then place it over the tip of the stapleso that the latter extends about 8 millimetres between the blades and mark this point on the outside of the cane with a pencil. Bind the cane on tightly with silk or thread (fig. 11, *v*), beginning at the pencil mark and securing below the cane with a hitch. To

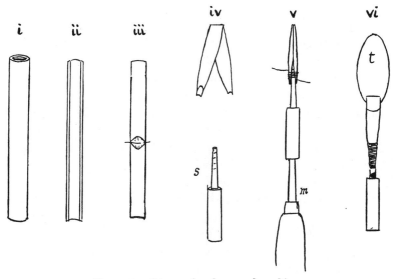

FIG. 11. *Stages in oboe reed-making.*

ensure tight binding, one end of the thread may be attached to a hook in the wall, to pull against.

Scraping. This is done with a scraping knife (Plate I, 16), with the reed well wetted. The knife blade is held upright across the reed, steadied against the thumb of the other hand, and worked with a rotary movement of the wrist, the cutting stroke always being towards the tip of the reed. A preliminary scrape may be given before *separating the tip*, which is done most simply with the metal tongue, using it like a paper-knife. The *tongue* (or *plaque*, fig. 11, *t*) is a thin, oval steel plate about 40 × 15 milli-metres, and it is always placed between the blade tips while scraping after the tips have been separated.

The upper parts of the blades are next scraped down until the reed will crow when blown in the mouth. At first the crow is a high, hard squeak; gradually it becomes freer. An important point is to work slowly, preferably in bouts lasting over several days, to allow the cane to settle after each small amount of scraping.

Reed-scraping varies considerably with different players. With the usual thin-gouged cane, the line above which the bark is removed may be given the form of a shallow U (commonest in England) or a deep V (in France). Above this line, the blades are scraped fairly evenly across, but the extreme tip may be made very thin right across. Tuning the reed is a matter of experience. In general, if notes are sharp, or the lower notes hard to produce, more is taken off the lower part of the scrape, continuing lightly upwards to avoid humps that would make the reed erratic. On the other hand, if the reed makes the notes flat, a millimetre or so may be chopped off the tip with a razor blade over a hardwood block, after which the blades may have to be scraped back a little to free the lower notes. This cutting the tip and scraping back is also how a worn-out reed can often be rejuvenated.

Many oboists on the Continent and some in England make the reed rather differently, gouging less deeply (e.g. to 25 thousandths of an inch, or thicker, depending on the consistency of the cane) and thus leaving the cane thicker. More has there-fore to be scraped off the outside, and the bark may be removed almost as far back as the binding. The blades are then scraped down gradually towards the tip in various ways, often leaving a thicker spine down the centre (as with a German bassoon reed).

To finish off a reed, or to touch up a bought reed, many players rub it with *Dutch rush*—a slender, greenish rush that hardens to form sharp silicaceous ridges. It is obtainable from many woodwind suppliers.

When the reed is satisfactory, a strip of *goldbeater's skin* about 50 × 10 millimetres is cut out and wound round the moistened base of the blades and the upper part of the binding, to keep the reed airtight.

COR ANGLAIS REED. Since a cor anglais reed does not fit directly into the instrument, but is placed on a metal crook, there is theoretically no need for a staple, and formerly, in the last century, it was made like a bassoon reed, i.e. without a staple (Plate VI). However, the cor anglais reed is too small to be really strongly held together by this method, and it is now always made on a short staple, the cane being tied on as with an oboe reed. The staple is about 25 millimetres long and needs, of course, no cork lapping. The cane strip before bending over is about 95 × 8·5 millimetres.

A cor anglais reed is always *wired*: two turns of fine soft brass wire are fastened round the reed below the scraped part. With pliers, the wire can be squeezed this way or that to adjust the opening and strength of the reed. The goldbeater's skin is applied over the wire. Some players wire the oboe reed similarly, for example when the tip becomes too closed up. In Vienna, the oboe reed is *normally* wired.

An *oboe d'amore reed* is made similarly, and is intermediate in size between those for oboe and cor anglais. A *bass oboe reed* is generally also made on a staple, but the *heckelphone reed* is more often made without a staple, like a bassoon reed, which it resembles in shape, though it is smaller—about 60 millimetres long and 12·5 millimetres across the tip.

BASSOON REED FROM GOUGED CANE. A holder for the gouged strip during the first operations may conventionally be made from 10 inches sawn off a broom-stick, with a 5½ inches curved recess cut in one side to take the cane.

Soak the strip thoroughly. Mark its exact centre, and make there, supporting the strip on the holder, a deep file-cut 3 to 4 millimetres broad (fig. 12, *i*). Re-mark the centre, and also mark the shoulder on each side (x, x)—which may be taken from a made reed, allowing for the width of the file-cut (which will not be part of the completed reed). Pare away the outer bark from these shoulder-marks towards the centre.

Soak again, and bend over the cane at the centre (*ii*) over a knife-blade or over a *shape*. Not all bassoon reed-makers use a shape, the classic method being to bend over a knife-blade and then shape with a knife by eye. The German type of shape (Plate I, 10) resembles an oboe shape, with clips for holding the cane after bending it over. Another type of shape is a long steel block narrowing towards each end, upon which the cane is shaped *before* bending over. If, after shaping the cane, the sides

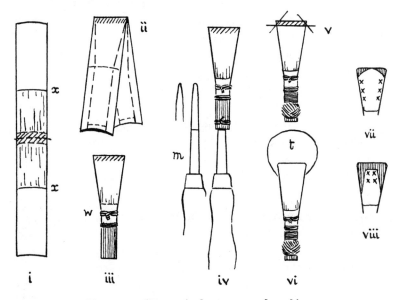

Fig. 12. *Stages in bassoon reed-making.*

of the blades do not come exactly together all along, it is best to start afresh with a new piece of cane, for the reed will leak. If the stem is too long, open out the cane and shorten the ends as necessary.

Wiring and introducing the Mandrel. Cut three 5-inch-long pieces of soft brass wire, about 22 gauge. Put on the first wire (*w*) just below the shoulder of the reed, winding two turns without overlap (or three if the wire is on the fine side) and twist with pliers to fasten *loosely*. Put on the second wire similarly, about 6 millimetres below the first.

Make about seven cuts up the stem of the folded cane with a razor blade (fig. 12, *iii*). This is to enable the stem to assume a tubular form when the mandrel is introduced. (Some make these cuts before putting on the second wire; others do not cut at all, but score the bark deeply with the razor blade.) Then put on the third wire close to the base of the reed, again fastening loosely.

After the cane has again been well soaked, the *mandrel* (*m*) is gradually worked in between the two blades. Much depends on the form of the mandrel, since it forms the throat of the reed. Some taper evenly all round; others (as Heckel's) are flattened towards the point. It should have a mark to show when it has been worked in as far as its designer intended. The danger in this operation is starting splits running up to the blades, but with practice this is avoided by judicious loosening of the wires (especially of the second). Afterwards, the cane is bedded against the mandrel all round, with the pliers. Leave at least twenty-four hours to dry, now and then replacing it on the mandrel to tighten the wires by degrees.

Binding. This requires about a yard of carpet thread. Hitch it over the bottom wire and wind a ball over it (one can unwind a made reed to see how this is done). Carry it up in single turns, not overlapping, but with each turn close up against the one before, and finish with a hitch close against the second wire. When dry, the binding is painted over with shellac or any other airtight solution.

Scraping. Separate the blades by chopping off the tip with a razor blade and mallet over a hardwood block; also chop a minute piece off each corner. During scraping the metal tongue (*t*) is always inserted between the blades, and the earlier stages are best done with the reed on the mandrel. As with an oboe reed, the more gradually scraping is done, the better. Most scrape with a knife as already described, but one of the most celebrated German reed-makers pares away with the cane with the knife and finishes with Dutch rush. This is Kurt Ludwig of Munich. His workshop is a sunny Bavarian garden. In it, is a table laid out with battalions of reeds in various stages of completion resting on pins. On one side a huge glass of beer. Calmly, without haste, each platoon of reeds is deftly operated on and moved up the table for attention next day. By contrast of method: the French player, seizing thirty-two bars rest in the opera pit to scrape down a freshly-bound reed to play the next show on. Music results from each method, but the first gives a reed that lasts longer.

As will be described in Chapter VI, two distinct types of bassoon are in use today—the German and the French—and reeds built for the one are not always easy to use with the other, though many players do so successfully in order to obtain special results. In a German-style reed, on which most of the British reed-makers concentrate today, the throat is rather more arched than in a French reed, the mandrel being designed accordingly. The blades are left comparatively thick down the centre, and the final scraping and adjustment is mainly along the sides of the reed and at the corners of the tip (fig. 12, *vii*). For a French-style reed the cane is gouged less thin. The throat of the reed is flatter, and the scraping is more evenly across the upper part of the blades, leaving the lower parts (furthest from the tip) quite thick and strong. Further scraping back on to this thick area will free the lower notes but, if carried too far, will spoil the high notes (*viii*).

The tip opening can be increased by pinching the top wire at the sides with pliers, or reduced by pinching the second wire at the sides or the top wire top and bottom.

Single reeds

CLARINET REED. It is an astonishing thing that while a clarinet reed is so straightforward an article, few players any longer make their own reeds except in countries where the German type of clarinet is used (since with this clarinet, mouthpieces are not only smaller than the ordinary, but vary in width). Neither is partly-finished cane procurable (as gouged cane is for double reeds), though it easily could be made so. Nor even are there professional reed-makers catering mainly for orchestral clarinettists. West of the Rhine all clarinet reeds are made by machine in the vast manufactories of Vandoren of Paris and others, and are marketed, at upwards from ten shillings per dozen, in five grades of strength—soft, medium soft, medium (the best to buy if in doubt), medium hard and hard—for dance-band, military band, and orchestral players without discrimination. However, some teachers are now teaching reed-making again.

The procedure, in brief, is as follows. The stick of cane is split into four strips, each of which is cut in half to make two reeds. The resulting short piece of cane (Plate VII) is trimmed to its correct overall size as a rectangle, and its inner surface is made perfectly flat and smooth by rubbing it either on a large fine-cut file, or on fine glass-paper laid over a flat sheet of glass. The point where the scrape is to begin is marked on the upper (i.e. bark) surface, and while holding the piece in a wooden jig, the cane is gradually scraped and filed away from the mark towards the tip, leaving it slightly thicker down the centre.

The tip is now rounded off with an emery bar or scissors, and the reed is tried on the mouthpiece and then further scraped until it sounds about right. Finally the tip is thinned almost transparent across the uppermost eighth of an inch with a fine file or sandpaper. Should the reed still prove too hard and windy, the lower part of the scrape must be thinned down more. Should it be too soft, buzzy and flat, the extreme tip is cut off, preferably using an adjustable *reed-cutter* (Plate VII). This tool, which is stocked by most dealers, makes an invaluable possession for a clarinettist, whether or not he makes reeds, since a good reed worn out through playing can generally be rejuvenated by cutting a millimetre or more off the tip, and the reed-cutter does this quickly and accurately.

SINGLE REEDS FOR OBOE AND BASSOON. These are mentioned as things of passing interest. In England in the early nineteenth century, local bandsmen would sometimes play the bassoon with an ebony or ivory mouthpiece of the clarinet type, made with a narrow bore below the chamber in order to fit on to the bassoon crook. Specimens of this mouthpiece are preserved in the Horniman Museum, London, and elsewhere. Today, a soprano saxophone mouthpiece will go fairly well on the bassoon, giving the whole compass easily, though the tone, while still unmistakably a bassoon's, is rather dull, flabby and defective in expressive range. But specially-designed mouthpieces for bassoon and for oboe have been made in America, chiefly intended for use in military bands that lack trained double-reed players. The oboe mouthpiece looks like a tiny clarinet mouthpiece, with a long narrow stem corked like an oboe staple, and a single reed barely an inch long and a quarter of an inch wide. It is illustrated in *Grove's Dictionary*, 5th edition (article 'Oboe').

Plastic reeds (single and double)

While plastic saxophone reeds are now well known and used considerably, much progress is said to have been made in America with plastic clarinet reeds; also with plastic bassoon reeds, which, however, seem to give a rather lifeless sound. The most successful plastic double reed, however, is that for the bagpipe practice-chanter (Plate XIX), now obtainable from bagpipe suppliers.

Bagpipe reeds

In every British kind of bagpipe and in most other Western European kinds, the chanter reed is double, and the drone reeds are single reeds of the ancient, pre-clarinet type.

CHANTER REED (fig. 13, *left*; also Plate XIX). This is made much as an oboe reed except that the gouging will have to be done by hand, using a gouge of suitable size, and finishing-off with glass-paper wrapped round a wooden block of the right shape. The ends of the strip are then trimmed, cut to a blunt point, the centre is nicked, and then, after thorough soaking, the strip is bent over.

The staple is made of sheet brass or copper, hammered round a mandrel and left unsoldered. The narrow end is slightly flattened, and the folded cane is tied on with waxed thread, starting at the top and reaching almost to the base of the staple. The reed is now left to dry.

The manner of scraping depends upon the type of bagpipe, but in general the cane is taken off evenly across and well back, which helps to give the flat shape with very narrow opening, necessary in a cane reed that is not controlled by the lips. In the small, powerful reed of the Highland pipe the cane is left fairly thick all over. In the delicate reed of a parlour pipe (as the Northumbrian small-pipe and the Irish union-pipe) it is scraped very thin, and to keep it dry, its crow is tested by sucking the air down through the staple.

The bottom of the staple is lapped for insertion into the chanter, and the wire is then put on the reed just above the

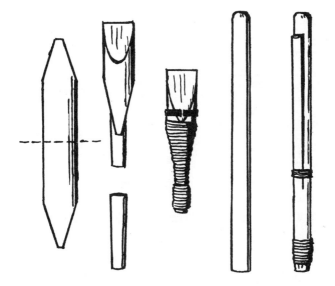

Fig. 13. *Bagpipe reed-making: chanter* (left) *and drone* (right).

binding; or instead of wire, a thin band cut from soft brass or copper may be bent round the reed. By pinching this wire or band, or by shifting it up or down the reed, the reed can be adjusted to speak at the desired wind pressure and to respond evenly over the whole scale.

DRONE REED (fig. 13, *right*). This is made of a complete tube of narrow-diameter cane, closed at the top by a knot, or with wax or cork. Elder shoots can also be used. The lower end is lapped for insertion into the drone. About one-quarter of an inch below the top end a transverse cut is made through the cane, and from this a long cut down the length of the cane makes the vibrating tongue or single reed. The length of tongue varies from 20 to 60 millimetres, and a few turns of thread are tied round its base as a tuning thread, moved upwards to sharpen the reed, and downwards to flatten it. If the latter fails to flatten it sufficiently, it may be scraped a little near the base, or a blob of sealing wax may be dropped on the tip. Similarly, for extra sharpening, the top part of the tongue may be thinned.

TABLE OF APPROXIMATE OR SPECIMEN SIZES OF BAGPIPE REEDS (mm.)

CHANTER

	Length of staple	Length of folded cane	Tip width	Average scrape (centre)	Total length of reed
Highland	20	30	11	15	45
Highland, practice-chanter	30	45	11	22	65
Northumbrian	22	42	12	18	52
Union	55	35	10	20	80
Union, regulators	55	35	10–14	20–23	80

DRONE

	Diameter of cane	Total length
Highland, tenor	9	100
Highland, bass	11	115
Northumbrian	5–6	60–70
Union	4	56
,,	5	80
,,	6	95

CHAPTER IV

The Oboe

The oboe, the second instrument of the woodwind and the first of the section's three reed instruments, is generally made of African blackwood (*grenadille* or *ébène* in French), a hard, dense wood from Central Africa or Madagascar, brownish when freshly worked, but pitch-black after polishing or exposure to sun. West Indian cocus has also been used, while formerly Brazilian rosewood was much favoured, especially for cors anglais. Recently some good instruments have been made of plastics.

The oboe has three parts: top joint, bottom joint and bell. Through these the bore expands at about 1 in 40 up to the flare of the bell, and with some makers the expansion is truly conical; but with others the expansion is more pronounced in the upper part of the bore—an ancient feature of oboe bores inherited from the fiery double-reed instruments of older times, whose bore had the profile of a sword. This short two-feet cone-bore, coupled to a double reed, is not one to yield a spectacular range in compass, and even after all recent improvements the oboe still has the smallest compass of the four woodwind instruments. But into this compass is packed a telling vividness and intensity of character unapproached by any other wind instrument. The oboe is the only woodwind instrument that it is virtually impossible to play without felt expression, and in its broad *espressivo* the tone can be swelled almost to bursting point without any trace of harshness creeping in.

To sound the oboe, the reed is first well wetted, either in the mouth, or, as Germans and Austrians often do, in a small pot of water placed on the music stand. Then it is pushed into the socket of the top joint as far as it will go, though if it has become too short through cutting down the tip (Chapter III), or if the staple is a short one, it may have to be inserted less than the full amount to prevent the instrument sounding sharp. With the oboe supported by the right thumb against the thumb-rest on the bottom joint, the scraped part of the reed is placed on the lower lip, the upper lip is closed over it, and both lips are curled back over the teeth while the corners of the mouth are closed round the reed to prevent air escaping. The tongue is moved against the reed for tonguing, as described in Chapter I. To do all this properly, the lip muscles have to be developed gradually through practice. At first it is rather tiring, and the tendency is to put too much of the reed in the mouth, and hence to blow sharp as well as noisily.

In the breathing, playing the oboe feels rather like swimming under water; the lungs must be well filled, but very little breath is expended. Therefore the accumulated stale air must be breathed *out* through the mouth before taking a fresh breath, or else the lungs will become tired. Most beginners would do this instinctively, but oboe tutors have always stressed it, since with incorrect breathing oboe-playing can become a strain on the lungs. Purely as a stunt, some oboe-players, past and present, have acquired the faculty of taking breath as glass-blowers and Oriental reed-instrument players do, namely by inhaling through the nose whilst actually blowing the instrument. For this, enough air is held in the cheeks to supply the reed (by tightening the cheeks) during the instant of breathing in through the nose. It is said that Reynolds, an oboist in the Hallé Orchestra many years ago, used to play the entire cor anglais solo on the stage in the last act of *Tristan* in this way, and there are bassoonists who can do it too.

Oboe designs and styles

The design of oboe that is used in the great majority of countries today, including France, England, Italy and the Americas, is French, evolved in the last century by the celebrated Paris firm of Triébert, whose work was carried on into the present century by their ex-foreman Lorée and his son. The bore is practically a straight cone, and the sound is clear, open and free, and perfectly homogeneous from bottom to top of the compass. Its various systems of mechanism are described later in this chapter. The style of playing it varies, on the whole, more between individuals than between countries. British playing, however, has developed a distinctive general character of its own, chiefly as the result of the brilliant playing and teaching of Leon Goossens, while an important contributing factor has been the widespread use for so long of the reeds manufactured by the late T. Brearley of Liverpool (who, like Goossens, received his early lessons from Reynolds). This school, with which every British concert-goer is familiar, employs a softish reed and produces a silvery, violin-like sound, characteristically accompanied by a slow vibrato. But some players have looked for a more flexible tone, capable of greater variation in dynamics and colour, and may obtain it with reeds of the thick-gouged, far scraped-back kind mentioned in Chapter III (if necessary, shortening the staple to counteract flatness). In England this second approach also hails from Lancashire, its acknowledged doyen being Alec Whittaker. Among the younger players its outstanding exponent is Sidney Sutcliffe, principal oboe in the Philharmonia Orchestra.

On the Continent and in America, while some players (e.g. Stotijn of the Amsterdam Concertgebouw) recall the broader British style last mentioned, the French oboe is mostly played in a more straightforward manner, with reeds often a fraction wider and with a darker tone, sometimes smooth and plaintive, sometimes reedy and 'pastoral', but sometimes, as often nowadays in France, loud and trumpet-like. Vibrato, if heard at all, is typically of the fast 'instinctive' kind, introduced to heighten a phrase at its climax, rather than of the slower, incessantly-continued tremulant so common in England. One may feel that one is hearing the oboe for a change, rather than the oboist.

East of the Rhine one may still sometimes hear the old German oboe, and to understand this instrument a short digression is necessary.

Most important woodwind innovations have been either French or German. Now in woodwind, as in so many things, the two nations have seen things differently. Whenever something new has appeared in the woodwind world, if it pleases the French, then it is likely to be viewed with suspicion in Germany, and vice versa. While Boehm's flute gained quick acceptance in France, there is something about it that kept many German players reluctant to adopt it for a surprising length of time. The Boehm-system clarinet and the large clarinet mouthpiece and reed of the Western countries are still strangers to orchestral circles in Germany, where older patterns have been developed independently. And to show that such examples do not merely reveal a conservatism on the German side, bassoons (like trombones) provide an instance of a radical German redesigning which the French in turn have so far refused to accept.

The explanation in every case may be sought in the sound. Matching the peculiar clarity of their music and their scoring, the French like wind instruments to give colourful, almost picturesque sounds, often rather thin in substance but always vivid in colour and highly individual for each particular kind of instrument (to enjoy these qualities at their very best hear, for instance, the Orchestre de la Suisse Romande, under Ansermet). The German ideal is quite different: a warm, mellow blend, in which, to French ears, all the wind instruments sound alike and equally thick and dull; and indeed, for one quite unaccustomed to them, it is even possible to confuse their broad, suave tones, all of which seem to be converging towards one universal, abstract notion of a beautiful, purely musical instrumental sound.

Let us now fit the oboe into this picture. Our modern oboe is, as we have seen, French, and the Germans, up to about thirty years ago, showed little interest in it. They had their own model; one of their conservative designs, retaining many features of the oboe of Beethoven's time: 'sword'-profile bore (cf. Plate XXIX); broad-tipped stiffish reed; and use of harmonic cross-fingerings from a'' upwards (Plate IX). Its tone is quite distinctive, preserving despite its enlarged bore (some 3 mm. wider at the bell tenon than in the French oboe), the classical oboe's flutiness, most noticeable on the D's and E's and on the

3rd harmonics just mentioned. Also, it blends superbly with the other instruments. But since then, there has been a change: the great majority of German oboists have changed over to the French type, which Richard Strauss, for one, preferred, Yet the old type lingered in several places, including Russia, where it may be heard—as till recently in the Leningrad Orchestra, going by former tape-recordings—in the pure German style of old. Pastoral reediness, refined silveriness are quite absent. The sound is so full and round ('manly', the latest Russian book on orchestration calls it) that on a held note it is easily mistaken for a clarinet. And since the flute there sounds practically the same as well, the effect in a piece like the second movement of Beethoven's Pastoral Symphony is perfectly extraordinary.

In Vienna too, the shrine of classical music, the classical oboe, in its Austrian form, has withstood the challenge of the French type. Wunderer, the former professor at the State Academy, insisted that this should be so. The retention even of external classical features is clearly seen in the standard Zuleger model (Plate IX): the bulbous top, which, they claim in Vienna, reduces condensation in the octave key; the bell-shaped bell with its internal flange; and the 'sword' bore, here about a millimetre wider than French bore at the upper tenon but over a millimetre narrower at the bell tenon. Viennese playing, though akin to the German, has its own lighter, more sparkling quality. The players, led by Hans Kamesch, principal in the Vienna Philharmonic (1955) and one of the greatest woodwind artists of the present time, use reeds scarcely wider than the French, though thicker-gouged and scraped further back. Their tone is sweet and tender, though with a splendid reserve of power, and it is a most exciting experience to put aside one's Western ideas of oboe-playing for a moment to hear Kamesch, with his Zuleger oboe, in his recording of Mozart's oboe quartet, or in the Furtwängler recording of the Serenade for thirteen wind instruments.

In technique there is not a lot to choose between these Germanic oboes and the French. Both go equally well up to the top G, and a difficult solo like the one in Rossini's *La Scala di seta* is brought off equally brilliantly by the leading performers on either instrument. But in the long run, the French oboe is perhaps technically the more flexible.

Deep Oboes

    Oboe d'amore, in A, a minor third below the oboe
    Cor anglais, in F, a fifth below the oboe
    Bass oboe, in low C, an octave below the oboe
    Heckelphone, in low C, an octave below the oboe

All these have metal crooks at the top end and bulbous bells at the bottom. No oboes of *higher* pitch than the ordinary have ever come into established use, though in the past the French built some D♭ instruments for military bands, and also an E♭ oboe (a minor third above the oboe; fig. 77), which might well have possessed interesting musical properties. Around 1850, Barret was trying to help Triébert sell it in England, offering to demonstrate it to any bandmaster who would care to call upon him at his residence in Regent's Park; but it never caught on.

COR ANGLAIS. Every oboist possesses this most glamorous of the woodwind 'extra' instruments (Plate VIII). In normal orchestral routine, the specialist on the cor anglais is the third player of the oboe team. He is usually called upon even in works like *William Tell* and *Carnaval Romain* overtures, in which the composer's idea was that one of the two oboists should change instruments in the middle of the piece; for suddenly to play cor anglais, in a solo, after perhaps an hour of hard oboe-playing, proves too risky in these days of high-precision performances. But in the choral works of Bach, as the *Christmas Oratorio* and the *St Matthew Passion*, principal and second oboists make no bones about doubling on cor anglais (for the *oboe da caccia* parts), and on oboe d'amore as well. The technical atmosphere is far more relaxed on those occasions than in symphony concerts and opera, while anyhow a long obbligato is a less nerve-racking thing for a player than the tense entries and solos of symphonic and operatic compositions. In light orchestras, and small pit orchestras, playing from special or reduced orchestrations and having only one oboist, the latter is as a matter of course expected to have a cor anglais among his (her) kit.

The cor anglais is generally supported by a sling round the neck, though many prefer it without. The reed goes on a four-inch-long crook. The reed has been described in the last chapter but it may be noticed here that as with the oboe itself, the sound produced on the cor anglais in England is rather different from that normally heard elsewhere. Instead of the brilliant solo tone that we are accustomed to hear from it in the orchestra, most players abroad go more for an impersonal 'pastoral' quality, thicker and reedier, and, incidentally, superior in effect when the composer's allusion is pastoral, as so often it is (e.g. in the slow movement of Berlioz's *Symphonie fantastique*). In Germany and Austria the cor anglais sometimes sounds nearly as dark and velvety as the bassoon.

The fingering systems of the cor anglais are the same as for the oboe except that the standard cor anglais has no low B♭, its bottom note being *b*, sounding *e*. Some composers, including of course Mahler, write the B♭, and one of Mahler's B♭'s has a most charming effect through its absence: in the *Song of the Earth* (1st movement), where the composer directs the player, should he have no B♭, to play B instead, which is what we always hear, Mahler's typical bugle-call theme becoming quaintly altered.

OBOE D'AMORE (Plate VIII). This favourite of Bach and his German contemporaries (Chapter XI) became forgotten in the classical period but was revived for the performance of Bach's works in 1878 by Mahillon of Brussels. Mahillon's first restoration had an ordinary oboe-shaped bell, like some original eighteenth-century French oboi d'amore in the Paris Conservatoire Museum. He fitted his then-normal simple-system keywork and added the low B (sounding *g♯*). About ten years later, Lorée in Paris, and Morton in London began to make it as we now know it, with bulbous bell like the old German specimens in museums, and full mechanism. Today every oboe-maker will make an oboe d'amore to order. In England, oboe d'amore owners do a brisk business around Christmas and Easter hiring out their instruments to colleagues for the Bach works, and therefore both thumb-plate and Conservatoire actions (see below) are often fitted together on the same instrument to suit all customers. The approximate length of an oboe d'amore, less crook, is 25·5 inches. The slightly bent metal crook measures about 2·5 inches overall.

A few modern works have made use of the revived oboe d'amore, the best-known examples being Strauss's *Sinfonia domestica*, in which the instrument represents the child; Debussy's *Gigues*, with a long solo motif; and Ravel's *Bolero*, in which it follows the E♭ clarinet to recommence the tune for the second time round.

BASS OBOE AND HECKELPHONE. Instruments pitched an octave below the oboe had been constructed spasmodically from the late seventeenth century onwards, though without receiving much attention. Then (1825) came the *hautbois baryton* of Triébert and Brod, with upturned bulbous bell (fig. 77). In 1889 Lorée rebuilt it in straight form, and it is this design that is occasionally seen played today, usually described in England as the *bass oboe*. Its lowest note is the low B. It looks like a long cor anglais, except that the crook bends first forwards and then backwards towards the player. Also its sound is very much like that of a cor anglais.

The *heckelphone* (Plate X) is quite a different proposition. The French bass oboe just described conforms with a classical principle of deep reed-instrument construction: when you double the length of an instrument, you will not seek to double the diameter of the bore, but only its cross-sectional area, if even that. In the bass oboe, the cross-sectional area of the bore, say at the sixth hole, is about double that of an oboe at its sixth hole. This is the proportion that was evidently found to give the musical quality and the technical feel best matched to those of the small instrument, but it leaves the large instrument some-what deficient in weight of tone and penetrating power.

The heckelphone was brought out in 1904 by Heckel of Biebrich, the German firm so famous for its bassoons. The object was purely practical: to provide a bass oboe-ish sound that would be effective in large orchestras and in the massive orchestration that composers were rejoicing in about that time. Heckel (Wilhelm, senior) said that Wagner had first given him the idea, in 1879. In this instrument, it is as if an oboe were doubled in length without reducing the angle of its cone; at the sixth hole its *diameter* is approximately double that of an oboe's at the same hole. To feed this large bore, the crook is wide and the reed is a comparatively big one of the bassoon kind, and the tone, in the true words of its creator, is 'voluptuously sonorous yet sweet; blooming and rich in harmonics, and so manly and baritone-like that one might be listening to a male voice'.

It is straight, four feet long less crook, and sturdily built of maple varnished Heckel's well-known brilliant crimson. The bell is a four-inch bulb with a two-inch hole at the bottom and a one-inch hole in the side, and has a short metal foot to rest on the floor. The compass is down to its low A (sounding A), the keys for this note and the B♭ being actuated by the right thumb. In the keywork, the rings and plates of ordinary deep oboes are replaced by Heckel's own arrangement of buttons and three-quarter rings, the buttons actuating the axles that close the primary note-holes while the three-quarter rings, pivoted on the opposite side of the instrument, play the normal role of rings. The fingering is French or traditional German as ordered.

In 1905, the year after its completion, the heckelphone made its début in *Salomé*, after which Strauss wrote for it again in *Elektra* and some other works. English parts labelled 'bass oboe', as in Delius's *First Dance Rhapsody* (1908) and Holst's *The Planets*, are played on either bass oboe or heckelphone, whichever the player happens to produce, which is nowadays usually the heckelphone. It has been said that in both these works the part was written with the heckelphone in mind.

Piccolo Heckelphone. This is well worth mentioning as an interesting might-have-been (Plate X).

The Heckel family has filled a place in recent times rather like that filled by the Sax family a century ago. Each in turn cleaned up untidy corners of the woodwind, and also thought out fresh inventions to fill out the section where it seemed to them weak, whether in orchestra or military band. Sax normalized the bass clarinet, and also invented the saxophone to strengthen the middle and lower registers of the military band woodwind. Heckel standardized the contrabassoon, produced the heckelphone, and then pounced upon a point of weakness in the high woodwind register, namely the lack of a soprano instrument sufficiently powerful to ring out a theme above the rest of the instruments in bands and in the swollen tuttis of late Romantic orchestration. Mahler would expensively throw on to the melody, in unison, as many as twelve of the ordinary soprano woodwind (four each of flutes, oboes and clarinets), while Bruno Walter is one world-famous conductor who has sometimes felt the need for reinforcing the high flutes with a clarinet playing in its high register or with an E♭ clarinet (e.g. in the second movement of Beethoven's Fifth Symphony in the passage that begins twenty bars before the *più moto*). Heckel offered assistance in the *piccolo heckelphone*, a wide-bore instrument pitched in F (an octave above the cor anglais) with compass written *b–e'''* and sounding a fourth higher. It has the heckelphone's perforated bulbous bell, and simple keywork with automatic octave keys.

It was said to have been successfully tried out at the local opera in Wiesbaden in the high dramatic oboe solo in the second Act of *Fidelio*. This must have been most exciting. But in his 1931 catalogue Heckel claimed no further success for it other than Strauss's use of it for the trumpet part of the Second Brandenburg Concerto, and, today, with the tendency to revert to economical classical orchestration, the piccolo heckelphone has probably missed its chance. Moreover, an oboist would have to handle it and it might prove a tricky instrument to control at short notice.

Oboe mechanisms

Mechanisms of the French oboe fall into several classes, distinguished mainly by the method provided for making c'' and $b'♭$ and their octaves.

SIMPLE-SYSTEM OBOES (Triébert's *système 4* of c. 1843, etc., see fig. 77). These have long been out of date. Hundreds of them survive in second-hand shops, but in England almost all of these are sharp-pitch. There are two side keys (middle joint of finger IV), one for $b'\flat$; and the other for c'' for use mainly in trills, etc., this note normally being cross-fingered. In the upper octave, both notes are sweeter and steadier when cross-fingered, as is also the B and sometimes the A. The simple-system oboe thus has the following important cross-fingerings in the low and upper registers:

c''	o . o / o o o	(*N.B.* on German instruments, o . o / . . o)
(a''	. . o / . . . C)	
$b''\flat$	. . o / . . . E$\flat$ }	(E$\flat$ key is sometimes not
b''	. o . / . . . E$\flat$ }	necessary)
c'''	o . . / . . o	

In some instruments, including those by Mahillon, and the former 'military model' of Hawkes and other British makers, the two side keys are replaced by a single key incorporating the 'Barret action' (said to be one of Triébert's inventions). In this (fig. 14, *left*) the C and B$\flat$ holes are brought round to the front (x, y) and are coupled together. The long side touch is rigid with y, and when pressed, opens it. But when the touch is pressed while finger II is raised (releasing its ring), key x—the C key—is free to rise under its own light spring. Hence with the fingering . o o / o o o the side key gives C (x and y both open), and with . . o / o o o it gives B$\flat$ (y open; x kept closed by ring II).

THUMB-PLATE SYSTEM (Triébert's *système 5*, 1849). This (fig. 14, *right*) is the system that is still used by the majority of British oboists. It was made up to the war principally by Louis, later merged with Rudall Carte; and Boosey & Hawkes. To these is now added T. W. Howarth & Co. Also, large numbers of French-built oboes have been converted from Conservatoire system to thumb-plate system by repairers, to customers' orders.

For C and B$\flat$ it has the above-described Barret side key, but this is used only for trills. Main control of the action passes to the left thumb and its *thumb-plate*. The thumb normally rests on the plate. When lifted from it, the C and B$\flat$ keys become free to rise under their own springs: when finger II is raised, both rise (C); when finger II is down, only the B♭ key rises (B♭). In order that the side key shall be able to perform its trilling function while the thumb is resting on the plate, the connection

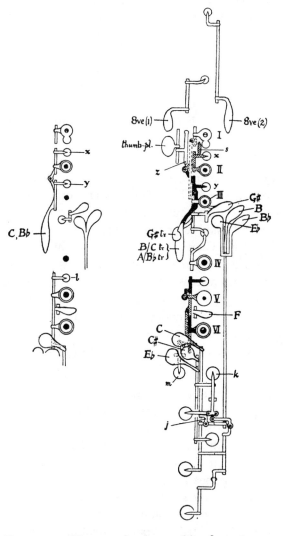

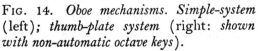

FIG. 14. *Oboe mechanisms. Simple-system* (left); *thumb-plate system* (right: *shown with non-automatic octave keys*).

between the latter and the C and B♭ keys is through a stiff needle spring arranged under the bar z as a flexible lever. Thus the side key can be depressed without forcing up the thumb-plate.

Most current models of thumb-plate oboe also include the following devices.

On the bottom joint:

1. *Low B–C connection* (j). The low B key automatically closes the low C key, in order to avoid having to slide the right little finger in slurs at the bottom of the compass (e.g. *B–C♯*; *B♭–E♭*).

2. *Articulated E♭.* An E♭ (or D♯) next to a C♯ or the low C is made with the duplicate E♭ touch for the left little finger. To facilitate rapid movements between these notes, and to give a *C♯/D♯* trill, the action of this key (k) is 'articulated' or 'split', so that the low C or C♯ key will automatically close the E♭ hole while the left hand E♭ touch remains held down. (Extra left little finger keys sometimes fitted in addition to those shown in fig. 14 are a duplicate F touch or 'long F' and a duplicate C♯ touch of 'long C♯', the latter being incorporated in the Reynolds model used by Goossens. The oboe d'amore in the Plate has the long F.)

3. *The brille* (so named after the German word for a pair of spectacles). This is shown in its simplest form in fig. 14, *left*. A small vent key l serves to sharpen the fingering . . . / . o o into a true F♯ (otherwise it would be flat, as it is on the recorder). It normally stands open, but it is closed for the lower notes by rings for V and VI, and also by the low C key to help certain high notes. In most modern oboes, however, finger V has a perforated plate (cork- or rubber-padded) instead of a ring, in order to correct the top D, for which note the plate is closed by the low C key. Consequently, plate V and ring VI must be arranged to close the brille vent l independently (fig. 14, *right*).

4. *Forked-F vent.* To avoid sliding the sixth finger, the forked F (. . . / . o .) is used in both registers instead of the F key

when F is next to D or E♭. This fingering generally needs extra venting lest the note be dull and flat. Hence there is usually a 'forked–F vent'—an open key (*m*) on the right hand side of the instrument about level with the E♭ key. For lower notes it is closed by plate V. Sometimes, even on otherwise fully-equipped oboes, this vent is lacking, in which case the forked F's are vented by opening the E♭ key, or brought under control by practice and careful choice of reeds.

On the top joint:

5. *Articulated G♯.* While the G♯ touch (left little finger) remains held down, the G♯ key itself becomes closed when finger IV is lowered, through the small arm connected to ring IV. This provides a perfect F♯/G♯ trill (by finger IV) and facilitates certain movements between G♯ and the low notes. Some thumb-plate instruments have a duplicate G♯ touch for finger IV—a small key overlapping the long side key (fig. 14, *right*)—useful in other trills. Incidentally, these two G♯ touches, like the two E♭ touches, make possible a 'double trill' —a *tour de force* by which an oboist can mesmerize his audience at a recital; the two alternative touches are used alternately, so that each finger moves with half the speed of the trill, with the most extraordinary visual effect imaginable.

6. *The thumb-plate action* for C and B♭, combined with the side key for trills, has already been described. The small spatula *s* soldered to the C key is for counteracting the thumb-plate in the trill A♯/B: finger I is extended on to the spatula to hold down the C key while the thumb-plate is released and finger II is lifted, the trill being made with the latter finger.

7. *Half-hole plate* (finger I). The first three notes of the upper register—*c″♯, d″* and *e″♭*—are obtained not with an octave key, but by 'half-holing', i.e. by rolling finger I downwards on to the extension of the plate in order to uncover the small perforation. To proceed higher up the scale, the finger re-covers the perforation while simultaneously the thumb touches its octave key (still holding down the thumb-plate).

Some players, however, prefer to have plate I connected to ring III (as shown dotted in fig. 14) or sometimes to ring II.

This enables half-holing to be done by lifting the finger instead of rolling it. The inclusion of ring III and the bar extending upwards from it also affords provision for future addition of automatic octave keys (see below) should this ever be desired. On the other hand, the arrangement can interfere with the classic fingering for the high C♯ (i.e. with the C key, see fig. 15a), since this note really requires the full opening of hole I. Hence a screw-adjustment is sometimes fitted by which ring III can be set to hold plate I nearly down but not quite, making a sort of compromise. The cor anglais (thumb-plate system) analogously has for finger I either a 'split plate', for the oboist who rolls his finger to half-hole, or a 'fixed plate' closed by III or II, for a player accustomed to the above-mentioned connection on the oboe. (Another small difference of keywork in the cor anglais is the usual addition of a small open vent-key for A, placed on the right hand side of the top joint near its lower end and closed automatically by ring III.)

8. *Open c''♯* (all fingers off). This gives the B/C♯ trill with finger I, and also an emergency alternative to the full fingering of *c''♯* ($\frac{1}{2}$ .. / ... C♯) in fast passages of the kind B–C♯–B– C♯–D, in which the first of the C♯'s may be taken 'open'. Most players, however, make a point of using the full fingering in all circumstances.

9. *Octave keys.* The bottom octave key (left thumb) is used from *e''* to *g''♯* and from *e'''♭* upwards; and the top octave key (middle joint of finger I) from *a''* to *c'''*. Since water condensed from the breath is liable to block these keys, an oboe-player carries about with him a packet of cigarette-papers, a piece of which, placed under the clogged key, draws the water out. Also, the hole of the top octave key is fitted with a special metal bush to discourage collection of water in it.

These octave keys can be *non-automatic* (or 'simple'; as they are shown in fig. 14), *semi-automatic* (as in fig. 16, *right*); or *full automatic* (fig. 16, *left*). Some players prefer the first, with its two quite independent octave keys. But by far the most popular arrangement (and on the Conservatoire system too) is the second, the semi-automatic octave keys, whereby the top key can be pressed for *a″* and upwards without removing the thumb from the bottom key; the switch-over of the vents being effected automatically on pressing the top octave key. Full automatic octave keys have pretty well gone out of favour save in Germany. Only one touch is needed (left thumb), the octave vents being automatically switched over on passing above *g″♯* by the release of ring III. Frequently, to suit those brought up on non- or semi-automatic octaves, the two touches are still provided (as shown in fig. 16), and then it does not matter which one presses.

With full automatic octave keys, the G♯ key, when pressed, holds down ring III. This is in order that it shall be the bottom octave vent, not the top, that opens for high *f‴*, for which this key is used but finger III is raised. But there are other high fingerings, e.g. for *f‴♯*, in which finger III is raised and the G♯ key not pressed, and it is still the bottom octave vent that is required to open. Full automatic octave keys therefore interfere with these fingerings unless a special reversing key is fitted (a second touch for the thumb) which reverses the entire action of the mechanism. (Also, the fingerings given in the chart for the top two semitones are not available with automatic octaves.)

10. *Trill keys* (one or two, neither shown in the diagram) for trilling over the break in the registers, e.g. C/D.

On *simplified thumb-plate models* (low-priced models by Selmer and others, costing around £48, as against from £90 to £200 for the full 'artist's models') there may be simple octave keys, and the following may be omitted: forked F vent, perforated plate for V (the original ring being restored), and G♯ trill key. In short, a useful revival of Triébert's original thumb-plate design of 1849, perfectly adequate for all but high-class professional work.

CONSERVATOIRE SYSTEM. This is Triébert's *système 6*. It derives its name from its adoption by the Paris Conservatoire in 1881 as official model in place of the thumb-plate system. It is now the standard system in most countries. In England several players have always used it. Among the present French makers

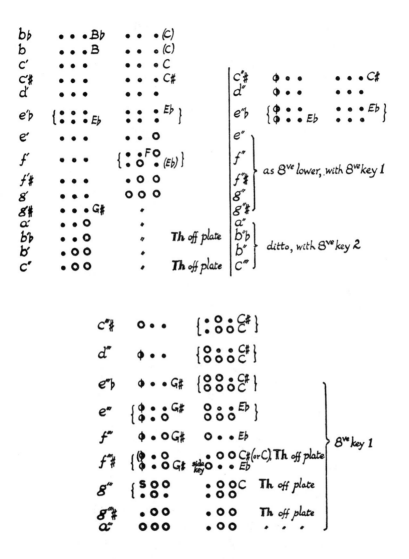

FIG. 15a. *Chart for thumb-plate oboe. Half-filled circle: uncover the perforation in plate I; S: with finger I, cover the plate and also depress the spatula s. (The top two notes are included for completeness only; they are difficult, and composers scarcely ever write them.) N.B. Alternatively in the first e'''♭ fingering, also cover V and release octave key.*

are Rigoutat, Marigaux, Jardé, Selmer and Triébert (Couesnon), while the older makers Lorée and Cabart now make chiefly for the foreign market. In America, makers have also produced a simplified model for beginners and bandsmen. The Conservatoire system can also be ordered from the British makers.

The left thumb has only the octave key. The C and B♭ action is by putting down finger IV. This tilts a lever on the right hand side of the top joint (*n*, fig. 16) to release the C and B♭ keys

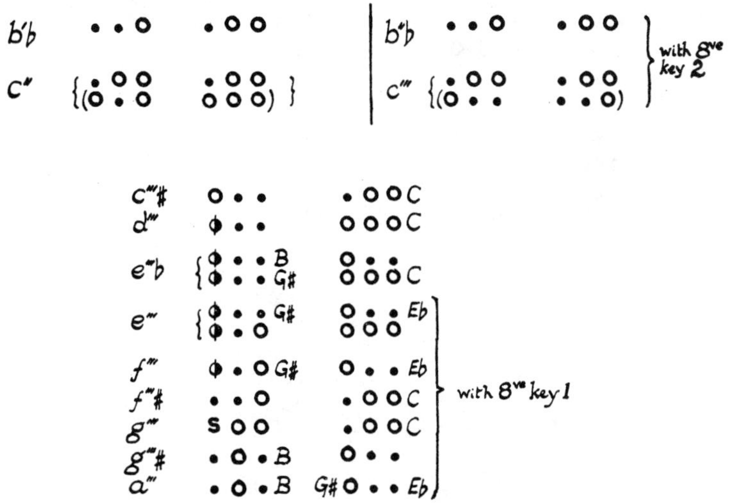

FIG. 15b. *Conservatoire-system oboe: the important differences from the thumb-plate model in the lower two octaves, and fingerings for the high register.*

just as lifting the thumb does on the thumb-plate system. Thus . o o / . o o gives the C's, and . . o / . o o the B♭'s. For the right hand notes, the B♭ key is kept closed by ring III. On account of the closure of hole IV, Conservatoire action considerably reduces the venting of B♭, giving this note, particularly in the low register, a pleasantly mellow quality recalling that of the plain fork-fingering of earlier times.

The original model of the Conservatoire system, which some still prefer, has rings (see fig. 16, *left*, for the top joint). But in 1906, Lorée, in collaboration with the elder Gillet, then oboe professor at the Conservatoire, introduced the *Gillet model,* which has perforated plates instead of rings for II, III and VI in order to obtain some better trills. A plain plate is provided for

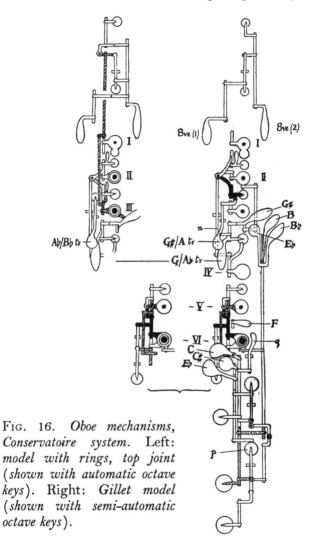

FIG. 16. *Oboe mechanisms, Conservatoire system.* Left: *model with rings, top joint (shown with automatic octave keys).* Right: *Gillet model (shown with semi-automatic octave keys).*

IV, to match the others. This (fig. 16, *right*) has now become the standard instrument in France and has gained much favour in America and elsewhere. Michael Dobson, whose set of instruments is illustrated in Plate VIII, is among the first British oboists to adopt it.

Conservatoire system mechanism. On the bottom joint:

1. *Articulated C♯ key.* A disadvantage with the low B/C connection on the ordinary thumb-plate model is that it rules out independent use of the B key on the high notes (e.g. top E♭). On this account, the Conservatoire system generally has, instead, an articulated C♯ key (*p*, fig. 16) to help slurring on the bottom notes in a different way, making possible C♯–B without releasing the C♯ touch, but leaving the B key otherwise uncoupled.

2. *The 'banana key'* (C/D♭ *trill*). This small lever next to plate VI (*q*) closes the low C key. When finger VI is extended to hold it down, the trill in question can be made with the right little finger on the C♯ key.

3. *D♯/E trill* (*Gillet model*). The plate VI is of compound construction, having an outer ring encircling an independently-hinged bush. The left hand E♭ key, when pressed, holds down this bush which makes a small-sized aperture giving a correctly-tuned E with the E♭ key open. Thus the trill is perfectly made with the finger VI while the left hand E♭ touch is held down.

4. *Closed forked F vent.* For some mysterious reason an open-standing F vent spoils the Conservatoire-system B♭. Hence it is arranged to lie normally closed. It is automatically opened by finger VI for the forked F, and is closed again by V for the lower notes.

On the top joint:

5. *Side keys.* The lower is a duplicate G♯ touch, for the G/A♭ trill. The small overlapping key is (1) on the model with rings, a plain B♭ key intended solely for the A♭/B♭ trill, being tuned to give a correct B♭ while the left hand is fingering G♯. But (2) on the Gillet model, it is a *third* G♯ touch, intended for the trill G♯/A; it opens the G♯ key and also lowers plate III, so that while fingering A, a trill can be made with this key alone. (The A♭/B♭ trill is made on the Gillet model by fingering G♯ with the left hand and trilling with finger II alone; the left hand G♯

110

key is arranged to hold down plate II, whose small perforation suffices to give the B♮ in this trill. The same connection permits use of this G♯ key for the A♯/B trill, circumventing the need for moving finger I onto the spatula.)

6. *The Conservatoire C and B♭ action* has been described already, but note also the alternative cross-fingerings in the chart, which may sometimes come in useful. (The *second spatula*, soldered to the B♭ key (fig. 16, *left*), is sometimes present as a relic from an earlier version of the system in which any one of the right hand fingers could actuate the C and B action; this spatula was then needed in order to keep the key closed during the high D/E trill.)

7. *The 'third octave key'* (not shown in fig. 16) is a second touch for left thumb, opening a vent a little higher up. It is sometimes fitted to help high notes from top E upwards.

A recent addition to French instruments is a low B♮ vent key on the bell. After the pitch was officially raised to $a' = 440$ in 1939, the French makers found that the corresponding shortening of the bell (about one-quarter of an inch) had an unsettling effect on the note E. Therefore they retained the old $a' = 435$ length of bell and fitted this small vent key, which opens when the low B♮ key is pressed in order to bring this note up to the new pitch.

OTHER OBOE SYSTEMS. In England one may still occasionally see an oboe built to the *Barret system*, with thumb-plate duplicated by right hand action for any of the four fingers of that hand, but no 'Barret' side key. It is mentioned again in Chapter XII.

Though more and more Germans are playing on the Conservatoire system, in some *French-style oboes built in Germany* the C and B♭ action is neither by thumb-plate nor by Conservatoire action, but by a 'Barret' side key duplicated by a left thumb key. The latter is *pressed* for C or B♭, not released, as the ordinary thumb-plate is. This arrangement perpetuates the German tradition for a closed B♮ key for the thumb (similar to that on the eight-keyed flute). Similarly, these instruments usually also have the duplicate F key or 'long F', used in preference to the forked F, and full automatic octave keys.

The *earlier types of German oboe*, with the wide bore, are illustrated in Plate IX by a model still taught in Russia. French influence is shown in several small points, as the lay-out

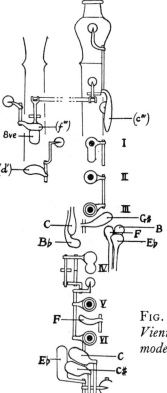

FIG. 17. *Diagram of Viennese oboe (Zuleger model)*.

of the little-finger keys. The fingering is that of the simple-system oboe described first in this section (p. 101), though with even greater emphasis on the use of the harmonic cross-fingerings from *a''* to *c'''*, these being always employed save in those quick passages in which they would prove cumbersome.

The mechanism of the *Viennese oboe* remains Germanic throughout. Fig. 17 shows that of the current Zuleger model (Plate IX). It has long F and long E♭ keys, and side keys for B♭ and C, alternative to the cross-fingerings. In the upper register, the octave key (thumb) is employed up to *a''* inclusive. Then follow harmonic cross-fingerings without the octave key. The key located in a similar position to that of the French top octave key is a special key to help the high C. The key whose touch overlaps the touch of the octave key, helps top F. The lowest thumb touch opens a key that helps the half-holed Ds under certain conditions. The instrument's most remarkable mechanical feature is its *closed brille*. The brille key (F♯ vent) lies normally closed. When finger IV is lowered, it becomes free to rise under its own spring. On other notes, the lower rings and the right little-finger keys close it again. The benefit is that it preserves the classical venting of the notes made with the left hand only.

Boehm-system oboe. This is generally taken to mean the Klosé-Buffet design brought out at the same time as the Boehm-system clarinet. It is briefly described in the last chapter. Several catalogues of the nineteen-twenties still listed it, and some Spanish orchestras and bands use it. In Spain one may come upon, today, many relics of French fashions of the past, just as past German fashions survive in Russia, on the opposite end of the woodwind's fundamental Franco-German axis. Elsewhere there have also been 'half-Boehm' and 'sax-fingered' models, with F♯ and F made *à la Boehm* and various other modifications. They have never caught on, however, and are not seen in orchestras.

The Shawm today

The oboe today plays a diminishing part in military band and other outdoor music; many military bands abroad dispense with it entirely. The proper double-reed instrument for outdoors is the *shawm*, one of the oboe's predecessors, and a wider-bore, far more powerful instrument that was always a band instrument, far too fierce and penetrating to be employed in music of milder kinds.

This most desirable instrument had become generally extinct by the beginning of the eighteenth century, and now there is only one place in Europe where it has lived on in its ancient role; and not merely lived on, but been developed mechanically along the lines of the other woodwind instruments. This is Northern Catalonia—the north-east corner of Spain from Barcelona northwards to the French frontier, and across it into Roussillon, the district of the French Catalans with Perpignan its chief city. There one hears the shawms as the melodists of the *coblas*, the bands that play for the sardana dance. They are supported by two trumpets, a valved trombone, two bass flugel horns in C (virtually euphoniums built in bugle shape) and a string bass. Also, there is the leader of the band, who plays a special form of pipe and tabor, the fluviol (Chapter IX).

Two sizes of shawm are used (Plate X), named *tiple* (Spanish for 'treble') and *tenora* ('tenor') and there are two of each in a band. The instruments are known to the musicians by no other name, though Spanish musicologists describe them by the old Spanish shawm name *chirimia*. Their reeds (Plates VI, XIX) are short and triangular, and have a wider opening than any other kind of double reed. Each reed is made on a short peg-like wooden mandrel which is kept in the reed until it is to be used. The reed is then placed upon a short conical staple upon which is permanently mounted a thick wooden cylinder, the *tudel*, better known to wind-instrument historians by the old French term for it, *pirouette*. The pirouette is recessed on its upper surface to make room for the base of the reed, and the player, holding the instrument well up, almost horizontally, rests his lips against it while also gripping and controlling the reed like an oboist. With this arrangement he can keep the strong reed vibrating at its full power without his embouchure muscles quickly becoming tired. To keep the reed firmly fixed on the staple, wedges of cork or wood are pushed down into the recess in the pirouette, but some of the players now use a metal pirouette provided with a set-screw to grip the short stem of the reed.

Tiple and tenora are both transposing instruments; the tiple (*c.* 22 inches long) is in F, a fourth above the oboe, and the tenora (*c.* 33 inches long) is in B♭, a tone below the oboe. Their modernization began in the last century with the musician Pepe Ventura, and led to their being fitted with a simple-system key-work, with a half-hole plate for obtaining the lower part of the upper register, and an octave key for use above g''. Both instruments have extension keys, actuated by the little fingers and the left thumb; the tiple down to its written a (sounding d') and the tenora, which has a long metal bell, down to its $f\sharp$, sounding e. As for high notes, José Coll, principal tenora in the Cobla Barcelona—one of the leading bands, recording regularly for Columbia (and one of the few bands that does not play at sharp pitch)—gives charts up to written e''' for the tiple and g''' for the tenora, and such high notes are indeed heard in solo variations.

The sound of these shawms is unbelievably exciting. Constant Lambert and de Sévérac are two discriminating musicians who have lauded it. Their effect is of tremendously loud, full-throated oboes—the tiple the clearer and more trumpet-like, and the tenora the more sensuous and reedy. Yet on both, the players command a full dynamic range down to *mezzo-piano*, which the first tenora continually exploits with uninhibited abandon in the solo passages, of which he has the lion's share and delivers with a rich oboist's vibrato. The instruments have, indeed, the full expressive range of the oboe stepped up to out-door strength, and great would be the day if ever they came to be tried in the northern countries, to add their fiery glow to the rather pallid hues of our military bands.

Musette

In the eighteenth century, the *musette* was a small bagpipe, but the chanter was often taken out and played without the bag, in which case a wooden cap was put over the reed to preserve it. Played either way, this was the original instrument of the *bal musette*, French country-dancing. During the last century the bag and wooden cap became forgotten, and the musette became a small oboe-like instrument pitched in G (a fifth above the oboe). It was still used for the bal musette, though today this has become something rather different and its chief instrument is the accordion. These later musettes were exported to England as late as the 1930s for sale as musical toys, though their sales cannot have been large and there was always the difficulty and expense of reeds (cf. p. 330).

CHAPTER V

The Clarinet

This, the third of the woodwind primary tone-colours, has a cylindrical tube (about four millimetres narrower than the flute tube) of African blackwood, which has replaced cocus; though possibly none of this jungle wood can rival the old Turkish boxwood, which for some reason gave especially fine results in clarinets, Boehm-system included. Many fine players have played on ebonite, which gives a sweeter though rather smaller tone than wood. Metal, on the other hand, does not seem to offer the right resistance, giving a tone that feels to most players rather vapid and uninteresting, and it is not used for high-class work.

The wide over-blowing intervals of the clarinet—a twelfth, and above that, a sixth, due to its 'stopped pipe' acoustical properties (Chapter I)—give the instrument the largest compass of all the woodwind; the lower and upper registers alone cover three octaves all but two notes. This is however accompanied by a very much more marked difference than on other instruments between the tone-colours of the registers. Where the registers join, their tone-qualities meet without sharpness, yet quite distinctly, like the colours of the rainbow, contributing much to the instrument's individual character.

As on every reed instrument, the great register is the upper register, here the overblown twelfths. Can one possibly imagine Mozart or Brahms having written a principal slow-movement theme for their clarinet quintets in any other register? It was for this upper register that the clarinet was invented, and from it, it derives its name: to early eighteenth-century ears it suggested the far-away sound of a trumpet (*clarino*), softened and sweetened by distance. It was its liquid beauty in this register that earned it its place in the orchestra, and this too is the register that always stands out most vividly in one's memory of every fine player.

The low register, which a beginner learns to sound first, is traditionally known as the *chalumeau* register, after a little kindred instrument played at the time of the clarinet's invention. Being at the twelfth below the 'clarino' register, the low register reaches notes half-way down the bass stave—low notes for an instrument only 26 inches long. To bridge the gap or 'break' between these two registers, the upper is played right down to its bell note (*b'*)—a unique feature among woodwind techniques —and to meet it with the adjacent *b'♭*, the low register is carried up into the 'throat' of the instrument by small closed keys. This arrangement makes clarinet-fingering seem difficult and cumbersome at first. But in fact it proves so efficient that the clarinet is rated among the most agile of musical instruments, and all proposals for new mechanism to simplify 'the break' have been flatly turned down by the mass of players, past and present.

Above the upper register is the high register, in which the tone rapidly deteriorates in quality. The notes above *g'''*, up to the top *c''''*, are hard and squeaky and are little employed except in bravura passages and massive *tuttis*.

B♭, A and C clarinets

The common clarinet is the B♭ clarinet. This is the clarinet of dance bands and military bands. But for orchestral work a player also needs an A clarinet (just over an inch longer), making a pair of instruments; the one that is to be used is specified in the part. They have the same bore, and the same mouthpiece and barrel are generally used for them both, being changed over as the parts require.

This employment of two instruments arose in early times when it was scarcely possible to play in remote keys on the clarinet. In music in flat keys the parts were written for the B♭ instrument; in sharp keys for the A; and this remains the normal practice among composers in most countries although the technical reason for it is no longer urgent. There is a small difference in tone-quality between the two instruments, the slightly darker sound of the A being most noticeable in the lower part of the upper register. But so small is the difference that in certain countries—Italy and Spain—the A is dispensed with entirely; every part written for it is transposed at sight (reading a semitone lower) on the B♭ instrument, which then has to have an extra key (low E♭ key) to reach the bottom note of the A clarinet. The Italians claim that this is the logical thing to do now that modern clarinet technique has made it possible to play fluently in the remotest keys. They claim too that one instrument can better be kept in tune through a performance than two. Certainly these players manage the A parts perfectly well, and one never hears an accident on account of the formidable transposition. All the same, players north of the Alps, British included, prefer to retain the A and sometimes even use it for a passage written for the B♭ in order to obviate some technical difficulty, for instance in the last Act of *Carmen*, where a whole-tone trill on $f''\sharp$, virtually impossible on the ordinary systems of clarinet, becomes, on the A, an easy trill on g''. Moreover, the A is virtually indispensable for the two great quintets and Mozart's concerto.

Beginners who cannot afford a pair straight off, start with a B♭ and pair it with an A later on. There is no binding need for the two to be of the same make. Ideally they should be, but there are plenty of first-class players who use an odd pair.

Formerly, up to about 1900 in England, an orchestral clarinettist also had a *C clarinet*, which is often written for by classical composers in movements in the keys C and G. But today, C clarinet parts are played on the B♭ instrument (the player reading the part a tone higher) or, in sharp keys, very often on the A (reading a minor third higher). The reasons for abandoning the C, apart from the fact that it is comparatively seldom demanded, were firstly that its tone lacks the dignified mellowness of the B♭, being in comparison hard and chirping; and secondly that it needs a different mouthpiece, since its bore is over a millimetre smaller.

In Germany and Austria, however, Mahler and Strauss revived the C clarinet as a *special* instrument—as a tone-colour in its own right—and today in those countries the C is numbered with the E♭ and the D instruments as one of the 'small clarinets', and is handled mainly by the players who specialize in these. (But the real home-ground of the C today is in local bands in the southern Teutonic regions; for instance a café band in German Switzerland, where one may see the clarinettist, after he has laboured through a number of commercial dance orchestrations on a Boehm-system B♭, happily seize his old simple-system C to reel off a string of *Ländler*.)

Mouthpiece, bore and tone

The clarinet has five pieces: bell, bottom joint, top joint, barrel (which must be pulled out a little when necessary to counteract rise in pitch through heat), and mouthpiece. The latter is usually ebonite, though other materials have their devotees: 'crystal' (i.e. glass) in Italy; plastics (especially in America); cocus-wood, or cocus faced with metal (old-fashioned German).

The reed is clamped to the mouthpiece with the screw ligature, with the tip of the mouthpiece level with the tip of the reed (or, if it suits a particular reed better, just proud of the tip of the reed). The player puts the uppermost half-inch or so of the mouthpiece, reed downwards, between the lips, with the lower lip curled back to form a cushion between reed and teeth. Some curl back the upper lip to cushion the top of the mouthpiece as well, but others place the upper teeth directly on the mouthpiece. There have been local traditions in the past about this. Today the second is the most taught, though some will find the first suitable. The grip on the mouthpiece is assisted by the pressure of the right thumb against the thumb-rest on the bottom joint, while the sides of the mouth are puckered round the mouthpiece to prevent air escaping or the cheeks puffing out. It helps the tone to keep the throat perfectly relaxed. Should a beginner still scarcely be able to produce a sound after a few days, there is no need to feel discouraged; probably the sound will be all the better in the end. Any pain or swelling of the lips or right thumb soon passes off once and for all. The tongue-stroke against the reed should be quite light; it is the breath that sets the reed in vibration.

To save time when looking for suitable reeds out of a box of new ones, each reed can be roughly tested, after wetting it in the mouth, by holding it against the mouthpiece with the thumb and blowing a few notes fingered with one hand only. If no promising reed can be found, others must be adjusted (see Chapter III). But if no reed ever seems to go satisfactorily or the instrument seems impossible to play in tune, the probability is that the mouthpiece is of unsuitable pattern or has an unsuitable *lay*. The lay is the shape of the gap between the reed and the table of the mouthpiece. It becomes visible when the mouthpiece, with reed on it, is held sideways up to the light. The gap at the tip averages one millimetre, though some like it more open, others more closed. The *length* of the lay (or 'spring') is measured from the tip back to the point where the mouthpiece bears away from the reed. It varies from less than 10 millimetres (short lay) to 25 millimetres (long lay; i.e. about one inch), with medium lays (*c.* 15 millimetres) in between. Re-laying a clarinet mouthpiece is one of the woodwind repairer's constantly-demanded jobs—a skilled operation of hand-grinding on emery laid over glass or marble, progress being tested with feeler gauges.

To gain a broad idea of the implications of mouthpiece design, instrument design and choice of reed—all of which are bound up together—we may look at certain distinctive national schools of clarinet-playing. As usual with wind instruments, two extremes are represented by the French and the German.

The *French school* uses a Boehm-system clarinet with a comparatively narrow bore for modern times (about 14·9 millimetres). The bell-expansion starts from a little way above the lowest hole. The top end may also expand, from the neighbourhood of the speaker key to about 15 millimetres in bore at the top of the barrel, where it meets our ordinary mouthpiece of the wide, broad-slotted type, introduced by French and Belgian makers a century ago mainly with the idea of filling out the sound in the low register. French tradition is for a short lay and a soft reed, and the net result is a tone that inclines to sound thin and pinched, and often distinctly reedy in the upper register. Moreover, the tone becomes difficult to swell effectively in cantabile passages in that register. Otherwise the French style can sound very musical and expressive, and it is the style that now prevails on the whole in Italy and America.

In England, the great majority of players use the Boehm-system instruments of Boosey & Hawkes, which have a wider bore than the French (exceeding 15 millimetres) and no expansion at the top end. The same type of wide mouthpiece is used, but generally with a medium length of lay and a medium-hard reed, following the tradition set by Charles Draper and continued by Frederick Thurston, and producing that firm, clear clarinet sound which characterizes most, but not all, British orchestras. Draper himself used French instruments by Martel, and the clarinets made by Louis (London) were modelled on these under his direction.

A present tendency in England, however, is the use of a longer lay and a harder reed, recalling the earlier British school of Draper's equally famous predecessor, Lazarus, who recommended a lay one inch long. The main object of this (notably achieved by Bernard Walton, principal clarinet in the Philharmonia Orchestra) is to carry the full liquidness and expressive power up to the top of the upper register—especially on the crucial note c''', a note that is, by nature, brittle and lifeless with the Boehm system.

The *German clarinet*, used also in Austria, Russia and (though now challenged by the French model) in Holland, is normally a non-Boehm instrument with complex and variable keywork (see further on), and with a greater length of cylindrical bore than any other type of clarinet. It is cylindrical from the mouthpiece down at least to the level of the lowest hole, while also the bell flares less on the inside than in other clarinets. The mouthpiece is comparatively narrow and pointed (Plate VII), with a smaller slot. On this goes a small, hard reed, generally tied on with five feet of special silk cord (*Blattschnurr*), the mouthpiece being grooved on the outside to prevent the cord slipping upwards. Average dimensions of this reed are as follows (with those of a

French reed in brackets), in millimetres: length, 62 to 65 (68); tip width, 12 to 12·5 (13·5); length of the scrape, 30 (about the same). In this form of bore, mouthpiece and reed, something more than elsewhere has been retained of the clarinet of the time of Beethoven and Weber, though the actual bore-diameter has been considerably increased to keep up with the general growth of orchestral loudness over the last century and a half, and may now exceed 15·5 millimetres.

With this equipment, the best German players can obtain the broadest and creamiest sound of any. The change of colour over the break may be rather more pronounced than with other designs; but the instrument possesses the weight to balance the thick-toned German bassoons, horns and rich string-playing, and the tone can be swelled on every note in the upper register from a pianissimo echo-tone to a wonderful *forte* without trace of shrillness. So often in other countries the clarinet sounds pale beside the oboe—its sister instrument that is played with such luxuriant expression; and an appassionato solo is apt to sound disappointing (e.g. in the slow movement of Beethoven's Ninth Symphony). But rarely so in Germany and Austria. True, the German style is not always displayed to its best advantage; for example, Mühlfeld, the first to play the Brahms quintet, is remembered in Vienna as having been admired more for his technique than for his tone, which was heavy and over-predominating. But when the late Leopold Wlach soars above the Vienna Philharmonic in a recorded Strauss tone-poem, or fires the impassioned gypsy moods of Brahms's quintet, one recognizes not only a superb artist, but also something extra which the German clarinet alone provides.

High and deep clarinets

THE SMALL CLARINETS. The chief of these is the *E♭ clarinet*— the only one used in England, where military bands include it as a regular member, though latterly the tendency has been to dispense with it except on the march. Berlioz brought it into the orchestra (*Symphonie fantastique*, 1831), after which it was little used until Mahler. Mahler hits off its very individual nature to perfection in 'The Hunter's Funeral' (the third movement of the First Symphony), with two E♭s playing in thirds like classical woodwind instruments, and in the motif played above the canon (fig. 18). Most composers since Mahler have employed it in one work or another.

An older instrument, and the one most used by German composers before Mahler (e.g. Wagner, in *The Valkyrie*), is the *D clarinet*, built a semitone lower. Strauss continued to score for it, and many German orchestras always employ it instead of playing its parts on the E♭ clarinet. Players find the D a very much sweeter instrument to handle than the E♭, and it is now regularly being used at Covent Garden.

E♭ clarinet reeds are stocked by the leading instrument suppliers. They are about 60 millimetres long and 12 milli-

FIG. 18. *A characteristic motif for the E♭ clarinet, from Mahler's First Symphony, 3rd movement. (By courtesy of Boosey & Hawkes Ltd.)*

metres across the tip; but German reeds are smaller, e.g. 54 × 10·5 millimetres, and *hard*.

Further ascent among the small clarinets brings us to the *A♭ clarinet* used in most large Continental military bands to help with the highest passages in transcriptions of orchestral works. Notwithstanding its minute size, the French and Italian makers manage to fit full Boehm mechanism to it (Plate XII). Its lowest note is the same as that of the flute, while its top G sounds *e''''♭*, i.e. well up into the piccolo range. Naturally the high notes are rather hard and piercing, but of course that is what the band needs them to be. Lower down, the instrument gives the quaintest sound—some idea of it can be gained by playing a clarinet record at practically double speed—and we might well ask to enjoy it in the rendition of eighteenth-century parts for the chalumeau, to which the A♭ clarinet is the nearest modern equivalent. Like the other flat-key clarinets, the

Ab has a fainter companion pitched a semitone lower—the G clarinet, which now seems to exist only on paper (e.g. in the stage band parts of *Norma* and *La Traviata*).

The pinnacle of the clarinets is reached in toys like the 'red hot fountain pen'—a keyless, penny-whistle-sized clarinet which jazz connoisseurs may remember as a novelty instrument of many years ago. Joe Venuti could imitate it in harmonics on the fiddle.

TABLE OF CLARINETS

(Extinct or very rare sizes in brackets)

	Actual sound of		Approximate total length, in inches	
	the open G	*the lowest note*		
Ab clarinet	$e''\flat$	c'	14·0	Continental mil. bands
(F clarinet)	c''	a	17·3	Bands of 150 years ago
Eb clarinet	$b'\flat$	g	19·3	
D clarinet	a'	$f\sharp$	20·5	German orchestras
C clarinet	g'	e	23·5	„ „
Bb clarinet	f'	d	26·5	
A clarinet	e'	$c\sharp$	27·8	
(Clarinet d'amour in Ab or G)	$e'\flat, d'$	c, B	31	Extinct; see Chap. XI
Basset horn in F	c'	F		
(F alto clarinet)	c'	A		Formerly in Continental bands
Eb alto clarinet	$b\flat$	G		Military bands
Bb bass clarinet	f	$C\sharp (C)$		
(A bass clarinet)	e	$C\sharp$		Occasionally still in Germany
Eb contrabass clarinet	$B\flat$	G'		
Bb contrabass clarinet	F	D'		
Bb sub-contrabass clarinet	F'	D''		New

BASSET HORN. Most of the deeper clarinets that we know are nineteenth-century French inventions with the bore enlarged in proportion to the depth in pitch. Thus the alto and bass clarinets, —instruments originally designed to supply military band-masters with fat, resonant tones useful in the transcription of string parts of orchestral works—have bores of 18 millimetres and 20–23 millimetres respectively.

The basset horn, however, is an eighteenth-century idea, and is quite different. It is a clarinet pitched in F (a major third lower than the A clarinet) and traditionally made with the same bore as an A or B♭ clarinet and played with the same mouthpiece. Thus, for example, the Uebel instruments of the Vienna Philharmonic have a 15 millimetre bore, though in the French instruments hitherto used by most London players the bore is 16 millimetres, and Schmidt too has enlarged the bore for power in the large modern orchestra. With its old bore the basset horn is just a *long* clarinet, lengthened in the tube and having the finger-holes lower down. Its upper-register tone fully conserves the clarity and melodiousness of the clarinet, having none of the alto and bass clarinets' wide-bore throatiness. Its quality, as compared with that of the B♭ clarinet, might be described as like that of an A clarinet but much more so.

Its compass has always been extended down below its low E (sounding *A*) to a low C (sounding *F*). This is done with four extra keys—on German instruments, all four for the right thumb; on French, two for the thumb and two for the little fingers. A curved barrel brings the instrument into a comfortable playing position, as on all modern deep clarinets. Sometimes this barrel is of wood, and sometimes it is of metal, in which case it is usually called a crook. French instruments have an upturned metal bell (Plate XI); Germans often used to have a straight-downwards wooden bell, as on the clarinet, but now have a metal upturned bell which is in a sense a dummy, for the lowest note issues through a large vent-hole at the base of the bottom joint, in order to equalize its quality with that of the other notes; the bell then acts as a general reflector, lifting the sound off the floor.

The basset horn has two major composers: Mozart and Richard Strauss. Mozart's basset horn works include the *Requiem* (in which there are no ordinary clarinets); several operas, including the *Magic Flute*, and *La Clemenza di Tito*, which contains an obbligato that once used to be popular at concerts; various short pieces, including the three beautiful

Andantes for two clarinets and three basset horns; and the great *Serenade* in B♭ for thirteen wind instruments. It is in this last that the basset horn has its sublimest say, above all in the *adagio* movement, with its trio of soloists, oboe, clarinet and basset horn (Boskowsky plays it in Furtwängler's great recording) over a moving bass and softly-throbbing inner figure of accompaniment on the other instruments; a jewel in wind music, comparable with the Air of Bach's Third Suite in string music.

Strauss scored for basset horn in almost every opera from *Elektra* onwards, and thanks to the popularity of these two composers a pair of basset horns can now be produced when necessary in every big musical centre, and the days of faking their parts on clarinets are over.

When looking for second-hand basset horns, one must take care to avoid a rare but none the less existing type of German E♭ alto clarinet with extension down to its low C like a basset horn. Six fingers on the basset horn sounds (at concert pitch) *c*, and the open note sounds middle *c'*; on this other instrument they are B♭s.

BASS CLARINET. Modern bass clarinets are derived from the 1838 design of Sax, which displaced earlier models, many of which had bassoon-like butt joints (for a full account of early bass clarinets, see Rendall, *The Clarinet*). It is uncertain whether it was one of the latter or on an early straight model that the pioneer *obbligato* in Meyerbeer's *Les Huguenots* was first played.

The bass clarinet is in B♭, an octave below the B♭ clarinet. In France and in England (in the fine instruments of Boosey & Hawkes) it has a large bore, up to 23 millimetres. Bass clarinet reeds can be bought in Paris, and an emergency substitute is a tenor saxophone reed. German instruments traditionally have a narrower bore (*c.* 20 millimetres) and smaller mouthpiece, for which the players mostly make their own reeds; the example in Plate VII is from the Amsterdam Concertgebouw Orchestra and is for a Mollenhauer bass clarinet. The German tone is less powerful than that of the French design, but no less effective, having a compact, telling reediness below the break and greater brightness above it. Heckel, however, has departed from this tradition, and makes a very wide bore, feeling that increased tonal weight is desirable.

The chief fingering difference from the ordinary clarinet lies in the common use of two speaker keys. Both are actuated by the left thumb and the upper one is used from $e''\flat$ upwards. With automatic mechanism these keys can be made to change over with a single touch for the thumb, so making the bass clarinet an easy doubling instrument for a dance-band saxophonist. But it interferes with the production and intonation of certain notes in the high register, and so most orchestral bass-clarinettists retain the two independent keys. There is also a modern German design with *three* speaker keys, all changed automatically, to clear the wolf notes in the region e''–$g''\sharp$, which incline to kick and to lose tone when made with the ordinary top speaker key.

There is much difference of opinion as to the proper lowest note of the bass clarinet. (1) In many older and military instruments, it is E as on the clarinet (sounding *D*). (2) For orchestral work, however, a bass clarinet needs a low E♭ key in order to reach the bottom E of parts written for the virtually extinct bass clarinet in A. In the Wagner operas, for example, this note is too important to be omitted in performance. (Only a few German opera houses still possess an A bass clarinet, and even so the odds are that the player will play everything on the B♭, as is done elsewhere.) Every orchestral bass clarinet in France, England, etc., has this extra key (for right little finger on Boehms, but often for right thumb on other systems). (3) In Germany, bass clarinets have hitherto normally been built down to their low D (sounding *C*, a useful and appropriate note for a bass instrument to go down to). (4) A long-established custom in the Eastern European countries is to extend the bass clarinet in basset horn fashion down to its low C. This accounts for the low Ds and Cs that occur quite often in Russian scores, and this extended compass is now finding favour in Germany. The Berlin Philharmonic, for instance, use a bass clarinet built down to its low C, by Oehler. On the standard Western instrument, nothing can be done about the Cs, but a quick way of dealing with Ds (e.g. in *Petrushka*) is to drop the mouthpiece cap into the bell and finger the low E♭. This makes a rather stifled note, however, and a better way is to drop in a cardboard tube about 4 inches long. If D and E♭ occur together, an accomplice is needed, to insert or remove the tube in time with the music. Many Western designs, however, now descend to the low C.

Unlike the oboist's cor anglais, the bass clarinet is a specialist's instrument that the great majority of clarinettists never touch. It is a difficult instrument to play well, with a full clear sound in all registers. When well and thoughtfully handled, however, an entry of the bass clarinet is really something to look forward to, whether in the deep wind harmonies of Wagner, Delius and Puccini, or in a solo obbligato like the one in the last Act of *Aida*.

ALTO CLARINET (formerly better known in England as *tenor clarinet*). This has always been purely a military-band instrument, normally built in E♭, though some German and older French instruments are in F. The approximate reed-size is: length, 72 millimetres; tip, 14 millimetres. It was Muller, inventor of the thirteen-keyed clarinet, who first proposed the alto clarinet, as a kind of wind viola for band transcriptions, and in this capacity the old 'soup ladle' lasted in the British service well into the present century, though it has since been replaced by the more powerful alto saxophone. The big military bands in America, Italy and Spain, however, still often have it. An example is the municipal band of Venice, which plays several evenings a week during the summer in the Piazza, with the customary Italian military band repertoire of operatic selections, Wagner overtures and special clarinet solos, all executed with that conscientious musicianship typical of every grade of Italian wind player. It may be seen with the following instruments, formed up in concentric semicircles facing the conductor and St Mark's:

innermost row: 2 flutes, 2 oboes, A♭ clarinet, 2 E♭ clarinets;
second row: 14 B♭ clarinets;
third row: 3 soprano and 1 alto flugel horns, 4 horns, 2 alto

clarinets, 2 bass clarinets, soprano, 2 alto, tenor and baritone saxophones; also a bass sax. reading from the same part as a contrabassoon;

fourth row: 3 trumpets, 2 B♭ bass trumpets, 2 tenor trombones (valved or slide, depending on who turns up), 1 F bass valved trombone, 1 BB♭ contrabass valved trombone, 2 tenor horns, 1 euphonium, 4 brass basses, and 4 string basses;

in front: timpani, side drum, and bass drum with cymbals.

CONTRABASS CLARINET. This is a good instrument that should receive wider attention. The supra-treble register of the woodwind is well enough provided for by the piccolo; but it cannot be said that the sub-bass is equally well served by the contrabassoon—an instrument that ceases to be effective as soon as the orchestra approaches a mezzoforte. One remedy for this deficiency would be to double the contrabassoon with a contrabass clarinet, following the line sometimes taken in big Continental bands. In large-scale transcriptions for these there is usually included a 'reed contrabass' part intended for whatever deep reed instrument the band happens to possess (e.g. sarrusophone; see next chapter). If the band possesses more than one sort, then all the better, and they are thrown on to this part together (as for instance in the Italian band cited above). Among such instruments in France and Germany, there is occasionally a contrabass clarinet.

Several modern makers have shown that the contrabass clarinet is a sound practical proposition. Some, as Selmer, have concentrated on a *contrabass in E♭*. This, though its bottom note sounds no lower than *G'*, has an advantage in that bass parts in bands can easily be sight-read by imagining treble clef instead of bass clef and adjusting the sharps and flats as necessary.

But most have concentrated on the full *contrabass in B♭*, an octave deeper than the bass clarinet and two octaves below the ordinary clarinet. The German designs are on the whole the neatest, keeping (in wood or in metal) to the plain shape of the bass clarinet. The Hüller instrument illustrated (Plate XIV) stands 57 inches tall, resting on the ground through an adjustable peg, like a cello. It has 28·5 millimetre bore, and its reed is

97 millimetres long and 19 millimetres wide across the tip. Its sound is clear and musical right down to the bottom E (sounding the lowest D of the piano). Even the deepest notes can be played as lightly and as staccato as could be desired, while the technical flexibility throughout is all that one could possibly wish for. It was recently used in London for a performance of Schönberg's *Five Orchestral Pieces* (in which the composer has somewhat perversely scored for contrabass clarinet in A), and played on that occasion by R. Temple Savage, Covent Garden's wizard of the bass clarinet and the owner of the instruments in Plate XI.

So successful are these contrabass clarinets that it is not surprising to read that *sub-contrabass clarinets*, an octave lower still, have been built. A recent example is the *octo-contrabass* clarinet by Leblanc, in BBB♭, of metal, five feet tall and descending far below the piano keyboard down to the bottom of the 32-foot register of the organ—the deepest orchestral or band instrument yet contrived.

Clarinet mechanisms

In the following descriptions the keys are named according to the notes they give in the *upper* register except for the A and A♭ keys for finger I, which are used only in the lower register. To obtain the upper register on any clarinet, the left thumb keeps the thumb-hole closed and opens the speaker key with its merest edge; simultaneously, the lower lip presses tighter on the reed and one 'thinks' the note that is being aimed for.

BOEHM-SYSTEM CLARINET (Plate XI and fig. 19, *left*). This system, inspired by the ring-mechanism of Boehm's conical flute of 1832, was brought out in 1843 by Klosé, then professor at the Paris Conservatoire, working in collaboration with the maker Buffet. It is now the standard system in France, the Latin countries and both American continents, while in England it has become by far the most-used system and the only one in regular manufacture. Among present French makers are Selmer (with a second factory in America), Buffet, Marigaux, Leblanc, and Couesnon. In England, Boosey & Hawkes. There are several first class Italian makers, and German makers will supply the system to order. A new instrument costs (1955) from £24 to £120, according to the quality of the materials and workmanship.

1. *Little-finger keys.* An alternative touch is provided for B, C, and C♯, but not for E♭. With these, sliding a little finger from one key to another is largely avoided by using the two little fingers alternately. Normally B is taken with the left hand;

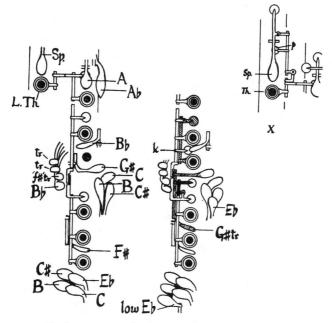

FIG. 19. *Boehm-system clarinet mechanism.* Left: *standard or 'plain' Boehm;* centre: *full Boehm;* X: *example of an 'improved B♭' device.*

C with the right hand (unless next to E♭); and C♯ normally with the right hand since it occurs most commonly next to B, but if next to C or E♭ it is taken with the left hand. The player gets to recognize groups like B–C♯–D♯, where the B must be with the right hand, but in some passages, sliding the right little finger cannot be avoided, e.g. B–C♯–D♯ *repeated.* A conundrum like B–D♯–G♯–B–D♯ may be solved by use of a cross-fingered g''♯ (· · ○ / · · ○).

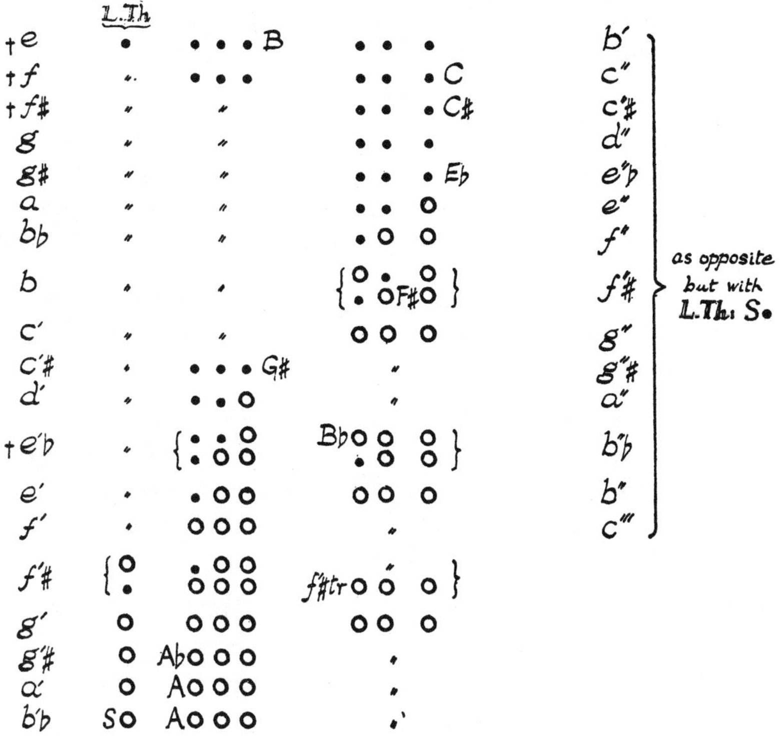

L.Th

†e • • • • B   • • •   b′
†f • • • •   • • • C   c″
†f# • • • • C#   c′#
g   • • •   d″
g#   • • • Eb   e″b
a   • • ○   e″
bb   • ○ ○   f′
b   { ○ • F# ○ }   f′#
c′   ○ ○ ○   g″
c′# • • • G#   g″#
d′ • • ○   a″
†e′b { • • ○ / • ○ ○ } Bb ○ ○ ○ / • ○ ○ ○   b″b
e′ • ○ ○   ○ ○ ○   b″
f′ ○ ○ ○   c‴
f′# { ○ / • • ○ ○ / ○ ○ ○ } f#tr ○ ○ ○
g′ ○ ○ ○ ○   ○ ○ ○
g′# ○ Ab ○ ○ ○
a′ ○ A ○ ○ ○
bb S○ A ○ ○ ○

as opposite but with **L.Th: S●**

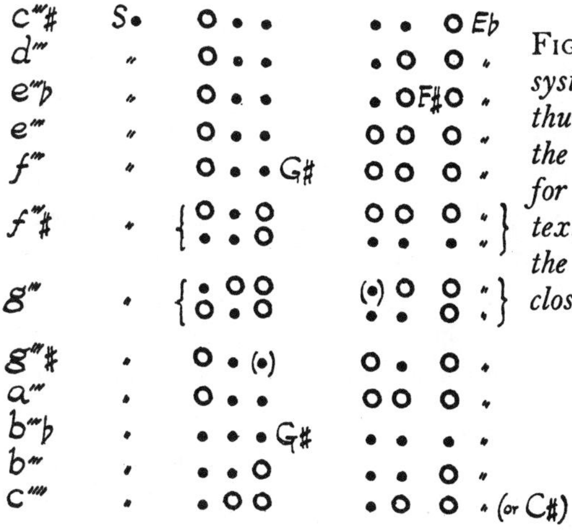

c‴# S● ○ • •   • • ○ Eb
d‴ ○ • •   • ○ ○
e‴b ○ • •   • ○ F#○
e‴ ○ • •   ○ ○ ○
f‴ ○ • • G#   ○ ○ ○
f‴# { ○ • ○ / • • ○ }   ○ ○ ○ • / • • • • }
g‴ { • • ○ ○ / ○ • ○ ○ }   (•) ○ ○ • }
g‴# ○ • (•)   ○ • ○ •
a‴ ○ • •   ○ ○ ○ •
b‴b • • • G#   • • • •
b‴ • • ○   • ○ •
c⁗ • ○ ○   • ○ ○ • (or C#)

Fig. 20. *Chart for Boehm-system clarinet. L. Th: left thumb; S: speaker key. For the use of the alternative keys for the notes marked †, see text. N.B. On many models the Eb key should remain closed for e‴b.*

2. *The F♯ key* (finger VI) is needed next to F in chromatic passages. Sometimes, also, it gives a better note than the usual fingering (. . . / o . o).

3. *The three B♭'s.* Either of the keys may be used as convenient, but the side key is on the whole preferred. The Boehm 'long' action . o o / . o o (or, after F♯ . o o / o . o) is useful in quick slurs and arpeggios from the right hand notes.[1]

4. *The other side keys* (finger IV): the second key is mainly for low register *f'♯* after *f'*; the upper two keys are for trills across the break.

5. *Throat notes.* The A♭ key is worked by the middle joint of finger I, and the A key by a small rolling movement of the same finger. The *b'♭* (A key and speaker key together) is apt to be weak on the A clarinet, and is better made on a held note with the lower of the two trill keys instead of the speaker.

The 'Full Boehm' (fig. 19, *centre,* and Plate XII). The preceding standard or 'plain' Boehm shows the system exactly as Klosé and Buffet designed it with such masterly restraint over a century ago; the major fingering advantages of Boehm's flute are incorporated in the clarinet with mechanism that is a model of simplicity and reliability. However, some players, especially those who play A parts on the B♭ clarinet, use the more elaborate model known as the 'full Boehm'. In addition to the standard mechanism, and (if required) the low E♭ key on the B♭ instrument (right little finger) for reaching the low E of the A clarinet, it has the following. *Duplicate E♭ key* (*e''♭*) for left little finger, especially required in conjunction with the low E♭ key, e.g. to be able to play, on the B♭ clarinet, the straightforward low E to A slur of the A clarinet. *Articulated G♯,* for trilling *f''♯/g''♯* with the right hand alone (cf. oboe) and making the A clarinet *g''/a''* trill practicable on the B♭. In addition there is generally an *extra G♯ key* (cross-key for V). *The ring for III* (sometimes

---

[1] Boosey & Hawkes have recently added to this action a simple device for improving the trill A♭/B♭. The G♯ key raises the link between the joints, thereby holding down the ring-controlled B♭ key so that the trill can be made with finger II alone.

fitted to plain Boehms) closes the open B♭ key (the key between rings I and II) to provide a forked B♭, useful in arpeggios of E♭ and of the diminished seventh on G. To vent this fingering in compensation for the closure of hole III, there is a small vent-key (*k*, fig. 19), kept closed on other notes by rings II, IV, etc.

Improved b′♭ mechanism. This is a separate idea that German makers of Boehm clarinets are especially keen on. It can take several forms, one of which is sketched at *x*, fig. 19. When the speaker is pressed and the thumb-ring is released, an extra vent (*p*) opens automatically to open out the tone of the *b′♭*. In another arrangement there is a key that opens *instead of* the speaker-hole when speaker and A keys are pressed together.

Schmidt Reform-Boehm clarinet (Plate XII). The most recent interesting development of the clarinet. With the object of rectifying certain faults of the normal Boehm, and also of wedding Boehm fingering to the German type of bore and mouthpiece in the best manner, the late Schmidt of Mannheim produced this new design, in which the holes are set out according to revised principles arrived at after many years of research and experiment. The bore is of the largest German size (15·75 millimetres), and cylindrical to the lowest tenon where there is an abrupt step to the wider bore of the bell, which has a vent-hole for *b′*. It has several additions to the normal Boehm mechanism. (1) Since hole VI is made smaller than usual, there is an automatic vent key for *e″* further down on the right hand side of the bottom joint. (2) A small vent for *f″♯* is attached to ring IV, which remains *up* when this note, or *b*, is fingered. (3) F♯/G♯ trill. Hole III is smaller than usual, but a small adjacent vent key makes up the correct venting for *a″*. This vent key is closed not only by ring III, but also by rings IV and V, in which event (finger III being raised) hole III emits a *g″♯*. The trill in question is thus made by . . . / o . o and trilling with finger III. The device similarly provides an A♭/B♭ trill by . . o / . o o and trilling with finger II. (4) An improved *b′♭* device, similar to that described in the preceding section.

This Reform-Boehm has already come into wide use in

Holland, where it has brought about a truce in a battle that has been going on for some time between the Boehm-system clarinet and the normal German models.

'NON-BOEHM' SYSTEMS. These are direct descendants of Muller's pioneer thirteen-keyed clarinet of about 1810. Their fingering differs from that of the Boehm system principally through the fact that ... / . o o gives F♯ instead of F (in low register, B instead of B♭), and that the thumb gives f'♯ instead of f'. The various types may be grouped thus:

Simple or Albert system
Clinton model
Full German models (Oehler, etc.).

As compared with the Boehm, (1) several cross-fingerings of the ancient kind (i.e. like those of the recorder) play an important part in the fingering, and these, while they give superb notes in the upper register, give poor notes in the lower unless tuned by added vent keys (as some of them are in the Clinton and Oehler models, etc.). If not vented they are only good for fast arpeggios and the like, where a poor note is less likely to be noticed. On the other hand the vital high c''', whether cross-fingered or keyed, is immeasurably superior to the same note on the Boehm—an incalculable aid to expressive playing. (2) The stretch for the hands is rather wider, and may inconvenience a person with small hands, especially on the A.

Simple system: the 13-keyed clarinet as remodelled by Albert of Brussels about the middle of the last century (Plate XII). In spite of the general adoption in England of the Boehm system within the last forty years, the simple system is still played by many, and no beginner should be afraid of using it should a good flat-pitch pair become available. This is no unlikely event, for the system was still manufactured in the 1930s. Many Continental manufacturers make it still. It is important that the instrument should include the *patent C*♯ (fig. 21, *extreme left*; shown next to it is the appearance of the bottom joint without it). This involves a duplicate C♯ hole (*l*, fig. 21) controlled by the C key.

It abolishes the need for sliding the left little finger from key to key when going from B to C♯; pressing the B key *only* gives C♯, while pressing the C key as well gives B as usual.

The following additional mechanism on the top joint is sometimes found in Continental instruments.

B♭ side key: a third side key for finger IV, with its touch below those of the trill and C keys. It is very useful, especially in the low register where the forked *e′♭* is too sharp; without the extra side key this note has to be made almost always with the cross key, which so often involves an awkward slide for finger III.

Rings for I and II: the top-joint brille. A small vent, with its key soldered to the edge of ring I, brings *f′♯* in tune without the help of the side C key (which otherwise has to be opened to bring the note up to pitch). From *f′* downwards, the vent is kept closed by the rings.

Rings for I, II and III: top-joint brille combined with improved left-hand fork. Another small vent, soldered to ring II, is closed by ring III in order to secure reduced venting for the forked *b″♭/e′♭*. On French instruments these extra rings are hinged on the right hand side of the instrument, like the bottom-joint rings; but on German, on the opposite side (as in fig. 23), so that for each hand, the rings are pivoted on the same side as the hand is held.[1]

Clinton model (fig. 21, right; Plate XIII); a clarinet devised about 1885 and first made by Boosey. The names of well-known players who use, or have used, it would make an impressive list (though Pat Ryan, the principal in the Hallé, plays the simple system), while at least one player has changed to the Boehm and then later gone back to the Clinton. The chief differences from the preceding are as follows:

Forked-F vent. This converts the fork . . . / . o . into a completely vented fingering fully available for *b♭* in the low

---

[1] German catalogue descriptions in English are not always very easy to follow. E.g.: *Clarinet, grenadil wood, 17 keys, 2 holes in F flat, 4 rings, 3 trillers on the upper piece, triller in B–C flat, levers in E flat and G flat, 4 rollers.* Presumably one of the four-ring models mentioned above.

register. Hole V, from which the note issues, is moved a little further down the joint (almost level with the F key) and is covered by a plate with an upwards extension so that finger V may still fall in its natural position. While this finger is raised, the vent key (*m*) stands open, to compensate for the closure of hole VI. For the lower notes the vent is automatically closed by finger V.

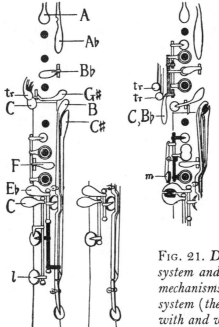

FIG. 21. *Diagram of simple system and Clinton clarinet mechanisms.* Left: *simple system (the lower end shown with and without the patent C♯);* right: *Clinton model.*

Re-sited G♯ key (first introduced by Sax). The G♯ hole is drilled through the tenon and socket that connects the joints (correct alignment being ensured by a metal stop on the outside). Alternatively the two joints may be made in one piece. The re-siting greatly improves the note in the low register (*c′♯*). (Most full Boehms also incorporate this modification.)

Barret Action, adapted from the oboe to make *c‴* and *b″♭* (in the low register, *f′* and *e′♭*) with a single side-key. It is also sometimes added to the plain simple system. The small keys between the left hand holes are normally kept closed by the

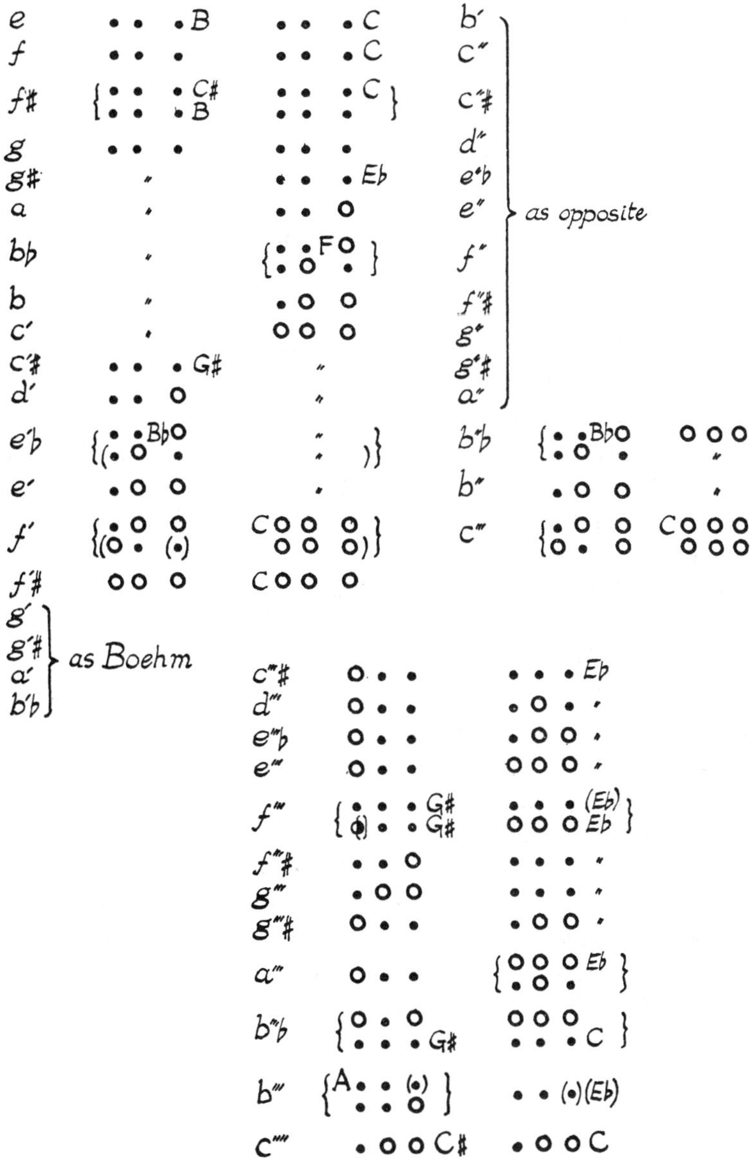

e • • •B   • • •C   b′ ⎫
f • • •   • • •C   c″ ⎪
f♯ {• • •C♯   • • •C }   c♯″ ⎪
     • • •B
g • • •   • • •   d″ ⎪
g♯   ″   • • •E♭   e♭″ ⎪
a   ′   • • O   e″ ⎬ as opposite
b♭   ′   {• •FO }   f′ ⎪
                 • O •
b   ″   • O O   f♯″ ⎪
c′   ′   O O O   g″ ⎪
c♯″ • • •G♯   ″   g♯″ ⎪
d′ • • O   ″   a″ ⎭
e♭ {• •B♭O   ″)}   b♭″ {• •B♭O   O O O
    • O •   • O •   ″
e′ • O O   ′   b″ • O O
f′ {• O O   C O O O}   c‴ {• O O   C O O
   (O • (•)   O O O O)}   O • O   O O
f♯ O O O   C O O O
g′ ⎫
g♯ ⎬ as Boehm   c♯‴ O • •   • • •E♭
a′ ⎪   d‴ O • •   ○ O • ′
b♭ ⎭   e♭‴ O • •   • O O ′
               e‴ O • •   O O O ′
               f‴ {• • •G♯   • • (E♭) }
                  (⊙) • •G♯   O O O E♭
               f♯‴ • • O   • • • ″
               g‴ • O O   • • • ″
               g♯‴ O • •   • O O ′
               a‴ O • •   {O O O E♭ }
                                • O •
               b♭‴ {O • O   {O O O }
                    • • •G♯   • • •C
               b‴ {A• • (•) }   • • (•)(E♭)
                   • • •O
               c‴′ • O O C♯   • O O C

Fig. 22. *Chart for simple system and other non-Boehm clarinets. In the left-hand column, the thumb-hole is closed until g′; in the right-hand and bottom columns, the thumb-hole is closed and the speaker key is opened.*

master-spring of the long side key. When the latter is pressed, either both the small keys (for C) or only the lower (for B♭) open, according to whether finger II is raised or not. Ring III permits the side key to be held down through trills, tremolos, etc., involving G or A♭ and B♭ in the upper register, simplifying many passages.

Lengthened A♭ touch, so that this key may be operated by finger II when so desired.

A later Clinton model, used by a few, is the Clinton-Boehm, with the little-finger keys arranged as on the Boehm system and with articulated G♯ key. Other 'half-Boehms' have been brought out in Germany.

Oehler system, etc. In Germany, the advanced mechanical evolution of the clarinet has paralleled that of the oboe in France, having led in a similar way to a complicated non-Boehm instrument that has not yet settled down in one final pattern fixed in every detail. Basically it is the Albert simple system incorporating all the extra devices described earlier under Simple System (patent C♯, side B♭ key, three top-joint rings; also forked-F vent). In addition it has inherited various things from the earlier German system (*c.* 1860) of C. Baermann, son of the Baermann for whom Weber wrote the concertos.

The best-known design in German orchestras is that of Oehler, Berlin (Plate XIII). The designs of other well-known makers, as Schmidt (Mannheim), Uebel (Markneukirchen), Mollenhauer (Cassel) and Koktan (Vienna), are often referred to as the 'Oehler system', even though each maker may have his idiosyncrasies over certain details, as for instance in the arrangement of the forked-F vent.

The Oehler mechanism includes the following devices (fig. 23).

On the bottom joint:

1. *Patent C♯.*

2. *Duplicate E♭ key* for left little finger, often with a duplicate F key beside it.

3. *Forked-F vent*, much like that of the Clinton except that Oehler has moved hole V to the right hand side of the instrument

and covered it with a lightly-sprung open key (n); thus plate V has no hole under it, but it closes both the little keys at the side.

4. *High E correcting device:* a small vent soldered to ring IV, which is lowered by the E♭ key. The purpose is to provide normal venting for g'', but diminished venting for e''' (... / o o o E♭), which otherwise tends to be sharp. (On the Baermann clarinet, the E♭ key closed the brille for the same reason.)

On the top joint:

5. *Improved left hand fork:* the fork-fingering, by means of ring

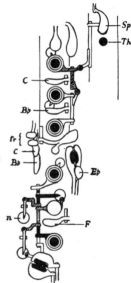

FIG. 23. *Diagram of Oehler-system clarinet.*

III, closes the little vent soldered to ring II, giving an improved note in the low register.

6. *Top-joint brille* (involving rings I and II) combined with Baermann's *corrected open C♯* as follows: the open fingering for $c'''♯$ is a good note for many passages, but this top-joint brille makes it too sharp. Therefore ring I, which carries the brille vent, is automatically lowered by the speaker key. The A key also lowers it to prevent a' becoming sharp.

Some German clarinets now have a small closed key on the bell, to be opened by the right thumb. The player opens it if he feels that his *b'* or *e* is too flat, which, with the long cylinder of the German bore, it is prone to be. Like the French oboe-makers, the German clarinet-makers like to keep a maximum tube-length even if it introduces a slight problem in the tuning.

Saxophones

Patented by Adolphe Sax in Paris in 1846, the saxophone has a wide conical brass tube expanding at about 1 in 18, coupled with a single-reed mouthpiece similar to that of the clarinet. It overblows the octave like the oboe, with two automatic octave keys, but otherwise it is fingered much like the clarinet. Also, the embouchure is like that for the clarinet, but is looser and, up to a point, easier to acquire.

Sax, the son of the Brussels wind-instrument maker Charles Sax, was himself a maker of woodwind (especially of clarinets) and of brass of all kinds (including his own saxhorns—the prototypes of our brass-band tenor horns and baritones). He was also a clarinettist. Unfortunately he left no account of his discovery of the saxophone, but we may imagine that he began by experimenting in the field of woodwind-brass hybrids, for instance, trying out clarinet mouthpieces on the ophicleide—which may be shortly described as a euphonium with padded keys instead of valves.

The new invention was envisaged for military bands, in which, in the 1840s, increased use of chromatic brass instruments had upset the classic balance between brass and woodwind. Saxophones, by supplying a powerful, filling-out reed tone—almost an open-air string-tone—would pull the band together, as the French military authorities immediately recognized by authorizing their adoption by bands in the year following the patent. Many other countries came to follow the French lead, though never Germany. In British bands, the former prejudice against them has been dispelled sufficiently to admit an alto saxophone and a tenor regularly and a baritone occasionally. American bands also use these, often in considerable numbers and sometimes adding a soprano. It was ultimately from the band that the saxophone found its way into jazz.

The complete family of saxophones, with the sounding compass of each member, is as follows:

E♮ sopranino ($d'♭–a'''♭$), *rare*   B♮ tenor ($A♭–e''♭$)
B♮ soprano ($a♭–e'''♭$)   E♮ baritone ($D♭–a'♭$)
E♮ alto ($d♭–a''♭$)   B♮ bass ($A'♭–e'♭$)
              E♮ contrabass ($D'♭–a♭$) *very rare*

In each case the compass is *written $b♭–f'''$* in the treble stave.

It has not been thought necessary, in this book, to illustrate all these sizes, since each is standardized for all practical purposes, while most can readily be inspected in a shop or a dance band. The first two are quite straight (looking like conical metal clarinets). The rest have turned-up bells, and, from the baritone downwards, a loop next to the crook. Callers at Buffet's shop in Paris will remember the giant contrabass saxophone standing in the corner of the showroom, with its colossal mouthpiece and tattered reed on which generations of visitors have had a respectful and unproductive blow. In point of general utility in dance and other bands, the alto claims first place, closely followed by the tenor. The baritone would come third.

In addition to the above series, we should notice certain survivors of Sax's alternative set, which was pitched in the keys of F and C (instead of E♮ and B♮). Best-known of these is the 'C melody' saxophone—a tenor in C supplied for those who work in hotel orchestras and so on, and wish to read from piano copies without transposing. Quite rare is the C soprano, on which military band oboe parts could be read without transposition; and also the F 'mezzosoprano' (Plate X), Conn's adaptation of Sax's original F alto.

Through jazz, the tone of the saxophone has been considerably opened out by enlargement of the bore and modifications to the mouthpiece. Old saxophones sound curiously mute by comparison, yet interesting as showing the tone of the instrument at the time of its early adventures in Paris a century ago—'soft and penetrating in the higher part, full and rich in the lower, their medium has something profoundly impressive' (Berlioz). Out-of-date saxophones are quickly recognized by the absence of automatic octave keys, patent high F (Fig. 24 *x*), articulated G♯, and the low B♭. For comparison with the modern instrument, an example is shown in Plate X.

One most striking thing about the saxophone in modern times is the way each principal size developed an individual

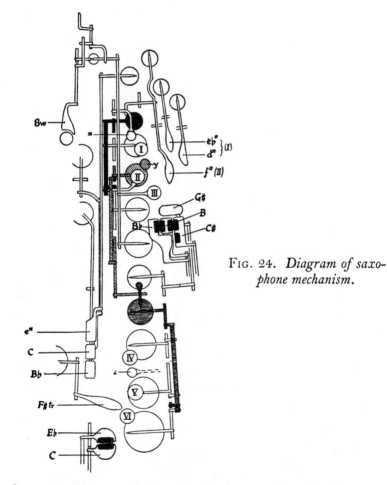

FIG. 24. *Diagram of saxophone mechanism.*

character of its own during the classic age of jazz in the 1920s and 1930s. The alto, with its clear but rather monotonous solo-tone settled down as the chief saxophone in ensemble work (the basic section having two altos and a tenor). The expressive tenor, whether husky and almost speech-like in the hands of

Hawkins, or more urbanely romantic with Featherstonehaugh, inevitably became the great solo instrument of the family, taking its turn with clarinet, trumpet and trombone. Next to it, for solos, came the baritone, on which Ellington's Carney improvised

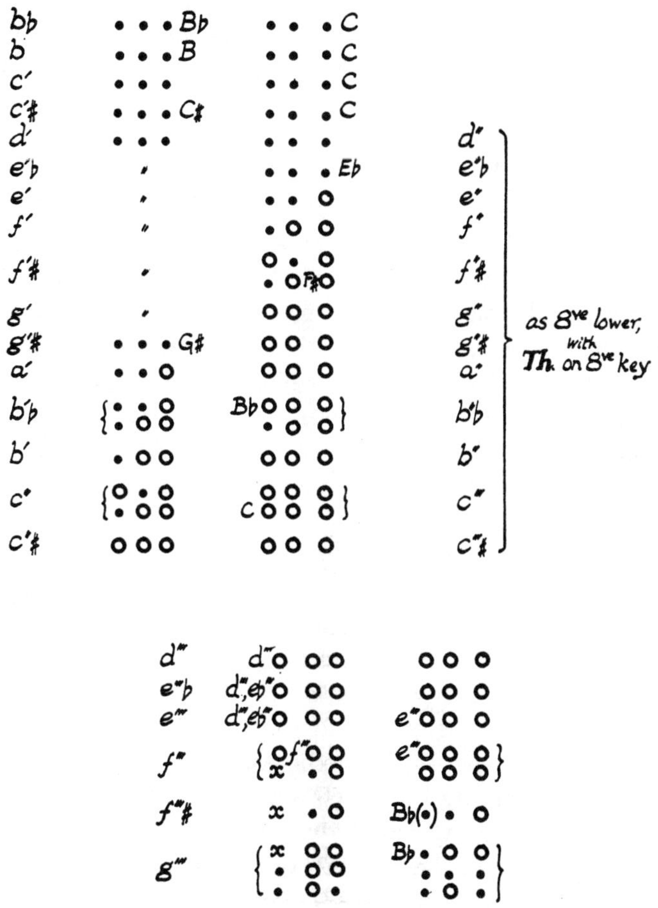

```
b♭      • • • B♭      • • • C
b       • • • B       • • • C
c′      • • •          • • • C
c′♯     • • • C♯       • • • C
d′      • • •          • • •        d″  ⎫
e′♭     ʹ              • • • E♭     e″♭ |
e′      ʺ              • • ○        e″  |
f′      ʺ              • ○ ○        f″  |
f′♯     ʹ              ○ • ○        f″♯ |
                       • ○♯○             |
g′      ʹ              ○ ○ ○        g″  |  as 8ve lower,
g′♯     • • • G♯       ○ ○ ○        g″♯ ⎬  with
a′      • • ○          ○ ○ ○        a″  |  Th. on 8ve key
b′♭    {•:•○   B♭○ ○ ○}             b″♭ |
        •:•○     • ○ ○              |
b′      • ○ ○          ○ ○ ○        b″  |
c″     {○:•○   c○ ○ ○}             c‴  |
        •:•○      ○ ○ ○             |
c″♯    ○ ○ ○          ○ ○ ○        c‴♯ ⎭

d‴     d̄○ ○ ○        ○ ○ ○
e‴♭    d̄♯e♭○ ○ ○      ○ ○ ○
e‴     d̄♯e♭○ ○ ○      e○ ○ ○
f‴    {○f○ ○        e○ ○ ○}
       x • ○          ○ ○ ○
f‴♯    x • ○          B♭(•) • ○
g‴    {x ○ ○        B♭ • ○ ○}
       • ○ ○          • • •
       • ○ •          • ○ • •
```

FIG. 25. *Chart for saxophone. (The octave key remains pressed for the notes in the bottom column.)*

with perhaps the lightest and most breathing sound ever conjured from a deep wind instrument, and lastly Rollini's superb 'pizzicato' slap-tongued bass supporting small combinations, sometimes with a marvellously dignified and relaxed solo. The soprano, save in the hands of a few like Bechet, was outshone by the clarinet and little heard in those days.

Among concert artists Sigurd Rascher leads the soloists while Marcel Mule's Quatuor des Saxophones de Paris (soprano, alto, tenor, baritone) must be counted among the most sensitive wind ensembles existing. In the orchestra, Honegger, in *Jeanne d'Arc au bûcher*, makes fine use of three altos (replacing horns). With a single saxophone, British composers have been outstandingly successful, as Walton in *Belshazzar's Feast*, and Vaughan Williams, first in *Job*, where an alto represents the hypocrite, and later in the Sixth Symphony, in which the saxophone is a tenor, and quickly makes its appearance in an arresting theme that could hardly have been announced on any other musical instrument. In this last example especially, one feels that Berlioz's prognostication is fulfilled—that composers 'will hereafter derive wondrous effects from saxophones which it would be rash to attempt foreseeing'. If more music uses the saxophone like this, the instrument may in time become promoted from a rare 'special' to a regular 'extra' in the clarinet department of the woodwind.

SAXOPHONE MECHANISM. Figure 24 shows the typical layout. The normal F♯ is . . . / o . o, the key being for trills with F natural. The normal B♭ fingering is with the side key, and the normal C fingering is with the o . o / o o o cross-fingering, the side C key being for use in rapid alternation of B and C. The small plate *y* (finger II) is for the A♯/B trill, and *z* (not always fitted) is a duplicate G♯ touch also for trilling. A neat device found on American saxophones enables E♭ to be fingered . . . / . o . through the addition of a small E♭ key on the left-hand side of the instrument. This key opens automatically when finger V is raised, plate V being meantime held down by a connection from plate VI.

The upper register is carried up to top F, still in second harmonics, by a cluster of three side keys for the left hand and one for the right hand. Plate *x* (the 'patent F') simplifies the fingering of top F, especially next to C in arpeggios. There is no regular high register of third and fourth harmonics, though experienced players are able to creep up even to the F an octave higher still, by means of complex cross-fingerings and special embouchures. The two semitones above the ordinary top F, up to the G, are, however, much used by some soloists, and specimen fingerings for obtaining them are included in the chart. At the bottom of the compass Selmer have for some years lengthened the bell of the baritone saxophone to provide a low A (L. thumb key) giving low C in actual sound. Also to be noted is the Houvenaghel system, *le Rationnel* (Leblanc, Paris), described in its original form by J. A. MacGillivray in *The Galpin Society Journal*, XII (London, 1959).

Finally it may be added that the saxophone mouthpiece varies considerably in interior design. The old rounded 'tone chamber' has been choked by various flat surfaces and shoulders in order to give a brighter, more penetrating tone, though it has also been discovered in America how to obtain this effect with an approximation to the classic tone chamber.

Tarogato

This is best-known today as one of the instruments used for the second stage call in the last Act of *Tristan*. It is a kind of B♭ soprano saxophone made of wood (Plate X), with vent-holes in the bell, plain finger-holes, and keywork arranged in German simple-system fashion. The mouthpiece fits *into* the instrument, instead of over it as on the saxophone, and an ordinary clarinet reed can be used on it.

The name originally belonged to a species of shawm romantically associated in Hungarian national lore with the soldiers of the younger Rakowsky (*d.* 1735) in his struggles against the Hapsburgs. Specimens are preserved in the Budapest Museum. A century afterwards, this original tarogato had retired to a rustic oblivion in which it remained undisturbed until fresh national spirit moved certain Hungarian musicians to revive 'national' instruments. This was in the 1890s, and it quickly led to the elaboration of the cimbalom from a simple folk dulcimer to the substantial piece of furniture used by Hungarian bands today. The tarogato, however, with its fierce double reed, was judged, no doubt prudently, as likely to prove too much for even the most fervent patriot, and accordingly the present 'easy-blowing' single-reed mouthpiece was substituted. The instrument was manufactured by Schunda (Budapest), and even curved-crook tenors and basses were advertised. Today it is heard as a folk instrument especially in Rumania. It has an amusing 'woody' tone, mellower than that of the soprano saxophone.

It is said to have been Richter's original choice at Bayreuth for the second stage call in *Tristan*. Wagner marks this 'cor anglais', but observes in the preface that it would be better if 'a special instrument of wood be made for it after the model of the alp-horn, which, on account of its simplicity, should be neither difficult nor expensive'. As may well be imagined, opera-houses have had great fun with this. The usual substitute at Covent Garden has remained Richter's tarogato, but in Barcelona they use the *tiple*, while in Vienna, Wlach himself crawled out of the pit to play it on a soprano saxophone. In Germany, the call is commonly played on a trumpet with felt mute. But at Bayreuth and certain other houses, Wagner's 'alp-horn' idea has long been roughly followed, using a straight wooden trumpet in C, with bulbous bell, rather wide trumpet mouthpiece, and a short brass section containing one whole-tone valve, and this certainly gives the best effect. As usual, Wagner's idea works.

CHAPTER VI

The Bassoon

The bassoon,[1] fourth and last primary tone-colour of the woodwind, is a conical-bore, double-reed instrument like the oboe, but as well as being an octave and a fifth deeper in its basic scale, it produces a sound of entirely different character. The bore expands at only about half the angle of the oboe's, and is doubled back on itself to make a long bass extension (the total tube-length is just over eight feet). Moreover, most of the finger-holes are deep drillings running slantwise through as much as two inches of wood (see Plate **XXIX**), so that the venting of the notes is comparatively weak, and large amounts of energy are passed down to the lower parts of the tube, including the long doubled-back extension, to set up powerful resonances that strengthen the sound in a characteristic way. The bright reediness of the oboe is transformed into a dark mellowness—a strange, unique quality impossible to describe adequately in words, but something between a male voice and a horn, and in many ways sweeter and more pleasing than either. Sacheverell Sitwell, discussing the concertos in his book on Mozart, wrote, 'with the bassoon, it is like a sea-god speaking'.

The great solo register, as a glance at any classical score will show, coincides exactly with the compass of the tenor voice, and it is the continual use of the bassoon as a tenor melodist that makes it so rewarding to play in the orchestra. Its archaic

[1] Ital. *fagotto*; Germ. *Fagott*. The traditional English military-band pronunciation with Z sound may be quite old: 'Spent with the singers when the new Bazoon came 2*s.* 6*d.*'—at Hayfield in Derbyshire, 1772 (McDermott).

function as bass to the woodwind remains important, but subsidiary to its tenor role. Above the tenor range, the high register is usually considered to extend to *e''* or *f''*. Heckel, the celebrated German bassoon-maker, advertised a top *a''♭* in his fingering chart, and somebody once actually heard him get it with a special reed, but mercifully nothing above *e''* has been written in an orchestral part. In a solo passage, the highest really comfortable note is *c'''*, though many well-known solos ascend to *d'''*.

Assembling and sounding the bassoon

The bassoon has five pieces: the metal *crook*; the wing or *tenor joint*; the double joint or *butt*; the bass or *long joint*; and the *bell*. Also required is the *sling*, and with bassoons of the German type, the wooden *hand-rest*. 'French' and 'German' denote the two types of bassoon in use today. They are described separately further on.

From the crook, the bore runs down through the tenor joint and butt, and then ascends up the wider bore of the butt and through the long joint and bell. The six principal finger-positions communicate with the descending bore, and the ascending portion is controlled mainly by the right little finger (with the F key) and the two thumbs.

The instrument must be put together correctly, else the joints may become strained. *First,* the sling is donned. This is a cord carrying a hook and an adjusting bead; the cord makes one loop above the bead, and two below carrying the hook (fig. 26). It is normally put over the neck, though some put it round the right shoulder. Ladies, not as a rule having coat-collars, fit a band of broad material to the sling to prevent it cutting into the neck (and the same for the cor anglais). *Second,* while holding the butt in the right hand with its narrower bore lowermost, the tenor joint is pushed in with the other hand, its concave inner surface being aligned concentrically with the large bore of the butt. Remove the crook-key protector (a lapped wooden peg inserted into the top of the tenor joint when the instrument is dismantled). *Third,* while still holding the butt in the right hand, the long joint is pushed in. French bassoons have a catch to hold it tight against the tenor joint; German usually have a projecting edge on the tenor joint which comes against a metal plate screwed to the long joint. *Fourth*, the bell is pushed on, and with a German instrument the hand-rest is put into its socket on the butt. Finally the crook is inserted, pointing half round towards the back, i.e. to the thumbs side of the instrument.

The assembled instrument is now hooked on to the sling by the ring at the top of the butt, and a reed (Chapter III) is put on the crook, which should first be moistened in the lips so that the reed grips better. (To strike the true point of balance, several players of the German bassoon have recently taken to slinging

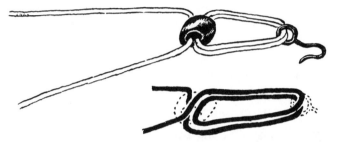

Fig. 26. *Sling for bassoon, saxophone, etc. Diagram showing method of threading cord through hook and adjusting bead.*

the instrument higher up, by means of a ring carried on a 4-inch-long extension plate or rod fixed to the band at the top of the butt. Others recently have discarded the sling, for instance in America sitting on a strap attached to a hole in the butt cap.)

Whilst playing, the butt is firmly held against the right thigh by the pressure of the lower part of finger IV. On the French instrument this is applied directly against the wood of the butt, but in German through the hand-rest. The upper part of the instrument is held up by the lowest joint of finger I against the long joint—not by the left thumb, which has far too much work to do operating the keys. The sling must be adjusted by the bead so that both blades of the reed feel properly under control, the lips being curled back just over the teeth, and the corners of the mouth being closed round the reed in the usual manner for playing a reed instrument—but not too tightly, for it is a good thing to feel that the cavity of one's mouth is well arched and expanded, since this helps the tone.

If a bassoon feels a shade too flat or too sharp on all the notes (assuming that a correct embouchure has been developed), one may try a crook of different length. Heckel numbers his crooks: No. 0, the shortest, No. 1, short, No. 2, longer and the one normally used in England, and No. 3, the longest. French crooks are not numbered, but repairers know all about lengthening or shortening them as may be necessary. It is also worth remembering that quite apart from pitch, a bassoon may play better with one crook than another, and professional players often test each other's crooks on their respective instruments.

Even more than on other wind instruments, the lips have to work all the time to get notes in tune. At first it may seem that almost every note on the bassoon requires a different embouchure, especially on the older French- and English-made instruments; but in course of time, this 'humouring' largely becomes subconscious. Another important means of humouring the notes is by use of the lower keys. On most notes it will be found that the quality, and also sometimes the pitch, are considerably altered when one of the keys on the long joint is pressed, and all bassoon players make regular use of this in order to fill out the tone of weak notes, to rectify notes that incline to 'fly' or blow sharp, and so on. For instance, on a French bassoon, if a weak or unsteady B♭ or A can be corrected by pressing the low E♭ key (or any other key on the long joint) then that key should be included in one's regular fingering for the note, even in fast passages. On all bassoons the tenor F benefits from filling out by pressing one of these keys. The low E♭ key especially is so valuable in toning-up weak notes that it has been referred to as the 'doctor'.

The Buffet and the Heckel

While it has been emphasized in the preceding chapters that French woodwind sound differs from German, the differences between the instruments themselves is not so fundamental that a player of a French instrument may not now and then sound almost as if he were playing on a German, and vice versa. With the bassoon, however, the difference is always unmistakable, whoever the player may be.

Of all our present woodwind, the *French bassoon* is that which has been altered least since the time of Beethoven. Weak notes of old have been greatly improved and the overall sonority has been developed, but with deliberate avoidance of all but the gentlest modifications to the bore and to the holes and mechanism. It is of rosewood (or, occasionally, of ebonite, for use in tropical climates), with the expanding bore ending with a practically cylindrical bell. The bottom of the butt is closed either with a plain cork or by a metal U-tube.

The leading maker is Buffet-Crampon of Paris. Another favourite maker among British players up to the 1930s was Mahillon of Brussels, whose instruments those formerly made by the London manufacturers closely resemble. In France, Spain and Italy, the Buffet is standard. Elsewhere west of the Rhine it has lost ground, or is beginning to lose ground, to the German bassoon. Even in Italy, by tradition very much a Buffet country, the players at the Scala, Milan, have recently changed over to the Heckel. England, after having also been a French-bassoon country for nearly a century (except for an isolated German-bassoon cell at Manchester) underwent a sweeping German invasion early in the 1930s, largely precipitated by the visit to London of the New York Philharmonic Orchestra with Toscanini; players changed over to the German bassoon in dozens, and it has now become by far the commoner of the two. Most beginners seek to procure one (they cost from £125 upwards, new) and Boosey & Hawkes, the only British firm now making bassoons, no longer make the French model. Yet a great many British players, including several of the finest and most sought-after (headed by Cecil James, principal in the Philharmonia Orchestra) have remained true to the Buffet, and indeed, when one hears them, one wonders why this swing-over to the German instrument should have taken place. But there is a reason.

The *German bassoon*, standard east of the Rhine and in

America, is the eventual outcome of bandmaster Almenraeder's drastic remodelling of the classical bassoon about the time of Beethoven's death. How he improved the instrument technically in many ways but at the same time spoilt its tone, and how it took two generations of the Heckel family to restore this, is told in Chapter XII. The modern German bassoon is the triumph of the firm of Heckel (Biebrich-am-Rhein, near Wiesbaden), who are still its leading makers. Many others manufacture it too, following Heckel's model: Mollenhauer, Mönnig, Hüller, Kohlert, and others. But the majority of leading players have used a Heckel. The Adler instrument, a little less open in tone, is well-known in England through its use by Archie Camden and Gwydion Brooke. Schreiber (Markneukirchen), was one of the earlier makers to produce a comparatively cheap model and other manufacturers have since followed. Several American firms make the Heckel model (e.g. Fox), and at least one of the French manufacturers now makes it for export.

It is of European maple, with the bore almost evenly conical throughout. The tenor joint, sometimes also the small bore of the butt, is lined with ebonite, since unlined maple is liable to develop whiskers through the effect of moisture. The bottom of the butt is closed by a metal U-tube which can be removed for occasional cleaning after pulling off the protecting cap with a sharp tug. The bell is characteristically, though not invariably, surmounted by an ivory ring, an old German feature.

Comparing the two types, their fingerings differ without giving either a decisive advantage. The great point in favour of the Heckel is that from top to bottom of the compass, and from *piano* to *forte* the tone is uniformly *effective* in the orchestra. And, going with this, it is a comparatively easy matter always to have a reed handy that will produce its clear, telling quality reasonably satisfactorily, without the tone becoming forced, nasal or stuffy. It is possible, but much harder, to be certain of corresponding results on the French instrument, which is the more sensitive to the vagaries of reeds, and has weak spots in each register which a reed that falls short of the optimum will show up. This is the real reason behind the successes of the Heckel outside its home territory; it makes life easier for the orchestral player.

Against this, the tone-quality of the French bassoon is by nature the more subtle and vocal. The sound of course varies with different players and in different countries. The French players prefer a rather dry, reedy tone, which artists like Dherin and Oubradous nevertheless mould into an extra-ordinarily expressive sound with their feeling, breathing and vibrato. In England, and also in Italy, the players have sought a rounder, mellower sound, free from reediness (today in England frequently using German-type reeds); vibrato is either not used, or is reserved for very special occasions. But in whatever way it is produced, the sound of the French bassoon is never uninterest-ing. That of the German, on the other hand, tends rather to become so, and to lack variety. Clear and ethereal though it is on the upper notes, the middle and lower parts of the compass tend to sound wooden and monotonous, especially in chamber music and solos. It takes a thoughtful approach to avoid this; to make the legato sympathetic and singing, and the staccato light and vivacious. The shape of the reed therefore varies con-siderably.

The late Strobel of Vienna, said to have had the finest tone of all Heckel-players of his day, made a very broad reed, 17 millimetres across the tip. This model is still used by Oehl-berger and his fine team in the Vienna Philharmonic. It makes the tone warm and human, though on the thick side (truly German in fact, blending naturally with its Germanic neigh-bour instruments in the orchestra). The well-known reeds of Ludwig of Munich show an average width (Plate VI). Many, however, make them much narrower, and in America, where the German bassoon is particularly well played, the modern ten-dency is said to be for a reed as little as 14 millimetres across the tip, and perfectly circular in the throat, instead of slightly flattened as is more usual. This introduces an interesting touch of vocal hollowness into the tone, and causes the instrument to blend very well with the prevailing French style of the other woodwind in American orchestras.

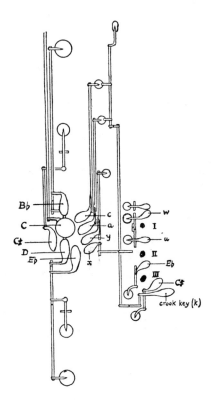

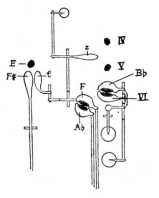

FIG. 27. *Diagram of French bassoon keywork (Buffet). Thumb keys and hole shown on the left; finger holes and keys on the right.*

It is a curious thing that the two types of bassoon, neither of them perfect nor sounding exactly like the other, go remarkably well side by side. They have been frequently seen thus in

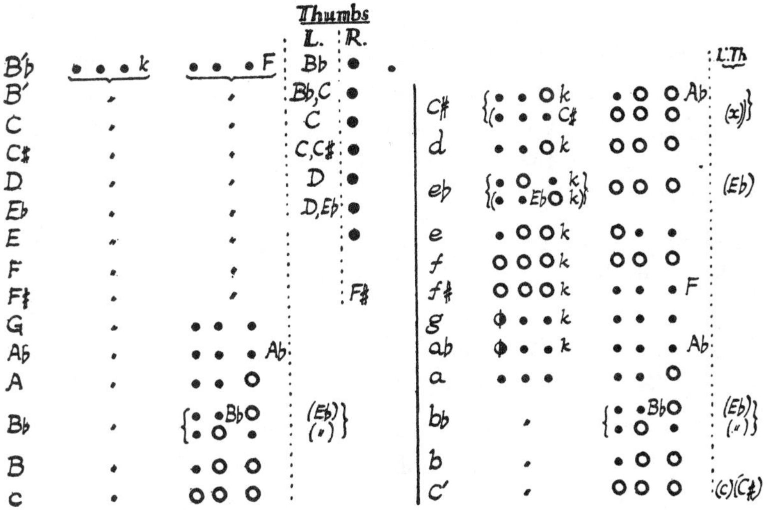

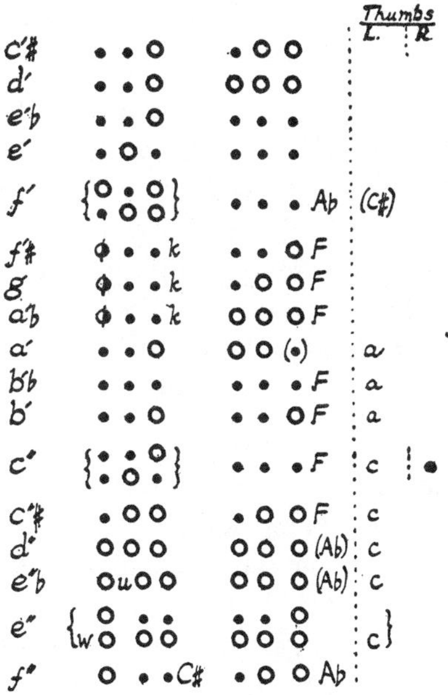

FIG. 28. *Chart for French bassoon. k: close the crook key. Keys, etc., indicated in brackets suggest ways of tuning notes (individual instruments differing in this respect). Note also the following trills (trill with fingers indicated by x):*

$e/f\sharp$ .oo|xx.F
     (or o.o|etc.)
f/g oxx|...
$e'\flat/f'$ xxo|...
e'/f' x.o|...A♭
$e'/f'\sharp$ xxo|...A♭
f'/g' finger the F and
        trill with w
        (fig. 27).

English orchestras, and it is usually held that the best effect is when the Buffet is on top and the Heckel underneath, though of course this also depends upon the players.

Bassoon mechanisms

FRENCH BASSOON (fig. 27). The *crook key* (left little finger) is kept closed from the bottom note up to *a♭*, and then again for *f'♯, g'* and *a'♭*. (The alternative crook key touch for left thumb, *x*, if present, is for use when making *c♯* pianissimo with the keyed fingering.)

Cross-fingerings alternative to keyed fingerings are available for the B♮'s, where both fingerings are indispensable; and also for the C♯'s and the middle E♭, where many players prefer the cross-fingerings on account of their mellower sound, though the French use the keyed fingerings freely.

Half-holing (for *g*, etc.) is by rolling finger I downwards to uncover the upper part of the hole.

High A and C keys. There may be from two to four thumb keys on the tenor joint. The essential ones are the two harmonic keys (*a* and *c*, fig. 27), used in the high register from *a'* upwards, and also sometimes for steadying tenor notes like *a* and *c'* (e.g. when slurring up from the low register).

Trill keys, etc. The small keys for fingers I and II can be used for trills over the break, e.g. E/F♯ (though these trills also have other fingerings), and for obtaining extreme high notes from *e''♭* upwards with all holes uncovered. The trill key *y* for the left thumb, if fitted, is the 'Creation key', facilitating quick alternation of *e'* and *g'*, as in the 'doves' passage in *The Creation*; also, it gives a top *f''* in conjunction with the small keys. The trill key *z* on the butt (finger V) is especially valuable for the *g'/a'* trill.

The Buffet F♯/G♯ trill device: in this, the key-arm of the F key is sprung to *close*, the key normally being kept open by the stronger spring of the F touch. Pressing the extra touch *t* for the right thumb holds down the F touch, allowing the F key to close and thus disengaging the little finger for trilling the A♭ key, which has a projecting lug so that every time it rises, it opens the F key with it. (Some players, however, permanently disengage this mechanism, having the F key re-sprung to open as normally.)

Finger-plates and rings. On the Buffet, the plate for VI (with roller for sliding to the B♭ key) dates from about forty years ago, when hole VI was moved further down the butt to help steady the A's. Earlier instruments, and also most of those by other makers, have either a plain hole or a simpler form of plate. On many of the older Buffet instruments, however, one also finds the rings introduced by Jancourt and adopted by the Paris makers for some years, e.g. half-hole plate for I held down by ring for II; and a vent key for the B naturals (formerly inclined to be flat) closed by a ring for V.

GERMAN BASSOON (fig. 29).[1] *Connections through the butt:* Three pieces of mechanism on the butt involve connection between front and back by means of thin rods that pass through the wall between the two bores. These rods are usually of a flexible material like soft vulcanite, to avoid risk of their jamming. They are as follows: 1, for the front B♭ touch to actuate the B♭ key, which is on the back; 2, for plate VI to close its key, which is also on the back; and 3, for the thumb F♯ key to close the F key.

The alternative keys on the butt. Both F♯ keys, front and back, close the F key, so that F♯/G♯ need involve no sliding of the little finger. Most players normally use the thumb F♯ and the little finger G♯ (as indicated on the chart) and are thereby further prepared for A♯ with the thumb in passages in the keys of B and D♭. The thumb key is likewise normally used for B♭, being the handiest next to A♭ and the notes below (no forked B♭ is used on this system). Nevertheless, just as on the Boehm-system clarinet, passages occur when sliding a finger cannot be avoided (e.g. B♭–A♭–G♭ repeated).

The middle C♯'s. The simple cross-fingerings are not used, and furthermore, the plain fingering with the left hand only is generally avoided in both octaves, since the more complicated fingerings give clearer notes and better in tune (see the chart).

Keyed e♭. The left thumb C♯ key becomes an E♭ key when

---

[1] German bassoons have also been made with an approximation to French-system keywork, for export. With a good instrument this is perfectly satisfactory. The sound remains that of a German bassoon.

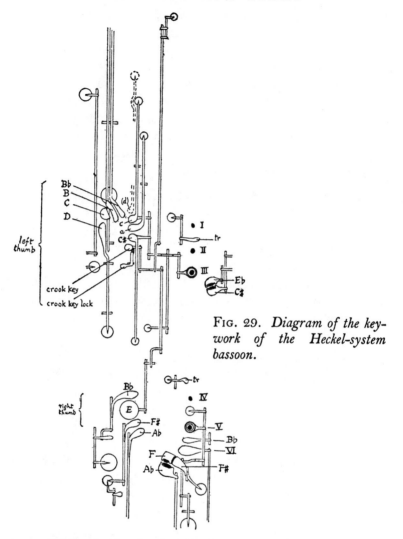

FIG. 29. *Diagram of the key-work of the Heckel-system bassoon.*

finger III is raised, releasing its ring—a useful *e♭* in chromatic passages. (The other ring, for finger V, permits a vent key to open when this finger is raised and the F key is depressed, to bring *g'* in tune with the normal fingering.)

Use of the left thumb on the tenor notes. This forms the most difficult part of the fingering. The crook hole is smaller than on the French bassoon and less efficient as an octave vent. It is too

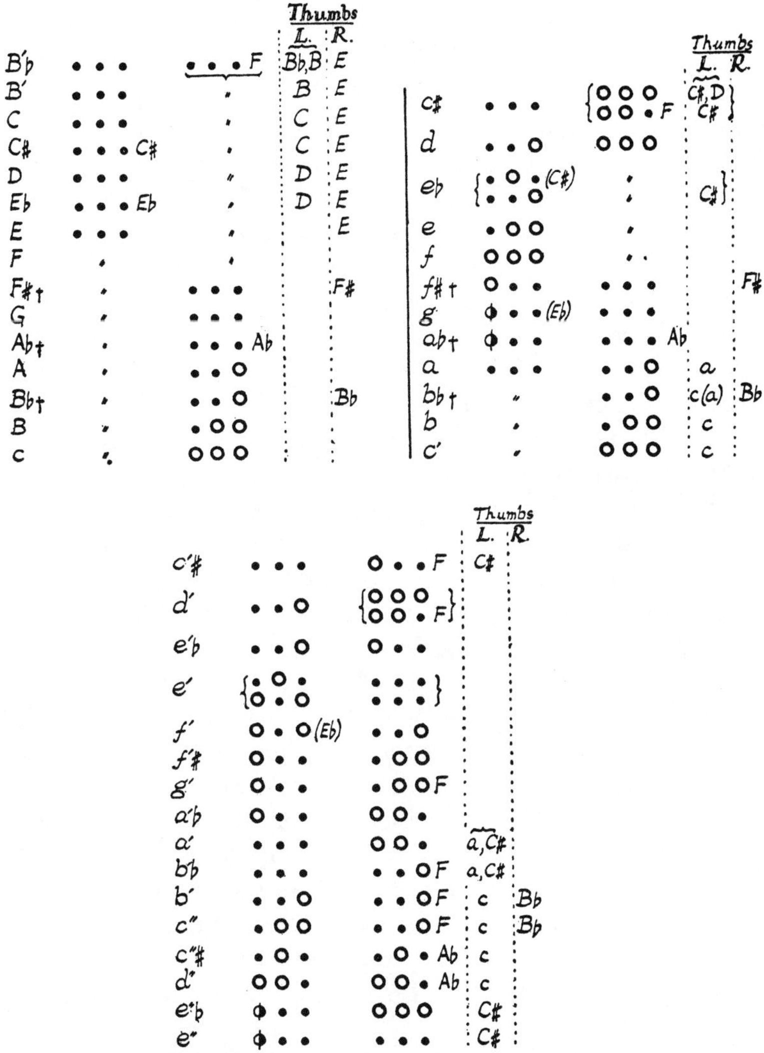

Fig. 30. *Chart for German-system bassoon. See text for the use of the crook key and of the alternative keys for the notes marked* †. *Note also the following trills (trill with fingers marked x):*

e/f♯	with trill key for II, or o . o | x . . F♯
f/g	as French system
e'♭/f'	as French system
e'/f'♯	. o . | . x x
f'/g'	o . . | x x o

small to give adequate help to the notes from *c'* down to *a*, and if it is made larger, these notes only become unsteady and windy. The result is that when they are attacked, they are apt to sound for a split second in the low register before settling in the upper, making an audible grunt or croak which has to be avoided at all cost. It is avoided as follows. For *c'* and *b* the high C key is opened (*c*, fig. 29), and for *a*, the high A key (*a*); for *b♭*, whichever gives the note best in tune. This is normal technique on the German bassoon, cumbersome though it is. One has to be very lively with the left thumb, especially if there are C♯'s in the passage as well, or if the crook key is to be closed. Since, however, the German crook-hole is so small, it is possible up to a point to disregard the crook key. Formerly, indeed, there was no key to close the hole, and for *pp* passages in the low register, which are unsafe with the hole open, it was temporarily closed with a pin that the player carried in the lapel of his coat. An advance on this was a pad cemented in a brass clip. Better still, a small sprung lever mounted on the crook, to be flicked closed for a quiet passage on the lower notes. Many players have retained this lever, some keeping it closed all the time, so that they must always finger *d'* with the fingering ..o/oo.F, which gives this note without the crook-hole open.

With the normal thumb-operated crook key (*piano-Mechanik* it is called in Germany) the crook-hole is kept closed from *a♭* down to *F*. Below this the E-plate (right thumb) closes it automatically. In addition, a spring-lock is fitted to hold down the crook key on slurs down at the bottom when the left thumb is unable to manage both the crook key touch and its keys on the long joint (e.g. the *pp* slur from *B♭* to low *C* at the beginning of *Siegfried*).

Several *extra keys* and gadgets can be fitted optionally, e.g.: *high d'' key* for left thumb (indicated in broken line in fig. 28); *middle d/e♭ trill key* on the tenor joint (either for III, or with the touch extended over the butt, for IV, like the side key on the flute); connection by which the E plate holds down the F key for the trill on low E/F♯; *A♭/B♭ trill key* (another thumb key on the butt) to do away with the poor trill made by trilling finger V while fingering A♭; combined key for low E♭ and D♭; etc.

Low A. Wagner and Mahler are the chief low A writers, the former in his third bassoon parts only. Instruments with this note are supplied to order by Heckel and others (Plate XV). Their bell is about 6½ inches longer than the ordinary and the open low A key is operated by either the left thumb or the left little finger. Failing this, an excellent low A may be made with a roll of paper in the bell, while some players can produce quite a good A by fingering low B♭ and drawing back the lips to slow down the vibration of the reed.

Mutes. To help pianissimo on the low notes, a French player may sometimes be observed to stuff his handkerchief in the bell. This makes an effective mute, except that one cannot then play the low B♭ and the B becomes dangerous. An improvement is the kind of mute often used in Germany, for example the following from the Berlin Philharmonic: a 3-inch length of brass tube, about ⅜ inch less in diameter than the bore of the bell. Sufficient felt or wool is tied round the tube to hold it lightly in the bell mouth, half in, half out, and with this simple device the low notes become safe down to the softest *pp* without damage to the attack or the tone-quality.

Contrabassoon

This, also often called by its older name *double bassoon,* is an octave lower than the bassoon; its deepest notes provide the woodwind's rendering of the bottom notes of the piano. Such low frequencies, sustained on a wind instrument, have to be heard to be believed.

One design of contrabassoon is used throughout modern orchestras, namely Heckel's. Most of the instruments in use today are by Heckel himself, though several other makers now copy the design. It is not by any means a scaled up replica of the ordinary bassoon, for the holes are placed approximately in their acoustically-correct positions, and are closed by finger-plates turning on long axles. However, Heckel has preserved something of the bassoon's character through his retention of narrow, deep drillings for the left hand holes.

There is no crook key, nor high A and C keys. Instead, the

left thumb has two octave keys, the lower of them used from g to c' (as written, but sounding an octave lower) and again from high $a'\flat$ upwards; and the upper key, from d' to g' ($c'\sharp$ is best made without the octave keys, by fingering low F and opening the middle C$\sharp$ key). Otherwise the key system is like that of the bassoon, German or French system as ordered, and slightly simplified. The fingering in the upper register is more straightforward than on the bassoon, because simple second harmonics are used right up to f', and then third harmonics to top of $b'\flat$ (the highest note required, though c'' comes easily enough as a fourth harmonic).

Downwards, many instruments descend only to the C (with a wooden bell pointing upwards). But the parts frequently demand the low B$\flat$, and this is supplied either by a bent-over wooden bell (as in Plate XVI), or by a tall metal bell, which, however, tends to obstruct the view of the brass players behind—and this becomes worse with the low-A bell that so many foreign orchestras quite unnecessarily invest in for the cost of a few extra marks.

'The double-bassoon is a large and ponderous instrument with a heavy and obtrusive tone', says a recent book, echoing the statements of all orchestration books, ancient and modern. If only it were! As for the alleged ponderousness, technique on the Heckel contrabassoon is as fluent and flexible as that on the bassoon itself; e.g. the difficult bassoon cadenza in Rimsky-Korsakov's *Sheherezade* is actually child's play on the contra, and Beethoven's hectic passages up to top A with the cellos and basses are all perfectly feasible. But as for 'obtrusive tone', the only trouble with the contrabassoon is simply that it is not loud enough in the orchestra. With properly-made reeds, its tone throughout is warm and musical, like thick velvet. But only the lowest fifth has sufficient volume to tell in ensemble passages above the level of *mezzopiano*. An attempt to make more noise can be made with a French-style reed, but produces only the shattering, pitch-less buzz of a large reed that has failed to come properly to grips with the air-column. There are, admittedly, some conductors of the French school who relish this horrible noise. But nothing can be more objectionable in works by composers who have understood the instrument differently, like Brahms, Strauss and Puccini. The first and last movements of Brahms's First Symphony, and the see-saw pedal at the end of the 1st Act of *Tosca*, cry out for the fullest and firmest organ-like notes that the instrument will deliver, and the only way of obtaining them is laboriously to play in the stiffest German reeds, made of the best cane, and not to touch them with the scraping knife unless they refuse to loosen-up with month after month of playing.

Very occasionally (e.g. in Madrid) one may still see one of the old French contrabassoons, some 6 feet 9 inches tall, constructed rather like a bassoon, and mostly with plain finger-holes and going down to C. Usually it has some good steady notes along with a lot of very bad ones for which the best fingerings have to be found by experiment. It needs a French-type reed and a certain amount of buzz suits it. Another obsolete design, used in England around the latter part of the last century, is Morton's copy of Haseneier's formidable invention, the *Contrabassophone*. This had a bore double that of the bassoon in diameter (cf. the heckelphone)—a far wider bore than in any other contrabassoon—and finger-holes wide in proportion. Where the other contras may wheeze and buzz, the contra-bassophone roars. It can be played almost up to a tuba fortissimo; *piano* is the difficulty.

Notwithstanding the many fine points of the Heckel-type instrument, it must be conceded that a really satisfactory type has yet to be evolved. That this should be no impossibility was demonstrated a few years back by the London player and reed-maker James O'Loughlin, who made a contrabassoon for himself using bits of an old sharp-pitch bassoon for the narrower parts and tubing of plastic for the larger. When after weeks of keen anticipation in woodwind circles the instrument was first produced at an engagement, it was agreed by all present that in spite of its odd, home-made appearance, it was superior in tone to any contrabassoon that they had ever heard before.

Sarrusophones, etc.

Sarrusophones (Plate XVI) are a family of double-reed instruments with conical brass tubes patented by the French bandmaster Sarrus in 1856, ten years after Sax patented the saxophones. His idea was to preserve the usefulness of the double reed in military bands, which, in France, had already ejected the bassoon as being too quiet, and were having doubts about the oboe.

In bore, they are wider than oboes and bassoons, though nowhere near as wide as the saxophones. But as on the latter, the holes are large, and are placed in acoustically logical positions and covered by plates hinged on axles. The fingering is also like that of the saxophones (though usually with simple-acting octave keys) and the tonalities, ranges and transpositions are the same (six fingers being written d').

The sarrusophones were first put into production by Gautrot of Paris (subsequently Couesnon). The Bb soprano is straight, like a brass oboe. Eb alto and Bb tenor are folded once, like small bassoons. Eb baritone, Bb bass and the Eb, C and Bb contrabasses are folded again for compactness. From alto to bass they have short bassoon-like crooks. The contrabasses have coiled crooks. Their reeds are like bassoon reeds, varying in size with the different members of the family (a complete set is drawn half-size in Lavignac's Encyclopaedia; Plate VI shows the reed for the large military Contrabass in Bb).[1]

The tone in the lower and middle parts of the compass is considerably more powerful than that of the oboe or the bassoon, bestowing upon a band a cheerful reediness which the smoother, though in some respects not dissimilar tone of the saxophones does not. Their failure to have secured a permanent place in bands must be mainly due to the fact that their *useful* compass is severely limited on account of the ineffectiveness of the higher notes. These notes are too dull and faint for satisfactory rendi-

---

[1] Approximate measurements, in millimetres, of tip-width, blade-length to first wire, and total length: soprano, 9, 20, 55; alto, 13, 25, 55; tenor, 15, 27, 60; baritone, 17, 32, 70; bass, 19, 40, 80; Eb or C contrabass, 22, 44, 85.

tion of orchestral oboe and bassoon parts, and consequently, as Franko Goldman has pointed out, one would need at least two different sarrusophones to deal effectively with a single wood-wind part. They have been fairly tested in the past. For instance in some big Italian bands even up to the 1920s, a tenor (or bari-tone) and a bass sarrusophone were allotted the orchestral bassoon parts in transcriptions of Puccini operas (in which, incidentally, the voice parts are rendered by brass soloists), while a contrabass would help with the *contrabasso ad ancia* or 'reed contrabass' part. In Paris, the civilian band, the *Fanfare la Sirène*, still musters a team of sarrusophones, including soprano (for orchestral oboe parts) and alto. But generally today, 'sarrusophone' means simply the contrabass, which is still manufactured and is employed in a number of the larger French and American bands. It can add magnificent extra weight, sonorously reedy, to the bass of the full band's harmony, while yet, with practised handling, it can be played softly as a contra-bass to the band's woodwind. Latterly, single-reed mouthpieces have been tried on it.

For a long time the contrabass was also used in French orchestras for contrabassoon parts, with the full connivance of Saint-Saëns and other leading French composers of the time, all of whom took a great interest in the instrument and wrote *contrebasson* parts envisaged for performance on the sarrusophone. It has recently been replaced by Buffet's copy of the Heckel-pattern contrabassoon, yet according to one who often used to sit near it in the Paris orchestras, the sarrusophone made a very reasonable, contrabassoon-like sound in this role (but then, as already noticed, the French like a good rattling sound in the 16-foot register of the woodwind). In Spanish orchestras, the contrabass sarrusophone is still commoner than the contra-bassoon; it is sometimes a C contrabass, sometimes the more handy E♭ contrabass, whose lowest note is $D'♭$. (The contrabass sarrusophones are best regarded as non-transposing, reading from bass clef like a contrabassoon.) On the large military band B♭ contrabass, the bottom note is $A''♭$—the deepest note given by any reed instrument save the still-experimental sub-contra-bass clarinet.

CONTREBASSE-À-ANCHE OR CONTRABASSO AD ANCIA ('reed contrabass', Plate XVI). This is a double-reed instrument of brass, made in a tuba shape, and is a mixed product of several inventors (Cerveny, Mahillon, etc.). It has a short crook, and a series of closed keys covering very large holes. The instrument's unique technical feature is that each hole is so big that, when opened, the note requires no further venting from holes further down. For each note, therefore, *one* key only is opened at a time, so that the instrument is fingered somewhat like a piano. To assist the illusion, the touches of the main series of keys are so arranged that the little finger of the left hand (the instrument being slung in bassoon fashion) has the key for the lowest fundamental, and the right little finger that for the highest, the other fingers falling in between in the order of a pianist's fingers. 'The player can acquire great proficiency with only a few days' practice' (Mahillon, 1896), and all that a pianist would find strange at first is that his left hand is held palm-uppermost. There are in addition, two octave keys, and also some thumb keys, including that for the bottom note, D', this key differing from the rest in being an open key. The instrument takes a very large double reed and makes the loudest noise of all the 16-foot double-reed inventions. Even some provincial Italian bands have found it *troppo aspro*.

PART TWO

History

CHAPTER VII

The Primitive Flute World

Tens of thousands of years ago, upper palaeolithic man, crouched in his rough shelter, noticed that certain kinds of object, like a hollow bone, a dried-up fruit shell or a piece of hollow cane, might give a sound if blown upon in certain ways; a flute-sound, and the sound interested him. No doubt a note had already been produced accidentally now and then by earlier men, for instance, while picking a bone; but it would have been passed over without particular notice; even up to the present time there have remained a few primitive peoples who do not make flutes, among them the Australian aborigines and the Fuegians. They represent the flute-less advance-guards of mankind. Only to the expanded consciousness of the superior palaeolithic peoples of some twenty thousand years ago, the fact that a dead bone or cut plant apparently possessed a voice of its own became interesting, and the customs of primitive flute-users today reveal that the first significance to be attached to the phenomenon was magical. The natural material was then deliberately fashioned into a flute by the tribal medicine man, to aid him in his communications with the world of spirits, to cure sickness, stop rain and so on. Thus, like the drum, the flute was invented to serve primitive magic and ritual. So too was the trumpet, which first appeared in its rudimentary forms scarcely later than the flute. And even in high civilization, wind music has not entirely shaken off its earliest associations. In the church organ we still have our religious super-flute, and in the military band our ceremonial super-trumpet.

Flute typology shown in whistles

In this earliest stage, the flute is scarcely more than a little one-note whistle. Yet its variety in form is astonishing. Almost every known flute sounding-arrangement is employed somewhere or other in the world by primitive men in their magic

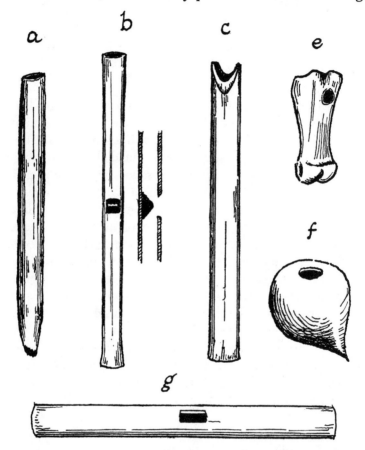

FIG. 31. *A selection of primitive whistles, illustrating different sound-generating arrangements.*

whistles. Several of these arrangements are illustrated in fig. 31, among them some that are virtually unknown in Western civilization, though our ancestors may have employed them in some remote era and subsequently given them up.

The 'Bushman's flute' (*a*) of an ostrich quill shows a form of *stopped vertical flute,* closed at the bottom end and held approximately vertically against the lower lip. It is not blown quite as we sound a note on a fountain-pen cap, but with a primitive embouchure formed by sticking out the tongue a little way and curling it into a wind guide. The American Indian medicine man's 'Mataco whistle' (*b*) is a bird-bone *flageolet,* voiced by a hole in the middle under which there is a lump of resin which deflects the breath on to the farther edge of the hole (as shown in the sectional drawing). It can be blown from either end, so that if the hole is off-centre it gives two notes, which some medicine men make use of when directing a dance, or a battle.

The bamboo whistle from South-east Asia (*c*) represents the genus *notched flute,* that is, an end-blown flute in which sound-production is facilitated by a notch cut in the rim of the tube opposite the point where it is held to the mouth. The instrument is held forwards like a recorder, and the lower lip almost covers the tube while the breath is aimed at the base of the notch—lip aperture and notch combining to form something not unlike the voicing of a flageolet. In the example shown, the bore is so small that a shallower notch is cut on the opposite side to assist the embouchure, but some fully-fledged notched flutes are shown later on (fig. 36).

Next, two examples of the *globular flute* in whistle form, the widespread ancestor of the ocarina. The Brazilian whistle (*f*) is made of a one and a half inch purplish dried fruit-shell, and the note is made by blowing flute-wise across the hole. Its equivalent in bone (*e*) is the 'phalange whistle' of a reindeer foot-bone, found in considerable numbers in European Upper Palaeolithic sites, including the painted caves of the Pyrenees. Like the paintings themselves, these whistles could not have been made without much time and care; it cannot have been easy to cut a neat round hole in an inch-long bone with a flint tool, and this surely indicates that the reindeer whistle had some great ritual or magic importance. It has been suggested that these remote part-ancestors of ours blew these whistles (note, about d'''') in chorus in their innermost, secret caverns where the paintings are. Other typical primitive noise-makers have been found with them: bone scrapers, and bull-roarers whirled round on the end of a cord.

Lastly the *transverse flute* (of which our own flute is one example), represented by another whistle from Brazil (*g*). Usually, of course, the mouth-hole of a transverse flute is placed close to one end, so that the full sounding-length of the tube can be used. But before flute *music* was envisaged, the hole was made in what was then the obvious place for it—in the middle, as we see it here. Sometimes both ends are open; sometimes one is stopped. Later in this chapter we shall see how tunes can be played on such an instrument.

Musicologists have not yet reached complete agreement about the evolutionary order of these various sounding principles. Curt Sachs has suggested that the rudimentary flageolet (*b*) was the earliest. Others have pointed to the stopped whistle (*a*). However, it is not difficult to imagine ways by which one might have quite naturally given rise to another. The transverse whistle might have been discovered through accidentally sounding a note whilst blowing away the chips during the manufacture of whistle (*b*). Some bones naturally develop a notch as they dry out. And so on.

Flute music without finger-holes

'THE MAN' and 'THE WOMAN'. The notes or calls sounded on these primitive whistles are not, of course, music. But when two bamboo flutes giving different notes are blown continuously one after another throughout a tribal ceremony, we may say that we are confronted with a kind of music—probably the most ancient and primitive wind music that there ever was. The longer of the two flutes is called the man, and the shorter, the woman. They are sounded vertically, transversely or otherwise. They are tremendously sacred, and taboo to women and children on pain of death by poisoning or strangulation; one explorer in New Guinea could obtain a specimen only on the strict understanding that it would never be shown to any women.

These archaic flutes are innocent of finger-holes. The music is made entirely with the natural harmonics of the two tubes.

That man should have come to know about harmonics so early on is by no means difficult to understand; any trial with a piece of bamboo, with the interior knots burnt out, will clearly show how no human being could possibly remain ignorant of harmonics once a tube reaches about two feet in length. You just cannot help blowing them. Moreover, the primitive savage further noticed that if the tube is considerably larger, the harmonics are very much stronger and more imposing. The 'man' and the 'woman' are not of our common woodwind size, but giant flutes reaching five or even seven feet in length and often well over an inch in bore, and their most readily-blown harmonics can sound terrifyingly loud, almost like a bugle, but far more blood-curdling.

Among some tribes, the two performers do not seem to aim for any particular harmonics, and in New Guinea there are huge stopped vertical flutes, sometimes notched, played like this. The two men, puffing alternately as hard as they can with a primitive embouchure extremely wasteful of breath, stamp round each other in a circle, twisting and turning in the effort to find more breath (Plate XVII, *top inset*). But in fig. 32 (1), also from New Guinea, the two flutes are *tuned*, having been cut so that selected harmonics fit a simple melodic scheme. The instruments in this instance were giant transverse flutes with mouthholes almost an inch across (Plate XVII, *left*), though this huge aperture is reduced with the fingers while playing. The man with the shorter flute blew only his fourth harmonic (g') while his mate with the seven foot long F flute blew his 4th and 5th. They began with phrase **a**, repeating it until one man gave the signal by pressing on the other's foot, whereupon they embarked upon **b** or one of its variants **c**, **d**, finally returning to **a**. This is a very simple example, but none the less it represents a beginning. Other New Guinea tribes are said to make more complicated tunes, even using two pairs of flutes together.

A similar technique is found among the Indian tribes of the Amazon and Orinoco—among primitive Mongoloid men instead of primitive Negroid, but whether the two people learnt it from a common source aeons ago, or whether they evolved it independently, is a deep question to which an authoritative answer can hardly as yet be given.

These South American Indians employ pairs of giant hole-less flageolets—enormously enlarged versions of the flageolet whistle described earlier—with a band of leaves tied round the upper part of the voicing hole to guide the wind over the block on to the far edge of the hole. In fig. 32 (2), from one of the recordings of the Piaroa Indians made by Pierre Gaisseau on the recent French Orinoco–Amazon expedition led by Alain Gheerbrant, the two instruments are again tuned, this time to a minor third apart. With this tuning they make up between them

FIG. 32. *Duets with hole-less giant flutes; 1, New Guinea, after Bateson; 2, Upper Orinoco, from a recording by P. Gaisseau, (reproduced by courtesy of the Musée de l' Homme, Paris).*

that tetratonic scale (pentatonic less one note) that is so typical of primitive song, but whether the flute tunes or the songs came first is another difficult and controversial question. The tune in the example is accompanied by another pair of archaic wind instruments—huge trumpets of coiled bark, blown with a primitive, half-formed embouchure and alternately producing grunting notes or moans in the bass register.

FLUTE BANDS AND PANPIPES. Another widespread kind of ceremonial music with hole-less flutes employs a set of several instruments each tuned to sound one given note (its fundamental; harmonics not being used). This sort of performance is remembered in European musical history in the Russian regimental horn bands of a hundred and fifty years ago; each man was issued with a horn that gave one note, to be sounded at its proper place in the music (and if one man received a flogging for a misdemeanour the band was without an F sharp for the rest of the week). This 'Russian band' method is fairly common among primitives and is employed by them with many different types of instrument. Probably best-known are the flute bands of South Africa, originally Hottentot but now found among many Bantu peoples in Bechuanaland and the Transvaal.

These bands have been fully described by Professor Kirby. There may be as many as twenty-four instruments in a band, all of them one-note vertical flutes from 6 inches to 54 inches long, typically of river reed and stopped at the lower end with a fibre stopper that can be pushed up or down for tuning. The embouchure is of the kind already noticed for the 'Bushman's flute'—the tongue being curled into a channel and slightly protruded against the top of the flute, which is blown with great force while the players, each with his one-note flute, move slowly round in a circle. The set of flutes is commonly tuned to a tetratonic scale extended over several octaves, e.g. from d''', c''', a'', g'' in the highest octave (the smallest four flutes) down to d, c, A, G in the longest and deepest flutes. The top group, which includes the leader of the band, leads off and then the lower groups join in one after another until everyone is playing. So they continue, endlessly repeating their same short phrases (e.g. fig. 33, *top*) until the leader's group ceases, whereupon the lower groups drop out in order, leaving the lowest to finish alone, as in a round. The tone of the flutes is reedy and vigorous, and the deepest flutes sound unbelievably like a bass clarinet.

There is no space here to go far into the complex and fascinating subject of primitive *panpipes*, which represent a third way of making flute-music without finger-holes. The two great pan-piping regions of the world are Melanesia and the north-west quarter of South America, and here the variety of the instruments and tunings is quite astonishing, while they are played not only singly, but also in ways that show clear connection with the ancient fluting methods described already. For instance, in duet, with one panpipe of a pair supplying notes missing from the other; the haunting melody in fig. 33, from another Orinoco recording by Gaisseau, was somehow played by two boys with six-cane panpipes. And also, in bands with panpipes of different sizes, recalling the octave groups of the South African flute band; the longest cane may exceed four feet.

Moreover, while the panpipe is known among ourselves simply as a small row of vertical flutes, each stopped at the bottom by a knot in the cane, the Melanesians frequently add a

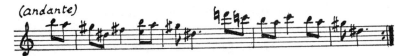

Fig. 33. Above: *South African flute band—example of a tune* (*from a Gallo recording*). Below: *A panpipe tune from the Upper Orinoco* (*from a Gaisseau recording*).

parallel row of open-ended pipes, and these are sometimes heard to sound feebly, yet distinctly, in the upper octave as the over-flow of the player's breath strikes them. South American Indians may add a parallel row of half-length stopped pipes, with the same effect. In Melanesia, there are even panpipes consisting *only* of open pipes (as in the old Chinese ceremonial panpipe) and the player stops each pipe with his finger as he wishes to sound it.

Some panpipes are tied in a bundle instead of in a row, and here one meets many more surprises. Professor Kunst has described from Flores (Indonesia) a bundle-panpipe which was produced only to be untied, and its four small canes handed out to a group of men who then proceeded to perform in the Russian band manner. In another, more sophisticated Asiatic type, the centre cane is charged with gunpowder, and the panpipe sent into the air as a musical rocket.

THE HARMONIC FLUTE AS A SOLO INSTRUMENT. With the wide knowledge of flute harmonics shown by primitive peoples in their ceremonial music, it is not surprising to find that they have also evolved ways of utilizing them in solitary flute-playing. It is said that one of the New Guinea blowers of the stopped vertical flutes described on page 175 would, when off-duty, make quite elaborate tunes on the harmonics of one flute alone. But the recognized solo technique is considerably more ingenious. It is founded upon intercalation of the open and stopped harmonics obtained by opening and stopping the lower end with the finger.

FIG. 34. *The solo harmonic flute.* Top: *derivation of a harmonic flute scale;* centre: *a Swazi tune, after Kirby;* below: *a tune from Gabon, from a recording by Rouget.*

Consider the harmonics obtainable from a vertical or transverse flute about 31 inches long, which is about the longest that the arm can manage. Its stopped fundamental is about A♭ and its open fundamental an octave higher. The two series based upon these fundamentals are given in fig. 34 (*top*), with a scale on the right that demonstrates how they fit together as the lower end is alternately stopped and opened, to make a useful scale of notes for tune-making. A cross marks the stopped notes and a circle marks the open ones.

Zulu and Swazi herd-boys are said to be the experts with this technique, using vertical flutes and a strange embouchure in which the top of the flute actually enters the mouth between slightly-parted lips to rest against the upper teeth. Hugh Tracey has written that some of the best Zulu music is theirs, and Professor Kirby gives a number of examples in which harmonics as high as the 11th stopped and the 6th open are reached. Fig. 34 (*centre*) shows one of the simpler examples, while below it is a still simpler effort recorded by M. Rouget from a player on a 17-inch-long vertical nose flute in Gabon (French Equatorial Africa) with the open fundamental sounding sharp.

Flute tunes are made in this way all over the world; even in Europe, for Bartók found in the Carpathians tunes in which the Rumanian shepherds' alp-horn is imitated on a hole-less vertical

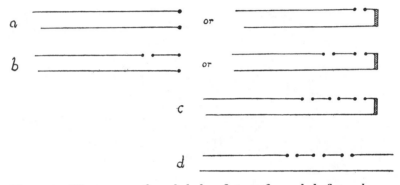

Fig. 35. *The progress from hole-less flute to finger-hole flute, shown diagrammatically.*

flute. In the East the technique is employed mainly by young men for recreation and courting. Their tunes are said to consist of a few notes but to be none the less 'sweet and musical', while they have the curious property of being recognized, though never heard before, by the particular women to whom they are addressed. Perhaps she recognizes her name from the rise and fall of the tune. Often the flutes are transverse flutes, in which case the open lower end may be replaced by a stopped end with a side hole just above it, which technically comes to the same thing (Plate XVII; also fig. 35, *a*). The embouchure end, on the other hand, is very often open, so that from the Western point of view the flute is built the wrong way round. While playing, this open end is closed with the hand or a lump of mud.

Finger-holes

The scope of a harmonic flute is often seen to have been extended by the boring of an extra hole or two, giving additional open fundamentals to fill certain gaps among the notes. The arrangements shown diagrammatically in fig. 35, *b* (with two open fundamentals) and *c* (with three) are especially common in Melanesia, mainly on notched flutes (Plate XVII), and South Africa, on transverse flutes. The stopped harmonics are still employed, being obtaincd by closing all the lower apertures. Both hands are often used, even when there is only one side hole.

But with three or more side holes, the stopped notes become confusing. Fig. 35, *d* illustrates the higher stage in which they are no longer used—the pure finger-hole technique employed by ourselves and by every other civilization exclusively, and by the less advanced peoples on the fringes of civilization very commonly. But the latter may in some cases have acquired the technique through contact with the higher peoples, among whom it was developed very early. The ancient civilizations—Egypt, Sumeria, China—each entered history already provided with three- or four-holed open-ended flutes, while bone specimens of far earlier date have been found in European prehistoric sites (fig. 36, 4), and these may be the distant cousins of the similar, though much later flutes of the extinct civilizations of America. A memory of the primitive stopped end, however, appears to be preserved in numerous instruments (e.g. certain cane flageolets of the Near East) in which the lower end is terminated by a perforated knot, instead of by a clean cut through the hollow cane.

Fig. 36 shows a selection of flutes from different parts of the world, with an English B♭ flute (1) for comparison of size. The Turko-Balkan *kaval* (3) is a wooden vertical flute and a modern descendant of the ancient Egyptian long vertical flute of cane. It is used by folk who employ many small intervals in their music, and the inter-hole distances are correspondingly small; two fingers may have to be raised together to make a whole tone. The kaval is one of the most beautiful of flutes, though often a reedy, breathy tone is preferred, at times accompanied by a drone hummed by the player. But it is the most difficult to

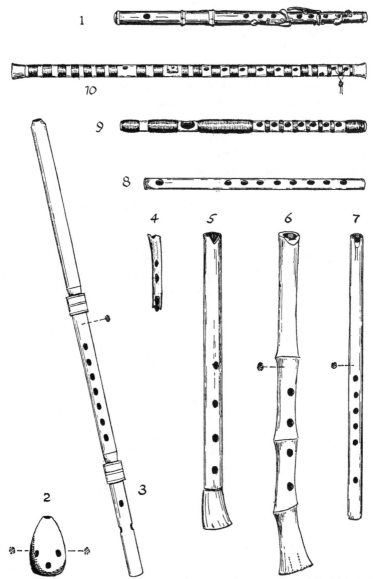

FIG. 36. *A selection of higher finger-hole flutes.* 1, *Western B♮ flute*; 2, *Chinese* hsuan; 3, *Balkan* kaval; 4, *prehistoric bone flute, Europe, after Seewald*; 5, *West African notched flute*; 6, *Japanese* shakuhachi; 7, *Peruvian* kena; 8, *the classical Indian flute*; 9, *Japanese* fuyé; 10, *Chinese* ti.

sound and takes years to learn. Though we classify it as 'vertical' (as opposed to 'transverse') it is generally held forwards or sideways, with the top end, which is bevelled off all round to a sharp rim, placed against the aperture of the lips, which is narrowed much as it is in our own flute-playing. The bevel is not vital, however, and many of the cane vertical flutes (*nay*) of modern Egypt, North Africa, etc., have plain-cut top ends.

In contrast, nos. *5* and *6* are two flutes that have been evolved to suit the wide basic intervals of pentatonic music. Their inter-hole distances are very wide and the first and third fingers of each hand are used to cover the holes. On the West African notched flute (*5*), lifting one finger after another gives approximate one-and-a-quarter tones, which the players may or may not try to humour by lipping into the whole-tones and one-and-a-half tones of the music. The Japanese *shakuhachi* (*6*) is more carefully tuned, giving a fairly accurate basic pentatonic scale $d'\,f'\,g'\,a'\,c''$ (continued upwards by over-blowing), other notes being obtained by cross-fingering and lipping. It is a notched flute with the notch reduced to a bare minimum, and rivals the kaval in the ethereal beauty of its sound.

The Chinese are also a pentatonic people, but their flute *ti* (10) came, like our flute, from Central Asia. It has the normal inter-hole distances of a diatonic flute, and two fingers must be raised together to make the larger pentatonic interval. Its bamboo is bound with lacquered thread between the holes to make the tube wall firmer and the sound fuller, while a membrane of bamboo, cocoon or paper, glued over a hole a little way below the mouth-hole imparts a reedy quality, said to make the sound carry better. No. 9 is its Japanese derivative. No. 8 is the traditional Indian flute, which belongs to the same family, and nowadays may often be heard in Indian films, very sensitively played in diatonic music. Its eighth hole is used only in certain modes, the little finger of the upper hand then taking hole IV. Each of these last three flutes has about the same pitch as our B♭ band flute sketched at the top of the figure. Another normal-interval flute now used in pentatonic tunes is the Peruvian notched flute *kena* (7), a descendant of the old Inca flutes, of whose music nothing is known.

On these diatonic flutes with equidistant holes, lifting one finger after another gives a diatonic scale only approximately. One finds oneself landed, as recorder-players well know, with roughly three-quarter tones among the whole-tones (especially upwards and downwards from . . . / . o o), and before the keys and other improvements of the nineteenth century, all Western players had to humour these false intervals by cross-fingering or lipping. Oriental flutists still have to.

Finally (2) an example of finger-holes applied to the globular flute, in 'that peculiar egg-shaped thing made of earthenware' as an early visitor described the Chinese *hsuan* or goose-egg, preserved up to recent times in the ancient ceremonial music and played there in unison with many other curious wind instruments. The two thumbs operate the two rear holes. As with the ocarina (fig. 76), which is a nineteenth-century development of the traditional earthenware carnival whistle of Italy, the greater the volume of the instrument, the deeper the note. Also, the greater the sum area of apertures (including the mouth-hole, or in case of the ocarina, the voicing hole), the higher the note, so that the holes may be uncovered in different orders to give the same series of notes. The *hsuan* is manufactured today as a souvenir object, and gives a feeble sort of sound across the upper part of the treble stave.

Some special exotic forms

NOSE FLUTES. In Western popular imagination, tropical fluting is linked inseparably with the nose flute; yet by and large, sounding a flute with the nose is far less common among primitive peoples than mouth-blowing. Obviously the nostril is a less efficient projector of the breath than the aperture of the lips, and this on the whole outweighs a special recommendation of the nose, mentioned by Professor Sachs; namely that its breath is held to contain the soul.

Among specialized nose flutes, the end-blown type, characteristic of the aboriginals of Malaya, Borneo, etc., has a small, neat hole pierced in the knot at the top end—the nose-hole. With one nostril usually plugged with a rag or piece of tobacco, the flute is held sideways under the nose. The tone is clear and bright and players sometimes perform to large audiences. A peak of woodwind virtuosity was illustrated by a photograph in the *Tatler* some years ago (January, 1909): an itinerant musician in India playing the nose flute, and at the same time, with his mouth, sustaining a drone on a chanter-less bagpipe.

More celebrated, however, is the side-blown nose flute, the national wind instrument of Polynesia. Plate XVII shows an instrument of the classic two-holed type, brought back from Tahiti by Captain Cook himself. It is held forwards, a little to the side, with the nose-hole (visible just below the stopped top end) under the right nostril. The hole a little way further down is for the left hand, whose thumb is meanwhile closing the left

FIG. 37. *Phrases from the nose-flute* hula, *after Emerson.*

nostril. Far away, close to the open lower end, is a hole for the right hand (though some flutes have extra holes here). Consequently the instrument gives two deep fundamentals and one much higher, e.g. f', g', and a'', though overblowing the first two to their octaves makes three consecutive notes. The phrases in fig. 37 give an idea of how these notes were employed in old Hawaii, where this flute, like each other instrument, was dedicated to its particular *hula*. The performer, a woman, started 'slow and languid' and then gradually increased the speed. In remotest Mangareva, in the South Pacific, the same instrument was recently reported still to be played in its ancient manner. In other islands, it has been revived in various ways.

CENTRAL-EMBOUCHURE FLUTES. It was noticed in the first section of this chapter that the mouth-hole of a transverse flute is not necessarily placed near one end. It may be at the centre.

In several parts of South East Asia the instrument, so constructed, is played as a hole-less harmonic flute, open-ended for finger-stopping at *both* ends.

Let us examine an 18-inch-long specimen from the Shan States of Burma. The mouth-hole is half an inch off-centre, making one side of the flute a little longer than the other. The notes obtainable are then as follows:

1. Both ends stopped: the longer half takes command; fundamental e'; harmonics (stopped pipe) b'', $g'''\sharp$.
2. Both ends open: the longer half again takes command; fundamental (open pipe) e''; harmonics e''', b'''.
3. Stopping the shorter half: this half just manages to take command; fundamental $f''\sharp$; harmonics $c'''\sharp$ $(a'''\sharp)$.
4. Stopping the longer half: the shorter half still takes command, now as an open pipe; fundamental $f''\sharp$; harmonic $f'''\sharp$.

Thus with the harmonics the player has a useful pentatonic scale, b'' $c'''\sharp$ e''' $f'''\sharp$ $g'''\sharp$ b''', and very well in tune.

The extraordinary collection of archaic wind instruments that was employed in the Chinese ceremonial music up to the time of the last emperor, included up to the eighteenth century a flute with three-finger-holes each side of the embouchure, representing the highest stage reached by the central-embouchure flute. The two hands were held in front of the instrument (i.e. with their palms facing the player), and the fingering is based upon the 'both ends open' phenomena on the hole-less model just described; i.e. the note is given by whichever side of the flute is the longer when measured from the mouth-hole to the nearest open finger-hole. Say the group of holes on the left is a little further from the mouth-hole (x, fig. 38) than that on the right. With all fingers off, the note is given by the tubing from x to $l.1$, this being longer than x to $r.1$. To descend the scale, first close $r.1$. The note is now given by x to $r.2$, this now being the longer portion. Next close $l.1$, making x to $l.2$ the longer portion. And so on, closing $r.2$, $l.2$, $r.3$, and finally $l.3$, which gives the bottom note. A replica made of a piece of cane makes an amusing toy though not much of a musical instrument since poor overblowing restricts the compass, and this is presumably why the central-embouchure has never come to anything in the end. Assamese tribesmen, however, were recently still making it, with two holes on each side of the mouth-hole.

RINGED FLAGEOLETS, etc. Lastly, here are some examples to show how our Western method is not the only way of making a good flageolet.

A simple voicing of resin block with leaf adjusting ring has

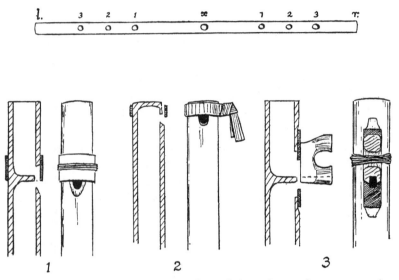

FIG. 38. *Central-embouchure flute* (above), *and some exotic flageolets:* 1, *Burmese* palwee; 2, *Javanese* suling; 3, *Apache flute, North America.*

already been mentioned earlier on. This is clearly a far simpler way of directing the breath on to the edge than our method of inserting a carefully-fitted, non-adjustable wooden block into the interior of the tube. Geographically, the wooden block belongs to the belt of old civilization from China and India across to Europe and North Africa. The leaf ring and its elaborations belong to South East Asia, Indonesia and both Americas. The Negro peoples rarely make flageolets.

In the Burmese *palwee* (fig. 38, 1), used in some kinds of

orchestra, a knot in the cane (or sometimes a wax partition) forms a deflector underneath a long oval voicing-hole. A leaf or paper ring (or even a metal plate) is secured to cover the upper part of the hole and to extend over the width of the deflector, to direct the wind on to the lower edge of the hole.

In the Javanese *suling* (2), the only wind instrument in the celebrated gamelans, the upper end is closed by a knot. On the outside, a short shallow channel is cut, leading to the voicing-hole which is just below. To roof this channel, a band of rattan is tied round the top end.

The North American Indian 'lover's flute' or Apache flute (3) shows one of the many more complicated variants of the first example. Again a knot in the cane or an artificial partition forms the deflector and is situated underneath a long slot-like hole. Placed over the slot is a metal plate with a smaller slot cut in it, and the lower edge of this slot is the sounding edge. To roof the upper part of the superimposed slots, there is a saddle-shaped piece of wood, held in position with a thong or string.

More remarkable flageolet constructions may be seen in Jaap Kunst's book on the instruments of the Indonesian island of Flores; not only simple flageolets, but double and triple flageolets, and bass flageolets with crooks formed of several interconnecting bamboos. Altogether, we must concede that, save for their ignorance of mechanism, there is very little that the tropical peoples do not know about how to make a flute.

CHAPTER VIII

Early Reed Instruments and Double-piping

While so much of the earliest development of the flute class is laid out before us among the living peoples of the world, the earliest stages in the evolution of the reed instrument are lost in the unrecorded past. Primitive races, except where they have copied from civilization, scarcely know reed instruments, their ignorance of them standing in strange contrast with their extraordinary inventiveness in the matter of flutes. With a few exceptions, as those pairs of one-note reed-pipes *uanas* which South American Indians must have invented for themselves, primitives have not carried the vibrating reed idea beyond the squeaker stage—equivalent to the earliest whistle stage in flutes: grass-blade squeakers of various kinds, used for imitating spirit voices and so on. The reed instrument proper—a vibrating reed coupled with a tube—is evidently a product of the ancient peoples of the Eurasian continent.

How old it is, is difficult to guess, for reed instruments have no bone pre-history stretching back a hundred centuries before the dawn of civilization, as the flutes have. All the prehistoric bone pipes are plainly flutes of one kind or another. But this is understandable, for although the Romans called their reed instrument by the bone name *tibia* (according to their tradition the first were of deer-bone), and although pastoral reed instruments like the Near Eastern *zummara* and the Western horn-pipe have often been made of bone, this material does not belong as naturally to the rudimentary reed instrument as it does to the rudimentary flute. The reed instrument in its simplest forms is

189

necessarily of vegetable material, since the vibrating reed is made by cutting, or flattening out, one end of the pipe itself. These simplest forms, which no doubt represent the ancestral forms, are still made by village boys all over the civilized world from corn stalks, rice stalks, or thin river reeds, either by flattening one end to make a *double reed*, or by cutting a tongue in the side of the stem below a knot (which closes the top end) to make a *single reed*. With three or four small finger-holes added, this becomes the 'pipe of green corn' of Chaucer and the 'oaten pipe' of Milton—quite an amusing and instructive bit of instrument-making to occupy the idle moments of a wind-instrument historian on a country holiday.

Reeds, single and double

At some time before the birth of civilization, some peoples among the mother races of Near Eastern civilization must have proceeded to the next stage, by which the rudimentary reed pipe is improved to become a more substantial musical instrument; namely, making the reed separately from the pipe. An obvious advantage of this is that when the reed wears out, or becomes damaged, it is not necessary to throw the entire instrument away. The pipe-maker could then settle down to make the pipe more carefully, with wider choice of bore-diameter and materials. Meanwhile the performer gained a means of tuning the pipes by pushing the reeds further in or out—an indispensable provision when he took to playing two pipes at once, as will be described shortly. Both of the two kinds of reed, single and double, became improved in this manner and were so employed by the ancients.

The ancient form of *single reed* is best known to us today as the drone reed of our bagpipes (Chapter III, also fig. 40, *i*). No early specimen has reached us, but certain instrument-forms prove beyond doubt that this reed has always remained substantially the same. It is made of cane, except that in northern countries it may be cut from an elder shoot, pushing out the pith, or even from a goose quill. There are small variations in the cutting; the vibrating tongue may be cut upwards or downwards; the upper end of the reed is normally closed by a knot in the cane, but wax or even the tip of the player's tongue may serve instead.

Fig. 39 shows some less common constructions of the single reed found among old European folk instruments. In the wooden Swedish pipe (*ii*), said to have been used for frightening bears, the reed-blade—a separate slip of pinewood—is tied over the obliquely-cut end of the pipe, thus anticipating the clarinet reed-and-mouthpiece assembly, though not necessarily directly. Still more like the clarinet is reed *iii*, in which the usual all-cane

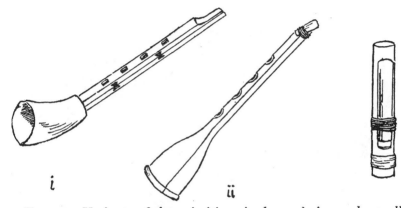

FIG. 39. Variants of the primitive single reed: i, *wooden wall pared down* (*Denmark*); ii, *wooden reed tied over oblique cut* (*N. Sweden*); iii, *cane reed on ivory holder* (*Czech bagpipe*). (i, *Brussels Museum*; ii, *Stockholm Museum*; iii, *Pitt Rivers Museum, Oxford*.)

single reed is developed as an ivory or metal holder over which a cane blade is tied.

In ancient civilization, as also in the Orient today, a *double reed* was made like the rudimentary double reed already described, namely by flattening one end of the material. When the latter is fresh-cut cane or some other resilient plant stem, the flattened end must be held in a clamp while it dries out and sets.

A primitive form of this reed survives in the whit-horn (fig. 40, *ii*)—a one-note reed horn of coiled willow bark pinned together with blackthorn spines; it is still made in several parts of Europe and Asia. The reed, which one Oxfordshire village called the 'trumpet', is a 2-inch long tube of bark worked off a small willow branch. One end of this is pinched flat, and the other is pushed into the horn. In England until quite recently the whit-horn used to be blown round the village on Whit Monday, accompanied by one-note willow May whistles, to rouse the inhabitants for the Spring festival. It sounds rather like a vintage motor horn.

The bamboo Chinese reeds shown in Plate XIX are of the same kind, for a musical pipe called *kuan-tzu* (and the reed for the corresponding Japanese pipe *hichiriki,* fig. 44, *b,* is similar).

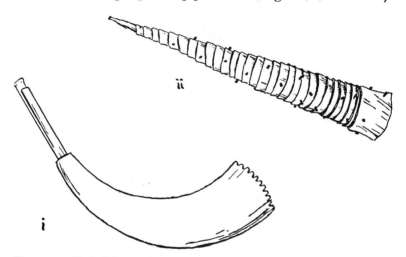

FIG. 40. *Primitive reed horns; i, with single-reed and cow horn, Argentine (formerly made also by shepherds in Gascony and Spain); ii, with double-reed, whit-horn, Oxfordshire.*

With the pipe itself, these reeds are directly descended, thanks to traffic on the Old Silk Road across Central Asia, from ancient Graeco-Egyptian patterns, and fig. 41 shows two of the rare survivors of the latter. These are believed to date from Ptolomaic Egypt of the last few centuries B.C., and were constricted to a waist by a thread ligature that was presumably put on the young plant while it was growing. In the larger specimen we again see the mark of the clamp that held the tip in shape. This ancient or 'long stemmed' type of double reed is inserted directly into the pipe; the short reed mounted on a metal staple came later (see 'Shawm', p. 228).

Our woodwind double reeds are of course made entirely differently: by bending double a long strip of the material. This mode of construction can be traced in actual specimens back to the sixteenth century (Plate XXII) and by inference to the Middle Ages; but not to antiquity, and it seems quite unknown outside the West. However, among the manuscript notes of the

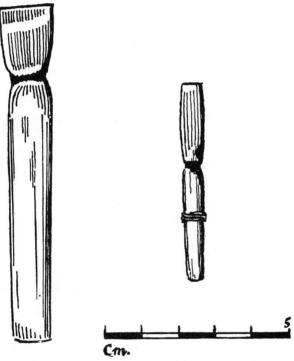

FIG. 41. *Ancient double reeds, Egypt (Brussels Conservatoire Museum).*

late Dr Balfour of Oxford, who collected a great deal of information about primitive reed instruments, there are references to another way of making the whit-horn reed, namely by bending over a strip of willow bark and poking this into the horn. The joined end was then presumably parted to separate the two blades, as we do with our cane today.

(While the Far East borrowed the double reed from the West, its original contribution to reed music is the *free reed*, which we now know so well in our mouth-organs, accordions, harmoniums, etc.; we borrowed the reed from China some hundred and fifty years ago. The brass tongues in the oriental mouth-organs are 'free' to vibrate to either side of the slots in their holders, but in the Western instruments they keep to one side, so that 'free' is perhaps a misnomer. The free reed does not couple very satisfactorily with a finger-hole pipe, though certain Burmese hill tribes manage to get results from this combination.)

Double pipes

The ancients used the reeds in slender cane pipes (Plate XVIII) approximately from 4 to 11 millimetres in bore—far narrower than flutes—or in pipes of wood or metal in which the narrow cylindrical bore of cane was reproduced. All behave as 'stopped pipes', with deep fundamentals for their length (like a clarinet). But the striking thing about them is that they were almost invariably played in pairs as *double pipes*; that is, two pipes blown simultaneously by one player.

This seems to have been adopted by all early reed players as the natural thing to do. Possibly it arose from our inborn tendency to pair wind instruments in some way (we have noticed it already with primitive flutes). And with reed instruments it is so simple for the pair to be blown by one person. There have been variety artists who can not only play two clarinets at once, but smoke a cigar at the same time. And clarinets are heavy instruments; a pair of the light-weight ancient reed pipes are nearly as easy to handle as a pair of flageolets (as one can discover for oneself with two thin canes and a couple of old drone reeds or bassoon reeds), while the simultaneous sound of the two pipes renders unaccompanied piping more vibrant, interesting and self-supporting, like people singing together. It is true that with certain arrangements of the pipes, pairing limits the number of fingers available per pipe, but during the three- and four-holed stage of finger-hole technique, which is represented by the greater part of antiquity, this need scarcely have been counted an objection. At any rate, to play on two reed pipes was the general rule, not only throughout antiquity but well into the Middle Ages. Playing on a single pipe as the regular thing came in only quite late; in the West, not until about the twelfth century A.D. The history of reed instruments begins with a four thousand-year long 'double pipe era', traces of which survive in some of our folk instruments today.

From the aspects of playing technique, double pipes may be grouped in the three main classes distinguished diagrammatically in fig. 42, and in the following table (which is most easily understood if, while reading it, one waggles one's fingers over imaginary pipes):

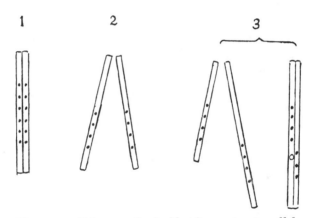

Fig. 42. *Scheme of double-pipes:* 1, *parallel;* 2, *divergent;* 3, *unequal.*

1. *Parallel pipes* (two pipes lashed or waxed together) — Hands placed *one above the other*, each finger covering both pipes (unless one is a drone) — *Single reeds* (e.g. zummara, hornpipe)

2. *Divergent pipes* (two separate pipes of approx. equal length) — *Hands level*, one on each pipe — *Double reeds* (e.g. Greek aulos; today extinct, though the arrangement survives in some double flageolets)

3. *Unequal pipes* (one longer than the other; usually divergent) — Hands *one above the other*, *one on each pipe* — Anciently with *double reeds* (e.g. Phrygian aulos); today, folk instruments with *single reeds* (e.g. launeddas).

PARALLEL PIPES are, on the whole, instruments of a lower grade, and have seldom featured prominently in music. The commonest number of holes today is five or six, giving a series of notes across the compass of the treble stave, with no over-blow. Often the strong bleating sound is made more interesting through a tremulant secured by tuning the pipes just off unison so that their notes 'beat'. The tuning is done by pushing the reeds in or out, and it may take a considerable time; one folk-music explorer in the Balkans witnessed a man take over an hour tuning before he began his piece. Sachs has traced one wide-spread form back to ancient Egypt; the *zummara*, a simple instrument resembling fig. 42, No. 1, which the Egyptian pipe-maker still makes, sitting in his stall in the market, with a knife for cutting the holes and a heated iron wire for removing the knots. Beside him is his supply of cane and a display of finished zummaras, arghuls (in which one of the two pipes is a long drone) and other varieties, which boys and peasants buy very much as people buy mouth-organs and tin whistles in Western music shops.

While this instrument is also made by shepherds in many parts of Eurasia, a type better known in European lore is that in which bells of cow horn are attached to the bottom ends of the pipes, making a *hornpipe*. In Plate XVIII, the ramshackle article from Morocco shows the primitive hornpipe, found also elsewhere, as in Albania. The Basque example—a pastoral instrument which is still occasionally heard—shows the finer construction, with a single bell common to both pipes, typical of the West and exemplified also by the former British hornpipes referred to in the next chapter. The horn bell is also widely found on primitive cane and wooden trumpets, and would have first appeared on these. It represents the germ of our own wind-instrument bells (compare *i* and *ii*, fig. 39). The hornpipe too is very old, though how old is not known. Possibly it arose in connection with the pastoral rites of some early type of culture, like, for example, the megalithic (which would place the horn-pipe's arrival in Britain, Scandinavia and the Baltic somewhere about 2000 B.C.) though there is no evidence for it before classical times.

The Basque hornpipe, also the Welsh species, *pibcorn*, has an additional horn at the top end. This protects the reeds and keeps them comparatively dry, which must have improved their performance. Many Eastern species similarly have a gourd enclosing the reeds. But a more important development has been the fitting of a skin, provided with mouthpipe and valve, over the reeds, introducing the *bagpipe*—the primitive bagpipe of India and the Near East, either with one single-reed cane chanter, or, as a true bag-hornpipe, with twin pipes and horn bells.

The main characteristic of bagpiping is, of course, that the sound continues while the player takes breath. On a bag-less reed instrument it is possible to achieve the same effect only by breathing in through the nose while still playing (as described concerning the oboe in Chapter IV). Now this is yet another curious technical extravagance, like blowing two pipes at once, that early reed-instrument players seem to have favoured very widely. Most Oriental pipers still patiently acquire this difficult art, but the West has long preferred the simpler expedient of the inflated bag, and it is only in bagpipe form that the hornpipe has grown up into a substantial Western musical instrument. This is in the fine bagpipes of Central and Eastern Europe. In these, the chanter has generally become reduced to one single, cylindrically-bored, wooden pipe, though sometimes the parallel bore is retained as an auxiliary drone. Hornpipe ancestry is proclaimed by the up-turned or turned-out end of the chanter—a reminiscence of the primitive cow-horn— also by the ancient single reed hidden inside the chanter stock and the plaintive tone given by the narrow cylindrical bore. The old Polish bagpipe in Plate XIX is really a super-hornpipe, and makes a fine contrast with the primitive specimen from Morocco in·the preceding Plate.

It will be observed that the Basque hornpipe has fewer holes in one pipe than in the other. This is to introduce an articulated drone effect, which may be simply illustrated on the Yugoslav *diple*—a hornpipe with the two bores made in a single piece of wood (fig. 43). The right hand fingers cover the highest three holes, giving in descending order, say, g'' f'' $e\flat''$ and d''. The left hand fingers cover hole IV, both holes V, and both holes IV, giving *c″ b′ a′*. The lowest hole on the left hand bore is only used for tuning the note above, i.e. as a vent hole. The effect of this lay-out is that the lowest three notes, from *c″* to *a′*, are always in unison on the two bores, while from *d″* upwards the left hand bore sounds *c″* as a drone. Since the reeds cannot be tongued on this hornpipe, the instrument is graced as in bag-piping, by putting down two or three fingers, usually including the lowest two, in which case the drone note and the melody note are simultaneously graced by the low *a′*. The effect recalls

FIG. 43. *Articulated drone effect on hornpipe* (*Yugoslav* diple; *after Broemse*).

that of Greek and Bulgarian folk fiddlers, whose drone note is continually interrupted with the bowing.

THE DIVERGENT PIPE was the specialized wind instrument of the ancient Near Eastern and Mediterranean civilizations. Though today extinct, possibly no wind instrument has ever received comparable honours and held a monopoly of wind music for so long a period of time. One after another the ancient nations came to adopt it, and after the old vertical flute dropped out of the picture in the second millennium B.C., the divergent double pipe remained as the only wind instrument normally used in music—and in music of every kind. It is the 'pipe' of the Bible, the *aulos* of the Greeks and the *tibia* of the Romans; the wind opposite number to the lyre and the harp, with which it was often played in consort. One might ask what possessed the ancients to adopt this pungent species of wind instrument so exclusively, and to cherish it so devotedly. Perhaps it answered to the dynamic, creative elements in their nature, while the more passive, accepting nature of primitive peoples finds its echo in the music of flutes.

As for its reeds, it is certain that the Greeks used the double reed. Theophrastus mentions, in his *History of Plants*, that a pair of aulos reeds was made from a single internode of cane (which varies from 6 inches to 9 inches long) and that where this was cut in two, to make the two reeds, the ends towards the cut formed the 'mouth' of the 'tongues' of each reed; or as we should say, the opening of the blades. Clearly a pair of flattened-end double reeds of the kind shown in fig. 41. The cane for aulos reeds was cut, incidentally, from the same plant that supplies our reed cane today; the best was said to come from around Lake Copias, forty miles north of Athens.

Among the fifty-odd cane pipes found in Egyptian tombs— nearly all of them double-pipe components with three or four holes (Plate XVIII)—many had fragments of straw-like matter adhering to one end, thought to be remains of reeds like the smaller example in fig. 41.

On the strength of these data, it is therefore inferred that the venerable silver pipes of Ur, dating from a thousand years earlier (*c.* 2500 B.C.; the earliest specimens of a civilized wind instrument) were also sounded with double reeds, and indeed that the divergent pipe was so sounded from the beginning. The ancients, among whom music was a profession and an art, no doubt preferred the double reed to the single in virtue of its greater flexibility. The two kinds of reed, as they were then known, both produce basically the same kind of tone-quality in the pipe; it ranges from a deep droning in a long pipe to a plaintive screaming in a short pipe (as the Japanese hichiriki). But double reeds would have given the artist more scope, with better control over pitch, greater dynamic range, and also (though we do not know whether he took advantage of it) readier overblowing.

Greek Aulos. This of course is the double pipe that we should most like to know about, and it is sad that no completely fitted-up specimen has reached us. The only specimens from the classic epoch of Plato and Aristotle are the wooden pipes—the Elgin auloi—in the British Museum (Plate XVIII), found in a tomb of the fifth century B.C. near Athens along with the remains of a tortoise-shell lyre. The two pipes are beautifully made, with neatly undercut holes and polished cylindrical bore (9 millimetres now, though no doubt they have shrunk after 2,400 years underground). They are about 14 inches long including the bulbous wooden barrels (which the Greeks, like some modern clarinettists, called sockets) and represent the most usual size of the aulos as it was used in private music, in the theatre to lead the chorus, and at the professional contests. There were, however, smaller and larger instruments for music of special kinds. The Elgin barrels have decomposed at their top ends where the reed would have been inserted, but their bore is just about right for holding a reed of the larger size shown in fig. 41. This is the reed that the aulos appears to have in vase paintings, and the player's cheeks are often shown puffed out as if breath were taken in through the nose in the manner already alluded to.

On each pipe one could play an entire octave with one hand, because the holes evidently give a pentatonic scale. Sachs has shown that the strings of the Greek lyre were tuned similarly. Trials of replicas of the Elgin pipes, using reeds of the Chinese *kuan-tzu* type, gave *a c' d' f'* (or *e'*) *g' a'*. This is leaving out the lowest hole, as one is obliged to do when fingering with one hand, but of course including the thumb-hole, which is between holes I and II. The stretch for the hand is formidable; the fingers have to be laid well across the pipes—as the players are doing in the vase paintings. However, the paintings also indicate that the little finger was occupied most of the time supporting the instrument from below, in which case the stretch becomes nothing like so painful. With the combination of large reed and small pipe, embouchure action suffices for filling the gaps in the scale when required; classical authors mention pinching with the lips to sharpen, and also spreading the pipes further apart, or raising them up, thereby presumably bringing the reeds into a different contact with the lips. Later instruments (e.g. the pipes from Pompeii, of Caesar's time) have revolving metal rings, evidently for pre-setting the pipe in the desired key. Other late instruments appear even to have sliding keywork, possibly sprung for instantaneous action, like our woodwind keys.

To judge from the surviving pieces of Greek music (three examples are printed in Davison and Apel) this one-octave compass would have sufficed for much of the music. However, there are hints that the total compass was larger. Overblowing is possible on the narrow Egyptian pipes, and with only four holes one can even make a continuous scale in the treble register by playing on the 3rd and 5th harmonics in tabor-pipe fashion. On the wider-bored aulos this seems more difficult; but then we do not know the secrets of its reed-making, which was said to have involved great skill.

About the employment of the *two* pipes together, Greek writers preserve a sphinx-like silence, which perhaps suggests that it involved nothing of theoretical musical interest. Theophrastus just mentions that from a pair of reeds cut from a cane internode, the half furthest from the root made the softer reed and this was used in the right hand pipe, and vice versa. This may be taken to imply some sort of heterophony. Sachs has concluded that on Egyptian double pipes one pipe sustained a drone; and on the aulos a drone is again a possibility. The drone deliberately added to a melody is no primitive thing, but a folk and professional product of the Indo-Mediterranean belt of civilized populations. But did the second pipe *only* drone? One might have thought that the celebrated artists who drew enormous crowds to the Athens Odeon to hear, say, a star rendering of 'Apollo and the dragon', did everything humanly possible with their eight fingers and thumbs. Moreover it is across the old Greek area, from the Black Sea to Italy and Sardinia, that living double-pipe tradition today exhibits an intricate mixture of drone and polyphony that is approached nowhere else in the world of folk music, as the section below, on unequal pipes, will show.

Monaulos. Under the Ptolemys, Egypt took to playing on a single aulos pipe, monaulos, of which some specimens have come down to us (e.g. in the Brussels Museum, fig. 44, *a*). The instrument is historically important since it represents perhaps the main direct link between the double pipes of the ancient era of reed-instrument history and the single pipes of the modern era. The monaulos was of course fingered with both hands, and each hand was provided with holes similar to those to which it

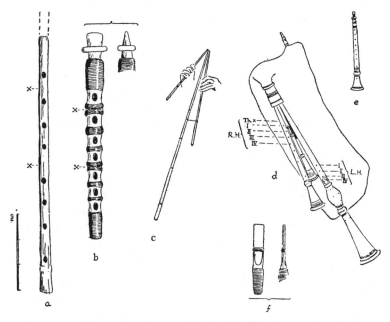

Fig. 44. Monaulos (a) *and* hichiriki (b); launeddas (c); zampogna (d, *with reed*, f) *and* ciaramella (e).

had been accustomed on the ordinary double aulos; i.e. the monaulos included a thumb-hole for each hand. That for the upper hand lay between holes I and II, and that for the lower hand between holes IV and V. The instrument's Japanese descendant, hichiriki—one of the most interesting woodwind 'living fossils'—keeps them both, but in practical piping the lower thumb-hole is quite unnecessary, and elsewhere it has vanished from pipe-fingering. The aulos-position for the upper thumb-hole, however, remains characteristic of Near-Eastern and Asiatic reed instruments in general today, though these are no longer cylindrical pipes, but shawms (see next chapter).

UNEQUAL PIPES. These seem to represent a cross between the parallel and the divergent forms of the double pipe. Holding one hand above the other comes from the parallel; placing the hands on separate pipes comes from the divergent. Some Egyptian divergent sets had unequal pipes. The Phrygian aulos that became so popular in later classical times, carried a horn bell on the left hand pipe (the longer one).

On the unequal pipes, double-pipe technique becomes very interesting. As we observe it today in folk instruments, the two pipes are generally tuned in fourths, with the left hand pipe usually the deeper-pitched (though not necessarily the longer in total size). There are from three to five holes per pipe, and below them one or more vent holes for tuning the bottom notes of the pipes. Usually wax is used for stopping these vents when necessary, but the Phrygian aulos had a row of mushroom-like pegs, as if for the purpose of pre-setting the drone note that could be obtained by covering all holes on one pipe or the other, momentarily or otherwise.

Unequal-pipe technique is roughly summed up by the following generalized example of a pipe in G—a common key for it (fig. 45). The scale is divided between the two hands. The right hand, on the higher-pitched pipe, gives, ascending, g' to d''. The other gives d' to a'. Both pipes sound continuously, so that while playing a melody in the most straightforward way (i.e. without harmony) one or the other of the pipes must sound a drone note for part of the time, and the obvious drone note then to choose is the tonic, g'. This gives the basic scale shown.

An illustration of this compound drone technique occurs in the introduction of fig. 46. But mostly the pipes are played in harmony, as in fig. 45, done on the Russian unequal parallel pipe *brelka* (single reeds, and horn or coiled-bark bells). This ten-bar morsel, as Russian as could be, was noted down in the last century, but the instrument was still heard recently. Some time ago Andreev, the person who popularized the balalaika, unsuccessfully tried to push forward the brelka too, urbanizing it with rosewood construction and some simple keywork.

The excerpts in figs. 46, 47 are no less typically Italian, at any rate of Italian double-piping as heard on the Sardinian *launeddas* and the Italian bagpipe *zampogna*, both of which have been known in the West in one form or another at least since the thirteenth century. The launeddas (divergent, with single reeds; fig. 44, *centre*) is actually a triple pipe, having a

FIG. 45. *Basic scale on unequal pipes.* Below: *a tune played on the Russian brelka.*

long drone cane attached alongside the left hand cane by wire struts. Thus the player has three reeds in his mouth at once. The effect is a rich burbling, full of life. A short, spirited excerpt from a recording of the launeddas appears in *Grove's Dictionary* (5th edition) in the article *Aulos*. Every trick displayed would have been perfectly possible on the ancient Phrygian aulos, though how far the Roman pipers went towards such polyphony, we shall never know. Classical sources merely allude vaguely to a deep buzzing or droning of the left hand pipe as compared with the high ringing of the right hand pipe.

The zampogna (fig. 44, *d*) shows the same technique transferred to the post-classical conical-bore pipes. It is a bagpipe with two chanters (divergent) and two drones, all four of these pipes being housed in a single stock and all four sounded with long, narrow-bladed double reeds of the usual modern Western construction (*f*).

It is found in two main forms, in both of which the right hand (shorter) chanter has a thumb-hole for obtaining the fifth

Fig. 46. *The opening of a siciliana on a Sicilian bagpipe.*

of the scale while the little finger gives the leading-note: (1) The solo form, with the chanters pitched in fourths; see fig. 46, an example from Sicily. (2) The accompanying form, played in duet with the folk shawm *ciaramella* (mentioned again in the next chapter); this has the chanters pitched in octaves, and includes a little-finger key of sixteenth-century pattern on the longer (left hand) chanter. There are two sizes of this accompanying form, one built an octave below the other. The deeper size makes an imposing instrument, with the left hand chanter

FIG. 47. *Two examples of* zampognari *music:* (a) novena *song;*
(b) *saltarello.*

(called the *trombone*) reaching 5 feet in length, and it sounds like an organ.

Though frequently played by street musicians (with the

FIG. 48. *Technique of the English Double Flageolet.*

shawmist leaving off every so often to take the hat round, the bagpiper meanwhile keeping the music going in two parts by himself) these are above all Christmas instruments, and are properly played by shepherds. The *zampognari* (sometimes called *pifferari*, 'pipers') come down from the villages into the towns during the *novena*, the nine days before Christmas. Their music is immortalized in the pastoral symphony (the *pifa*) in the *Messiah*. Fig. 47 *a* is a novena song; alternately the shawmist plays and sings over the unending accompaniment of the bagpipe; *b* shows the admirably simple manner in which this same large-sized bagpipe accompanies a quick saltarello played on the shawm.

Double flageolet

As well as reed instruments, flageolets are well suited for double-piping and are so used widely over Eurasia. Still quite common in English antique shops is the boxwood Double Flageolet by Bainbridge, London; a popular musical toy in the early part of the last century. It is designed for playing in thirds and sixths. Fig. 48, *i* shows the fingering of the two pipes (from Brigg's Preceptor). The numbers 1 and 3 indicate the opening of the top front key on each; 2, the octave key on the back of the right hand pipe; 4, the low key on the same. *ii* gives the two usual scales for the pipes together, the letters L and R indicating which pipe sounds the upper note. *iii*, from Egan's Preceptor of about 1820, shows an example of what they used to play on it. In his *Triple Flageolet*, Bainbridge added to the rear of the two pipes a closed boxwood cylinder with keys, to be operated by the wrists, giving various bass notes on the principle of the ocarina or globular flute.

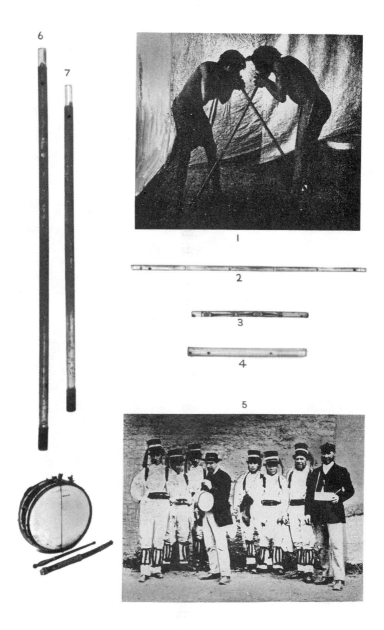

XVII. FLUTE ANCESTORS

1, Sounding ritual flutes without holes, New Guinea (*Nova Guinea*, vol. III); 2, transverse flute with one hole (Assam hills); 3, notched flute, stopped, with one hole (New Britain); 4, nose flute (Tahiti, collected on Cook's first voyage)· ,, Joe Powell, last of the old taborers in England, leading the Bucknell Morris, *c.* 1870; 6, 7, pair of ritual transverse flutes without holes, the larger nearly six feet long (New Guinea); *bottom left:* pipe and tabor (Oxfordshire, collected 1886)

Nos. 2–7 by courtesy of the Pitt Rivers Museum, Oxford. 1 and 5 reproduced by kind permission of Messrs. E. J. Brill, Leyden, and the English Folk Song and Dance Society

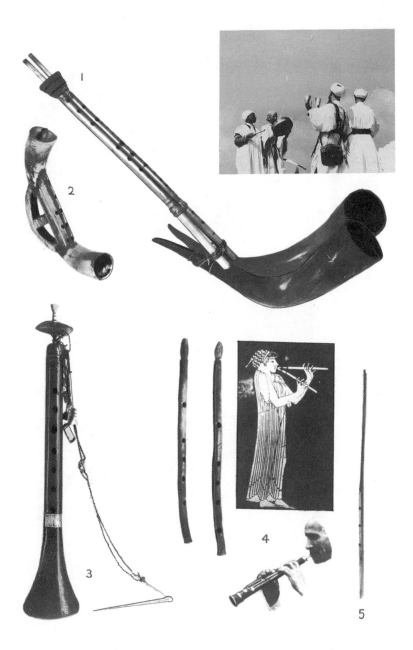

XVIII. REED INSTRUMENT ANCESTORS

Above, left to right: 1, primitive hornpipe, Morocco; 2, Basque hornpipe; *inset*, a Moroccan hornpiper.
Below, left to right: 3, Persian shawm (*surna*); with spare reeds and mandrel; 4, the Elgin *auloi* (double
pipe), Athens, *c.* 400 B.C.; *inset*, an aulete, from a Greek vase painting, British Museum; 5, ancient
Egyptian reed pipe (a double-pipe component). *Bottom right:* Spanish *dulzaina*
Nos. 1 and 2 by courtesy of the Pitt Rivers Museum, Oxford; Nos. 3–5 by courtesy of the
British Museum

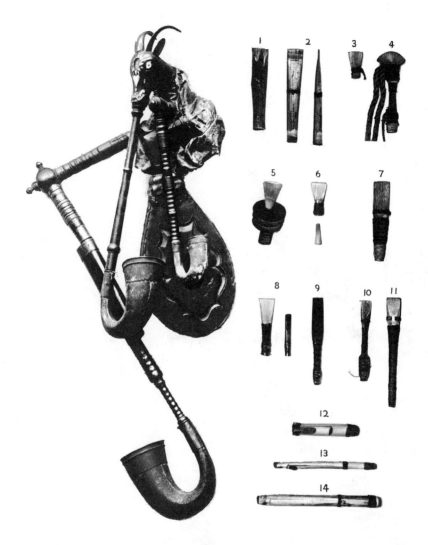

XIX

Left: 16th-century Polish (possibly Bohemian?) bagpipe, bellows-blown. *Right:* reeds of woodwind precursors. *Top row (double reeds):* 1, English whit-horn (reed of willow bark); 2, Chinese *kuan-tzu*, an aulos descendent (bamboo reed, full and side views); 3, North African shawm (maize reed); 4, Burmese shawm, *hne* (reed of palm leaf). *Second row (cane double reeds):* 5, Catalan shawm, *tenora*, showing reed mounted in pirouette; 6, Catalan shawm, *tiple*, with wooden keeper-peg shown below it; 7, Italian *ciaramella*. *Third row (double reeds):* 8, Highland bagpipe (chanter) and (to right) copper staple; 9, plastic reed for Highland practice-chanter; 10, French bagpipe, *cornemuse* (chanter); 11 Irish Union pipe (chanter, showing copper adjusting band). *Bottom row (single reeds):* 12, Egyptian parallel double pipe, *zummara·* 13, Union pipe, small drone (tongue tuned with a wax blob); 14, Highland bagpipe, tenor drone

XX. CORNETT

Left to right: cornettino dated 1518, and treble cornett (author's collection); X-ray photograph (E. Halfpenny) of treble cornett, 1605, Christ Church, Oxford. All three instruments of wood, leather-covered, silver-mounted. Mouthpieces not original

XXV. THE CLASSICAL BASSOON

Four-keyed bassoon, pear wood, *Milhouse*, *Newark*, *c.* 1780 (Cave collection)

XXVI. TWO EPOCH-MAKING WOODWIND DESIGNS

Above: six-keyed flute, stained boxwood, *Gedney, London*, dated 1769, with its box and alternative top joints (Champion collection), the prototype of our 'simple systems'. *Below:* conical Boehm flute, boxwood, *Boehm, Munich, c.* 1832 (Morley Pegge collection); Boehm's first new design, introducing the modern ring mechanism

XXVII. THE CLASSICAL CLARINET

Five-keyed B♭ clarinet, boxwood, *Mousseter, Paris, c.* 1780 (Bate collection). The
long keys are extendable for insertion of an A joint

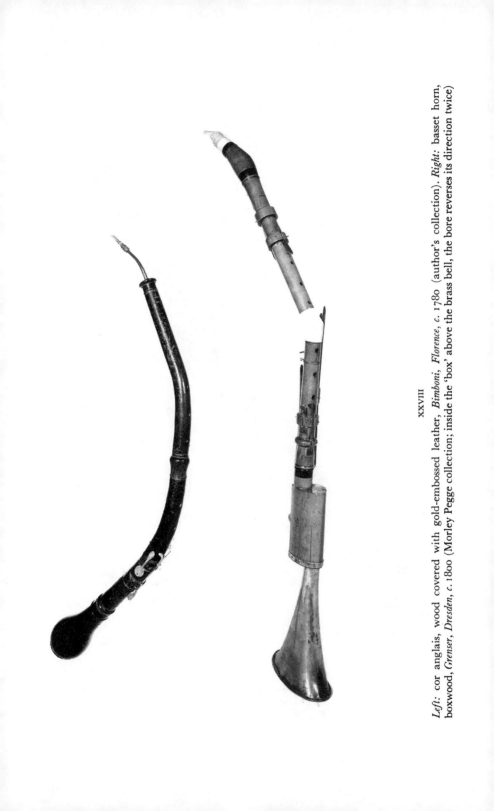

XXVIII

Left: cor anglais, wood covered with gold-embossed leather, *Bimboni, Florence, c.* 1780 (author's collection). *Right:* basset horn, boxwood, *Grenser, Dresden, c.* 1800 (Morley Pegge collection; inside the 'box' above the brass bell, the bore reverses its direction twice)

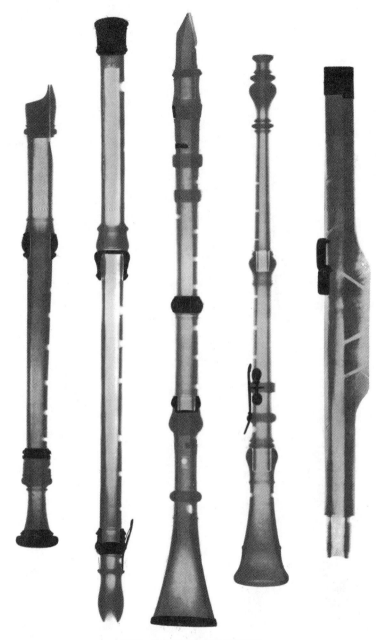

XXIX. X-RAY PHOTOGRAPHS

by Eric Halfpenny of 18th-century woodwind. *Left to right:* 1, treble recorder, *Bressan,*
c. 1740 (cylindrical head joint, the rest contracting); 2, one-keyed flute, *Rippert, c.* 1700
(the early form, with middle joint in one piece; bore as above); 3, five-keyed clarinet,
Miller, c. 1780 (cylindrical bore; the barrel and mouthpiece are from another clarinet
of the period); 4, two-keyed oboe, Collier, *c.* 1770 (conical bore, with 'bee-hive' or
'sword' bore-profile in top joint, step at the bell tenon, etc.); 5, tenor joint of eight-
keyed bassoon, *Goulding, c.* 1800 (conical bore; showing the deep, oblique drilling of the
finger-holes, still characteristic of the bassoon). (The instruments have mostly been
photographed by joints and the prints subsequently pieced together.)

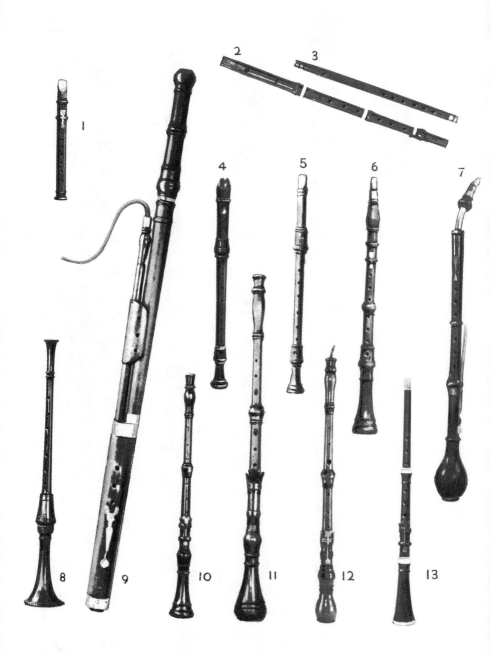

XXX. OTHER 18TH-CENTURY WOODWIND TYPES

1, two-keyed chalumeau (reproduction of former Munich specimen); 2, one-keyed flute, *Potter*; 3, B♭ fife, *Wiltshire*; 4, treble recorder, *Bressan*; 5, two-keyed clarinet, early type resembling recorder, *J. C. Denner*; 6, two-keyed clarinet, later type, *J. Denner*; 7, clarinette d'amour, *Venera*; 8, treble *deutsche Schalmey*, *Haka*; 9, three-keyed bassoon of earliest type, *J. C. Denner*; 10, three-keyed oboe of Bach-Handel period, *Boekhout*; 11, tenor oboe of Bach-Handel period, *Wyne*; 12, oboe d'amore, of Bach-Handel period, *Eichentopf*; 13, two-keyed oboe, English 'straight-topped' model, *Astor*

XXXI SOME OTHER EARLY MODELS

1, eight-keyed flute, 'Nicholson's Improved', with the wide holes, *Clementi*, 1825; 2, four-keyed serpent, English, *c*. 1800; 3, Breton *bombarde* (a folk instrument); 4, the classical contrabassoon, *Lempp*, Vienna, *c*. 1800; 5, early simple-system oboe (10 keys), *Stengel*, *c*. 1825; 6, Muller-system clarinet (13 keys and two thumb branches), *Stengel*, *c*. 1825; 7, English 13-keyed clarinet, *Key*, 1835; 8, an early form of Sax's bass clarinet, *Sax*, Brussels, *c*. 1840

XXXII. WIND PLAYERS OF THE VIENNA PHILHARMONIC ORCHESTRA
preparing to perform a Mozart serenade. (Foreground, *left*, Hans Kamesch; *right*, Leopold Wlach)

CHAPTER IX

Medieval Wind Music

The primitives play flutes; the ancients played reed instruments; but we, like the Orientals, play both.

This we must ascribe ultimately to the fact that our musical ancestors, so far as everyday instrumental music goes, were the aboriginal, Celtic and Germanic tribesmen who dwelt and moved about in the European hinterland during classical times. Like the Greeks and the Romans, these were lyre-players, but their lyres were of ruder kinds. Likewise they were wind-players, not of the classical aulos, but rather of those lesser instruments which the Greeks and Romans, once they had erected their civilizations, relegated to the background as folk instruments. A good example is the panpipe. To Rome, this was hardly more than one among those rustic instruments that the poets alluded to casually as *calamus* (cane), *fistula* (pipe), *avena* (oat) and so on. But among the peoples beyond, from North Italy upwards, the panpipe counted for very much more; engravings on bronze vessels show it being played at feasts beside the lyre, as the aulos was in the grand civilizations (Blume's new *Musik in Geschichte und Gegenwart*, article 'Flöte', reproduces some of these engravings). Double pipes of the hornpipe kind must have been played too, though no direct evidence of this has yet been found. Bone flageolets with two or three holes have been found in graves, and cane ones would have been made too in regions where the plant grew suitably.

Many centuries later, in the times of Charlemagne and Alfred, the prominent wind instruments, apart from the organ and the horn, were still just hornpipes and panpipes, though

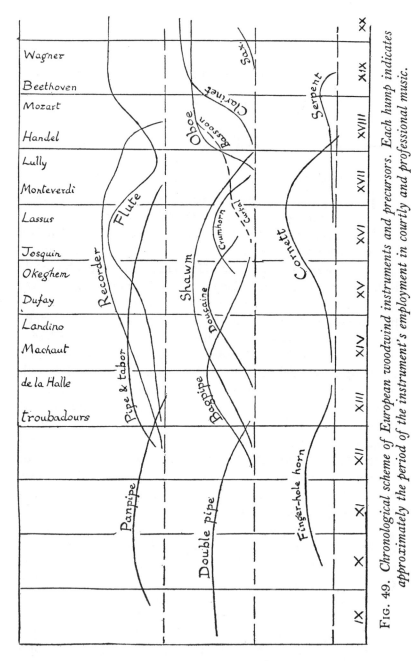

Fig. 49. *Chronological scheme of European woodwind instruments and precursors. Each hump indicates approximately the period of the instrument's employment in courtly and professional music.*

just afterwards, from the tenth century, pictures also show the forerunner of the cornett—the cow-horn with finger-holes.

These instruments, destined to survive in the modern West only as rare and vanishing shepherds' instruments, seem to have been the best wind instruments that the generations who built the Norman cathedrals possessed. The great medieval wind instruments enter the scene with the Gothic, during the twelfth and thirteenth centuries: pipe and tabor, superior flageolets (including the prototype of the recorder) and flute; also the expanding-bore reed instruments—the shawm and the Western bagpipe. These were the instruments that took the leading share after harp and fiddle in the minstrels' concerts of the thirteenth century, the music that rang through every castle hall on every festive occasion.

We say, mainly on the evidence of pictures and carvings, that they came in with the Gothic. But were they all really so new? It is strange that the pipe and tabor, and the bagpipe—so much the favourite wind instruments during troubadour times—should already have been characterized as *peasant* instruments. This seems rather to imply that they had been lurking on Western soil for some time before the earliest-known depiction and literary mention of them in the twelfth century; for folk instruments do not grow up overnight. How long back into the six or seven hundred years of the Dark Ages and Early Middle Ages each type had already been known, if only as a submerged local species or as something slowly pursuing its own course of development from an Eastern or Southern prototype, these are among the most difficult questions in European organology.

However, problematic though their origins are, the instruments themselves—or most of them—can be studied at first hand; for in the quieter, remoter parts of the Continent, medieval wind instruments live on today as folk instruments, unchanged save perhaps for a small modification here, or a sign of degeneration there. Hence we can watch and hear medieval types of instrument actually being played, and often in circumstances that seem to mark a local 'closed tradition' in which the music itself may not be very different from that which the local minstrels played seven centuries ago (e.g. in East Europe and across that belt of country from the South of France to the West of Spain). Here is material of real importance towards reconstruction of the sounds of medieval music, a branch of practical musical research that grows yearly more active.

Short encyclopedia of medieval wind instruments

BAGPIPE. To describe this most variable of wind instruments in all its numerous forms would take a book to itself. Yet, even apart from its leading place among the instruments we are now considering, the bagpipe's part in the evolution of our reed instruments is in many ways so important that a brief sketch of its workings and construction cannot be omitted.

Bagpipes fall into two principal classes distinguished by the bore and reed of the chanter (the melody pipe, as opposed to drones): (1) With cylindrical bore and single reed. This class includes the elementary bagpipes found in Asia and North Africa, and all the European bagpipes east of Germany and Italy; these were mentioned in the last chapter. (2) With expanding bore and double reed. This includes all the typical Western European bagpipes, and it is these that most concern us here. (Ethno-musicologists often term the first kind of chanter a 'clarinet' and the second an 'oboe'; this is neat and concise, but the terms would read so oddly in a book about woodwind that they have not been used.)

Whether the first bagpipe recorded in Europe, the pipe of the Roman *utricularius,* was of the first kind or of the second or Western kind is scarcely possible to guess. But one can say that the common medieval bagpipe appears in pictures so much like many Western bagpipes of today (especially the Spanish) that it is reasonable to suppose that it resembled them in its important details.

These are shown typically in fig. 50. The bag is held under the left arm with the drone over the left shoulder. It is inflated through the *mouthpipe* (or blow-pipe, 7), which has a non-return valve consisting of a leather flap secured by a tack, or lapped in a nick in the wood. This valve prevents the air flowing back into the mouth (which can be literally a nauseating experience with a village-made bagpipe of uncured goatskin,

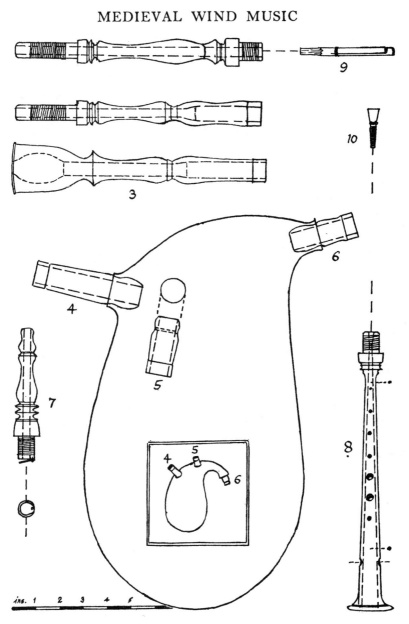

FIG. 50. *Spanish bagpipe* (gaita gallega) *by Carril, Santiago de Compostela. 3, the three-jointed drone; 4, 5, 6, drone, mouthpipe and chanter stocks; 7, mouthpipe; 8, chanter; 9, drone reed; 10, chanter reed.* Inset: *more traditional positions for the stocks.*

when the valve is not acting properly). The air in the bag is fed to the pipes by a steady pressure of the left elbow, and some Spanish pipers even sing to their own accompaniment in between re-inflations of the bag with the breath. *Bellows* for the right arm, replacing the mouthpipe, date at the latest from the sixteenth century (see Plate XIX), and today may be found with bagpipes of many nations.

The *bag* was originally, and sometimes is still, of the whole skin of a sheep, goat or kid, with the chanter mounted at the neck and the other pipes at the fore-legs. Hence the goat's head carved on many chanter stocks (Plate XIX). But generally, the bag is of two pieces of skin cut out to shape, stitched together and then turned inside out. Also, nowadays, bags are often made of mackintosh material, in which case the two pieces are joined on the outside with adhesive strips of the same material. Yet other bags are of moulded rubber, while for an emergency replacement, almost anything may be used, e.g. in Italy an old lorry inner-tube.

The *stocks* are the tubular wooden sockets in which the pipes are held and their reeds protected (fig. 50; 4, 5, 6). They are bound into their respective holes in the bag with strong thread. The side holes (for mouthpipe stock and, usually, drone stock) are cut in the bag with diagonal cuts to form triangular fillets which can be bent up for tying round the stocks. The cloth or velvet *bag-cover* fits over bag and stocks like a jumper and is laced along the edge below the chanter stock. In the Middle Ages it was usually dyed some bright colour, red, blue or green.

The *chanter* (8) normally has seven holes in front and a thumb-hole above them behind. In 'folk' and other outdoor types its bore is steeply conical (from one-eighth of an inch to seven-eighths of an inch is traditional in Scotland), giving the loudest and most penetrating sound possible in a high treble scale, of which the six-finger note is regarded as the normal key-note (see table, p. 218). The little finger gives the leading-note below (except on the Highland pipe where it gives the tone below). The neutral third (four fingers), characteristic of most of our woodwind instruments in their keyless stage, is sharpened into a major third on some pipes by making holes V and VI especially large. Any holes below VII (little finger) are 'vent-holes', provided to tune the lowest note. Though normally only the fundamentals are used, giving a compass of nine notes, many chanters can be made to overblow the octave by sharp arm-pressure on the bag. The Spanish *gaitero* features this in his opening flourishes, rising as high as the fourth of the scale in the upper octave.

Since a bagpipe cannot be tongued, articulation, when needed, is by *gracing*, i.e. by flicking the fingers to interpolate one or more grace-notes. This gives the effect of attack and makes possible repetition of the same note. To help this, the chanter may be played in partly 'covered' fashion, uncovering only the holes that are necessary to make the note clearly, and keeping the fingers down on the lower holes. As an illustration of gracing on the familiar Highland pipes for those who have not realized its intricacy, the following are the opening bars of 'Highland Laddie', from Logan's Tutor (1923 edition):

FIG. 51. *Example of gracing on the Highland bagpipe.*

But such intricate gracing is a comparatively recent development. In most 'folk' bagpiping it is done more simply and sparingly.

For soft indoor practice of the fingering and gracing without the bag, both Scottish and Spanish makers supply a *practice-chanter*, with narrow cylindrical bore and long-bladed reed enclosed in a wooden cap. It sounds an octave below the real chanter.

The *drone* first appears in medieval pictures latish in the thirteenth century, though in so many different forms that it can scarcely have then been a fresh introduction. Also, the peasantry already knew it; in Adam de la Halle's pastoral play *Robin and*

Marion (*c*. 1275), Robin, the rustic hero, runs off to fetch his tabor and his *muse au grand bourdon*, 'bagpipe with the big drone'. The drone idea was very popular in music of the troubadour period and just after, when so much rested upon solo, unsupported performance. Fiddlers used a bourdon string (open drone string), and so too, probably, did hurdy-gurdy players, while it is thought that the little portative organ had a drone pipe or two. There can be no questioning that for a full and satisfying accompaniment to a simple air, the drone is hard to beat. Even today, old traditional airs that we have grown accustomed to stuff with conventional harmonies on piano or accordion, often gain fresh life when played over a simple drone. To medieval music it means far more, and it may even be introduced to enrich a piece written in parts (as for example the well-known two-part piece that occurs in the same manuscript as 'Sumer is i-cumen in': no. 41a in Davison and Apel's *Historical Anthology of Music*).

In view of its function as a supporting pipe, a drone is constructed differently from the chanter, having a single reed of cane or elder (the double-reed drones of the zampogna are exceptional) and a cylindrical bore made in three or two separate joints with long tenons for pulling out in order to tune the drone to the chanter. In some of the louder bagpipes, each joint of the drone has a larger bore than the one above it—a 'stepped' cylindrical bore (fig. 50; 3).

A *single drone* (the commonest arrangement in the Middle Ages) is nearly always tuned two octaves below the chanter key-note. In many medieval miniatures it is coloured gold or silver and shaped like the medieval trumpet, with balls over the joints and a banner flying at the bell; evidently such drones were of metal (and perhaps reserved for royalty and nobility).

In the splendid array of instruments that illuminates the Escorial Library's famous MS., Alfonso the Wise's *Cantigas de S. Maria* (*c*. 1270), one also sees a bagpipe with the drone placed parallel with the chanter in the same stock, exactly as in the present French *cornemuse* or *cabrette*. This drone sounds one octave below the chanter key-note, but today, in the Cantal region around Aurillac, when the cornemuse is intended for playing with the hurdy-gurdy for the bourrée, the latter instrument provides the drones and the drone on the bagpipe, if kept at all, is a dummy.

Two drones are also seen in the *Cantigas* manuscript. With two drones the tuning is either in octaves (e.g. *c, c'*) or in fifths (*c', g'*; or an octave deeper). The old English bagpipe which vanished in the eighteenth century, seems, from pictures and figurines, sometimes to have had the second tuning, with two little drones beside each other in the same drone stock. When playing in the plagal mode (with three fingers as the key-note) the smaller drone would be pulled out to sound F instead of G, as is done on the Northumbrian small-pipe today. *Three drones* are post-medieval. They appear in seventeenth-century Germany (e.g. with tuning *c, g, c'*), and soon afterwards in Scotland (*A, a, a*).

All bagpipers, even the wildest shepherds in the southern mountains of Europe, tune their drones with the greatest care and with complete absence of hurry, for everything in bagpiping depends upon the drone being exactly in tune with the chanter. The drone is usually tuned against the fifth of the chanter scale, since this note requires only one hand, leaving the other free to manipulate the drone slides. Perhaps we may picture the medieval bagpiper completing the tuning and at the same time loosening up his reeds in an extended tuning prelude or *tempradura* appropriate to the coming lay and drawing the audience into its mood. Medieval fiddlers and harpers, certainly, made such preludes, just as Spanish bagpipers and guitarists, and Arab lute-players, to name but a few, still do today.

BLADDER-PIPE. In this an elastic bladder replaces the bag of a bagpipe. In the West of Europe today, it survives only as a toy found in bagpiping regions like Brittany and Sicily, where it is made by fixing a mouthpipe and a miniature wood or cane single-reed chanter in an ordinary rubber balloon, for sale from a tray at markets and fairs. In the East of Europe, however, one of the ancient forms has just survived in Poland as a very rare shepherd's instrument; a hornpipe-derivative, consisting of a wooden pipe with curved horn bell and a single reed, held in a sheep's bladder (fig. 53, c).

During the Middle Ages and Renaissance, instruments of this kind seem to have been fairly popular, though less so than the bagpipe. The *Cantigas* MS. shows two types, one with curved end, apparently made entirely in wood (like its derivative, the sixteenth-century crumhorn), and the other straight,

TABLE OF THE PRINCIPAL WESTERN BAGPIPES

As shown in the sketch-map, fig. 52 (which gives their home regions only). (N.B. Until the eighteenth century, most of the blank areas of the map were bagpiping regions too.)

Number on map	Species	Chanter keynote	Drone(s)	Mouth or bellows
1	Spanish (*gaita gallega,* Galician bagpipe)	c'' or $b'♭$	1: c or $B♭$	Either
2	French (*cornemuse,* or *cabrette*)	Varies, e.g. g'	2: e.g. g, G; or 1: g	,,
3	Breton (*biniou*)	$b''♭$	1: $b♭$	Mouth
4	Highland	a'	3: a, a, A	,,
(4a)*	Irish war, and Brian Boru	$b'♭$	2: $b♭$, $B♭$	,,
5†	Irish Union pipe	d'	3: d', d, D; also 3 regulators	Bellows
6†	Northumbrian small-pipe	g' (cylindrical)	3: g', d', g	,,
7	Italian (*zampogna*)	Two chanters, see Chap. VIII	2; with double reeds	Mouth
8, etc.	East European bagpipes with cylindrical chanters and single reeds, including: Czech *dudy*, Polish *koza*, Hungarian *'duda*, Yugoslav *gajda*, Dalmatian *diple*, etc.			

* These are twentieth-century adaptations of the Highland bagpipe inspired by some early engravings, to be (as it was claimed) 'more characteristically Irish than the ordinary fife and drum, or brass band'.
† See Appendix 2.

and apparently with a short drone parallel with the chanter. Probably bladder-pipes varied regionally as much as bagpipes, and the Western examples, like the Western bagpipes, may have had double reeds. They were mainly folk instruments.

BOMBARDE. (1) The Renaissance tenor shawm; see below, *loud music.* (2) Today a small Breton folk shawm, 12 inches long, with detachable bell. Six fingers give $b'\flat$ and it is always played in duet with the miniature Breton bagpipe *biniou*, which is pitched an octave higher. The music (gavottes, etc.) is played continuously on the biniou while the bombarde joins in at specified places. Since about 1930, however, the little biniou has been largely replaced by the Highland bagpipe (re-tuned in the key of $B\flat$), and since this plays in the same octave as the bombarde, the effect of the latter is entirely lost.

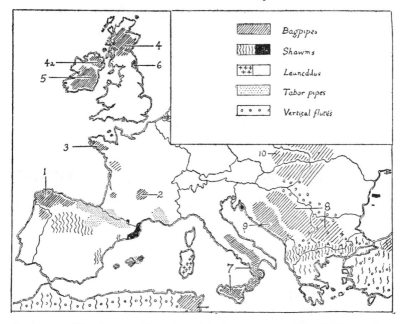

FIG. 52. *Sketch-map of various folk instruments. (Probably readers will be able to fill in further areas from their own observations.) For the numbers, see adjacent table.*

CORNETT. The finger-hole horn is a strange type of instrument apparently unknown outside Europe, save for an instrument of a South Indian tribe, the Toda; (the African side-blown horns with a finger-hole in the tip constitute quite a different class of instrument). Though sounded as a true horn, with the lips against a mouthpiece cavity, we shall mention it, and its successors, by virtue of its 'woodwind' finger technique and its place in music.

The finger-hole horn, when first depicted in the tenth century, appears very much like an instrument still made by shepherds, though now very rarely, in Norway and Sweden, and also in those remote districts lying on the boundary of Spain and Portugal: a cow or goat horn with a row of three or four large finger-holes in the side, and the tip cut off to make the mouth-piece (fig. 53, *a*). It gives four or five clear, far-carrying notes of remarkable equality, pitched in the upper part of the treble stave. For recent examples of its tunes, see: Norway, *Journal of*

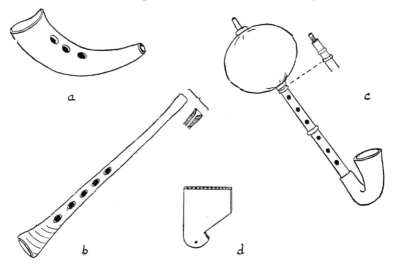

FIG. 53. *Cornett precursors* (a, *Swedish finger-hole cow horn;* b, *Russian* rozhok *of wood bound with birch-bark*); *bladder-pipe* (c, *simplified sketch of Polish type*); *Pyrenean boxwood panpipe* (d).

the English Folk Song and Dance Society, 1935; Spain, *Anuario Musical*, Barcelona, 1947.

In the Middle Ages it was made with more holes and must have proved quite a useful and attractive instrument for the time, but during the troubadour period it began to be replaced by those straight and curved wooden designs that were later to rise to such heights of musical fame under the name *cornett* (next chapter).

A co-ancestor of these is the alp-horn. This, which is found in

Scandinavia, the Pyrenees and the Carpathians as well as in Switzerland, exhibits a simple built-up method of construction known all over the world in primitive trumpets; also here and there in pipes (e.g. those sketched in fig. 39). The log of wood is sawn in half from end to end, and the expanding bore is marked and cut out in each part. These are then bound or glued together again, and the instrument is usually wound over with birch bark. As a short finger-hole version of the alp-horn, the early cornett lasted into modern times as a Russian folk instrument (fig. 53, b): the *rozhok* ('little horn'; cf. 'cornett', which means the same thing), some 16 inches long, with five or six holes, and formerly played in village bands in harmonized melodies similar to the brelka tune in fig. 45 in the last chapter.

DOUÇAINE (*dulzaina, doucette*). A problem. See later in this chapter, *soft music*.

FLAGEOLETS. The time-honoured village custom of making willow May whistles suggests that the West has long been familiar with the 'block' method of constructing a flageolet: i.e. by shaping a wooden plug and driving it into the top end of the instrument to make the wind channel (as on our recorders). An early musical form of the same instrument is the cane 'shepherd's pipe' still found in several parts of Europe. It averages 8 inches long and has any number of holes that the maker chooses to burn in it. It was the six-holed instrument of a Sicilian goat-herd that provided the prototype of those pleasant-toned bamboo pipes that British schoolchildren have been making under the instruction of Margaret James's *Pipers' Guild Handbook*.

No doubt many medieval flageolets were much the same, though made also of wood. Others perhaps already possessed the recorder characteristics, e.g. contracting bore, and the eight holes of a bagpipe's chanter. The actual name 'recorder' is late fourteenth century and may denote 'keepsake'.

In pictures and carvings one notices on the whole more of the *double flageolet*; either with separate pipes of cane or wood; or with both pipes carved and bored in a single piece of wood, and diverging sufficiently to enable the hands to be held level on them (very much as with the well-known Balkan double flageolet of today). Certainly, instruments of these kinds might seem to fit best into the general picture of thirteenth-century performance, which still, except for dancing, amounted mainly to a series of solo turns one after another. 'As they rose from dinner the hall resounded with the tuning of strings, each minstrel wishing at once to be heard' (Romance of Flamenca), and the fellow who pushed his way to the front was heard first. Now, harp, fiddle (with bourdon string), guitar, bagpipe, pipe and tabor, were all musically self-supporting instruments with which an artist could hold the attention of his listeners quite on his own; and the double flageolet might just have fallen into this category. When Tristan, disguised as a jongleur, performed a lay on the *flageol*, we may imagine that it was a *flageol doubliers*, its music filled out by the tremulant between the two pipes, and perhaps also with touches of drone, thirds or polyphony. The great days of the plain recorder came later, with the growth of organized part-music.

FLUTE. No traces have yet been found of the flute in Inner Europe before the Middle Ages, though the instrument had been known among at least two of the ancient Mediterranean peoples (the Etruscans and the Hellenistic Egyptians), while at certain Roman pastoral rites the flute was imitated in the *plagiaulos*—a monaulos with the reed inserted into a hole in the side near one end (which works perfectly well, though there has been no occasion to employ the arrangement since). After this, little is heard of the flute in West Europe until the twelfth century, by which time it had become established in Germany, apparently derived from the East: a Tartar instrument, akin to the Asiatic bamboo flutes; indeed in some medieval illustrations it is clearly made of cane, just as it still is in Turkestan. To the Germans of the period, the flute seems to have been a somewhat select or aristocratic instrument, played in chamber music beside the Minnesinger fiddle. It grew widely known west of the Rhine only during the fourteenth century.

HORNPIPE. During the early Middle Ages, most if not all of the peoples of Europe were probably playing hornpipes of one kind or another. The Anglo-Saxon *swegel horn* ('shin-bone and horn') would have been one kind. From pictures, a kind that might have been especially familiar to Continental audiences of touring troupes of entertainers, was a fairly long parallel double-pipe with one or two horn bells and with the reeds taken directly into the mouth. Its compass would have been about one octave.

Among the recent survivors are the former hornpipes of the Baltic countries and Scandinavia, with pipes made of wood or elder. Most had degenerated into single pipes, following the wane of the double-pipe era in the Middle Ages (see fig. 39, though these instruments are chosen to show freak constructions of the single reed). Another group is represented by the Celtic hornpipes that lasted in Britain until the eighteenth century, sometimes still as double-pipes: the Scottish *stock-and-horn*, of which Burns, after a long search, finally procured a sheep-bone and cow-horn specimen from Athole; and the Welsh *pibcorn*, of which some eighteenth-century specimens, apparently made by Anglesey shepherds, are preserved at the National Museum of Wales, Cardiff. In Wales, pipers, presumably pibcorn-players, followed the harpers and the crowthers at the medieval Eisted-fodd contests in a way that recalls the procession of lyre-players and auletes at the contests in ancient Greece. Later on, the pibcorn appears to have been superseded by a Welsh bagpipe (of which there are sketches in the sixteenth-century British Museum Add. MS. 15036), but within the last few years it has been revived to a small extent to give extra colour to Welsh folk music festivals, on one occasion accorded the full honour due to it as the one-time aulos of the North by having been entrusted, as the bills announced, to none other than 'Leon Goossens, oboe and pibgorn'.

PANPIPE. Since late antiquity the Western panpipe has been made in two ways. One is the common way of tying or waxing together a row of canes each stopped at the lower end by a knot or with wax. The other way is by solid construction, either in pottery, or by drilling holes down the thickness of a flat piece of wood, sometimes in the Middle Ages decorated to look like a book, no doubt a prayer-book. The solid construction is still carried on by shepherds of the French Pyrenees—very neatly, in boxwood (fig. 53, *d*), preserving the ancient favourite numbers of pipes, viz. seven or nine (though sometimes more), and giving a diatonic scale of treble stave compass (an 8½ inch deep panpipe tube sounds about *g'*). They play lively little tunes, incorporating much of Papageno's famous run-up, and the introductory flourish played on the small tabor pipe in Catalan sardanas may well be a memory of some ancient Pyrenean panpiping. Somewhat similarly, in Russia at the end of the eighteenth century, Guthrie found that an almost extinct seven-cane panpipe was being regularly imitated in village bands by a person whistling (British Museum Add. MS. 14390).

A fine East European panpipe that is far from extinct today is the twenty-one-pipe Rumanian *nai*, upon which Fanica Lucă and other virtuosi play even elaborate violin tunes, their performance culminating in bird-song cadenzas done with glissando, vibrato and every other possible trick. Drops of a semitone or more can be made on any note by raising the instrument, to cover more of the pipe with the lips.

PIPE AND TABOR. This unique one-man band is first heard of in the old terrain of the troubadour movement, the South of France and the North of Spain, and it is in these same regions that it is most heard today. The outfit (Plate XVII) comprises:

1. pipe (tabor pipe, three-holed pipe): a flageolet played with the left hand only;
2. tabor (pronounced 'tabber' by English folk music authorities): a small snare drum slung at the left side of the body or from the left arm; and
3. drum stick, held in the right hand.

The *pipe* (of wood, generally in one piece) preserves the cylindrical bore of the primitive cane flageolet, and the technique is founded on the readiness and good intonation with which a narrow-bore flageolet can be overblown to its higher harmonics. The fundamentals of a tabor pipe can be sounded, but are not used. The scale begins an octave higher, with the 2nd harmonics, and is continued upwards, by harder blowing, through 3rd, 4th, 5th harmonics and even higher. In this, the widest interval between registers is that of a fifth between the 2nd and 3rd harmonics, so that three finger-holes suffice to provide the four notes needed to make the scale continuous. This leaves one hand free to wield the drum stick. The holes are two in front for fingers I and II, and a thumb-hole above them at the back. The third and little fingers grip the end of the pipe from above and below except on Basque pipes, which have a holding-ring for the third finger.

The well-known French tabor pipe—the *galoubet* of Provence and the farandole (commemorated, on the piccolo, in *L'Arlé-sienne*)[1]—is a small-bore instrument (fig. 54, 1), 7·5 milli-metres bore, a foot long, and normally in D. The following is the typical fingering, with the thumb-hole indicated to the left of the oblique stroke:

Fingering	Note given as: 2nd harmonic	3rd harmonic	4th harmonic	5th harmonic	6th harmonic
• / • •	d'	a'	d''	$(f''\sharp)$	a''
• / • ○	e'	b'	e''	$g''\sharp$	
• / ○ ○	$f'\sharp$	$c''\sharp$	$f''\sharp$		
○ / • ○	g'		g''		
○ / ○ ○	$g'\sharp$				

N.B. All these notes *sound* two octaves higher. Further semitones can be obtained by cross-fingering and half-holing. Sometimes the low leading-note, $c'\sharp$, is made by half-closing the bell with the little finger. On other tabor pipes, the 'thumb only' fingering is often an F natural.

The tabor pipe formerly played for the Whitsun Morris dances in Oxfordshire and the neighbouring counties was of the same kind, made locally, or in London (e.g. by Potter, the fife, drum and bugle specialists), or imported from France. Much valuable information about it is preserved in the un-published note-books of Dr Percy Manning and other pioneer English folk-music collectors, now kept in the library of the English Folk Dance and Song Society, in London. Up to the 1860s every district had its piper—a shepherd or a labourer—

[1] The dates of the fêtes when the pipes—*tambourinaires*—perform may be found in the calendars of local events published by the French Railways, touring offices, etc.

who played for his own and the surrounding villages. They used to be heard in London when the country folk came up for the hay-making. Among their tunes were *Greensleeves*, *Shepherds Hey*, *The Maid of the Mill*, *Brighton Camp*, etc. But from the 1880s the fiddle and the concertina began to supersede the pipe and tabor, and by 1900 there were only a few aged players still

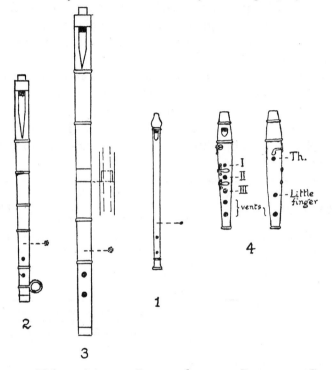

Fig. 54. *Tabor pipes:* 1, *Provençal;* 2, 3, *Basque;* 4, *Catalan fluviol.*

living. Several of their instruments are preserved, and since the revival of English folk dancing in the 1920s, Dolmetsch and Louis have made some pipes modelled upon them.

Spanish tabor pipes generally have wider bore and more powerful sound than the preceding, and perhaps more closely preserve the form of the ubiquitous medieval instrument. Especially interesting are the perfected pipes played in the Basque cities (fig. 54, 2), for these most closely resemble the large pipes of the Renaissance and of Tudor England. The principal size, *chistu*, is in G, 16·5 inches long, 13 millimetres bore with a compass a fifth below that of the French pipe. A metal mouthpiece projects at the top and the voicing edge is a long plate of German silver let into the wood—a common feature in Spanish tabor pipes, and a sensible one for an instrument subjected to much rough usage. A vibrato is made where possible by shaking finger II. In municipal pipe and tabor bands as that of San Sebastian this pipe is accompanied by a fat-toned bass pipe, *silbote*, in C a fifth below (fig. 54, 3). It is made in two joints, totalling 24·5 inches and has a 16·5 millimetres bore. In some arrangements the G pipes play the melody in thirds while the silbote provides a sort of flute-band bass. The silbote player is excused taboring, and while the tabors (*tamborils*) of the other pipers mark the main rhythm, an independent side-drummer, the *atabalero*, is responsible for the more subtle beatings. In medieval pictures too one sometimes sees this auxiliary drummer.

Tabors vary in size and shape in different regions from the shallow English tabor, decorated with red, yellow and green Morris ribbons, to the deep-shelled Provençal *tambourin*. Medieval tabors were on the whole more like those of Spain, about as wide as deep. The tabor is suspended in many different ways, hung from the left arm, slung round the shoulders, hooked on a belt, etc., and it is usually beaten in fairly straightforward rhythms to guide the dance, as two-in-a-bar in six-eight time, or in dactylic rhythm in two-four. No medieval beatings are recorded, but those given in Arbeau's *Orchésographie* (1588) are all of the same simple kind. The medieval pipe and tabor was also intended primarily for dance music, like the *tresques* in Robin and Marion, though *estampies*, which were rated more as concert pieces, were also performed on it.

The tabor is not the only percussive instrument that is or has been used with the pipe. A feminine alternative to the pipe and tabor in the fifteenth century was the pipe and triangle. Today, on both slopes of the Pyrenees one finds the pipe and stringed drum (with some six gut strings stretched over a three feet long soundbox and tuned to the keynote and fifth of the pipe, and beaten with a stick). In the New World, the pipe with ordinary tabor has been widely adopted by the Indians of Mexico, who, on certain festive occasions, play it while hanging upside-down from a maypole; but the Negro population of Brazil has adopted the pipe and gourd-rattle.

A singular kind of tabor pipe is found in parts of North-east Spain and in the Catalan sardana bands (fig. 54, 4). It is barely seven inches long, with three finger-holes in front and two behind. Of the latter, one is for the thumb, and the other (situated between holes III and IV) is for the upper surface of the little finger. Also unlike the normal tabor pipe, the fundamentals are used, augmented on the sardana model, *fluviol*, by three keys. The instrument is really a species of *French flageolet* though this is played with both hands, the upper for I and II *plus* thumb-hole above as in a tabor pipe, and the other for III and IV (this no longer a vent) with thumb-hole between. Small bird-flageolets, made from the late seventeenth century for persuading cage-birds to sing, use the same arrangement, which allows thick fingers to play a very short pipe.

SHAWM. In the mixed and varied typology of ancient wind-instrument history, the outstanding fresh contribution of post-classical times is the reed instrument sounded with a double reed carried on the narrow end of a conical metal staple. The body of the instrument usually, but not always, continues the bore-expansion of the staple. The eventual outcome of the idea is, of course, our oboe, and also the bassoon, in which the staple takes the elongated form of a crook. Among older types of instrument, it has been employed in the chanters of Western bagpipes, and over the entire realm of civilization, from England and Morocco in the West to China and Java in the East, in the instruments of the *Shawm* tribe, of which two notable European survivors—the Catalan *tiple* and *tenora*—have already been described in Chapter IV.

By mounting the reed on a staple, the principal advantage gained over the older method of inserting a long-stemmed reed directly into the pipe was probably very much quicker and easier reed-making. But of the early history of the idea, virtually nothing is known. We have only the notion, based on general historical grounds, that the parent instrument of the staple-bearing kind is the Middle Eastern shawm *surna*, a variety of which, frequently heard at our folk-dance festivals, is the Macedonian *zurla*. According to a Mohammedan tradition, the surna was invented in Baghdad in the time of Harun-al-Rashid. Against this, Curt Sachs' identification of a shawm-like instrument on a Jewish coin of the second century A.D. would put the invention some six centuries earlier. It seems likely, however, that Sachs was mistaken.

The surna is of wood, often still turned on the ancient bow-lathe. An example is shown in Plate XVIII. Loosely mounted on the staple is a wide disc of metal, bone or mother-of-pearl, against which the player puts his lips, totally engulfing the reed inside the cavity of his mouth. From the staple may hang a festoon of shawmist's accessories, as spare reeds and reed-making tools—a mandrel (a metal or wooden spike) and a cane clamp. The Oriental shawm reed (Plate XIX) is of rush, maize straw, pala grass, etc. To make it, a short length of the material is first squashed quite flat and left to dry and set. Then, after soaking, its lower end is opened out and bound over the mandrel, and the upper part is restored to the flattened shape in the cane clamp. The mandrel is also used for clearing a reed that has become too closed-up and water-logged. Also shown in the plate is an alternative construction found mainly in Burma and Siam. Four or six strips of smoked palm-leaf are superimposed, bent over and cut to shape, and bound over a mandrel inserted between the middle two pieces of leaf. This makes a double reed, each blade of which is composed of two or three thicknesses of palm-leaf; an excellent reed, with which the players obtain a range of two octaves or more, and every mode of articulation and expressive nuance known to wind-playing.

The surna was a ceremonial and military instrument, played in bands with trumpets and drums. When, during the later Crusades, it became adopted in Europe, it was kept in the same role, but we must suppose that some top-end remodelling took place; for in the West, as far as we know, the instrument has always carried some kind of turned wooden 'pirouette' instead of the surna's loose disc. Conceivably this is because the European prefers to secure lip-control over his cane reed; the pirouette may then be seen as a device for bringing the disc up above the reed's stem.

But while the above inferences may be held satisfactorily to explain the provenance of the Western ceremonial 'band shawm', as we may describe this instrument, we have still to account for the possibility that medieval Europe had prior knowledge of the expanding bore and staple on the popular level, namely in the bagpipe, for which, with this bore, there is no counterpart in the Near and Middle East. This may lend support to Sach's view that the 'conical' pipe is older than we have hitherto believed.

Since a bagpipe requires neither disc nor pirouette, the cane is bound on to the staple, reducing the danger of it from falling off into the bag. Those little European folk shawms that also employ this construction of the reed—Italian *ciaramella* and Breton *bombarde*, both always played next to a bagpipe—are best regarded historically as detached chanters.

We may thus distinguish two shawm strains in the West: (1) The 'band shawm', derived from the Arabo-Persian surna, with detachable reed and (usually) pirouette; examples include the shawms described in the next chapter, and the Catalan instruments already mentioned. (2) The 'folk shawm', derived from the bagpipe, with the reed bound on the staple (and no pirouette); among the examples, the ciaramella (sometimes called *piffaro*, or *cornamusina*; fig. 44) is a particularly lively-sounding little instrument, about a foot long, with narrowly expanding bore and seven holes (rarely a thumb-hole, since it overblows to sound the upper tonic). The reed (Plate XIX) is like a bagpipe's, but is taken in the lips and tongued like an oboe reed. To woodwind history, both strains are important, for the oboe represents their eventual reunion.

Loud and soft instruments (1300 onwards)

During the troubadour age, wind instruments were used in music with great freedom. There are hints of segregation of the noisier instruments from those which matched the singer and strings, but hardly more. However, in the fourteenth century, with its greater emphasis on concerted music, the distinction became binding, and this is the first point to grasp when fitting old wind instruments, or modern substitutes for them, into performances of fourteenth- and fifteenth-century music.

The stricter observance of the distinction may have owed much to late thirteenth-century interest in Arab music-making. There had been nothing particularly Arab about either the provenance or the usage of the earlier 'Gothic' instruments, but now, towards the end of the thirteenth century, there appeared a fresh group of instruments, this time obtained direct from the Arab civilization. It included some of the principal stringed instruments of Arab chamber music, as the lute, and the Moorish fiddle *rubebe*; also the Saracen military band equipment, with long metal trumpets, the small Oriental kettle-drums *nakers*, and the band shawm described in the preceding section. With the advent of these came also the Oriental strict distinction between loud and soft instruments and music, and to appreciate what it signifies, we may first observe it as it still operates in the traditional music of the East today.

LOUD MUSIC (ORIENTAL). Anybody who has heard the old-style concerted music of the East must have noticed its broadest twofold division: artistic indoor music (soft), and ceremonial band music (loud). The outdoor band, heard at public and private functions of many descriptions, has its own instruments of which the chief is the shawm. With it are drums, and sometimes cymbals. The trumpet, the band's third type of component, is heard less now than formerly, but we must nevertheless notice its role; for in the East a trumpeter is a one-note man, and bass at that. Traditionally he is employed in pairs to sound a note that is roughly either one or two octaves below the key-note of the shawms. On this note, the trumpeters, with their long medieval trumpets, burst in intermittently with hoarse interruptions through which the shawmists unconcernedly play on. The shawm key-note is usually about *a'*, and in those Persian cities that still keep their medieval-style town band, one of the shawmists sustains a drone on this note (so that their combined effect resembles that of the two horns in the Trio of the second movement of Beethoven's Ninth Symphony, but a fifth higher). Describing the performance as he heard it long ago at Kirmanshah, Binder wrote: 'Every evening at sundown five or six musicians mount a small bandstand overlooking the terraces. The music begins with the small drum solo, soon joined by the big drum. Then these give place to melody on a surna, calm at first, then wildly abandoned. Finally all the instruments play together, the long trumpets adding their bellowing sounds to the devilish concert. The music stops; the trumpets give three last moans; a cannon shot, the sun is set, and the regimental bugles sound the governor's fanfare.' In the band of a Tibetan monastery, or of a Mohammedan chief in West Africa, shawm and trumpets are combined in just the same way.

LOUD MUSIC (EUROPE). The European band of the early fourteenth century, just after the last Crusade, took over the basic Oriental constitution outlined above. Thus the town band of Pisa in 1324 had one shawmist, one nakerer and two pairs of trumpeters. For a larger band, a bagpiper or a pipe-and-taborer, being readily available, might be added. These were military bands in the full modern sense, performing at state functions, cavalcades, tournaments and in battle. It is unlikely that their music was written down, so how 'Oriental' it may have first sounded is unknown. Possibly a more advanced trumpet-technique had already been developed in Europe on the alp-horns.

In Europe, by the Renaissance, another use had been found for the band: 'When people wish to dance, or to stage a grand celebration, the loud (*haut*) instruments are played, for their great noise pleases the dancers better; they include trumpets, tabors, nakers, cymbals, bagpipes, shawms and cornetts.' So runs the late fourteenth-century French poem *Les Echecs amoureux*. Then, as today, a loud band was preferred for formal dancing, and the medieval band forthwith began to be seriously Westernized. The early shawm was generally an instrument of about bagpipe pitch, but a longer shawm with keynote about the bottom of the treble stave now became the chief melodist, and longer still and a fifth lower was built a tenor shawm, *bombarde*. On the bombarde, to cover the lowest hole, there was made a key, protected by a slide-on wooden barrel (in French, *fontanelle*) perforated with rosettes of vent-holes that recalled the jets of fountains. This was the first woodwind key. Meanwhile, the trumpet was being made in folded shape like a capital S, and to this was adapted a sliding mouthpipe so that diatonic passages could be played on its lower harmonics: the *trompette des ménestrels* or musicians' trumpet, as opposed to the plain *trompette de guerre*. A further improvement of this during the fifteenth century produced the trombone ('sackbut'), also for this band. In Renaissance paintings one frequently sees the band—three or four men in tall hats, stationed in a gallery or in a raised pew against one wall of the hall.

The modern musicologists Besseler and Bukofzer have discovered a great deal about the performance of the band in the *basse danse* of the period. The bombarde gave out the long notes of the tenor part to the beat of the dance. This formed the framework of the music. It is not known quite what the trumpet did before it became a trombone and played a regular contratenor part, but the shawmist executed what can only be described as a hot chorus over the notes of the bombarde. Dr Bukofzer found in an Italian library a *basse danse* written down complete with one of these hot trebles. It is printed in his *Studies in Medieval and Renaissance Music*, p. 199, and it is interesting to compare it with a later version of the same tune, now with a contratenor part, printed in Davison and Apel, No. 102*a*. (As for the pitch in these examples, the treble and tenor parts comply with common fifteenth-century practice in being *written* at a deep pitch carrying them down to *g* and *c* respectively. The same deep pitches are given for shawm and bombarde in Agricola's fingering charts of 1528, but one can tell from the size of the instruments in later fifteenth-century paintings and in Agricola's own drawings that they actually *sounded* about a fifth higher, namely at the standard shawm pitches of the later sixteenth century.)

SOFT MUSIC (ORIENTAL). The soft or indoor music of the East is heard especially at receptions and dinner parties given by officials and wealthy people; also, in some places, in theatres and cafés. It is based upon stringed instruments, typically an orchestra of from two to five assorted strings. If a wind instrument is among them, which is frequently the case and is often obligatory, it is a member of the flute class: in the Far East, the flute itself; in the Near East, the vertical flute *nay*. Though there is no harmony in our sense of the word, each participating instrument plays the tune after its own allotted fashion, and the result is a bright heterophony, to which the drums, above their rhythmic function, add a remarkable effect of bass. Occasionally the flute is replaced by some soft-toned reed instrument, as for example the drone parallel double-pipe *arghul*, which has been heard in this role at a Syrian wedding reception. Its burbling contralto makes an interesting change from the high warbling of the usual *nay* and it blends just as well with the strings.

SOFT MUSIC (EUROPE). The poem *Les Echecs amoureux* continues: 'But when less noise is required one plays tabor-pipes, flutes and *douçaines*, which are soft and sweet, and other such soft (*bas*) instruments.' So here, as in many similar passages in poems and documents of the time, we may discover which instruments were used in *chamber music*, as when performing the ballades and chansons of Landino, Dunstable or Dufay. The *bas* instruments are closely analogous to those used in the soft music in the East. 'Other soft instruments' includes the strings and the portative organ. 'Flutes' includes recorder and flute. 'Douçaine' is the name of the soft reed instrument that went with them, but its identification presents us with a stiff puzzle today.

The only known description of it is in a few lines written by Tinctoris in 1488: the *dulcina* (he is writing in Latin) is a kind of shawm (*tibia*, in its late-medieval meaning), soft-toned, whence the name, and of limited compass (*imperfecta*); and it has seven holes plus thumb-hole, as a recorder (*fistula*). These brief particulars, taken in conjunction with the general picture of consort reed instruments in the following century, have been taken to imply that this dulcina or douçaine was of the non-over-blowing type with double reed, narrow cylindrical bore, and deep pitch for its length. Had Tinctoris described its pitch, he might have narrowed the problem for us. Unfortunately he does not, so that we cannot altogether rule out another possible answer, namely that the instrument was a kind of shawm, like the Spanish folk instrument that bears the name *dulzaina* today. This is a folk shawm, reputedly of Moorish descent, played without a pirouette. It is pitched a fourth above the oboe and has a broad double reed placed on a very wide metal staple. It is invariably accompanied by a side-drummer, and it is made keyless, or with simple-system keywork (Plate XVIII) or even in '*ultima systema*' with advanced mechanism. There are many examples of its tunes in the *Cancioneros* of Inzenga and Ledesma, and it is imitated on the high notes of two clarinets in unison in Debussy's *Iberia*.

This present-day dulzaina is a vigorous open-air instrument; but it may not always have been so. The *Cantigas* MS. shows some small pipes that look very much like dulzainas with bulbous bells, and similar instruments in Renaissance pictures might be douçaines of various sizes and pitches. But the fact of the matter is that we simply do not know what the douçaine was. The name may, as Sachs has suggested, even have covered a number of different softish reed instruments.

From soft music, the *loud* instruments were excluded. In those fifteenth-century paintings that show choirs of angels exhibiting every kind of musical instrument, soft and loud, it will nearly always be observed that the angels with loud instruments—shawms and trumpets—balance each other on opposite flanks of the picture, or form a group at the back; the distinction between *bas* and *haut* remains as evident as ever. When a picture appears to show a shawm-like instrument intruding amongst strings, it must be some sort of douçaine; the literary evidence admits no alternative.

From about 1350, wind consorts begin to appear, as three recorders, often heard at the Burgundian court in Dufay's time. But more commonly wind and stringed were mixed, as recorder and psaltery or rebec; lute and douçaine; psaltery, gittern and flute; pipe and tabor, recorder and harp; pipe and tabor, douçaine, lute and harp; etc., etc., these groups being both for chamber music and for quiet afternoon dancing in the garden.

After this, with the rise of the Flemish School of composition, our regular four parts came in—treble, alto, tenor and bass, with the last written down to the bottom of the bass stave. To fit these the *four-piece treble-to-bass consort* would have grown up roughly during the interval 1460–1490, producing the bass recorder, the consort of crumhorns and other new instruments described in the next chapter.

CHAPTER X

The Sixteenth Century and the Consorts

The sixteenth century has a special interest in that it is the earliest period in Western musical history to have left us a representative stock of its instruments to examine. And it is fortunate that it has done so, particularly as concerns the wooden wind instruments, for soon after Shakespeare's time these instruments—representing the culmination of the medieval types described in the last chapter—began to fall out of use, and sooner or later many of them became extinct, with the loss to music of several strange tone-colours. The principal species are listed below. Many of their names now have an antique ring, perhaps bringing to mind museum catalogues rather than practical music, though in this chapter the instruments will be examined mainly with reference to the latter:

Flute class: recorder, flutes
Reed class (consort instruments): crumhorns, curtals, etc.
    ,,   ,, *(band instruments):* shawms
Trumpet class (with finger-holes): cornetts[1]

[1] Sixteenth-century nomenclature is far from consistent or clear, but the following list gives the most usual names of the instruments in the various countries. Observe that 'hoboy' (*hautbois*) then meant 'shawm' (in Shakespeare's plays, for instance).

Recorder	flûte, fl. douce	flauto, fl. diritto	Flöte, Blockflöte
Flute	fl. d'Allemagne	fiffaro	Querflöte, Zwerchpfeife
Crumhorn, cromcorn	tournebout, ? cromorne	storto, piva torto, ? corna-musa	Krumbhorn
Curtal	fagot, basson	fagotto	Fagott, Dulzian
Shawm, shalme, hautbois, hoboy, wait	hautbois	piffaro	Schalmey, Bomhart, Pommer
Cornet(t)	cornet (à bouquin)	cornetto	Zink

Today, the major collections include those of the Vienna Kunsthistorisches Museum, and the Instrumental Museum of the Royal Conservatoire, Brussels (Place Petit Sablon). These two magnificent collections possess between them some 130 sixteenth- and early seventeenth-century wind instruments, mainly drawn from the ancient private collections of the Correr and the Obizzi families of Venice and Padua, and of the Archduke of the Tyrol at his castle, Schloss Ambras, near Innsbruck. Next in importance comes the collection now housed in the Biblioteca Capitolare at Verona, with some fifty wind instruments belonging to that city's ancient Philharmonic Academy and some others belonging to the Cathedral; and the Berlin Hochschule Museum, whose many notable specimens include a fine set of band instruments formerly preserved in the Wenzelskirche at Naumburg in Upper Saxony. More instruments of sixteenth-century local bandsmen are in the museums of Frankfurt, Nuremberg, Salzburg, Prague, Amsterdam and many other places, and there are some fine cornetts and other instruments in the Museum of the Paris Conservatoire. No English examples are known save for three cornetts: two trebles (particularly fine ones, Plate XX) at Christ Church, Oxford (in the Library), and a tenor at Norwich (in the Museum, Plate XXIII).

Besides actual instruments the period has left a number of tutors and descriptive works. Most informative of the earlier works is Agricola's *Musica Instrumentalis deutsch* (1528). There is nothing of comparable value until the great *Syntagma Musicum* (Vol. II, 1619) of Praetorius, German composer and court musical director. This work is an indispensable guide to the surviving specimens; it has been reprinted twice in Germany in modern times, though copies are now hard to obtain. Some of its plates are reproduced in this chapter (figs. 57–8, 61–3), resized to show the instruments at approximately the same scale throughout (the ruler-scales in the plates give the old Brunswick inches, twelve of which are roughly equal to eleven of ours). The *Syntagma* was followed a few years later by Mersenne's scarcely less valuable *Harmonie Universelle*, published in 1636, though much of it was compiled at least ten years earlier.

For further insight into the instruments as the musicians knew them, contemporary inventories are especially interesting. Many of these have been published in modern books and journals and we shall here quote two of them, translated, and slightly condensed to save space.

First, the 1569 list (from Turrini) of the instruments of the already-mentioned Verona Academy, whose performances were set beside those of St Mark's, Venice, and the Duke's castle at Ferrara, as the three best in Italy. The list has the extra interest that many of the instruments entered in it must still be there among those in Monsignor Turrini's care in the Verona Chapter Library. Some extra details from an inventory of a few years earlier are added in brackets in items two to four.

Accademia Filarmonica, Verona, 1569

5 sets of viols, a lira and a *rebechino*
7 lutes, a (two-manual) harpsichord, another harpsichord and a regal
a chest of 22 recorders (with crooks for the three deepest) and two incomplete chests
a case of 5 flutes (with the bass made in two pieces), another set of 5, and two incomplete sets
2 tabor-pipes; 2 tabors (*tamburi*)
5 crumhorns (*pivete*)
3 fifes (*fiffari da campo*)
3 trombones, with their crooks and tuning bits (*pezzi*)
5 tenor cornetts
4 silver-mounted ordinary cornetts
8 mute cornetts
3 dragon-belled cornetts (*con testa di bissa*)
1 curtal (*fagoto*) with its reeds (*canelli*)

The fifes would probably have been for processions (the Academy later bought an extremely fine Nuremberg trumpet too), and the tabor pipes for certain dances. But the rest of the wind instruments could scarcely be more typical of those used in concerts during the century. They were not all played at once. There would be five or six wind players who changed from one instrument to another as instructed by the musical director, who arranged the programme from the current repertoire of part-music—motets, madrigals and French songs—constantly redeploying his force of instrumentalists and singers between numbers, to suit the pieces and to avoid monotony of tone-colour. In a music-room—like the fine example preserved in the Castelvecchio at Verona—the performers sat round a long table on one end of which was placed a harpsichord taken off its stand. Sometimes at the other end, as at Ferrara, the musical director conducted with a baton.

Our second inventory is that of the instruments of the Berlin court in 1582, condensed from the original text printed by Sachs. This list states the pitches of the instruments, and to save space these are abbreviated below thus: B, bass; T, tenor; A, alto; D, descant. (In English nomenclature, which will be employed for the rest of this chapter, most of these 'alto' instruments would have been called trebles.)

Berlin Hofkapelle, 1582

6 positive organs, 4 regals, 4 harpsichords

5 new viols and some old ones

3 trombones, each with a crook (a double crook for the bass) and 7 tuning bits

7 crumhorns, 1 B, 2 T, 2 A, 2 D

2 tenor shawms (*Bombardte*) and 1 treble shawm (*discant Schalmey*)

7 recorders (*Handt-flöten*, 1 B, 2 T, 2 A, 1 D, and a tabor-pipe with them and another missing

8 recorders (*Brauhne-flöten*), 2 B, 3 T, 2 A, 1 D, and a small descant missing

9 flutes (*Querpfeifen*), 2 B, 4 T, 3 D

4 cornetts, two of them with keys, two without

1 tenor cornett with a key

7 *Schreipfeifen*, 1 B (without its brass *mundstuck*—crook?), 3 T, 2 A, 1 D; one of the tenors lacks its key, and all but one are without their *messinge Rorlin* (staples) and *uberröhren* (reeds, or caps?)

mentioned separately: 1 *Dulzan* (curtal)

This list includes the loud instruments of the palace band: the shawms, and perhaps the *Schreierpfeifen* (another type of reed instrument), though these last were evidently not kept in playing condition. Apart from these, the emphasis is upon the same instruments as in the Verona inventory: recorders, flutes, cornetts and crumhorns; and in other inventories it is just the same.

The instruments in general

In their construction the museum survivors show workmanship of the first class. Bores and finger-holes are beautifully executed and the keywork, what there is of it, can act extremely well. The smaller instruments are mostly of boxwood and the larger of maple. Nearly all are made as far as possible in one piece and finished very plainly on the outside. Ornamental turnery, so characteristic of the eighteenth-century instruments, belongs to jointed construction, and this is rarely found in the sixteenth century save in bagpipes and some unusual instruments.

In instruments exceeding about 30 inches in length, the seventh finger-hole (little finger) is covered by that key which first appeared on the Renaissance bombarde—an open key protected by a slide-on barrel (as in fig. 57, *left*); or, in the case of curved instruments and those of oval or octagonal cross-section (e.g. in fig. 61), by a perforated metal box that also can be slid off for inspection of the key-mounting, sewn-on leather pad, and brass leaf-spring bearing on top of the key-lever. The larger bass instruments are usually extended diatonically downwards to reach three deep notes—'diapasons'—below the seven-finger note. This involved fitting three more keys; normally one more for the little finger (its touch partly overlapping that of the first key), and two for the thumb of the same hand (as on the bass shawm in fig. 63). As with the 'short octave' at the bass end of early harpsichords, chromatic semitones were not provided for in this bass extension.

Among the survivors in the big collections, those of Venetian manufacture predominate, which is appropriate, since Venice seems to have been the principal focus of design during the period. German courts, for instance, frequently bought their wooden wind instruments from Venice, while Italians reciprocated by sending to Nuremberg for their trumpets and trombones. Venetian models must have been well known in England too. France seems to have been on the whole more independent, though there too, in Paris, they made *cornets, façon de Venize.* This, and the constant migration of players from one country to another, led to some degree of standardization in instrumental playing-pitch. It was higher than it is today. Recorders at Verona, identical in shape and in size with those in Praetorius's scale drawings at 'chamber pitch' (fig. 57), sound a good semitone above modern pitch; say about $a' = 470$. Many other specimens also sound about this pitch, though yet others are lower, probably having been built (as many inventories reveal) to suit the pitch of some church organ.

CONSORT SIZES. Since the music was selected from part-music composed in a vocal idiom, almost every species of instrument was constructed in a *treble size,* a *tenor size* (which also did for alto) and a *bass size,* each matched in compass to the range of the corresponding voice part in the general run of compositions. And since the performers kept changing instruments in the course of a programme, all instruments of a given size, say treble, were built in unison, so that the reading of the music— i.e. the fingering of the printed notes—was as far as possible the same on all of them.

To examine this we may take as a reference point the note given when six fingers are put down (plus the thumb if there is a thumb-hole). In every normal wind consort the treble instrument then gives a; the tenor gives a fifth lower, d; the bass a fifth lower still, G. On flutes and recorders these notes sounded an octave higher, but there is evidence that these instruments were freely combined with the others and with voices as if the octave difference did not exist.

The above three sizes, including two of the tenor size (for alto and tenor parts) constituted the standard equipment at the beginning of the century. Further sizes were added to some consorts as the century went on—descant and great-bass (as we will term them, making the best of the variable terminology of the period). These were at first built to continue the ladder of fifths upwards above the treble and downwards below the bass; six fingers giving, respectively, e' and C. But a fault with this was that when using all sizes together, the fingering of these additional sizes got rather complicated, the descant having to play, as it were, in too many flats and the great-bass in too many sharps relatively to their basic tonality. And so in many cases they came to be supplied alternatively at the fourth above and below the primary consort instead of at the fifth, thus; descant, six fingers d'; and great-bass, D (a 'quart'-bass instead of a 'quint'-bass). Beyond this only recorders ran to two extreme or 'octave' sizes: exilent (Praetorius's term for the sopranino, an octave above the treble), and the recorder Great Bass, an octave below the 'quint-bass' (as we must therefore name the ordinary great-bass size when talking of the recorder consort).

TABLE OF STANDARD CONSORT SIZES

With the pitch defined in terms of the six-finger note (giving the actual *sounding pitch* for flutes and recorders). The anomalies of the shawm nomenclature are commented on in the last section of this chapter.

	Exilent	Descant	Treble	Tenor	Bass	Great-bass	(Recorder Great Bass)
Recorder	a''	e'' or d''	a'	d'	g	c (quint-bass)	G
Flute			a'	d'	g		
Crumhorn		e'	a	d	G	D or C	
Cornett		e'	a	d	(trombones used)		
Curtal			a or g	d	G	D or C	
Shawm	a' (b')	e' (treble)	a (tenor)	d (basset)	G	D or C	

TECHNIQUE AND DIVISIONS. All the instruments were fingered basically like a recorder except for differences occasioned by the lack of a little-finger-hole or a thumb-hole in some types. Now with this fingering, as every recorder player knows, the principal scales turn on the *cross-fingerings*, which provide some of the best notes on the instrument and the best intonation. And so it was in the sixteenth century. Playing in the key of C on the treble cornett was like playing in B♭ on the modern treble recorder, i.e. with cross-fingerings almost throughout, including for pivotal notes of the scale like C, G and F. Fig. 55 shows the general scheme for a treble instrument.

Ancient tonguing has been glanced at in Chapter I. The remaining technical points are lucidly summed up by Agricola:

g		b′	
g♯		c″	
a		c″♯	
b♭		d″	
b		e″♭	
c′		e″	
c′♯		f″	
d′		f″♯	
e′♭		g″	
e′		g″♯	
f′		a″	
f′♯		b″♭	
g′		b″	
g♯		c‴	
*a′			
b♭			

FIG. 55. *Generalized chart for treble instrument with thumb-hole, based on sixteenth- and seventeenth-century sources. p: half-uncover thumb-hole. C: special cornett fingerings (mainly from Speer). Asterisk marks upper limit of treble crumhorn.*

first, learn to play a part just as it is written; *second,* learn to introduce the correct *musica ficta* accidentals, i.e. accidentals not printed in the part but nevertheless required by the music (e.g. certain flats; sharpened leading-notes); *third,* to make trills at the cadences; *fourth,* to fill in the melody here and there with the simple elements of *divisions*; and *fifth,* to make full divisions (known on the Continent as *diminutions*).

Throughout the old polyphonic age of musical history, and in every country in Europe, division-playing was the sauce without which a concert of music was not looked upon as palatable. Descriptions of division-making go back to the thirteenth century; and from then on to the seventeenth century they all boil down to much the same thing, while wind-instrumentalists made them after the same fashion as singers and players on other instruments.

A division is a simple kind of variation upon one of the parts

FIG. 56. *Example of divisions, from Girolamo Della Casa, 1584.* Top line: *the original printed treble part;* lower lines: *two alternative divisions. The tune is 'Suzanne un jour'.*

of a composition—usually the treble part—done by filling-in and decorating the written part with scales and grouplets of fast notes. In the period of Bach and Handel, composers themselves had come to write allegros largely in the manner of divisions (e.g. the long semiquaver runs in Handel's choruses, and the stretches of division-like melody in the allegro movements of concertos, like Bach's for the violin). In the sixteenth century similar runs and figures were supplied mainly by the player, who either extemporized his division as he went along, or prepared one beforehand. For beginners and amateurs, specimen divisions, that could be practised and learnt off, were printed in tutors and books of studies. Ganassi gives many for recorder players in his *Fontegara*. Fig. 56 is taken from the book of divisions by the Venetian cornett soloist Girolamo della Casa, one of the most celebrated wind players of the late sixteenth century. It shows two specimen divisions for the treble part of Lassus's five-part French song *Suzanne un jour* (only the first quarter of it is reproduced here). It will be observed that the example also demonstrates the correct sixteenth-century way of making cadential trills: by beginning on the upper note and fingering *in tempo*, sometimes with eight, sometimes with twelve notes per trill.

Recorders

The structural differences between the sixteenth-century (Plate XXI) and the 'baroque' designs of recorder have been touched upon in Chapter II. We have here rather to consider the musical employment of the sixteenth-century recorder consort.

The primary set of *c.* 1500 (treble, two tenors, and a bass) was best suited to compositions written in the 'low clefs' (the 'low key' as Morley calls them). These clefs were generally the same as those used up till recently for choral music, namely *soprano, alto, tenor* and *bass clefs*. In the usual practice of the century the parts were kept mainly within the boundaries of the clefs, seldom straying above or below by more than one leger line. Each part therefore had a compass of about an octave and a half, which suited recorders. But it was usual to include in one's set of recorders a second treble instrument to deal with unusually high alto parts, while it also came in handy for five-part compositions. This made five instruments in all, which the Norwich Waits in 1584 still considered as 'beeying a Whoall noyse' (waits, like the corresponding town-bandsmen on the Continent, were primarily shawmists, but used recorders at indoor civic receptions and so on).

In music written in the 'high clefs'—typically *treble clef*, *mezzosoprano clef* (C clef on second line from bottom), *alto clef*, and *baritone clef* (F clef on middle line)—the treble parts often run up to *g"* (sounding *g'''* on recorder), which might be a difficult note to play nicely, and is in fact a note higher than contemporary German fingering charts allow the treble instrument. This is no doubt why the descant recorder came to be included in so many sets about the mid-century and from then onwards.

One bought these small bass-to-descant sets complete from the maker—the only way, it was said, to ensure their being in tune together—and they arrived in a shaped wooden case resembling a huge black panpipe. Several of the cases have survived, some (at Nuremberg and Frankfurt) with the recorders still in them. But the instruments are never quite the same. Clearly there was no standard equipment in the second half of the century, though from inventories we may detect a possible favourite in two descants, two trebles, two tenors and one bass. Frequently a vacant cranny in the case was filled by some small pipe like an exilent recorder, a fife or a tabor-pipe.

Popular though these small recorder outfits were, the special joy of the sixteenth century was the Great Consort or *grand jeu,* on which music could be played at its written pitch just as it was sung or played on other instruments. The bass recorder then took treble, with the tenor recorder as the optional descant. For the lower parts there were those splendid Venetian quint-basses and the Great Bass, with their full woody tone (though they can be difficult instruments to get one's fingers round). Nor need the sound of the Great Consort be lost, for well-preserved instruments for copying are all extant together at Verona or Vienna.

The following list shows the standard sixteenth-century

recorder sizes, with approximate length and lowest note (actual pitch). Note that the treble was a tone higher than it is today. Only the two deepest sizes have brass crooks; the ordinary bass was blown through a slot in the rim of its wooden cap (fig. 57, 1).

exilent, 8 inches (*g″*)	tenor, 24 inches (*c′*)
descant, 11 inches (*d″*)	bass, 36·5 inches (*f*)
„ 12 „ (*c″*)	quart-bass, 49 inches (*c*)
treble, 17 inches (*g′*)	quint-bass, 56 inches (*B♭*)

Great Bass, 76 inches (*F*)

ditto with diapason keys, 103 inches (*C*)

Some treble, tenor and bass instruments are pitched a tone higher than usual, possibly to facilitate sight-reading when playing as a Great Consort.

Concerning the use of all sizes of recorder together, Praetorius recommends 'more especially the five deeper kinds, since the small ones scream so', and these five (i.e. from treble downwards) 'can very well be used alone without other instruments in a canzona or motet, giving a most pleasing soft harmony in a hall or chamber, though in a church the larger recorders cannot be heard very well'. When combining them with voices, he advises the use of a curtal (proto-bassoon) as their bass. But it is Mersenne who shows us the most tempting picture: 'the small consort and the great consort can be used together just as the small and large registers of the organ are.' We imagine descant and tenor in octaves on the top part, and similarly treble with bass, tenor with quint-bass, etc. on the lower parts, and perhaps the small exilent piping high above one of the parts at the twelfth. This should sound wonderful. Perhaps some day we shall have enough replicas of the deep recorders to enjoy it.

Flutes

At the end of the fifteenth century the flute began to benefit from a wave of real popularity through the great impression made by German and Swiss fife-and-drum music, while throughout the sixteenth century fife (fig. 57, 4) and drum remained the favourite popular dance music in Germany, corresponding to pipe and tabor in England.

The flute, like the fife, was an absolutely plain boxwood tube with six holes and the ancestral cylindrical bore of the Asiatic cane flutes. This makes a telling instrument; Rockstro has pointed out how the pure cylindrical bore can give a very powerful tone, with notes well in tune over a compass of three

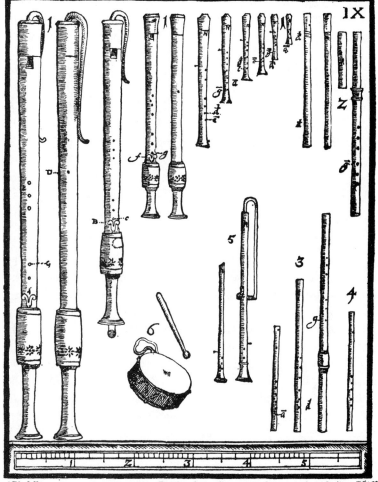

1 Blockflöten, ganz Stimmwerk. 2. Doltzflöt ♭ g. 3 Querflöten, ganz Stimmwerk. 4. Schweitzer Pfeiff. 5 Stamentienbass und Discant. 6 Klein Päuklin: zu den Stamentien Pfeifflin zu gebrauchen.

FIG. 57. *Praetorius:* 1, *Recorders.* 2 (top, right), Doltzflöten (*recorders made to be held like flutes*). 3, *Flutes.* 4, *Fife.* 5, *Treble and bass tabor pipes.* 6, *Tabor.*

octaves (two and a half are mentioned in the sixteenth century), though the quality is 'rather harsh' compared with that of the later conical bore. This, however, is a comparison that can be made between many sixteenth-century wind designs and their eighteenth-century successors. The earlier period liked clear, positive, organ-like *timbres*; the eighteenth century preferred instruments to have more resistance, enabling the player to coax from them every fine shade of spirit and expression. However, to make the most of the quality of the older flute, Agricola recommends playing it with 'quaking breath' (*zitternde Wind*) —the earliest-known mention of vibrato.

The consort set of flutes (fig. 57, 3) comprised the following sizes (sometimes evidently built a tone lower than shown):

	Lowest note (actual pitch)	Approximate length (inches)	Approximate bore (mm.)
Treble	a'	18	14
Tenor	d'	27	18
Bass	g	36 to 39	25

Thus the tenor is virtually the same instrument as our ordinary flute of today. The basses were often made in two joints. The sound of the complete consort, with all its instruments played mainly in the lower range of their compass, would have been thicker and heavier than that of the recorders, and was evidently held to be effective even outdoors.

The flourishing twentieth-century cult of the recorder for old music has quite unfairly pushed the flute out of the picture. The flute was well-loved not only in its consort, but also in small combinations with stringed instruments and the voice. There is that well-known painting, *c.* 1520, by an unknown French painter, depicting three ladies performing the French part-song *Jouissance vous donnerai*; the treble is being sung, the bass played on a lute, and the tenor on a flute (sounding the part an octave higher). In another painting the combination is the same save that the bass is played on a bass viol. A professional combination for light occasional music at Munich under the direction of Lassus was flute, cittern and virginals—a mixture that vaguely anticipates the later Tudor 'English Consort' for which Morley wrote his Consort Lessons. In this last, the only wind instrument to five strings is 'Flute'—a word that normally meant flute all through those times in England (as

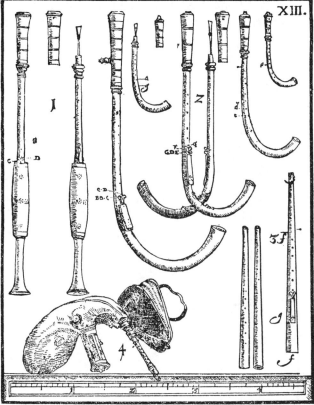

1 Bassett Nicolo 2 Krumbhörner 3 Cornetti muta stille Zincken. 4 Sackpfeiff mit dem Blasbalg

FIG. 58. *Praetorius:* 1. 'Basset: Nicolo', *an instrument apparently used with shawms or crumhorns.* 2. *Crumhorns.* 3. *Mute cornetts.* 4. *A bellows-bagpipe.*

opposed to 'Recorder'), while the two known pictures of the consort in action (both reproduced in Galpin's *Old English Instruments*) show the tenor flute. Again the flute part is a tenor part. Praetorius says that musicians were so accustomed to hearing alto and tenor parts played an octave too high on flute or recorder that they scarcely believed it when you pointed it out (cf. the deep effect of an owl hoot, also a high *oo* sound).

Crumhorns and other capped reed instruments

The crumhorn, a double-reed instrument with narrow cylindrical bore (Plate XXIII, fig. 58), appeared towards the end of the fifteenth century, evidently to meet a demand for an

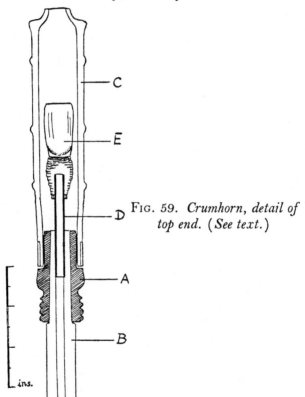

FIG. 59. *Crumhorn, detail of top end. (See text.)*

easy-blowing reed instrument on which four-part music could be rendered with good, harmonious effect just as it could be on voices, recorders or viols. Judging from its shape, the crumhorn was modelled on the curved-bottomed bladder-pipe mentioned in the last chapter (cf. fig. 53). Pictures suggest that this was a well-known popular instrument in Central Europe about that time, and no doubt (as also with some bagpipes) people used now and then to play it without the bladder, e.g. if this became punctured. The notes could then, of course, be tongued. However, either to simplify the embouchure, or to protect the reed from damage and excessive wetting, someone, very likely a German, introduced the *reed cap*. This is a wooden cap with a hole in the top to blow into, and it still allows the notes to be attacked and detached when desired. Whether the cap was suggested by some earlier instrument, or was inspired by the organ or the recorder, we do not know. We still have it in the bagpipe practice-chanter.

The normal construction of a crumhorn is as follows. The body consists of a length of boxwood, turned and bored, and the lower part bent round by steaming. The last two or three inches of the bore are funnelled out as a bell. Fig. 59 shows the detail of the top end: A, cap housing, tightly fitted over the body B; C, the cap (the bass is blown through a slot in the rim of the cap, and the great bass shown in Praetorius has a short projecting mouthpiece); D, the brass staple, slightly tapered to receive the reed E. The finger-holes follow the usual recorder arrangement.

The reed (Plate XXII) is made up like a bassoon reed, but is more evenly scraped across, like a bagpipe reed, to respond efficiently without the application of the lips. If one were to revive the crumhorn, plastic reeds should work as well as they do on the practice-chanter, and should last almost for ever.

The crumhorn was the favourite consort reed instrument throughout the sixteenth century. Every musical establishment possessed a set consisting of from four to twelve instruments made up from the following sizes:

	Lowest note	Approximate standing height (*inches*)	Tube length including staple (*inches*)	Bore (*mm.*)
Descant	c' (d')	13		
Treble	g	16	17	4 to 5·5
Tenor	c	24	26	6·5
Bass	F	32	36	8·5
Extended bass	C	38	43	8·5
Great-bass	C or B♭	44		
Extended great-bass	G' or F'	51		

In this list there will be noticed both plain and extended forms of the two deepest. The plain form has the usual little-finger key (for F in the bass size), while in the extended form the compass is augmented by three diapasons obtained in a most peculiar way. An E key overlaps the F key, and then, lower down, there are two small slider-keys that cannot be opened or shut without moving one hand away from the finger-holes. While the sliders are both open, the E key gives *E*. When the first slider is closed, the same key gives *D*. If both are closed, it gives the bottom *C*. Thus one could preselect a diapason to suit the tonality of the piece. Presumably this arrangement was considered preferable to fitting long curved keywork down the crumhorn's narrow body.

The Verona set of crumhorns, now restored to playable condition, had the primary four-piece composition of treble, two tenors and a bass. The showpiece, however, is the late sixteenth-century set at Brussels, reputed to have once belonged to Duke Alfonso II of Este, in Italy. Its flat, oblong fitted case, lined and padded with striped cloth, contains one treble, three tenors, one ordinary bass and one extended bass.

As compared with the practice-chanter, which is typologically the nearest thing to the crumhorn among present-day instruments and has the same compass as the treble crumhorn (though even smaller bore), the crumhorn is stronger, giving a full, singing tone. In 1500, one source describes it as 'loud'. Its volume range is limited, but the articulation, although the tongue does not touch the reed, is reasonably satisfactory. But the crumhorn possesses no speaker key, and therefore it cannot properly be overblown. Its compass is only nine notes, and therefore, as several musicians of the period emphasize, pieces to play had to be selected with this in mind. Sometimes a special morsel for the crumhorns was included in published collections of music (as Schein's pavan—which needs certain transpositions before it can be played on the standard crumhorns). But it is surprising how many unspecified compositions can be found to suit them. For instance in Antony Holborne's attractive *Pavans etc.* (1599) there are at least half a dozen pieces that do so, either entirely, or with alteration or omission

FIG. 60. *A piece suitable for crumhorns: 'The Widow's Mite' from Holborne's* Pavans etc., *1599.*

of no more than one or two notes in the whole piece (e.g. fig. 60). Perhaps they were designed especially for crumhorns.

The great virtue of the crumhorn is that it requires no special embouchure. It is as easy to blow as a recorder. It is, indeed, the equivalent among the reed instruments to the recorder among flutes, and it might well be revived as such, to offer school classes and family consorts a change from recorder-playing. The two instruments make a perfect contrast in tone and their fingering is the same. Also the notes of the crumhorn sound at vocal pitch, not an octave higher, so that on changing from recorders to crumhorns one experiences a change not only of tone colour but also of register, which is very restful.

About other kinds of capped reed instrument very little definite information is available. Also we lack specimens. They seem to have been well used nevertheless. Unlike the crumhorn, all were straight instruments. First, there was a consort of cylindrical-bore instruments about equal in overall length to the treble, tenor and bass recorders, though sounding an octave lower. No picture of them is known, but Praetorius says that they were stopped at the lower end, with vent holes in the side, and that they sounded like crumhorns, only softer and sweeter. He calls them *Corna-musen*. This term—an old bagpipe name— is very frequently met in Italian accounts of musical perform-ances in the second half of the sixteenth century. For instance at Munich, while Lassus was musical director there, the five-man team of Italian wind-players used to accompany the first course at dinner 'sometimes with *corna-muse*, sometimes with recorders, or with flutes, or cornetts and trombones in French songs and other light compositions' (from Trojano, 1569, a singer there, who adds that during the next course a string consort would play 'songs, motets or madrigals', and that finally, with the dessert, Lassus and his chosen singers would give a fresh work each day). The *corna-musa* was also used singly, in those strange mixed consorts that used to be put on towards the end of a programme (just as we today save up our more highly-coloured programme items for the second half of a concert). The following are three examples from Munich performances under Lassus:

1	2	3
harpsichord	4 viols	8 viols
trombone	4 great-consort	8 *viole da braccio*
recorder	recorders	(violins, violas,
lute	4 mixed wind:	cellos, etc.)
corna-musa	*dolzaina*	8 mixed wind:
mute cornett	*corna-musa*	*fagotto*
viol	flute	*corna-musa*
flute	mute cornett	mute cornett
		cornett
		tenor cornett
		flute
		dolzaina
		bass trombone

The instruments are listed in the above columns in the order in which Trojano gives them. In the first two columns the order possibly indicates the parts that the wind instruments were allotted to, reading downwards from bass to treble. The harpsichordist, and possibly the lutenist, in column 1 would have learnt the piece well enough to be able to support the ensemble in some manner anticipating the continuo of a few decades later. The titles of the compositions played by these consorts are unfortunately not recorded.

In two of these mixed consorts we find besides a *corna-musa*, a *dolzaina*. This is indicated in a brief account by Zacconi (1592) as having been another instrument of the same class, presumably some capped successor of the mysterious Renaissance douçaine. How it differed from the *corna-musa*, nobody knows. The douçaine-dolzaina class of instruments proves almost perversely mysterious. Of every other important Renaissance wind instrument several good pictures are known; yet of the douçaine, by all accounts one of the most important, we know not one definite illustration. Of every leading wind instrument of the sixteenth century we have not only pictures, but specimens; but of the dolzaina, so often mentioned, we have neither. Kinsky has, however, reasonably suggested that Praetorius's 'Cornamusen' (tail-less crumhorns) are really dolzainas, and that among Italian musicians *corna-musa* denoted something else, possibly the crumhorn, which is actually shown in the hands of the Munich musicians in a contemporary engraving by Hans Wagner.

Meanwhile, several German inventories, e.g. that of Berlin quoted earlier, mention a consort of *Schreierpfeifen* or *Schryari* ('crying' or 'screaming' pipes, fig. 62). These do not seem to occur in any known account of a musical performance, but Praetorius says that they could be used either alone or with other instruments. Here again we have non-overblowing capped pipes equal to the various recorders in size though sounding an octave lower; but they were 'strong and fresh' in sound. The tenor and bass sizes could have their nine-note compass extended upwards for two notes by two keys for finger I—keys also mentioned by Zacconi as an optional fitting to the dolzaina. Whether the tapered exterior of Praetorius's *Schreierpfeifen* betokens a contracting bore (an unusual thing in reed instruments) is impossible to say. In that event, the reed must have been of some very special kind. These may well have been organologically most interesting instruments and it is a pity that we know so little about their hidden detail. Sachs has suggested an Oriental origin.

Caps were also fitted to some *expanding-bore* chanters. The Berlin collection has a set from the church at Naumberg, and in France people liked to play a bagpipe chanter with a reed-cap instead of the bag—it sounded more lively that way, said Mersenne. Similarly, a kind of biniou-and-bombarde combination from Poitou was adapted for part-music by capping the bombarde (which played the tune an octave below the little biniou, as one may still hear in Brittany) and making special tenor and bass instruments to match. A detachment of these *hautbois et musettes de Poitou* was included in the French royal band and lasted there till Lully's time. They introduce the finale of his music to *Le Bourgeois Gentilhomme*.

Cornetts

Though known since the Middle Ages, the cornett, hybrid of woodwind and brass, hovered somewhat in the background until towards the end of the fifteenth century, when it was brought forward to take part in music of every kind, and to become, by the second half of the sixteenth century, the leading treble wind instrument of the day and the recognized instrument of the wind virtuoso.

The ordinary treble cornett (curved cornett, Plate XX) is made of plum, cherry or pear, following the primitive built-up construction outlined in the last chapter. After glueing up the two gouged-out halves, the outside is planed to an octagonal cross-section. Then the holes (six in front and a thumb-hole behind in the recorder position) are bored and slightly undercut. Finally the instrument is covered in thin black leather to preserve it. Sometimes the tube is bound in two or three places before glueing on the leather.[1]

At the narrow end, the socket for the mouthpiece is strengthened by a brass collar concealed under a silver or brass mount.

[1] The Christ Church cornetts, made in 1605, provide excellent specimen measurements for modern pitch. The bore diameters are taken from X-ray photographs by Eric Halfpenny (Plate XX):

Width at top, 19 mm.; at bottom, 38 mm. max. Thickness of walls, 5 mm. Diameter of holes (which are slightly undercut)—thumb-hole, 7 mm.; the rest, 8·5 mm. Mouthpiece socket, diameter, 11 mm., depth 19 mm. running into the bore without a step.

Distance from top end, along centre-line, in inches	Diameter of bore in millimetres, to nearest half-millimetre
0·8	7
3	9
6	11·5
8	14
9·9 (centre of thumb hole)	16
11·25 (,, hole I)	17·5
12·8 (,, ,, II)	20
14·5 (,, ,, III)	21·5
16·75 (,, ,, IV)	22·5
18·45 (,, ,, V)	24
20·2 (,, ,, VI)	25
22	27
25 (bottom end)	29

The cup-mouthpiece itself is of horn, ivory or bone, thin-rimmed and with a thread-lapped shank long enough to allow a little movement for tuning (Plate XXII). Players usually put the mouthpiece to the side of the mouth, where the lips are thinner.

Since there is no little-finger hole, the low *g*, bottom note of the old treble compass, was made by sounding the *a* (six fingers) with slack embouchure, and the note seems to have been used freely. The top note during the period was *a''*, but in the seventeenth century, the Germans, always altitude-record holders on wind instruments in former times, pushed it up to *d'''*.

The cornett's tone quality, as far as one can now attempt to reproduce it, combines a clear cup-mouthpiece tone, smaller and less ringing than the trumpet's, with the sweet, singing character of a woodwind instrument. In churches, where it was regularly played throughout the period to support the boys' voices, it must have rung with wonderful clarity—'like a ray of sunshine penetrating the gloom and darkness', wrote Mersenne. Another great point in favour of the cornett was its wide dynamic and expressive range. Altogether, it was praised in the very terms that were to be bestowed upon the oboe a hundred years later: it could be sounded as loud as a trumpet and as soft as a recorder, and its tone approached that of the human voice more nearly than that of any other instrument. Moreover, the flexible technique enabled the cornett player to excel in fast divisions; so also could his inseparable colleague, the trombonist: 'cornetts and trombones', writes Bottrigari in 1594 with the performances at Venice and Ferrara especially in mind, 'are played with such grace, taste and sure precision of the notes, that they are held the most excellent of the wind instruments in the profession. Their divisions are neither scrappy, nor so wild and involved that they spoil the underlying melody and the composer's design: but are introduced at such moments and with such vivacity and charm that they give the music the greatest beauty and spirit.' Among those whom Bottrigari heard, there would certainly have been Della Casa, whose specimen divisions have been quoted earlier.

On the other hand, as Mersenne points out, the *natural* tone of the cornett, when not sweetened by the player, is a little rough; and it seems that in England the instrument was less carefully controlled than, say, in Italy. In Campion's Masque at Whitehall in 1607, six cornetts, with six voices, were raised on a platform higher than the neighbouring string consorts, 'in respect of the pearcing sound of those instruments'. And fifty years later 'the cornet yieldeth a shrill-quakinge sound' (Sir P. Leycester), which suggests that on top of rough cornett-tone, the players were adding that quick, goaty vibrato that goes so characteristically with the instrument's modern brass-band namesake in England today.

Of the other sizes of cornett, (1) the *descant* or *cornettino*, 16·5 inches long, was used comparatively little and is rare in collections. (2) German inventories sometimes mention cornetts built one or two tones below the ordinary treble for use in church, e.g. on alto parts, and a few specimens have survived. (3) The *tenor cornett* (Plate XXIII), however, was used rather more, both when cornetts were played as a consort on their own (e.g. Walther's *Fugen* or canons, 1542, marked 'especially for cornetts', need a tenor for the bottom part), and also in mixed ensembles and wind bands. Its double-curved shape (length, 34 to 41 inches) brings the holes well under the fingers, and a key was often fitted to give a good *c*, the customary bottom note of tenor parts. The bore is proportionately wider than that of the treble cornett, presumably in order to favour the tone in the bottom register, though it gives the instrument a buglish quality that Praetorius did not like. He advised using a trombone if possible, and this was generally done. The union of cornett and trombones anyhow antedates the appearance of the tenor cornett by perhaps fifty years, and to the end of the cornett's musical lifetime its proper tenor, and bass too, was trombone; not deep cornett.

MUTE CORNETT. The straight cornett—a conical pipe turned and bored in boxwood in the straightforward way—was the principal German variety during the early part of the century, though later overshadowed by the curved form. But a special variety of it, the *mute cornett* (Plate XXIII), ranks as one of the most important and certainly one of the most beautiful of all the sixteenth-century wind instruments. Its bore expands from about 4 millimetres, beginning rather gradually. At the top end, there is cut a conical recess about 13 millimetres across and 9 millimetres deep, and this is the mouthpiece. With this primitive arrangement—practically the mouthpiece of the ancestral cow-horn and alp-horn—the ringing element is eliminated from the tone, which takes on a velvet, horn-like quality of indescribable beauty. The mute cornett was a favourite for blending with other instruments. Also it could be played extremely softly, and the unnamed Italian cornettist whom Giustiniani commended so highly for playing in balanced duet with a closed harpsichord may well have been using his mute cornett.

REVIVAL OF THE CORNETT. The cornett had become dropped from most music by the eighteenth century, either through its difficult technique, or through the success of the oboe as a solo wind instrument. Yet it survived in some local bands in Germany, and it is one of the tragedies of wind history that the live art of cornett-playing might have been handed down to us without a break, had it not been for the short gap in time separating two occurrences in the last century. In 1840 Kastner, the French composer and music historian, actually witnessed the town band of cornett and three trombones still playing their daily chorales in the old German manner from the church tower at Stuttgart. A mere thirty years later, Mahillon and Gevaert in Brussels had begun to turn their attention to the revival of extinct wind instruments demanded by the scores of ancient composers and one of these was the cornett, by that time evidently totally extinct save as a collector's piece. Mahillon therefore decided to construct a cornett of 'modernized' form (for Gluck's *Orfeo*): straight, with five keys for the semitones and the mouthpiece of a modern brass cornet. It did not work, however, and subsequent attempts to master the cornett—needed so badly, for example, in Monteverdi performances—have been made with facsimiles of originals. In this field Otto Steinkopf, of Berlin, is undoubtedly the pre-eminent performer.

Otherwise, the usual substitute for cornett is the trumpet, though the oboe has also been tried, while a soprano saxophone is perhaps best of all.

Curtals[1]

This term denotes the bassoon in its original form, made in one piece and looking like a large torch (Plate XXI, fig. 61).

The embyro of the bassoon can be seen in the early bagpipe in Plate XIX: half-way down the long drone there is a thick piece containing three parallel drillings that conduct the cylindrical bore down, up and down again, saving a foot or more in the overall length of the drone. Such doubling back of the tube is quite common in bagpipes, and the idea may well have originated in them. During the sixteenth century it came to be employed in various cylindrical-bore consort instruments that will be described later (sordone, racket, etc.). In the curtal, which first appears in written records about 1540, the bore that is doubled back, down and up again, is the conical bore of a shawm. Most curtals were bored out in a single piece of maple or pear of oval cross-section: but some were made in two halves, cornett-wise, including a fine example in the Frankfurt Museum, covered in gold-embossed leather.

The chief curtal was the bass size, about 39 inches tall, commonly known in England as *double curtal*, and in Germany as *Chorist-fagott* (being the size most employed in church music, e.g. as bass to cornetts and trombones). It has the pitch of our bassoon. On the front there are six holes and the F key: on the back, two thumb-holes and one key, giving E, D and C (the bottom note). Some are made left-handed. The reed was like a bassoon reed except for indication (e.g. in Mersenne) that it was sometimes made with a staple, like a modern cor anglais reed. The tone was also bassoon-like, though rather bottom-heavy, and in some instruments an attempt was made to remedy this by 'covering' with a perforated bell cap, foreshadowing

[1] Like *bombarde*, the name is borrowed from artillery; *curtal*, also *double curtal*, had previously denoted a type of short-barrelled cannon (O.E.D.). The German alternative name *Dulzian* must not be confused with Italian *dulzaina* (see earlier in this chapter). Around 1700, 'curtal' was sometimes used in England to denote the true bassoon.

some modern bassoon mutes. Praetorius states (and experiment confirms) that the upper register was practicable up to the *g'*.

Like other instruments of the period, curtals were also made in small and large sizes, but it seems that other than the ordinary bass size, only the quart-bass (53 inches or more) was commonly employed in music. The bassoon has never shone in

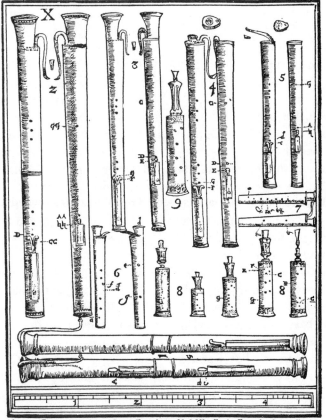

FIG. 61. *Praetorius:* 1. *Bass sordone (front and back).* 2 to 7. *Curtals or* Fagotten (2, *great-bass;* 3, *open* chorist; 4, *covered* chorist; 5, *covered tenor, evidently also called* Korthold; 6, *treble;* 7, *descant*). 8. *Rackets.* 9. *Great-bass racket descending to* C'.

small sizes. These produce a plaintive tone, deficient in body, though Schütz requires a tenor curtal (*c.* 26 inches, lowest note, *G*) in his setting of the Twenty-fourth Psalm. The midget curtals—the treble (18 inches) and the rare descant (14 inches) —seem to have been used only in certain countries (Germany and Spain) when something a little softer than shawms was required for use in church. There are trebles at Berlin and Brussels; also Augsburg, where the Maximilian Museum has a whole set including octave-bass, 73″ tall.

The pervading *deepness* of the sixteenth-century consort reed instruments is altogether a most curious thing. None of the usual types could reach the higher notes of the treble stave (the shawm could do so, and so could the bagpipe, but these were not used in the musical consorts). It was rather as if our own woodwind had grown to consist of ordinary flutes on the one hand, and only deep basset horns, heckelphones and bassoons on the other. Praetorius describes a promising-looking consort of oboe-like *bassanelli* (fig. 62) and several German courts owned a set of them: with double reed, straight-through conical bore, and soft tone. But they were deeper-sounding than ever; the bottom note (seven fingers) of each size was a fourth lower than that of the corresponding normal consort size, thus: in the treble (32 inches high less crook), *d*; tenor (44 inches), *G*; bass (64 inches), *C*. A kind of consort of bass oboes; and the rackets, mentioned in the next section, were even deeper.

Reed instruments with doubled-back cylindrical bores

These are first definitely reported in the later part of the sixteenth century. The chief of them was an instrument called *sordone* (or *Sordun*) in Italy and Germany, and *courtaut* in France: a wooden pillar (in France said to have been commonly obtained from old pilgrim's staves) with a narrow cylindrical bore running down and then up again and terminating in a plain side-vent near the top (fig. 62, 8). In the only surviving specimens—the bass and great-bass instruments from Ambras in the Museum at Vienna (Plate XXI)—the bores are 8 and 10 millimetres respectively. The reed was taken in the lips (though no. 7 in fig. 62 shows an exceptional form) and the tone, says Praetorius, resembled that of the tail-less crumhorns (i.e. a softish droning).

As with the capped instruments, the compass was limited to

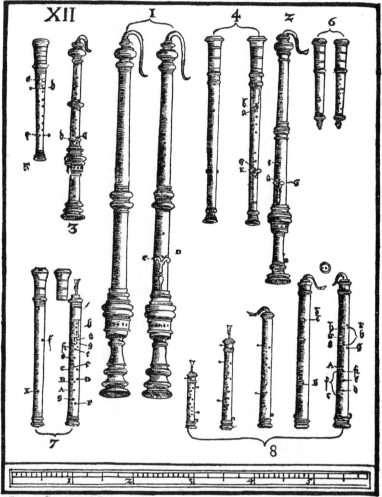

1 Bass vom Bassanelli 2 Tenor- und Alt-Bassanelli. 3 Discant-Bassanelli 4 Bass vom Schryari.
5 Tenor, Alt Schryari 6 Cant Schryari 7 Kortholt oder Kurz-Pfeiff 8 Ein ganz Stimmverk von Sordunen.

FIG. 62. *Praetorius*: 1 to 3. *Bassanelli*. 4 to 6. *Schreierpfeiffen*.
7. 'Kortholt' (*here a kind of capped courtaut or sordone*).
8. *Sordoni*.

the fundamentals and the highest hole was a thumb-hole. Consequently there was only one thumb left free to manipulate the ascending bore (in which were the holes for the deep diapasons) instead of two free thumbs as with a curtal or bassoon. The difficulty was neatly overcome, without recourse to key-work, by arranging most of the diapason holes as side holes, communicating with the ascending bore but covered with the little fingers and the middle joints of the first fingers. Following normal sixteenth-century practice, each side hole was duplicated on the opposite side to accommodate a left-handed player (surplus holes being waxed up), while on the courtaut shown by Mersenne the side holes are brought up into a better position by means of short projecting tubes called 'teats'. In the Vienna specimens, however, the side holes are covered by keys. The detail of the fingering varied. On Praetorius's sordoni (*Sordunen*, fig. 62), if we consider the tenor size with a right-handed player, the right little finger gives *c* (as on tenor recorder). Then, the right thumb gives *B♭*; the middle joint of finger IV gives *A*; the left little finger, *G*; and the middle joint of finger I, *F*, the lowest of these four diapasons. In France, the instrument was used with other wind instruments, particularly, says Mersenne, as bass to musettes. An instance of its employment in Germany is in a pavan that was played at the Cassel court on mute cornett, recorder, trombone, *sordone*, and bass viol (a copy of the music is in the British Museum, Add. MS. 33295).

The idea of the redoubled tube was carried a stage further in the *rackets* (fig. 61, 8), whose sound reminded Praetorius of a comb and paper. In the tenor racket, a five-inch tall cylinder of wood or ivory was bored with nine vertical drillings with about six-millimetre bore. These were connected in series to make up some 42 inches of total tubing, giving as bottom note *C*. On the bass it was *F*. Thus in contrast to the recorders, which sounded an octave above the written parts ('four-foot tone', as organists say), the rackets sounded an octave *below* ('sixteen-foot tone'). Finger-holes communicated with the drillings as required, and again the middle joints, as well as the tips, of certain fingers were employed to cover them. Sound was generated with a bassoon-like reed. Plate XXIII shows a latish example. A person playing the racket is seen in a painting of Lassus with his Munich musicians, reproduced in Hamel and Hürlimann, *Das Atlantisbuch der Musik.*

A length of cylindrical *metal* tubing can of course be bent into any shape you fancy. With this material it was but a short step from the eccentric ingenuity manifested in the racket, to carnival novelties and fanciful presents, like the quartet of small double-reed dragons (*Tartolde*) at Vienna, and the following consort listed in the Stuttgart 1589 inventory under the section 'war instruments':

'Eight pieces, viz.:

2 bass, one a boar lance, the other a musket
2 tenor, one a halberd, the other an axe
2 alto, one a crossbow, the other a broadsword
2 trebles, each a club'.

The Shawm band

With this we move into a different musical world, since in the sixteenth century the shawm was exclusively a band instrument. But it should not be forgotten in our general musical picture of those times merely because it was not admitted to the art of the consorts. Indeed of all musical sounds that from day to day smote the ears of a sixteenth-century town resident, the deafening skirl of the shawm band in palace courtyard or market square must have been the most familiar, save perhaps only for the throbbing of a lute through somebody's open window. A European town in the sixteenth-century must have sounded like present-day Barcelona or Gerona on a Sunday morning.

Since the fifteenth-century, the shawm, like other instruments, had developed a bass size. The bass shawm (German, *bass Pommer*) is a splendid instrument, six feet tall, and played with the bell resting on the ground to the side of the player. Unlike the smaller shawms it was played without a pirouette, with a reed like that of the curtal. The tone is fat and warm right down to the bottom *C*, and not unlike that of a modern German bassoon, though considerably stronger. But it is purely a bass instrument, and the tone rapidly falls away to a hoarse wheezing when one tries to ascend above *b* or *c'*. Like the other shawms it was very stoutly built to withstand the rough usage it received. Documents relating to the Augsburg town band reveal the sort of things that went on, as when, for instance, a dispute among the men reached a climax upon one of them aiming a blow at the bandmaster's son's head with a bass shawm—a thing that no modern bandsman would dare do with his instrument under any provocation.

Being employed in this ambit of their own, shawms deviated from the ordinary wind practice in several small matters: (1) The component sizes of a set were aligned rather differently, the treble having descant pitch.[1] (2) Extension or diapason keys were often fitted to quite small sizes to increase their availability on lower parts (e.g. the four-keyed tenor shown

[1] Approximate dimensions of treble shawm (Brussels Conservatoire Museum No. 176; Plate XXIII). For its reed, cf. Chapter IV, *The Shawm Today*.

Brass staple: 2 inches long; bore, 0·3 to 0·5 mm.

Wooden pirouette: 1·3 inches long; width at top, 1·2 inches (but cf. the larger pirouette in Plate XXII).

Body: width at top, 43 mm. Below this a slight waist, and then very gradual widening until the bell flare. Bell mouth, 4·5 inches.

Bore		Holes	
Distance from top of body, in inches	Diameter of bore, mm.	Distance of centres from top of body, in inches	Approximate diameter of hole, in mm.
at top	10 (socket)	I 3·9	5
1	5	II 5·3	5·5
3	7	III 6·7	6·5
6	9	IV 8·1	7·5
10	12	V 9·4	9
14	15	VI 10·7	8
16	17·5	VII 11·8 (offset)	8
18	21	dorsal vent 13·3	—
20	27	twin lateral vents 16·1	—
22	31	dorsal vent 19·4	—
bell (26)	90		

in fig. *63*). (3) The band seems to have bodily transposed its music a tone up. This arose from the fact that neither cross-fingering nor half-holing would give a satisfactory f' on the treble shawm. But by reading a tone higher this vital keynote fell on the excellent cross-fingering $\dots$ / . o . (actual sound, g').

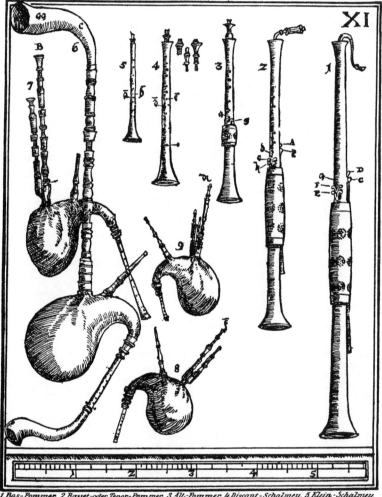

1. Bas-Pommer. 2. Basset-oder Tenor-Pommer. 3. Alt-Pommer. 4. Discant-Schalmey. 5. Klein-Schalmey.
6. Großer Bock. 7. Schäper Pfeiff. 8. Hümmelchen. 9. Dudey.

FIG. 63. *Praetorius:* 1 to 5, *Shawms.* 6 to 9, *Bagpipes.*

TABLE OF SIXTEENTH-CENTURY SHAWMS

The instruments cited in the right-hand column will give some idea of the various shawm pitches (actual sounds): i.e. six fingers on the treble shawm sounds e', as against d' on the oboe.

Number in Fig. 63	French and (?) English usage	German	Lowest note		Approximate body length		Instrument of approx. equivalent pitch
			1-key model	4-key model	1-key (inches)	4-key (inches)	
5	—	Small discant	a' (g')	—	19	—	Ciaramella, Highland bagpipe
4	Treble shawm	Discant Schalmey	d'	—	27	—	A tone above oboe
3	Tenor shawm	Alt-pommer	g	d	30	36	A tone above cor anglais
2	—	Tenor- or basset-pommer	c	G	43	51	Heckel-phone
1	Bass shawm	Bass-pommer	—	C	—	73	Bassoon
-	—	Great bass pommer	—	G' or F'	—	96–116	—

Of these sizes, No. 2 was fairly well known in Germany. In France a trombone took its place, and as for England, we simply do not know. But even in Germany, sizes 1, 3 and 4 seem to have been the most employed, and the following is a typical combination for the sixteenth- and early seventeenth-century shawm band:

1st treble	treble shawm
2nd ,,	cornett
alto	tenor shawm (No. 3)
tenor	,, ,, ,,
quintus	tenor trombone
bass	bass shawm

The French royal band was like this but had two players to each part, and fig. 64 shows a specimen of its music, played at the coronation of Louis XIII in Rheims Cathedral in 1610 (from Vol. I of the Philidor MSS., Bibliothèque nationale, Paris). At first sight it is not a distinguished piece. Yet it would be hard to imagine anything that suited the band better, and made its contribution to the solemnities more memorable. With the

Fig. 64. *A ceremonial pavan for shawm band, 1610 (Philidor MSS., Vol. I; Paris, Bibliothèque nationale).*

finer tricks of the composer's art kept down to a bare minimum, the piece represents ceremonial wind music in its purest tradition.

For other specimens of shawm band music, there are the wait's tunes listed by L. G. Langwill in *Hinrichsen's Musical Yearbook* for 1952, p. 178. Most of them are late seventeenth century, and would have been done on a four-piece band of treble shawm, two tenor shawms and bass trombone. Mr Langwill includes a rare original picture of them.

CHAPTER XI

The Eighteenth Century and the Classical Woodwind

The wind instruments of the consorts, described in the previous chapter, were succeeded, during the latter part of the seventeenth century, by the instruments of the woodwind. These are the products of the new era in the arts, and they included a new recorder and a new flute; the new French invention, the oboe; a new bassoon to replace the old curtal; and to these was added in due course a new German invention, the clarinet. The present chapter is devoted mainly to the classic eighteenth-century forms that these instruments soon attained—the designs that Handel and Bach, Haydn and Mozart knew and wrote for in music that remains so many wind players' best-loved music even today.

Specimens of the classical woodwind are naturally far commoner than specimens from the consort period. Many hundreds of them survive, not only in museums, but also, including many of the finest, in private collections, while fresh specimens continually come to light in small music shops, antique shops and auction rooms. Here an experienced collector knows how to distinguish true eighteenth-century instruments from the more common nineteenth-century specimens that often bear a superficial resemblance to them, the first thing that he looks for being the maker's name, generally stamped on an instrument. (A list of the chief English makers is given in Appendix 1.) Most eighteenth-century specimens date from towards the end of the century, but now and then an instrument from the Handel period turns up, adding zest to the collector's search.

Having found specimens and put them in order, the next thing to do is to explore their musical character. Much work has been done on this recently, and it may be claimed that practical musical research can seldom have proved more rewarding. Elementary though the old instruments appear to the eye, inwardly they are very subtle. Modern instruments possess many qualities that the old ones do not, but the converse is also true, and as one works patiently at the 'antiques' they reveal musical beauties that fully explain how it was that Mozart and the rest were able to put them to such superlative use. Certainly they are not easy to master. But in this connection we need only cite the case of the modern French bassoon, which, as we saw in Chapter VI, still lies so close to the woodwind of classical times in its technical feel. Of this instrument, Cecil Forsyth has written '. . . and imperfect it remains to the present day. This, however, is no drawback to the instrument. On the contrary, it has thrown on the instrumentalists the same responsibilities in the way of intonation as those incurred by the String-player. The consequence is that a good Bassoon-player is continually on the watch to overcome the natural deficiencies of his instrument, and however uncomfortable this mode of life may be to him, the artistic results are good beyond question.' Well, in the eighteenth century, the flute, the oboe and the clarinet were like that too.

Pitch. Most of the original woodwind models were evolved in Paris, and this is presumably why a French instrumental pitch, approx. $a' = 422$ (very nearly a semitone lower than modern pitch), became virtually a standard European pitch for the first part of the eighteenth century. But later in the century, though some institutions kept this pitch, the majority were playing sharper. For instance, a Paris bassoon player wrote in 1780 (in La Borde's *Essai*) that instruments by the old makers of the time of Rameau could still be used at the Opéra, but not at the *Concerts Spirituels*, where the pitch had risen. Most of the later English specimens are only a shade, if that, below modern pitch, and play well at this pitch with practice, suitable reeds and so on.

Jean Hotteterre

By the middle of the seventeenth century the prestige of wind playing had in most places sadly declined. The chosen instrument of the new musical styles initiated by the Italians was the violin; the only wind instrument that Italian composers came to employ with any enthusiasm was the trumpet, then comparatively a novelty in concerted music.

So the boy Lully, who was to become the first composer for the woodwind, no doubt set out for Paris with no better opinion than other Italians as to the possibilities of wooden wind instruments. What he saw there on arrival may not have immediately caused him to change his opinion; but he would certainly have recognized it as something that he had never conceived of before. In France the recorder was by no means one of the instruments 'of inferior kind' as Sir Peter Leycester noted it in England at that very time in his commonplace book. Nor was the bagpipe played only by the 'more Rusticall sorte of People'. Both were on the road to becoming the fashionable instruments of Parisian society. The recorder, we know. The bagpipe was the satin-covered, bellows-blown French parlour pipe, *musette*. Important people around the court had lessons on them and took them on picnics. Professionals featured them in the pastoral ballets. The musette especially; its rising vogue was coupled with that for provincial dances, as the bourrée and the gavotte—dances that are still played on bagpipes in parts of France today—while allied to it, in the royal band, there already existed that combination of vividly French regional character, the *hautbois et musettes de Poitou* mentioned in the last chapter. This peculiar spirit gave to French wind-instrument-making a stimulus that could be matched nowhere else at that time. It offered it a new direction, and instead of plodding on with the manufacture of the old consort and band instruments, the makers began to turn to remodellings and inventions along fresh lines.

Working in Paris about the time of Lully's arrival was a group of turners and woodwind-makers among whom the best-remembered today is Jean Hotteterre. He came from the Normandy village La Couture-Boussey, near Evreux, where wood-turning was the village craft and has remained so, with special reference to woodwind manufacture, ever since; Buffet, Louis Lot and Thibouville are noted modern firms who began there. Unfortunately, this crucial period in the seventeenth century is poorly documented from our present point of view, making it impossible for us to say definitely which individual maker or player was responsible for each of the vital woodwind inventions that originated during that time, all of them apparently in France and probably within that circle of Paris makers among whom we can dimly discern Hotteterre as the leader. The new products included: the recorder as we know it today; the conical flute; the oboe; and the true bassoon (as opposed to the old curtal). In other words, practically the entire woodwind of the eighteenth-century orchestra—an astonishing output for one small group of men. What was the approach that enabled them to achieve it?

The first thing we notice about the new designs is that in every case the instrument is constructed in several short joints, instead of as far as possible all in one piece as formerly. We notice also the characteristically ornamental appearance of the instruments, largely due to fashionable Renaissance turnery applied to the thickenings left in the wood or ivory to give strength to the sockets where the various joints met. This second feature therefore arises out of the first (and we may also find it on earlier instruments in which jointed construction had been toyed with though without establishing any lasting design, as in the bassanelli; also in the top and bottom caps of the sordone in Plate XXI).

But the Hotteterre multi-piece construction is further distinguished by a curious *internal* feature, namely, that the bore has a broken profile. It may change from joint to joint—e.g. cone and cylinder may meet end to end, or the bores of two joints may make an abrupt step where they meet. Such bore-construction naturally has some acoustic effect, but this is not a vital one. Thus, in our present instruments, we have kept all the Hotteterre joints, but have in nearly every case abandoned this feature of the Hotteterre bores; and although these bores successfully gave the musical results desired at the time, it is hard to imagine that their irregular profiles were arrived at through deliberate experiment in pursuit of musical objectives. They are, rather, distinctly primitive, and it is likely that the Hotteterres fell naturally into this way of construction because Jean Hotteterre was above all a bagpiper and bagpipe-maker.

In bagpipe-making, turning in short joints already had a long tradition, since socketed joints are needed at the stocks and in the tuning slides of the drones. And stepped bores are met in drones, and also in chanters when a separate bell is fitted. Jean Hotteterre, besides making instruments, played the musette in the court ballets, and was the bagpiper in the *hautbois de Poitou* group of the royal wind band establishment. No doubt before then, back in La Couture, he had made musettes and other bagpipes for the neighbourhood, for there were few country districts in seventeenth-century Europe where the bagpipe was not still the staple instrument for 'dances, weddings and other diversions' (Mersenne). His recorder design—probably the earliest of the important woodwind remodellings, and the design we follow today—seems to show the hand of a bagpipe-maker, especially with its cylindrical head joint, which, whatever its acoustical effect might be, takes after the chanter stock of a musette as if meant to match it. There are two of his recorders in the Paris Conservatoire Museum. But it was his next venture that laid the foundation of our woodwind.

The Oboe

Now and then an old shawm, called in France '*hautbois*', from the royal band would come into his workshop for repair or replacement. We might wonder what he and his colleagues used to think of its antique, monolithic build when they compared it with the neat elegance of their musette chanters. Anyway, they evidently set about designing an improvement on it according to their own ideas; a *new* hautbois that would be altogether more useful in the kinds of music coming into fashion. It would be flexible in dynamic range, and would possess a really good upper register—a register that had previously been badly neglected in reed instruments, but was now urgently required by the new musical styles.

No doubt experimental models appeared first, and certain curious instruments preserved in museums (e.g. at Paris) may commemorate some of them. The design that was eventually achieved—the oboe that Purcell and Handel came to know—had a bore only a little narrower than the average bore of a treble shawm, but made in three joints, with steps at the sockets (most noticeably at the bell socket, where the bore may suddenly enlarge by as much as three millimetres). The desired results in the upper register were secured mainly through finger-holes of reduced size in conjunction with a reed a good half-centimetre narrower at the tip than in that of the shawm (the earliest known width for an oboe reed is 9·5 millimetres, mentioned by Talbot in about 1696) and made, as it still is, on a staple inserted bagpipe-wise directly into the top joint of the instrument, the shawm pirouette being dispensed with. Since the new instrument was destined for playing with other concert instruments, its pitch was lowered by a tone, making the keys of C and F practicable at concert pitch, which they had not properly been on the treble shawm. In mechanism, there was at first only the C key, but to this was soon added the E♭ key to give that semitone above the six-finger note which is so bad on reed instruments as a half-holing. For a long time, this key was duplicated for left-handers, making the *three-keyed oboe* (but after about 1760 the duplicate key was usually omitted, making a *two-keyed oboe*). In most instruments, holes III and IV were twin holes, to help G♯ and F♯ (see the chart, fig. 66).

Thus, we may surmise in the absence of specific information, came about the invention of the oboe. As for the date, H. Prunières, Lully's modern editor, and Joseph Marx, who has recently made a valuable investigation of the subject, concur in the suggestion that it was very probably in 1657, in Lully's ballet *L'Amour malade*, that Jean Hotteterre and his colleague Philidor first publicly performed in the orchestra on the new instrument, and in doing so inaugurated the woodwind era.

From the first the oboe was a success, and as it quickly

became known in other countries it seems to have impressed musicians above all through the splendid expressive range of its sound. To the trumpet were allotted airs of joyous and brilliant character; to the flutes, those of the 'languishing and melancholy' kind; but the new oboe, like the human voice and the

FIG. 65. *An ornamented adagio for oboe or violin; Babell, London, 1726. The double tick indicates a trill.*

violin, could encompass every mood. In the matter of volume alone, it could be played nearly as loud as the trumpet and yet as soft as the recorder (as the *Sprightly Companion* of 1695 tells us —the first known oboe tutor, ascribed to Bannister). It had 'all the sweetness of the flute [recorder]' with a 'greater strength and variety of notes' (the *Tatler*, 1710), and about that same time Kytsch, the chief of Handel's earlier oboists in London, used to be engaged at two or three private parties every evening 'to play opera songs, etc., etc., which he executed with exquisite taste and feeling' (Burney, in Rees's Cyclopedia). Fig. 65, from a contemporary set of printed studies for oboe or violin, shows how Kytsch might have dealt with an adagio.[1]

Trials with well-preserved specimens of the early oboe wholly corroborate these assessments of its quality, and also tell us more. Its mean level of loudness is if anything less than that of the modern oboe; indeed Quantz, Frederick the Great's renowned flute-master, warned orchestral oboists to hold the instrument well up lest the sound be lost in the music stand—and yet orchestras were then softer than they are today. In character, the tone possesses a sweet, sympathetic quality that enables the instrument to blend in with other instruments just as naturally as the modern French oboe stands out in sharp relief; both are good instruments, but designed for different music, and nobody who has heard 'baroque' chamber music done with a well-played eighteenth-century oboe will ever again quite so much look forward to hearing it performed with a modern one.

A minor flaw in the tone of the Purcell-Handel oboe is a trace of huskiness, which became eradicated in later eighteenth-century designs chiefly through narrowing of the bore. Well-known to collectors is the English straight-topped model (Plate XXX), current from the 1760s to the 1790s. Vincent, pupil and successor of the celebrated San Martini and the last of the great Handelian oboists, adopted this model in his latter days. The bore is only slightly reduced, but the sound seems to become brighter. An English popular tutor of this period encourages the student to aim for the sound of a well-played violin, but by some accounts (e.g. Parke's) this model tended to sound a little too bright and penetrating. Meanwhile,

[1] In England, in the eighteenth century, the instrument was called *hautboy* or *hoboy*, words which, like *hautbois* in French, had previously denoted the shawm. These English names preserve the old French pronunciation of *hautbois*, as does also (as Sachs points out) the Italian name *oboe* (three syllables), which has since become the English word, though it sounds very odd with the English pronunciation of it. *Hoboy* was a much better word.

Fischer had arrived in England, bringing with him a Continental model which supplanted the straight-topped model towards the end of the century. This is the true classical oboe (Plate XXIV). It is easily recognized by the onion-like bulge at the top end and by its yellow, unstained boxwood (the earlier instruments having generally been stained dark brown with acid). Its bore is remarkably narrow—from a half to one millimetre less than that of a modern oboe—and its natural tone closely resembles that of the present Viennese oboe.

Fischer's playing was reported in those varying terms that will sound familiar to every full-blooded virtuoso on this extraordinarily expressive instrument. Some described his tone as uncommonly sweet, though capable of great power, but Mozart on one occasion wrote that 'his tone is entirely nasal, and his held notes like the tremulant of the organ' (Emily Anderson, *The Letters of Mozart and his Family*; as for 'tremulant', it is interesting to find that Garnier, the first oboe professor at the Paris Conservatoire, describes a shaking—*frémissement*—of the lips for a vibrato). Mozart's own favourite oboist was Ramm of the Mannheim orchestra, said to have had a beautifully pure and round tone, and unrivalled technique running effortlessly up to the top F, while his delivery of adagios was full of feeling and spirit. Mozart wrote the oboe quartet for Ramm and also gave him a concerto (believed to be the now-published one in C) which he played so frequently that it became, the composer said, 'Ramm's warhorse'. Like Fischer, Ramm would have played the narrow-bore oboe, possibly one of Grundmann's of Dresden, for these were especially admired in Germany. Of the playing of Bach's principal oboist at Leipzig, Gleditsch, no criticism seems to be recorded; but in the obbligati written for him to play, this humble town-bandsman is commemorated until the end of time.

The *reeds* used with the eighteenth-century oboes are known to have varied considerably among the players, but they all seem to have been broader than today, measuring from 8 to 10 millimetres (as against the modern average of 7 millimetres). The reeds shown in Plate VI include two out of several English reeds found with oboes of the straight-topped and narrow-bore kinds. They are made on unsoldered staples (as bagpipe reeds are still) and one is stamped with the name of a professional reed-maker, Taylor. The blades are scraped with the traditional

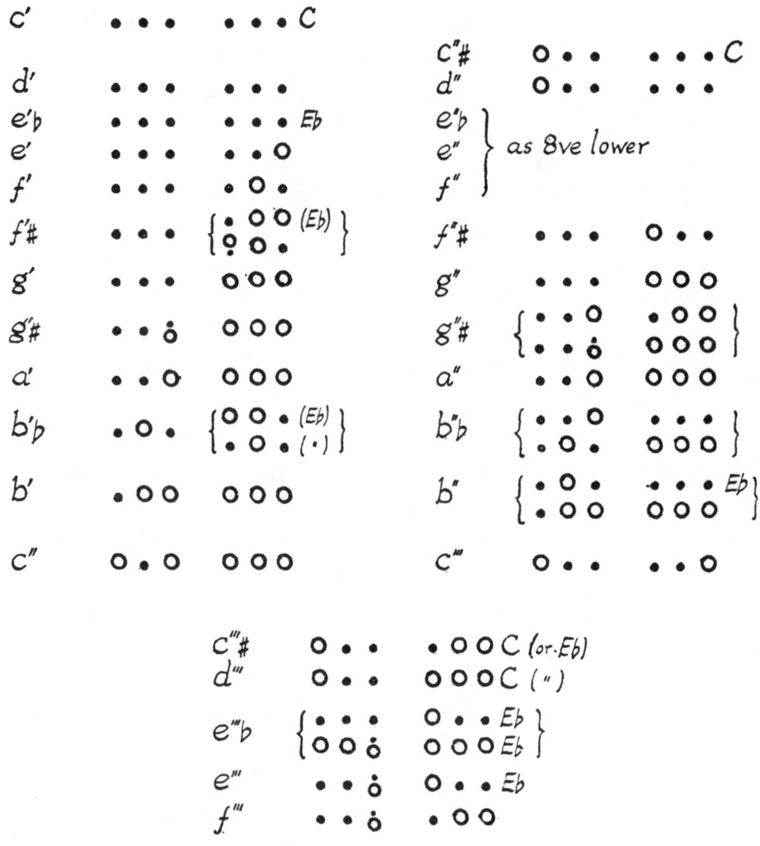

```
c'    • • •   • • • C          c"#   ○ • •   • • • C
d'    • • •   • • •            d"    ○ • •   • • •
e'♭   • • •   • • • E♭         e'♭  ⎫
e'    • • •   • • ○            e"   ⎬ as 8ve lower
f'    • • •   • ○ •            f"   ⎭
f'#   • • •  { • ○ ○ (E♭) }    f"#   • • •   ○ • •
                 ○ ○ •
g'    • • •   ○ ○ ○            g"    • • •   ○ ○ ○
g'#   • • ○̇   ○ ○ ○            g"#  { • • ○   • ○ ○ }
                                     { • • ○̇   ○ ○ ○ }
a'    • • ○   ○ ○ ○            a"    • • ○   ○ ○ ○
b'♭   • ○ •  { ○ ○ • (E♭) }    b'♭  { • • ○   • • • }
                { ○ ○ • (·) }        { • ○ •   ○ ○ ○ }
b'    • ○ ○   ○ ○ ○            b"   { • ○ •   • • • E♭}
                                     { • ○ ○   ○ ○ ○ }
c"    ○ • ○   ○ ○ ○            c"'   ○ • •   • • ○

              c"'#   ○ • •   • ○ ○ C (or.E♭)
              d'"    ○ • •   ○ ○ ○ C ( " )
              e'"♭  { • • •   ○ • • E♭ }
                     { ○ ○ ○̇   ○ ○ ○ E♭ }
              e'"    • • ○̇   ○ • • E♭
              f'"    • • ○̇   • ○ ○
```

FIG. 66. *Practical chart for two-keyed (or three-keyed) oboe, collated from contemporary sources. (The top two semitones are not given for the early and the straight-topped models.)*

bagpipe V-scrape that most French players still retain, but much further back, e.g. to 15 millimetres from the tip down the centre. Experiment shows that if successful results are to be obtained from the old oboe, with its peculiar bore and the player's reliance on cross-fingering for so many of the notes, a reed of this kind, or something approaching it, is essential. With the narrow, short-scraped present-day reeds, the old instrument is hopelessly erratic, but a reasonably satisfactory reed can be made from modern oboe cane so long as it is suitably shaped and the blades are scraped well back.

TENOR OBOE. Under Louis XIV, a new venture in military music was the establishment of regimental bands using the new oboes with side drums. The bassoon supplied the bass, and above this, to strengthen the harmony on the parade ground, Lully and other composers arranged three oboe parts instead of the orchestral two. Many of the marches and salutes are preserved in the Philidor manuscripts at Paris; several of them are printed in Kastner's *Manuel général de musique militaire*. In some marches all three oboe parts lie within the compass of the oboe itself; but in others the third part goes lower, having been written for the *tenor oboe*, in French *taille des hautbois*, or for short, simply *taille* ('tenor'). It stood a fifth below the ordinary oboe, with lowest note *f*.

Most other countries adopted the instrument for use in this same kind of band. Plate XXX shows a typical early Continental model, with the bell flared on the outside but hollowed to a bulbous cavity inside, foreshadowing the cor anglais bell. A bulbous bell is a very ancient and primitive thing, having its origin perhaps in the gourd bells of many primitive trumpets; but here, on the tenor oboe, it simply once again reveals the bagpipe strain in the oboe family. In the Italian bagpipe *zampogna*, for instance, the two chanters are often made in this way, flared on the outside but bulbous inside (see also the Spanish drone, fig. 50). The reason for fitting bulbous bells to tenor oboes is not known. Possibly such a bell was felt to give a resonance that helped to bridge the band's tone-colour gap between oboe and bassoon. During the eighteenth century in England, the bulb was discarded, leaving the tenor oboe or 'vox humana' with a plain and very narrow bell.

One of the best pieces for the oboe band is 'The Queen's Farewell' (fig. 67), written for Queen Mary's funeral by Paisible, one of the men who first brought the oboe over from

France. Its rich, almost Purcellian minor harmony has a nobly funereal effect on the snarl of four of the old instruments blown good and strong, including two-keyed tenor oboe on the third

Fig. 67. 'The Queen's Farewell'; Paisible, 1694 (from The Sprightly Companion). *To play tenor on cor anglais, read as treble clef in key of F.*

part and bassoon on the bass. On the other hand, the band might have been *muted*. Muting of wind instruments began with the trumpet, which was muted with a wooden mute at least as early as the sixteenth century for sounding military calls while close to the enemy, e.g. at sieges. Muting for funerals came afterwards, and was extended to the oboe band. There is a moving allusion to it in the St Luke Passion ascribed to Bach. In the entombment scene, every now and then the strings (marked *con molto lamento*) leave off to let through the phrases of a chorale played on the usual four-piece oboe band marked (in German) '*piano,* with the oboes even muted with paper'. Several earlier eighteenth-century opera composers demanded muted oboes occasionally (and Keiser, in *Otto,* muted bassoon). Besides paper, wool was used, pushed into the bell, not far enough to block the vent holes. Also one or two wooden oboe mutes have survived—solid pear-shaped objects to be jammed in the bell-mouth. These mutes are surprisingly effective, making the oboe whimper most pathetically.

DEUTSCHE SCHALMEY. Briefly to be noticed before leaving the subject of oboe bands, is a curious combination that immediately preceded general adoption of oboes by German regiments, i.e. from about 1680 to 1720. It consisted of two treble shawms of entirely new pattern, with a tenor shawm to match and an old-style curtal for the bass. This new shawm, described as *Deutsche Schalmey* (Plate XXX), was slender and graceful in build, not at all resembling the old pattern, and according to Talbot it was sweeter in sound. The pitch of the treble (24 inches long) was six fingers $=c'$ at the old high pitch. This was its lowest note, for the barrel was purely ornamental, having nothing beneath it but a large vent hole. The tenor, however, had the usual key here. Both were played with a pirouette, but the reed of the treble (from Talbot's measurements), was as narrow as an oboe reed, and the bore—in surviving specimens—is narrower than that of the narrowest two-keyed oboes. Possibly it represents a German attempt at a quick answer to the new French oboe. Specimens of these *deutsche Schalmeyen* are commoner in museums than specimens of the standard shawms of the earlier period, and must not be mistaken for them. The two instruments sound entirely different.

The Bassoon

Of the bass reed instruments that appeared under the Hotteterre régime, one did not last. This was a kind of bass oboe, straight, about 42 inches long, with a bassoon-like crook. It was three-jointed and ornamentally turned like an oboe, and holes I, III, IV and VI were covered with open keys to reduce the stretch for the hands; a sort of anticipation of the heckelphone, evidently meant to take the bass part in pastoral ensembles of musettes, recorders, 'cromornes', etc. One illustration of it is on the title-page of Borjon's musette tutor (1672). No actual specimen is known, but resembling it in many ways are those instruments in museums usually labelled 'basse de musette', though these have stouter bodies and bells. Their date and purpose have never been discovered, though there is evidence that links them with old churches in Switzerland.

The name *basson* already occurs at the beginning of the seventeenth century as a name for the curtal. But Mersenne describes as *basson* a special type of bass curtal with the bell lengthened to reach B'♮, presumably in order to match the compass of Louis XIII's cellos, which were tuned a tone lower than the normal. Remodelled in four separate joints, no doubt by the members of the Hotteterre circle, this became the true bassoon, which arrived in Purcell's London under the name *French basson*. It is first named in a Lully score in 1674, but it may well have been in use ten or more years earlier; we can only hope that some day fresh documents will come to light, to tell us more about these various French inventions.

A typical early example, still without an A♭ key, is the instrument by Denner shown in Plate XXX. Note the oboe-like turnery on the tenor joint, which was afterwards given up, perhaps because with the soft, light woods of which bassoons were made (maple, pear, etc.) it was found more practical to leave the joint thick-walled all along. The standard bassoon for most of the eighteenth century was the *four-keyed* instrument (with keys for A♭, F, D and the low B♭; Plate XXV), and Mozart's concerto (1774) was probably first performed on this.

The E♭ key began to be fitted at about that time, followed some ten years later by the F♯ key, making the common *six-keyed* bassoon of the end of the century. German makers, however, often fitted a thumb key on the tenor joint to help the high notes, before bothering to fit a key for *F♯*, for which note there was a fairly efficient cross-fingering. By 1800, English bassoons had begun to carry two of these thumb keys on the tenor joint, making an *eight-keyed* bassoon. The bassoon was slung by a short ribbon loop which the player hitched to one of the buttons of his coat. Many old specimens still have this loop tied to the ring on the butt, but of course it is little use with our light modern jackets.

In the bore, eighteenth-century bassoons vary, but as compared with today they are wider in the crook (which has no hole) and narrower in the butt and long joint, while the bell contracts to a narrow waist, no doubt partly to prevent the bottom notes blurting and partly to smooth out the resonance of the instrument as a whole. English instruments are peculiarly wide in the crook and tenor joint, and seem to have a richer tone than others.

The reeds in Plate VI demonstrate how the bassoon reed has diminished in size over the last hundred and fifty years with refinement of manufacture and regularization of the bore. To drive and control the somewhat bottled-up bore of the classical instrument, the blades must be comparatively massive; with a modern reed, especially with one of the German type, the notes of the old bassoon are harsh and brittle, and the tenor notes fly badly. The old English reed illustrated in Plate VI looks rather like a large-sized oboe reed. Its cane is gouged thinner than today, leaving correspondingly little to be taken off the outside, and the blades are longer and the throat is wider. It has only the top wire. Continental reeds, to judge by sketches in tutors, may have been gouged differently, but are otherwise not very different, though with two wires.

With a suitably-made reed, the old 'horse's leg', as people called the bassoon in England, sounds irresistibly sweet and beautiful; something like a well-played modern French bassoon, but a little softer, more firm and compact, and rather cello-like.

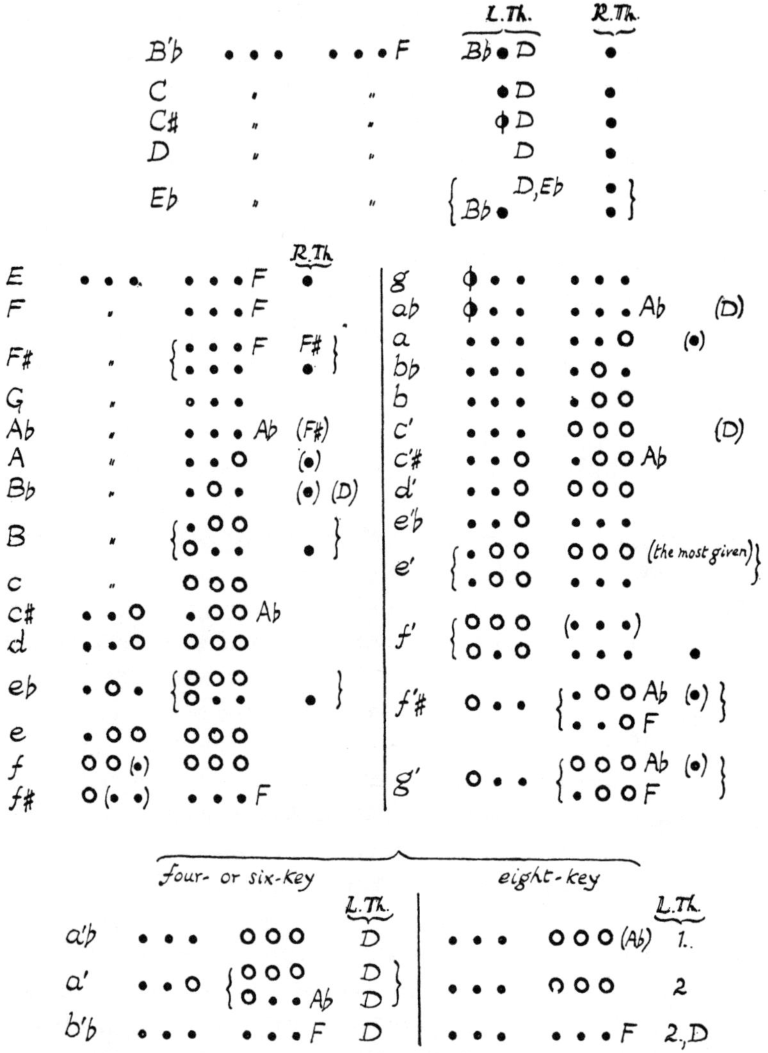

FIG. 68. *Chart for four- to eight-keyed bassoon. Keys or holes given in brackets are possible aids to unsteady notes. Of the alternatives given in the tenor register, those with the Ab key are English, those with the F key, Continental. Several further alternatives will be found in the old charts.* The top notes: *the thumb keys on the tenor joint (eight-keyed bassoon) are numbered thus:* 1, *the lower (shorter) key, and* 2, *the higher (which has the lower touch); without these keys these two notes are very difficult unless the reed is exactly right.*

Like the old oboe, it blends supremely well with every other instrument, while yet it possessed sufficient weight to have been a favourite solo instrument. It was said of Miller, the leading bassoonist in London throughout the middle part of the century, that 'the concertos at Vauxhall (etc.) and the solo parts allotted him by Handel in his oratorios and concertos, always excited attention, were heard with delight, and justly applauded for the sweetness of his tone and neatness of his execution' (Burney, in Rees). Another London player who must be mentioned is Holmes, whose tone 'resembled the most human voice'. It was Holmes who did the first performance of Haydn's *sinfonia concertante*, with Harrington on oboe. Whether he managed the high B♭s on the plain six-keyed bassoon, or whether he already had the thumb keys, we do not know.

German bassoons of the classical period show an unmistakable foreshadowing of the modern German quality. Why this should be can hardly be explained until eighteenth-century bassoons are subjected to methodical examination, but we may imagine that Ritter, for example, Mozart's closest acquaintance in the bassoon world, produced a clear, woody sound of distinctly proto-Heckelish quality. Mozart's concerto was written for an amateur player, but Ritter was one of the four original soloists in a *sinfonia concertante*, with Ramm of course on oboe, Punto on horn and Wendling on flute. The work may have been another version of the well-known K.297b.

Of course there were bad bassoonists then as there have been since. 'Snuffling' and 'goaty' are two words then applied to sub-standard bassoon tone, equivalent to 'rattling' or 'frying bacon' today.

SMALL AND LARGE BASSOONS. A surprising number of *small bassoons*, both English and Continental, have survived from the eighteenth century. Some are octave-bassoons or *fagottini*, about 25 inches tall and an octave above the ordinary, while others are tenoroons, usually built in G (though also in F, as later) and about 33 inches tall. Yet they do not seem to have been used much in music. No source mentions them as being so used, even in local bands, and they very rarely appear in scores (the *bassonetti* in a cantata by Zachau being one possible example). Possibly they were used for teaching boys on, for they started young in those days. Ritter, for example, began the bassoon at eight.

Among *large bassoons*, the instrument that Bach writes for down to G' in Cantata No. 31 (1715) may have been an old great-bass curtal. Talbot, however, mentioned a 'pedal or double bassoon' going down to F', and this may have been a 'semi-contra' bassoon, of which a few later specimens survive. This pitch—a fourth or a fifth below the bassoon—can give excellent tonal results, but it obliges the player, when reading from a bass part, to transpose his fingering, whereas a true contrabassoon, an octave below the ordinary, does not.

The earliest-known true contrabassoon is by Eichentopf, Leipzig, 1714. Next is Stanesby's nine-feet tall four-keyed *basson grosso* of Handel's *L'Allegro* and *Fireworks Music*, now preserved in the National Museum, Dublin. Both go down to the bottom B♭. But the first approximation to a standard type of contra-bassoon is the later Austrian model (Plate XXXI), looking like a tall, massive bassoon, with a butt joint at each end, and descending to bottom C. This is the instrument of the Viennese classics, and it was also extensively used in Austrian and Italian military bands. Its notes seem none too even and to lack power, though presumably after assiduous practice it produced a reasonably good effect, say, in the gravediggers' scene in *Fidelio*. And after all, one can hardly say much more for the contrabassoon today.

The Flute

The eighteenth-century flute was pretty certainly another of the Hotteterre family's rebuilds. They abolished the old cylin-drical bore (which was allowed to remain in the army fife) and substituted for it the bore and three-jointed construction of the Hotteterre recorder, making the so-called 'conical' flute. With this bore the tone becomes purer, free from fife-like shrillness; and since the bore-contraction has a flattening effect, the finger-holes can be placed closer together, in some cases by as much as half a centimetre, reducing the stretch for the hands.   But which of these considerations recommended the new proportions, or whether it was something else, is not known. The pitch of the favourite 'tenor' flute of the preceding era was kept (lowest note, d') and an E♭ key was added, thus making the *one-keyed flute*—the standard instrument for the greater part of the eighteenth century and that for which Mozart wrote his concertos (1778).

Though in the long run the conical flute has proved the least successful of the Hotteterre remodellings, people today who have heard the one-keyed flute in the hands of players who understand it have always been struck by the tender beauty of its sound; as with the other old woodwind instruments, its effect is never uninteresting. But of all of them, the flute was the hardest to play really well, and in tune.

Technique on these almost keyless old instruments depended absolutely on the chromatic cross-fingerings being good notes, and on the oboe and the bassoon, thanks mainly to the steadying effect of the old reeds, they were so. But on the one-keyed flute they were far less good. They could only be made into effective notes, in tune yet audible, by expert wangling of the embouchure, especially by turning the flute inwards to flatten the sharp cross-fingerings, which are in the majority, thus: c'' (fairly good), $b'♭$ (bad), both G♯'s and both F's (in each case very poor in the low register). For the F♯'s the straight fingering is flat (rectified by turning the flute outwards) while the cross-fingering is almost too sharp to be used at all, except as a leading-note in the upper register; but even so, the eighteenth-century flute player—especially the amateur, whom the Hotteterre grandson had begun to lure away from the recorder at the beginning of the century—was best off in keys like G and D, which most avoided the other bad notes. This fact has often been useful as a check on whether a piece marked *flute* or *flauto* is intended for recorder—as is usual—or for the flute (*flauto traverso* or *German flute*); the favourite keys for the treble recorder having been F and B♭. Another reason for avoiding flat keys lay in the frequent sharpness of high f'''—a note that young Hotteterre omits from his fingering chart altogether.

Since the entire range of an experienced flutist's power of lipping notes in tune was constantly brought into play on the cross-fingerings, some other provision became needed for meeting small variations in playing pitch (for instance somebody else's harpsichord). Hence from about 1720 (Quantz says) the previous middle joint was made in two pieces, an upper joint and a lower joint, the former being supplied in from three to six different lengths for tuning the instrument to various pitches without disturbing the response of those critical cross-fingerings that concerned the left hand holes. Three upper joints was the commonest provision, the shortest making the flute a good semitone sharper than the longest. At first they were numbered 1, 2, and 3 (this last the shortest). Later, as pitch rose, a sharper set became usual, numbered 4, 5, and 6 (a late eighteenth-century English tutor describes them as 'a flat pitch', 'concert pitch' and 'a sharp pitch' respectively). One had to remember to adjust the cork stopper after changing a joint; with the shortest it was screwed out and with the longest, screwed in.

Quantz mentions some special ways of using these alternative upper joints. A long upper joint, flat to the pitch, might be useful when playing the allegro movements of a concerto over a strong accompaniment, for then one could blow harder without going sharp to the orchestra. And also, when the keynote of a work was E♭ or A♭, a flat tuning would allow greater sonority on the A♭s. On the other hand, when playing an adagio, for which a darker, more closed quality of tone was sought, one might put in a sharp joint (or, if the sharpest was in already, screw in the stopper a trifle) to compensate for the flat, covered embouchure that produced this quality. Before attacking the final Allegro, one had to remember to change back to the original joint and reset the stopper.

SIX-KEYED FLUTE. Through its defective cross-fingerings, the flute became the first of the woodwind to accept the advantages of additional chromatic keywork.

Chromatic closed keys had already been known on bagpipes at least from the beginning of the seventeenth century. The French musette had several of them on the chanter. But on the woodwind instruments, tradition was set against this kind of key, admitting only the indispensable E♭ key and some equally indispensable keys on the clarinet. However, flute players' loyalty to the tradition, stretched to breaking point by the poor cross-fingerings, snapped when some London flute-makers

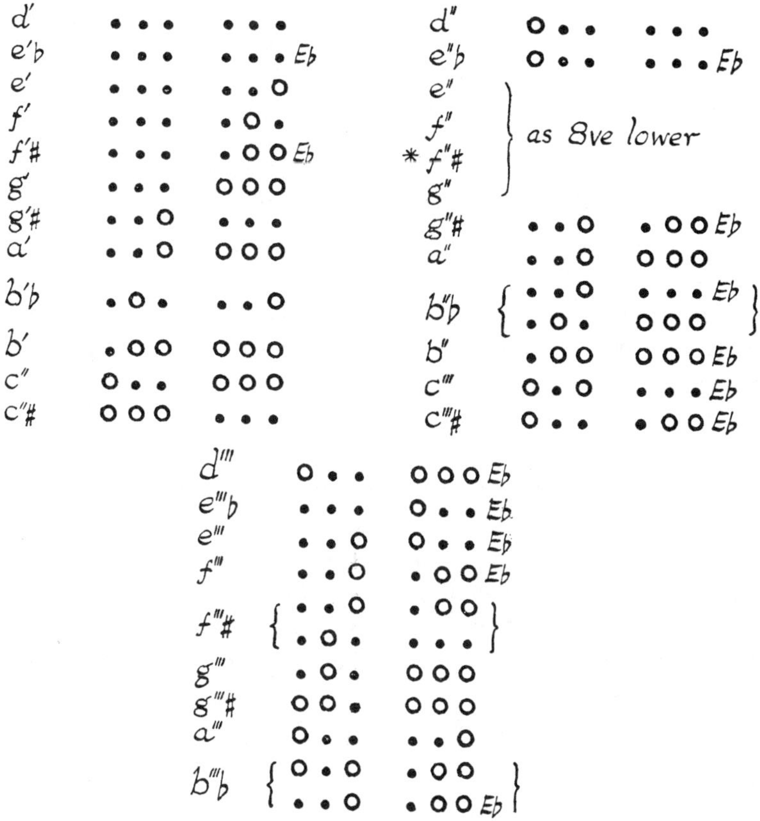

d′	• • •	• • •
e′♭	• • •	• • • E♭
e′	• • ◦	• ◦ ○
f′	• • •	• ○ •
f′♯	• • •	• ○ ○ E♭
g′	• • •	○ ○ ○
g′♯	• • ○	• • •
a′	• • ○	○ ○ ○
b′♭	• ○ •	• • ○
b′	• ○ ○	○ ○ ○
c″	○ • •	○ ○ ○
c″♯	○ ○ ○	• • •

d″	○ • •	• • •
e″♭	○ ◦ •	• • • E♭
e″		
f″	} as 8ve lower	
* f″♯		
g″		
g″♯	• • ○	• ○ ○ E♭
a″	• • ○	○ ○ ○
b″♭ {	• • ○ / • ○ •	• • • E♭ / ○ ○ ○ }
b″	• ○ ○	○ ○ ○ E♭
c‴	○ • ○	• • • E♭
c‴♯	○ • •	• ○ ○ E♭

d‴	○ • •	○ ○ ○ E♭
e‴♭	• • •	○ • • E♭
e‴	• • ○	○ • • E♭
f‴	• • ○	• ○ ○ E♭
f‴♯ {	• • ○ / • ○ •	• ○ ○ / • • • }
g‴	• ○ •	○ ○ ○
g‴♯	○ ○ •	○ ○ ○
a‴	○ • •	• • ○
b‴♭ {	○ • ○ / • • ○	• ○ ○ / • ○ ○ E♭ }

FIG. 69. *Chart for the one-keyed flute.* (*Some charts give the E♭ key to be held open throughout the lower two octaves except on the D's, as today.* * *As a leading note to g″, this note may be made . . . / ○ . . E♭*).

added three little musette-like closed keys to the one-keyed flute just before 1760. The keys were the cross F key, little-finger G♯ key, and left thumb B♭ key, thus making, with the old E♭ key, the *four-keyed flute.* And at last a fully reliable top *f‴* was possible, with the aid of the keys (p. 319).

The London pioneers, Florio, Gedney, and Potter, also resuscitated the earlier eighteenth-century idea of the C foot, which matched the flute's compass to the oboe's but had not until then received serious attention. This, with its two keys for C♯ and C, made the *six-keyed flute* (Plate XXVI), which is none other than the common simple-system flute of recent times minus the upper C key and the long F key, which appeared as optional additions at the end of the century. The three upper joints were still often provided, though now less urgently needed, and before 1800 the modern metal tuning-slide had been introduced, again first in England. The advanced musical possibilities of the new flute—e.g. freedom in tonality and modulation—are turned to splendid account in Haydn's Sonata; the work (arranged from a quartet) makes a sharp contrast with the previous one-keyed flute music, of which Mozart's pieces are the shining examples.

SMALL FLUTES AND FIFES. In Handel's time, *flauto piccolo* generally meant descant recorder, just as *flauto* meant treble recorder; but from Gluck onwards it signifies the orchestral piccolo, specimens of which have survived (one-keyed). The commoner eighteenth-century small flutes, however, were the military-band flutes, pitched in flat keys to be suitable for playing the tune an octave above the B♭ clarinets in marches and troops. There were two principal kinds: (1) the F flute or 'third flute' (a third above the ordinary flute), for which Bishop was later to write his well-known obbligato to 'Lo! Hear the Gentle Lark'. (For the obbligati to 'bird' arias, the smaller recorders and flutes were naturally chosen; but for doves, which coo in the lower part of the treble stave, not well above it, bassoons—as in Handel's *Floridante* and Haydn's *Creation*.) (2) Small B♭ and C flutes. All these were normally three-jointed one-keyed flutes. The C flute, a tone below the piccolo, is extinct, but the others survive among our six-keyed band flutes (Chapter II).

The *fife* was a different instrument, retaining sixteenth-century characteristics: cylindrical bore made all in one piece with a brass ferrule at each end, and no key (Plate XXX). In a baton-shaped metal case slung from his belt, a fifer usually seems to have carried two fifes, one in B♭, the other in C. A foreign example of a duty call is shown in fig. 70, and the English calls may be seen in printed fife tutors of the period. In England around 1850, the fife became replaced by the small B♮ flute (see above), but in many Continental countries it is still used today, sometimes with an E♭ key added (fig. 76) and with a pair of slinging holes at the lower end.

Chalumeau and Clarinet

Now and then during earlier eighteenth-century performances of opera and oratorio, the two oboists, in those days so often responsible for supplying any woodwind tone-colour that a composer might demand, would have been seen to take up little

FIG. 70. *An old reveille for the fife (Grand Duchy of Saxe-Weimar); from Kastner.*

instruments less than a foot long, and to produce upon them toy-trumpet-noises in the notes of the treble stave. These were *chalumeaux*—rudimentary, half-size clarinets.

In the seventeenth century the French word *chalumeau* meant either a bagpipe chanter; or 'pipe' in the general sense, and including the simple rustic reed-pipe with a single reed cut in a corn stem. Mersenne sketches the latter in his *Harmonie Universelle*, with three finger-holes and describes it as a 'chalumeau made of a corn stalk'. We can only imagine that the orchestral chalumeau arose out of this in course of woodwind-makers' search for novelties. The name suggests, but does not prove, French origin.

At its simplest, the chalumeau was a little cane pipe, 8 to 9 inches long, with six holes and thumb-hole, and the reed-tongue cut in the upper side of the cane at the top end. Bonanni describes it in his book on instruments (*Gabinetto Armonico*, Rome, 1722), and an instrument answering to his description was exhibited at the Royal Military Exhibition in London in 1890 and described in Day's catalogue as follows: of cane, $8\frac{1}{4}$ inches long with 15 millimetres bore, covered with red leather, and sounding from g' to g'' in fundamentals. The instrument also corresponds with particulars recently brought to light by Thurston Dart of the 'Mock Trumpet', for which books of tunes were published from *c.* 1698 onwards. The compass is here the same, and evidently the instrument was also leather-covered, for to sound it, 'put the trumpet in your mouth as far as the gilded leather and blow pretty strong' (*Galpin Society Journal*, VI).

Denner, the inventor of the clarinet, was said to have improved this little instrument. Possibly he was the first to make it like his clarinet, of boxwood, with a replaceable cane reed tied on; a little-finger hole; and two keys near the top, one in front and the other opposite to it on the back. Bonanni reveals that musicians called this form of the instrument *calandrone*—'the lark'—and that it gave a raucous sound, *poco grata*. There was formerly a specimen of this wooden *two-keyed chalumeau* at Munich (Plate XXX shows a replica). Its usual compass was from f' to $b''\flat$, or even to c''' (which no doubt would have been possible by opening the back key to overblow the bottom note to its twelfth), but a few of the operatic chalumeau parts demand instruments pitched a third or a fourth lower. Among the composers who wrote for it—usually for a pair—are Handel (in *Riccardo Primo*), Telemann, Vivaldi and lastly Gluck. Many of the chalumeau arias have pastoral texts, but not all; it is difficult to see exactly how composers regarded the instrument.

Diderot's *Encyclopédie* confirms that the chalumeau is correctly identified in this midget instrument. Moreover it was the fundamental register of the clarinet that afterwards came to be known as the 'chalumeau register', showing that the chalumeau itself was played in its fundamentals. For its usual compass with lowest note f', this would indeed require a tube no more than 9 inches long.

TWO-KEYED CLARINETS. The clarinet, Germany's great contribution to the woodwind, marks the first full exploitation in Western musical history—possibly in all history—of the upper register of a reed-sounded cylindrical tube. It was invented about the beginning of the eighteenth century by J. C. Denner of Nuremberg or his son. Doppelmayr's 'Historical Report of Nuremberg Mathematicians and Craftsmen,' 1730, names the father.

Denner was one of the leading German woodwind-makers of the end of the seventeenth century (he died in 1707, about thirty years after Jean Hotteterre). Surviving instruments carrying his initials include one recorder of the old pattern (dated 1682) and several of the new; a shawm of the old kind and a *deutsche Schalmey* of the new; a curtal, the bassoon already mentioned, and a racket; and, preserved at Munich, an elementary two-keyed C clarinet (Plate XXX). Recorders were evidently his speciality (Doppelmayr describes him as a recorder-maker), and it might conceivably have been while contemplating these that the idea of the clarinet occurred to him. His elementary design curiously resembles a treble recorder to look at, both in size and shape (especially in the foot joint) and in the slightly contracting bore. This also struck Bonanni, who calls the instrument *clarone* but confesses that he is unable to discover the inventor, though 'it appears to be a modern derivative of the recorder to give a louder and more vigorous sound; it is difficult to describe, but easy to recognize by its sound even when mixed with other instruments in *sinfonie*'.

A number of things might have suggested to Denner the clarinet's separate reed tied to a wooden mouthpiece, e.g. organ reeds (which have a separate reed of brass); or bagpipe reeds from neighbouring Bohemia, if reeds like no. *iii* in fig. 39 were already made at that time. He evidently applied it to the chalumeau first.

The Denner specimen shown is twice as long as the chalumeau, having fundamentals f to $b'\flat$. With suitable reeds, this design gives the upper register perfectly well by opening the key at the back. The *b'* is made by squeezing the *b'♭*. However, a more advanced two-keyed clarinet, with an oboe-like bell (Plate XXX), appeared perhaps during the 1720s, and this is the type more generally understood among historians by the expression 'two-keyed clarinet'. The note *b'* is still made as just described (or, in Majer's chart of 1741, as a flat-sounding harmonic of the low *f*). Yet the instrument gives remarkably good results as long as the music keeps close to its home tonality and mainly in the upper register; Frederick Thurston, who sometimes

FIG. 71. *Music for clarinets and horns from Arne's* Thomas and Sally, *1760.*

used to demonstrate early clarinets at recitals, said that certain types of passage in eighteenth-century concertos proved easier to bring off on a two-keyed clarinet than on a modern Boehm— for instance, quick broken-chord figures ('Alberti' kind) in the upper register.

This two-keyed clarinet was introduced to France and England by Germans who played it in partnership with the horn, apparently in vigorous open-air fashion. Their common band-stand routine, with the one pair of instruments picturesquely echoing the other, is demonstrated in the entry-music of a hunting party in Arne's opera *Thomas and Sally* (fig. 71). Both pairs of instrument are here in C, and their parts are marked 'with spirit'.

A better-known piece is Handel's *Overture* (*c.* 1740) for a trio composed of two clarinets and one horn (which plays the bass), all in D, the parts being written at concert pitch with two sharps, like Handel's D horn and trumpet parts in other works. The clarinet parts that occur in some of Vivaldi's concertos are also probably for the two-keyed instrument.

THE CLASSICAL CLARINET. Soon after 1750 came the improvement which gave the instrument its final basic form—elongation of the bell to take the long B key, so that *b'* could be made properly. Next followed the Eb key and after that the long C♯ key, making the classical *five-keyed* clarinet, known from 1770 at the latest (Plate XXVII). This would have been the instrument on which the Germans Tausch and Beer (for whom K. Stamitz wrote concertos) raised the clarinet to the rank of a solo instrument. Stadler, who with 'the soft vocal qualities of his tone which no one with a heart could withstand' (Rendall) won from Mozart the quintet and the concerto, may conceivably also have had the G♯ key, which became known on the Continent in the 1770s. In England, instead, the long trill key was added, though whether for the A/B trill, or for dodging the break in second clarinet parts, is not recorded. (In second clarinet parts, incidentally, low-register passages were sometimes written an octave higher and marked *chal.*, i.e. 'play in the chalumeau register'; this may later be countermanded by *clar.*, i.e. 'clarinet register'.)

The bore was narrow, measuring in the Bb clarinet only from 13 to 14 millimetres, as against some 15 millimetres or more today. Bb and C clarinets were the usual ones. The A clarinet was known, but as a comparative rarity (the only known English eighteenth-century A clarinet is one by Miller, in the collection of Messrs Glen, Edinburgh). Rather than an A clarinet it seems to have been usual to have an A joint for one's Bb instrument; the bottom joint was made in two sections, the 'middle piece' and the 'lower joint', and it was the middle piece (with the three right hand holes in it) that one could change to go into A. The small clarinet, used in large bands, was then the F clarinet; the E♮ appeared in the nineteenth century.

The ebony or boxwood mouthpiece was small and pointed (Plate VII), with a very narrow tapered aperture and a long lay. The reed was correspondingly small, narrow and hard, and was tied on with string as they still do in Germany. It was usual to play with the reed uppermost, as it had been on the chalumeau and its primitive forerunners, though some Germans are thought to have already been playing with the reed downwards as we do today. This point is returned to in the next chapter. Another curious thing about the reed is that several German sources through the classical period mention reeds of pine or fir (cf. fig. 39). In Schilling's *Lexicon* (1835) it is said that such reeds give fine tone and speak easily, but do not last. Fish-bone reeds are mentioned too. But it seems that cane was always the normal material.

The earliest detailed description of the reed is in Backofen's tutor (1803). Some, he says, thin it down towards the tip (i.e. a small, hard version of the modern reed). Others make the blade of equal thickness right to the tip (and he shows it so in his sketch, a good millimetre thick all the way along). It might be, he continues, thick the whole way across, or convex (in cross-section) on both surfaces, or flat on top and concave underneath (somewhat recalling the primitive single reed). At least one English clarinet survives (Brackenbury Collection) with an apparently original reed of the double-convex kind and nearly a millimetre thick down the centre right to the tip. But Muller, writing rather later (*c.* 1825), says that it is wrong to believe that a fine tone comes with a reed that is almost equally thick all along. It makes the *pianos* risky, the high notes piercing, and on account of the difficulty of blowing such a reed the mouthpiece-lay has to be too close. Better, he says, is a reed thinned towards the tip, enabling a more open lay to be used, making for more expressive playing and finer nuances, and also taking less breath. This last must surely have been that which Tausch and Stadler used. By modern standards it would still have been hard. All experiments with the old clarinets show that it is only with a long open lay and a hard reed that justice

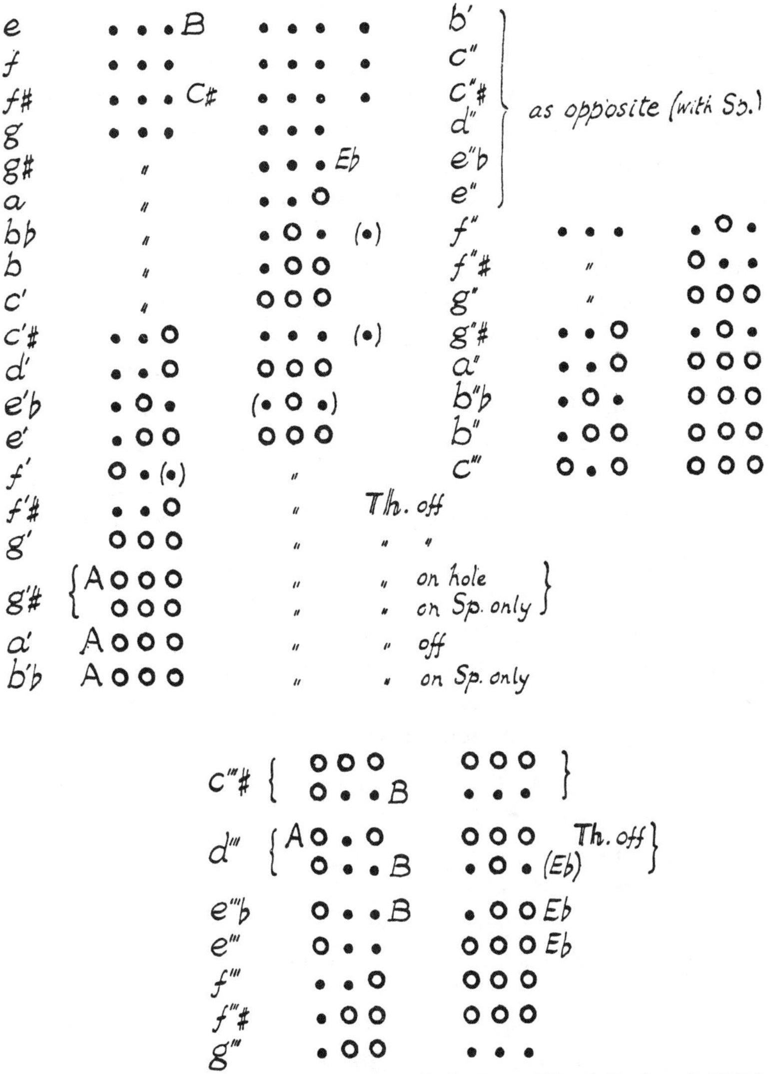

e	● ● ● B	● ● ● ● ●	b′ ⎫
f	● ● ●	● ● ● ●	c″ ⎪
f♯	● ● ● C♯	● ● ● ●	c″♯ ⎬ as opposite (with Sp.)
g	● ● ●	● ● ●	d″ ⎪
g♯	″	● ● ● Eb	e″b ⎪
a	″	● ● ○	e″ ⎭
bb	″	● ○ ● (●)	f″
b	″	● ○ ○	f″♯
c′	″	○ ○ ○	g″
c′♯	● ● ○	● ● ● (●)	g″♯
d′	● ● ○	○ ○ ○	a″
e′b	● ○ ●	(● ○ ●)	b″b
e′	● ○ ○	○ ○ ○	b″
f′	○ ● (●)	″	c‴
f′♯	● ● ○	″	Th. off
g′	○ ○ ○	″	″ ″
g♯	{A ○ ○ ○ / ○ ○ ○	″	″ on hole ⎫
		″	″ on Sp. only ⎬
a′	A ○ ○ ○	″	″ off ⎭
b′b	A ○ ○ ○	″	″ on Sp. only

Right-hand (upper) column:

f″	● ● ●	● ○ ●
f″♯	″	○ ● ●
g″	″	○ ○ ○
g″♯	● ● ○	● ○ ●
a″	● ● ○	○ ○ ○
b″b	● ○ ●	○ ○ ○
b″	● ○ ○	○ ○ ○
c‴	○ ● ○	○ ○ ○

c‴♯ {	○ ○ ○ / ○ ● ● B	○ ○ ○ / ● ● ● }
d‴ {	A ○ ● ○ / ○ ● ● B	○ ○ ○ / ● ○ ● (Eb) Th. off }
e‴b	○ ● ● B	● ○ ○ Eb
e‴	○ ● ●	○ ○ ○ Eb
f‴	● ● ○	○ ○ ○
f‴♯	● ○ ○	○ ○ ○
g‴	● ○ ○	● ● ●

Fig. 72. *Chart for five- or six-keyed clarinet. The left thumb* (Th) *closes its hole except where indicated otherwise, and from* b′ *upwards also opens the speaker key* (Sp.).

N.B. (1) Low register: *many of the cross-fingered notes are weak and muffled, and to prevent them being too sharp, the German charts, meant for learners playing with the reed downwards, generally give more holes covered than the English, as indicated in brackets.* (2) High register: *the notes are hard to tune, and charts here differ widely.*

can be done to their all-important upper register, where the tone
is smaller and more piping than on modern instruments, but the
cross-fingerings are first-rate and every note offers a resistance
that encourages the most expressive cantabile that it is possible
to imagine from a wind instrument. The clarinet has since
gained in sonority and flexibility, and also the old instrument is
defective in the lower register (where some of the cross-fingerings are worse than on the one-keyed flute); but in the upper
register, which matters so much more, the clarinet can never
have sounded more beautiful. When Mozart wrote his famous
remark to his father, 'if only *we* had clarinets', we must
remember that he referred not to the Boehm, nor even to the
Oehler, but to the simple boxwood instrument with narrow
bore, five brass keys and tiny hard-reed mouthpiece.

The d'amore instruments

The following list of wind instruments in the 1741 inventory
of the small court of Sayn-Wittgenstein at Berleburg, West-
phalia, gives a very good picture of the state of wind instruments
half-way through the period we are considering:

2 harpsichords; 3 clavichords (two in lacquer cases);
1 positive organ; 1 old harp;
5 violins; 2 violas; 2 cellos; 1 double bass;
3 *viola di gamben* of different sizes;
1 viola d'amour; 1 *piccolo* (violoncello piccolo);
1 viola pomposa; 1 string-spinning wheel.
3 bassoons;
8 large recorders (*Flaut-Doux*);
2 bass recorders (*Flaut-doux-Basson*) without crooks;
4 small recorders of various sizes;
1 ivory flageolet;
2 flutes (*traversière*), one ivory, the other black with silver
    mounts;
1 piccolo (*traversière*);
1 pair of *Flaute traversières d'amours*;
1 large *Fl. trav. d'amour*;
2 oboes;

2 pairs of *Hautbois d'amours*;

1 pair of *Wald-Hautbois* (oboi da caccia) without their brass crook;

1 *taille* without the brass crook;

2 pairs of clarinets in a recorder-case;

2 trumpets with their crooks;

5 pairs of *Wald-Horn* (horns), in C, D and F, and crooks;

1 small *Wald-Horn*.

Recorder consorts are still present; there is a pair of clarinets, no doubt used with the horns in the manner already described; and three pairs of *d'amore* instruments.

The idea of these last presumably originated in the viola d'amore, that peculiar instrument usually tuned to the chord of D major. The *hautbois d'amour*—as the oboe d'amore was better known—and the *flûte d'amour* were both pitched in A, a minor third below the respective ordinary instruments, and were calculated to produce at this pitch a soulful lovelorn quality in contrast with the bright extravert tones of the ordinary oboe and flute; a very eighteenth-century idea; while a handy thing about their being in A was that ordinary music written at concert pitch could be read on them simply by imagining the French violin clef (which puts G on the bottom line) instead of treble clef and subtracting three sharps from the key-signature. This is how Quantz says the flûte d'amour was used, and it saved transposition of the accompaniment.

The *oboe d'amore* is said to have been invented about 1720 in Germany. It is the only one of these instruments to have been scored for by composers. Bach employed it extensively and so did Telemann and others, while among the stacks of mid-century manuscript concertos for every wind instrument hidden away in German libraries, there are a number for oboe d'amore, and also for two oboi d'amore, in which (as in similar concertos for two flutes, two bassoons, etc.) the executants enjoyed a feast of playing in thirds.

The eighteenth-century oboe d'amore is 24 to 25 inches long, with a short brass crook. At least a dozen survive, mostly German and many of these by Eichentopf of Leipzig. These have squat bulbous bells, but some French instruments by Bizey have oboe-like bells. Evidently as with the tenor oboe, the bulb bell was not always considered essential. There are no signs of the oboe d'amore in England.

The *flûte d'amour*, to judge by the number that survive, must have been extremely popular. Quantz singles it out as the best of the variant forms of flute. Few composers seem to have scored for it. But the point of a *d'amore* instrument was not its deeper pitch, but its deeper tone-quality, and no doubt not only amateurs and recitalists, but opera-orchestra players too would change now and then to the flûte d'amour to give extra effect to an adagio or aria of sentimental character, transposing the part in the manner just described.

In England the flûte d'amour was known, but on the whole valued less than the 'B flat tenor flute' (English nomenclature, i.e. a *major* third below the ordinary flute), an instrument that became popular for playing the lowest part of amateur flute quartets on.

Lastly, the *clarinette d'amour* (Plate XXX), which appeared on the Continent in the 1770s, just before the oboe d'amore began to go out. Its usual pitch was G or A♭, thus providing for clef-transposition a third below the B♭ and C clarinets respectively, but some were made in F. Some specimens are straight with a curved brass crook. Others are angular. The bell is bulbous, or clarinet-like outside with a bulbous cavity inside. The approximate length for the G, excluding mouthpiece, is 30 inches. Again it must have been used for solos, since so few scores specify it. J. C. Bach while in Germany wrote for it in a march and also in his Mannheim opera *Temistocle* (1772), which contains three parts for *clarinette d'amour*, puzzlingly written as if for instruments in D.

The woodwind 'horns'

The Cor Anglais and the Basset Horn; two tenor-pitched instruments in F, a fifth below the oboe and the clarinet respectively.

The cor anglais began its life as the German *Wald-hautbois* or *Corne d'Anglois* of c.1720 onwards. A few composers, Bach among them, preferred the name *hautbois da caccia*. The instrument was another of the century's romantically conceived designs like those that we have just seen in the *d'amore* instruments, but in this case the romantic effect was of distant horns across forest glades. In Zedler's *Universal Lexicon* it is stated that Jagd-hautbois—meaning players—were taken out on hunting parties and played in the mornings and evenings before the quarters of the Chief Master of the Hunt. They may have featured a pair of *Wald-hautbois* on such occasions, though there is no proof of this.

No written particulars of the instrument's shape are known. However, a few collections possess specimens of a tenor oboe built in the picturesque curved antique hunting-horn shape. They show early eighteenth-century features of construction, and are generally accepted as being *oboi da caccia*. There is a pair at Bologna, rather roughly-made instruments of some softish wood planed to an octagonal cross-section (like the old cornett) and painted reddish-brown as if to imitate copper. They have wide bugle-like bells and would have matched the semicircular metal horns that were carried, according to Zedler, by certain hunt officials bearing the title *Flügelmeister*.

From 1760 little more is heard of the *oboe da caccia*, but a pair of *corni inglesi* begin to turn up in Viennese scores (e.g. in Gluck and Haydn), and a number of late eighteenth-century instruments are preserved—curved in shape, always with bulbous bells, and most of them either Viennese or Italian (Plate XXVIII). As far as we know, the *corno inglese* (cor anglais) was the same instrument as the *oboe da caccia*, save perhaps for detail of the bell; but why the 'hunting oboe' should have become the 'English horn' is a mystery. The instrument itself had no special connection with England; the only known early English specimen (by Milhouse) has the later, un-hornlike angular construction (like the basset horn in the same Plate). However, the Flügelmeister's metal bugle became, after the middle of the eighteenth century, characteristic of the English and Hanoverian light infantry and *Jäger* regiments and was described in the latter as *Horn*, so possibly this is where the connection lay.

The old method of constructing a curved woodwind tube has

recently been thoroughly examined by P. A. T. Bate with interesting results. In briefest outline, the favourite method consists in boring a joint in the straight, then cutting out several wedges almost right across the tube, and bending, glueing and securing to close the gaps. The construction is hidden in the finished instrument by wooden fillets and a leather covering.

As may be imagined (and Brod later confirms it), this construction is scarcely one to make for a full, vibrant tone. The tone is soft, with hardly a trace of reediness; it is, as La Borde (1780) says of the *oboe da caccia*, less sonorous and more velvety than that of the oboe. It is indeed very much like the sound of a distant horn. In the *William Tell* overture the solo cor anglais, in the curved form that Rossini would have known, would give an excellent imitation of the *Ranz des Vaches* on a distant alp-horn, an instrument that plays its tunes at much the same pitch as natural French horns do. The modern straight cor anglais was conceived more simply—as an oboe merely of deeper pitch—and Brod, its inventor, quite honestly described it as an *hautbois alto*. The old curved instrument was a typical romantic creation of the eighteenth century; the new straight one, a typical technical creation of the nineteenth century. In Italy, however, the curved form lasted until modern times, and there was said to have been an Italian player using it at Covent Garden at the beginning of the present century.

The *basset horn* was invented, according to the prevailing opinion, by Mayrhofer of Passau, Bavaria, in the 1760s: a deep clarinet in F (or alternatively, at first, in G) reviving the sixteenth to seventeenth-century idea of diapasons down to a low C. The tube was at first curved, like that of the cor anglais. Hence no doubt 'horn'. 'Basset' was an old German musicians' term for the lowest part in a high-pitched choir; and also for any tenor-pitched instrument with bass characteristics such as extended tube for diapasons (cf. table, p. 271).

On many old basset horns the extension is diatonic, with two thumb keys, for *d* and *c* (though the Mayrhofer instrument in the Hamburg Museum has one extension key only, giving *c*, and is also smaller). To reduce the overall length, the part between the B key and the metal bell was twice doubled back on itself in a flat block of wood of the shape of a pack of cards (basset cards, perhaps). Supplanting the curved form of the instrument, the angular form, with two straight joints connected by a short knee-joint, had appeared by 1782, in Vienna; this (Plate XXVIII) was simpler to make and better for sound. It was slung on a coat button. Then, says Backofen, if playing with the reed downwards, hold it to the right side, like a bassoon; but if playing with the reed uppermost, rest the bell on the thigh, or grip it between the knees (to suit which the brass bell had a flattened shape), though this, he admits, makes a stiff, morose-looking figure.

During the early decades of the nineteenth century, German military bands usually included a pair of basset horns to play simple harmony-thickening middle parts. But when valved horns came into general use in bands, the basset horns were dropped, and it was left to the concert popularity of a few classical obbligati to keep the instrument just alive until its revival towards the end of the century.

The Serpent

This instrument, related to the cornett, has claims to be included among the woodwind, having been manufactured in the classical period by woodwind-makers for use in military bands as a reinforcer of the bassoons. It was invented in French ecclesiastical circles in the sixteenth century and in France and the neighbouring countries its use remained confined to churches, where it was played alone or, less often, with other instruments, to keep the choristers on their notes. A century ago so many serpents were to be found in French and Flemish churches that the Brussels Conservatoire Museum strung two dozen of them together to make a chandelier.

These were all *keyless serpents*; great-bass cornetts of serpentine shape and huge conical bore, covered in black leather and sounded with a large, narrow-rimmed hemispherical mouthpiece of ivory or horn. The lowest fundamental was *C*, but most of the church work was done in 2nd and 3rd harmonics, in unison with the male voices. Notwithstanding the unscientific placing of the holes—bunched in two groups so that the fingers can cover them—the *serpent d'église* is quite a good musical instrument, though it takes a good ear to play it, since the notes are formed as much by the lips as by the fingering—far more so than on the cornett, on which, with practice, the lips adjust themselves unconsciously to the fingerings just as they do on flutes and reed instruments.

The serpent's tone-quality can be roughly imitated simply by blowing trumpet-wise into any long wide tube. The cup mouthpiece of the serpent merely focuses the sound-generating lip-vibration, giving the notes more bite and precision. The tone is richly woody, considerably louder than the bassoon's, though not as loud as the tuba's; in fact, an ideal tone for strengthening the bass in the classical wind ensemble.

It was the bandmasters in England who first thought of this. In England the serpent had been tried out in combination with other instruments from Locke's time, but without the success that would have gained it a place in the orchestra. But towards the end of the eighteenth century the larger military bands adopted it and soon produced a more or less standard *four-keyed serpent* (Plate XXXI), with a key for finger I (for B; the open note, all fingers off, being B♭), and an F♯ key for finger IV. The other two keys, both for the right thumb, were mainly for helping various notes that were otherwise hard to get clear and in tune. The fingering was largely empirical, and charts differ widely. But the effect of this serpent in militia marches of the late eighteenth century is excellent. The usual English band combination was: two B♭ clarinets; two horns; two bassoons (mainly in unison); one trumpet, with an exhilarating, epi-phenomenal fanfare-like part; and serpent *ad libitum*, written rather low, an octave below the bassoons where possible. The way the serpent blends in with the rest and pulls the whole ensemble together is quite extraordinary, and well accounts for the very great interest taken in this class of instrument in the early nineteenth century, when the Russian bassoon and the English bass horn and the *serpent Forveille* were brought out as handier versions of the serpent, held comfortably in bassoon fashion instead of rather awkwardly across the front of the body.

Performance

We cannot here go fully into the various eighteenth-century styles of performance of concertos and solos, though the subject really concerns the old instruments as intimately as fingerings, reeds, etc. But some of the main points may be noticed briefly.

All through the century, to play a solo literally, exactly as written, was considered very inexpert or faint-hearted, above all in the slow movements. The latter, Quantz points out, were so often boring to hear, through players not knowing how to fill them out and embellish them. Quantz's great work, *Versuch einer Anweisung die Flöte Traversiere zu spielen* ('Study of Flute-playing'), 1752, tells a wind soloist all the important things about solo performance in the 1730s and 1740s. Quantz is a safe man, as reliable as could be. He explains clearly what kinds of trills and mordents should be added by the player in allegro, andante, larghetto and grave movements of various characters in order to bring out these characters. For the treatment of adagios he gives two full-length examples; one of the French style, in which it was expected to find most of the necessary ornament already written in by the composer; and one of the Italian adagio, which depended for its effect on being lavishly filled in by the performer. Both these celebrated examples are reproduced by the Dolmetsch in *The Interpretation of the Music of the Seventeenth and Eighteenth Centuries*, one on p. 128, the other in the appendix volume of musical examples (with dynamic markings added by Dolmetsch).

However, with all this material, Quantz and the eighteenth century present the modern soloist with a problem; because that which was good taste in the eighteenth century, is no longer good taste today. Suppose somebody were to take the plunge, and publicly act upon Quantz's positive statement that in an Italian adagio it may truly be said that the performer does as much towards 'composing' the music as the composer himself. However well he did it, a present-day audience would probably think him childish or vulgar. People today like to hear music played exactly as it is written on paper, however boring an eighteenth-century audience would have thought it. So perhaps after all it is better for us not to study Quantz's examples, or

Babell's exercises (fig. 65) in the earlier whirlwind style of Corelli, or the eight crowded pages of ornament exercises in Ozi's official bassoon tutor for the newly-founded Paris Conservatoire.

Nevertheless, two characteristic examples from Ozi are given

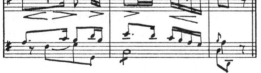

FIG. 73. *Two ornamentation exercises from Ozi's bassoon tutor* (*Paris, 1798?*).

in fig. 73, one slow, one fast. They show the style of ornamentation prevalent in France at the time of Mozart's death, and broadly applicable to all movements of his wind concertos. In each example, the lower line shows the written melody with the bass; the upper line, shows the suggested decoration. It must be remembered that this tutor was authorized for issue to students by a Conservatoire board consisting of the leading French composers and performers of the day.

Examples of *cadenzas* given in eighteenth-century tutors and exercises appear very much as we make them today, and (for wind instruments) quite short. One made a *messa di voce*—a long swell—on the initial note. Lorenzoni (flute tutor, 1779) emphasizes a point that is not always observed today: as the final trill of the cadenza draws towards its close, the accompanying instruments should supply the chord of the dominant seventh, although this does not appear in the parts. (Occasionally, however, these chords have been printed in, as in Jancourt's edition of Mozart's bassoon concerto.)

To trill properly in the eighteenth-century manner, starting the trill on the upper note, it is best to practise trills in even tempo, beginning with trills of eight regular notes, e.g. E D E D E D C D for a trill on D (cf. fig. 56 in the last chapter). Then, having once got the finger movement into a controlled rhythm, one can easily proceed to make trills of any length and speed, and regular or rubato as one pleases.

CHAPTER XII

Mechanization

The *Eroica* Symphony (1804) would have seen its first performance with woodwind instruments of the classical types described in the last chapter. Then things began to move rapidly. Nineteenth-century woodwind history is an action story of brilliant, dominating individuals—performers or craftsmen, sometimes both—and of their patented inventions through which the elegantly simple instruments of the past were transformed into the complicated tools of the woodwind section today. Chronologically, the story arranges itself into three principal phases, as follows.

1. First there came a period of some twenty-five years which saw the development of the basic 'simple systems'. With these, each instrument came to be provided with a set of simple closed keys following the example already set by the later eighteenth-century flute-makers. These gave an accurately-tuned keyed note for every semitone that had previously been unsatisfactory as a cross-fingering. Ten years after the *Eroica*, Beethoven's Seventh and Eighth Symphonies would have been introduced with eight-keyed flutes and eight- to twelve-keyed clarinets. Oboes and bassoons, on which chromatic cross-fingerings on the whole worked the best, were still mainly classical in design, but another ten years later, when the Ninth Symphony was produced, these instruments too had become available with extra keys. The following list of models supplied by Schott, condensed from price-lists printed in the Mainz journal *Caecilia*, shows what this well-known firm had to offer in 1825, the year after the Ninth Symphony.

MECHANIZATION

Schott, Mainz (1825)

FLUTES:

[Graded in price according to materials as follows, from cheapest to dearest:]

Boxwood, horn mounts, brass keys.

    ,,   ivory ,,   ,,   ,,

    ,,   ,,   ,,   silver ,,

Ebony   ,,   ,,   ,,   ,,

Cocus   ,,   ,,   ,,   ,,

Ebony or

  cocus, silver ,,   ,,   ,,

Piccolos, F, E♭ or D, 1 to 3 upper joints, 1 key.

    ,,   ,,   ,, tuning slide, 4 keys.

F Flutes, 3 upper joints, 1 key.

    ,,   ,,   ,, 4 keys.

Concert flutes, 3 upper joints, 1 key.

    ,,   ,,   ,,   ,, 4 keys.

    ,,   ,, tuning slide, 4 keys.

    ,,   ,,   ,,   ,, and C foot, 8 keys.

    ,,   ,,   ,,   ,, and B foot, 9 keys.

Walking-stick flute, 1 key.[1]

Flageolets, 0 to 3 keys.

OBOES:

Boxwood, 2 keys.

Boxwood or ebony, 14 keys, *new invention.*

Cor anglais, boxwood, 10 keys [this would have the angular form].

CLARINETS:

In B♭, C or E♭, boxwood, 5, 6, or 9 keys.

    ,,   ,, box or ebony, 12 keys, *new invention.*

In B♭ with A joint [5 to 12 keys, as above].

In F, boxwood, 5, 6, or 9 keys.

Basset horn, boxwood, 14 keys [angular form].

BASSOONS:

Maple, 9 keys.

   ,, with two tenor joints, two crooks, 9 keys.

   ,,   ,,   ,,   ,, 15 keys, *new invention.*

The same with silver mounts and ivory keys.

Contrabassoon, maple, 7 keys.

Serpent in bassoon shape [Russian bassoon], maple, 6 keys.

   ,,   ,,   ,, with dragon bell   ,,   ,,

---

[1] This is a flute that is also a walking-stick, with a wooden key simulating a knot in the stick. Fétis, the celebrated Belgian musical historian, is said to have carried one about with him. The flutist J. Clinton adapted the idea to British conditions in an *umbrella flute.* There were also walking-stick clarinets, some combined in the same stick with a walking-stick piccolo.

Translating the prices of the above instruments into the English values of the time, the cheapest piccolo cost 3*s*. 6*d*.; flutes from 6*s*. 4*d*. to £6; oboes from 25*s*. to £8 13*s*. 0*d*.; cor anglais £5; clarinets from 30*s*. to £11; basset horn 6 gns.; bassoons from 70*s*. to 7 gns.; contra, 7 gns.; the serpents from 5 to 6 gns.

The 'new inventions' presumably refer to Sellner's full simple-system oboe (newly introduced by the maker Koch in Vienna), the Muller clarinet (first devised in about 1810, in Paris), and to Almenraeder's newly-remodelled bassoon—a herald of the second phase in our story. Yet besides these advanced models, there was still a good sale for older designs, including those of simple classical pattern. Local bands and theatres, with their repertoires of old favourites and new light pieces, could still manage well enough with these, but to feel comfortable in the more ambitious orchestral works of the 1820s one becomes glad of a few extra keys, as trials with old instruments reveal.

The instruments of this period still have a generally antique appearance. The keys, for instance, are still pivoted on pins through the wood (or on brass saddles) as often as on the new pillars (which were then mounted on a metal base-plate screwed to the wood). The old flat keys with leather pads had, however, largely given place to the early forms of cupped key with stuffed pad, which Muller claimed to have invented in connection with his twelve-keyed clarinet. As playing instruments, those of this period can still be useful today, e.g. for classical music among friends. Their tone, provided that the correct fingerings are used, is often very beautiful. They must, of course, be reasonably well-preserved, and also close enough to modern pitch, the danger here being sharpness. About 1820 the London orchestras seem to have been playing at just below modern pitch (about $a' = 433$), but pitch was tending to rise, especially in bands, for which the majority of instruments were constructed. (By 1840, sharp pitch prevailed almost everywhere, and most mid-century instruments are far too high for playing on today.)

2. Next followed that period of intense activity which pro-

duced our modern designs. It covers roughly the 1830s and 1840s. Buffet brought out the needle spring (c. 1837), and pillars came to be screwed directly into the wood. Boehm introduced the long axle (1832) both for keys and for finger-plates and rings, which made possible not only his own new flute-mechanisms but also the Boehm-system clarinet (Buffet, 1843), the 'brille' F♯ device on oboes and clarinets, and Triébert's thumb-plate oboe (1849), not to mention the saxophone (1845) and the modern mechanism of all other woodwind instruments. These years also saw a great revision of woodwind bores in order to clear weak spots in the compass and to give a generally louder, more open sound. Clarinet bores and mouthpieces began to be enlarged to their various modern dimensions; Boehm worked out his cylindrical flute; Triébert began to straighten out the quaint bore of the classical oboe, coming continually nearer to a correct cone as he went on. Also from these years date the inventions that gave the modern form to the 'extra' instruments: Brod's straight-model cor anglais (Paris, 1839), which began slowly to replace the old curved and angular models; Sax's bass clarinet (Brussels, 1838); and in Germany, Haseneier's contrabassophone (Coblenz, 1847), the first successful scientifically-designed contrabassoon and the inspiration of many structural features of the Heckel design that eventually supplanted it.

Instruments of this period, and indeed also of the next, continued to be made generally of boxwood or ebony with brass or silver keys (though German silver began to be used in the 1830s). The workmanship is often superb and it is a shame that the instruments are now largely useless on account of their sharp pitch.

3. After this eruption of historic inventions there remained little useful to do except to refine, and to add various auxiliary keys and gadgets here and there. Certainly there was no lack of new and ingenious inventions during the second half of the century, but, generally speaking, they failed to catch on. An exception is Triébert's Conservatoire-system oboe of the late 1870s, while Heckel's important work on the Almenraeder bassoon also dates from the 1870s.

HISTORY

Since a comprehensive account of all these developments would fill a book in itself, the rest of this chapter is concerned mainly with the woodwind in England, which, as it happens, provides a good general view on account of the constant intermingling of native and Continental artists in English orchestras and the consequent impact of one foreign invention

TABLE OF LEADING PRINCIPAL WOODWIND PLAYERS IN ENGLAND, SHOWING THE ROUGH
DATE WHEN EACH SUCCEEDED TO THE LEADING POSITIONS

	Flute	*Oboe*	*Clarinet*	*Bassoon*
1790 to 1810	Ashe (6-keyed)	Harrington, T. Parke (2-keyed)	Mahon (5-keyed)	Holmes (8-*keyed, etc.*)
1815		Griesbach (2-*keyed, etc.*)	Willman (13-keyed)	Mackintosh (10-*keyed English*)
1820	Nicholson (7-keyed)			
1830		Grattan-Cooke (9–10-keyed) and Barret (Triébert)		Baumann (Savary)
1840	Ribas (8-keyed) and Richardson (Siccama)		Lazarus (12-keyed by Key; later Albert 13 key)	
1850	Carte (Boehm) J. Clinton (Boehm) Pratten	Barret; also Lavigne (Boehm-syst.)		
1870	Radcliff (Boehm) and others	Dubrucq sen. (*Triebert thumb-plate*)		Wotton (Savary)
1890		Malsch (Lorée thumb-plate)	also G. Clinton (Clinton model) and Egerton (Fieldhouse); Gomez (Boehm)	
1905	Fransella Murchie (Boehm)	also Lalande (Lorée Con-servatoire)	C. Draper (Boehm)	E. F. James (Morton) and W. James (Buffet)

after another. The table above broadly sums this up, showing some principal players and (in brackets) the type of instrument that each used in his prime (guesses, where the latter is not recorded, being indicated by *italics*).

Flute systems

THE EIGHT-KEYED FLUTE. Abjectly simple though this now appears beside the Boehm, it is nevertheless the model that carried the flute through the most glamorous period in its recent history. It was the flute played by early nineteenth-century performers whose names have become legends— Drouet, Furstenau, Nicholson, Tulou—and whose solo items were once clamoured for by concert audiences very much as the popular piano concertos are today.

To understand the instrument properly we must go back to those days. In technique, the keys of D and G were still the easiest for pure fireworks, and were therefore the favourites for those rather stereotyped airs with variations, among them Drouet's *Variations on 'God Save the King'*, which became the most popular flute piece of the day. But all keys were feasible, and Nicholson, the great English soloist, wrote that the key of A♭ is 'perhaps the most beautiful of which the flute is capable'. He himself used seven keys only, having considered the duplicate or 'long' F key unnecessary. After a Potter flute and then an Astor, he settled on the large-holed model which he and his father introduced in the 1820s, and Prowse manufactured, chiefly for sale by Clementi (*Nicholson's Improved Flute*, Plate XXXI).

Nicholson was the greatest flute virtuoso that England has ever known (with the comparatively small demand for woodwind solos today, players simply do not have the opportunity of becoming virtuosi in the old sense). The first outstanding thing about his playing was his tone. 'It is not only clear, metallic and brilliant, but possesses a volume that is almost incredible; and this too, be it observed, in the very lowest notes of the instrument', wrote his pupil, W. N. James. In Nicholson's own words, the tone ought to be 'as reedy as possible, as much like the oboe as you can get it, but embodying the round mellowness of the clarinet'.

The next thing was his style. He lived at the tail end of the centuries-long era of free ornamentation by solo players, and in two short pieces (fig. 74) from one of his tutors we can see something of his own method; first in a Mozart aria, with the ornament suitably restrained; and then in a popular air from the *Beggar's Opera*, very liberally embellished. Here and there will be noticed signs indicating special effects: the 'glide' (indicated by a crescent), and 'vibration' (wavy line). The glide was a portamento made by uncovering the holes gradually, and, he wrote, 'one of the most pleasing expressions of which the instrument is capable'. Vibration was a fingered vibrato in the

FIG. 74. *Two of Nicholson's flute solos, showing ornamentation, etc.*: 1, '*Ah perdona*', *from* La Clemenza di Tito, *Mozart.* 2, '*Cease your funning*', *from the* Beggar's Opera.

lower two octaves made by trilling on a hole or key well removed from the note-hole of the note in question (e.g. the E♭ key for the E's and F's, hole VI or V for the G's and A's, hole II for *d″*, etc., as given in his tutors). It was to have an

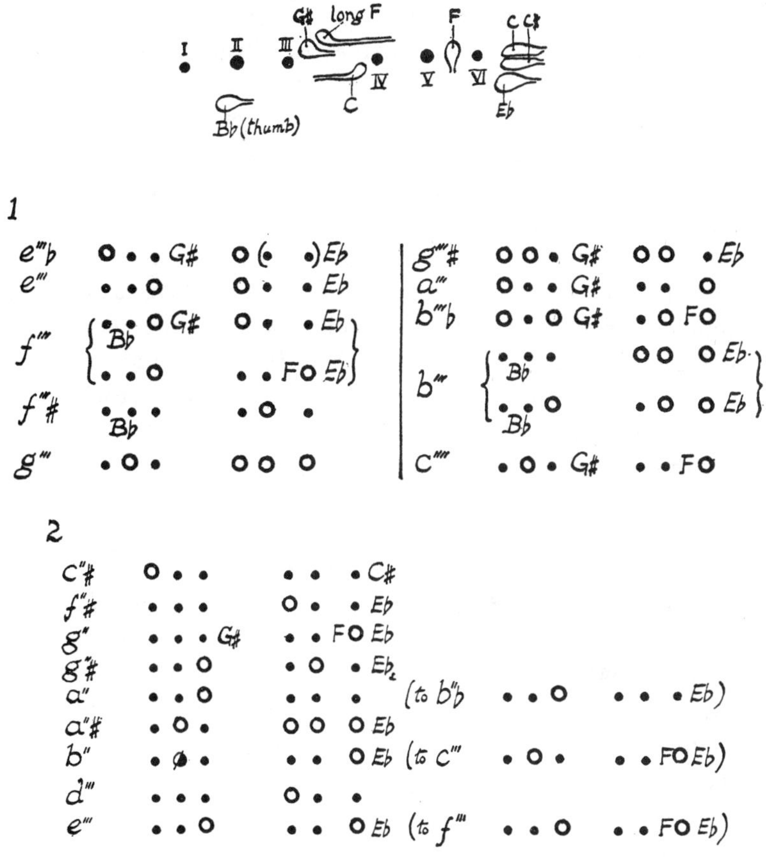

1

e‴♭	O • • G♯	O (• •)E♭	*g‴♯*	O O • G♯	O O • E♭
e‴	• • O	O • • E♭	*a‴*	O • • G♯	• • O
f‴	{•♭• O G♯ / B♭ ... • • O}	O • • E♭ / • • FO E♭	*b‴♭*	O • O G♯	• O FO
f‴♯	•♭• • / B♭	• O •	*b‴*	{•♭• • / B♭ •♭• O}	O O O E♭· / • O O E♭
g‴	• O •	O O O	*c‴*	• O • G♯	• • FO

2

c″♯	O • •	• • • C♯		
f″♯	• • •	O • • E♭		
g″	• • • G♯	• • FO E♭		
g″♯	• • O	• O • E♭		
a″	• • O	• • •	(to *b″♭* • • O	• • • E♭)
a″♯	• O •	O O O E♭		
b″	• ∅ •	• • O E♭	(to *c‴* • O •	• • FO E♭)
d‴	• • •	O • •		
e‴	• • O	• • O E♭	(to *f‴* • • O	• • FO E♭)

FIG. 75. *Eight-keyed flute.* 1, *Some fingerings for the high octave* (*see also fig. 69*). 2, *Sensitive fingerings for slurred semitones in slow pieces* (*from Nicholson*).

effect 'like a bell or glass', beginning slow and loud and then quickening as the note fell away in a diminuendo. These effects were clearly intended to give the playing the most free and singer-like quality, and with the same object in view, Nicholson,

Tulou and others employed sensitive, sharp-tuned fingerings to obtain the smoothest, most vocal legato over certain semitone intervals in slow melodies, e.g. between leading-note and tonic. The chief of these fingerings are given in fig. 75, and their employment as specified by Nicholson is indicated in the examples by the small stars or crosses. All these things help to reveal the carefully-considered approach through which Nicholson and his contemporaries earned such astonishing popularity on the old flute. It must be admitted, however, that Nicholson now and then aroused sharp criticism for excessive use of vibration and the glide, not to mention too lavish ornamentation and over-long cadenzas.

Nicholson died in 1837 and was succeeded by Ribas, with a powerful tone on the large-holed flute, and Richardson, who adopted the Siccama model—an eight-keyed flute with rings for I and II (to help $c''\sharp$ and c''), hole III lowered and covered by a lever (to improve A) and covered sixth hole (to help E; its full fingering is still included in the Otto Langey flute tutor, though the model has been out of use for many years). In 1850, Ribas, the more eminent player of the two, was succeeded by Pratten, the last noted English principal to use the eight-keyed flute. He rose to fame on the old large-holed model, but later changed to his cylindrical design described in Chapter II.

BOEHM. With his powerful, reedy tone, Nicholson may be said to have founded the traditional English school of flute-playing. But this was not all; for Boehm, looking back on his life, said that 'had I not heard him [Nicholson], probably the Boehm flute would never have been made'.

Theobald Boehm, of Munich, was a maker of flutes (with a partner, Greve) and also a professional player. On a visit to London in 1831 he heard Nicholson, whose volume of tone of the large-holed flute astonished him. He realized at once that he he could produce nothing to approach it on the German type of flute, which, though often provided with extra keys, was otherwise of a conservative design with small holes. When Boehm returned to Munich, his keen, analytical mind faced up squarely to the question of the large holes, and he quickly decided to incorporate them on a systematic basis throughout the instrument. Moreover, he went yet a step further: he conceived the idea of securing *full venting* for the notes by changing all the existing closed keys into open keys—i.e. into keys standing normally open.

This reversed key-system demanded some novel method of control, and for this Boehm embodied a mechanical device that had appeared already in rudimentary forms in the workshops of other experimental flute-makers: the now-familiar rings, through which a finger can operate a key in the same movement as closing its own hole. Thus he produced the *conical Boehm flute*, 1832, the greatest of all landmarks in the modern history of woodwind design (Plate XXVI).

In place of the old closed C key (side key for IV) he made an open C hole at the rear of the flute (actually a pair of small adjacent holes), so that closing hole I now gave C instead of B. This C hole also vented the open C♯, and the left thumb closed it to give B. The B in turn has for its primary vent an open hole on the front of the instrument replacing the old closed B♭ key at the rear. This hole was closed by ring IV for B♭, and by ring II for A. The A similarly has for its primary vent the open G♯ key, which reversed the traditional action of the left little finger. In this manner he worked his way down the flute, to produce the now familiar Boehm fingering. He would have liked also to reverse the E♭ key, but he refrained, fearing lest it might prove more than flute-players would put up with (although most of them even then pressed this key open for most notes). Indeed, as the conical Boehm quickly became known across Europe, many players were impatient even with the open G♯ key, and within six years, Dorus, a flutist at the Paris Opéra, had devised an ingenious closed G♯ key ('Dorus key') that did not encroach upon the full-venting principle. Thenceforth, the Dorus key was generally kept on the Continent, while Paris makers tidied up Boehm's own lay-out of the keywork, giving the conical Boehm flute its final form.

Search for yet greater volume and freedom of sound led Boehm next to reason thus, assisted by experiments with numerous bits of brass tubing:

1. Strength, fullness and clarity of the tone are proportional to the volume of air set in vibration; and a cylindrical tube contains more air than a contracting one.

2. Fundamental vibrations can be most perfectly elicited in wide tubes when there is a contraction at the mouth-hole; he said that his experimental tubes would not efficiently sound any fundamental below f' unless this contraction was present. Moreover, he had long wondered why the flute, alone among woodwind instruments, should have been blown at its wider end.

3. While the fundamentals were best when the contraction (which at first he made conical) began near hole I, the high notes suffered. Therefore he had to shorten the cone.

4. Now he discovered that this contraction must be curved, not straight, and that the best curve was one that approached a parabola.

With this, Boehm had found his *cylindrical bore* (1847), the bore of the flute today. The holes, he discovered, should have at least three-quarters of the diameter of the bore, making covered action (finger-plates) necessary. Hole I was an exception to the rule: for the sake of the upper D's it had to be smaller than the other holes, and placed rather high up the flute. Boehm's first instruments were of silver, though late in life he himself changed to wood, or silver with wooden head.

In England the cylindrical Boehm was immediately put into production by Rudall & Rose, who introduced the Briccialdi lever (B♭ by thumb alone) two years afterwards. Carte and J. Clinton were the first leading players to adopt it.

As a bird's-eye view of the flute in mid-Victorian times, the following section from Lafeur's catalogue of about 1870 may be of interest. Though the cylindrical Boehm was by then in use among the leading players, it is still featured as a novelty to general customers. The list is here somewhat condensed.

Cylindric Bore Concert Flutes (open or closed G♯).

   THE CELEBRATED CYLINDRIC BORE BOEHM'S
        IMPROVED SYSTEM CONCERT FLUTE:
   from solid 18-carat gold, down to B complete (£170); the same, made in white or coloured pure crystal [etc., down to the cheapest]; cocoa [cocus], to C (£18).

MECHANIZATION

Ordinary Boehm system Concert Flutes. Conical Bore [also in crystal, etc.]

Our own English London Best-Make Concert Flutes:
8-key, cocoa,
The most splendid English made PRATTEN pattern—to order.
Bushed holes (etc.).

Cheap Flute (very good)—8 key (28/-).

Special List of Cheap English Made Fifes and Flutes for Fife and Drum Bands

N.B.—The old-fashioned boxwood Fifes are now excluded from our list, the price of boxwood being almost as expensive as good cocoa wood, and far from being so good or so elegant.

Piccolo in F, E♭ or D, 1 key, cocoa; tuning slide extra.

B♭ Fife, 1 key.

F Flute, 1 key.

French Flageolets

Every flute-player should use this instrument. It is a most agreeable one with a small or large Ball-room Band, very easy to learn, and much less fatiguing than the Flute; more powerful and showy, and preferred to the Flute in all dancing rooms and private parties on account of brilliant and pleasing tone, it takes the same part as the Flute, Violin, or treble of the Piano. Next to the Boehm Flageolet Messrs Lafleur & Son recommend the 5-keyed Flageolet; all the ones with 6, 7, or 8 keys are of no use whatever. Our new Tutor by the celebrated Bousquet is the best book a beginner can refer to.

The *Alliance Musicale* new patent cylindric bore Boehm French Flageolet (ne plus ultra) of solid S.P. metal (12 gns.).
Ditto, ebony [etc.].

The regular ball business French Flageolet, with 5 keys and ring for C♯, ebony or cocoa.
Ditto, boxwood, brass mounted.

English flageolet (same fingering as Piccolo or Flute) with or without Flute head, *ad libitum*.

[down to]: Cheap, boxwood, 1 key, No Flute head (2/8d.).

The French Flageolet, or Quadrille Flageolet, with four holes in front and two behind, had been in great demand at dances and light music, and a popular solo instrument at Jullien's concerts, at which it was played by Collinet, who is said to have preferred only two keys on the instrument—the E♭ and G♯ keys in flute-language (the flageolet actually being pitched a fifth higher).

Fig. 76. *Miscellaneous flutes, etc., as manufactured in Germany c. 1890. Above, 11-keyed flute with ivory head. Left (downwards): simple-system piccolo with covered action; one-keyed fife (cylindrical); flageolet. Right (downwards): tin whistle, to be held sideways, imitating flute; swannee whistle; ocarina with tuning plunger.*

MECHANIZATION

Oboe systems

English audiences and critics of Beethoven's time were proud of the Philharmonic Society's woodwind principals—the players named against the dates 1815 and 1820 in the table of players on p. 316. They were all big-tone men. Apart, perhaps, from the marked individuality of Nicholson's style when he succeeded Ashe (who had a 'fine, rich sound'), contemporary comment leaves an impression that the section may have sounded very much like an old-school German or Russian woodwind section today.

The principal oboe, 'old Griesbach', as a critic of the time affectionately calls him, was pure German, from Hanover. He was said to have used a very broad and strong reed, and to have made a very full, rich sound resembling that of the clarinet of his colleague Willman. We do not know whether in due course he abandoned the classical two-keyed model on which he would have risen to his high position; but his immediate English successor, Grattan Cooke, played on the short-lived English simple-system oboe with up to ten flat or 'saltspoon' keys and the G♯ key on the bottom joint. Its lowest note was still C.

In the sharpest contrast with Griesbach stood the French soloist Vogt, who now and then came to London on concert tours. In the comparison, Vogt, with his delicate narrow French reed, sounded thin and reedy, though yet, as a critic wrote, his tone was possibly more the 'true tone' of the oboe. And in Paris, Brod considered that Germans made a hard, heavy sound with their too strong reeds.

While Vogt only paid visits, his pupil Barret came to stay, settling in London in 1829 following a dispute between the native players and theatre managements over fees. Then for nearly fifty years Barret held the principal positions in London, and during this long reign he established in England both the French style and the Triébert type of oboe, which in its various forms we use still. The following are the main stages in the evolution of this instrument.

THE TRIÉBERT OBOE. 1. Triébert *père*, a German by birth, served his apprenticeship in Paris and then, during the 1820s, made oboes there very much after the general Continental model of the time. Among the fourteen keys mentioned in Schott's list quoted earlier, four would have been Sellner's duplicate keys: extra touches for the c'' and $b'\flat$ keys, long F and long E♭. But most makers omitted these, producing a ten-keyed instrument (Plate XXXI) carrying, in addition to the two old keys: (*a*) The 'octave key' (as we should now call it), then used mainly for starting a slur upwards into the upper register and for helping high notes like top E and F. (*b*) The side keys for c'' and $b'\flat$; of these, the C key was intended mainly for quick alternation and trills with B, but the B♭ key gave a far better note than the old fork-fingering in the low register. Otherwise, for C in both octaves and for the upper B♭, the old cross-fingerings continued to take first place, just as they still do on simple-system oboes today. (*c*) An F♯ key on the bottom joint was opened by finger VII to bring the fingering . . . / . o o up to pitch in those days before the 'brille' rings. The remaining new keys—G♯, F, C♯ and low B—require no explanation. This would have been the type of instrument that Barret came to London with. Apart from the added keys it was still classical in build, and its reed was scraped back far further than now (to 11 millimetres from the tip in the drawing in Brod's tutor).

2. From this point onwards, old Triébert's son Frédéric commands the scene, starting with his *système 3* (*c*. 1840). This incorporated the second octave key, the half-hole plate, the brille (rings for V and VI) and the long E♭ key (left little finger). The brille, with its rings borrowed from Boehm's conical-flute mechanism, was applied by Sax to the clarinet at about the same time, and the next development with both instruments was a more extensive adoption of Boehm rings and mechanism, namely the Klosé-Buffet patent of 1843, announcing the Boehm-system clarinet and the Boehm-system oboe.

3. In its keywork, the Boehm-system oboe (fig. 77) closely follows Boehm's conical flute, with an open C key at the back, closed by the left thumb for B; an open B♭ key on the front, closed by any of the right-hand fingers (as on the Boehm clarinet); the usual Boehm F and F♯ arrangement; and sometimes side keys e.g. a B/C trill (as on the flute) or a B♭ side key. Triébert manufactured it as well as Buffet, yet, despite several

Fig. 77. *Various Triébert oboes, etc., from an advertisement of c. 1865.* Above, E♮ oboe (left) *and Pastoral oboe* (right). Below, left to right: *thumb-plate cor anglais; Boehm-system oboe; simple-system oboe; baritone oboe; Boehm-system bassoon.*

alterations to the bore, it seems never to have been really satisfactory. Barret wrote that though it prevailed for some years, 'it diminished the compass and entirely changed the quality of the tone'. The tone was bottom-heavy—loud and too free on the lower and middle notes and thin and characterless on the upper. Evidently the oboe proved more sensitive to small rearrangements of the ventages than the clarinet, on which the system is applied with comparatively small detriment to the tone-quality. In England, Lavigne, who was long the principal oboe in the Hallé, spent most of his life persevering with the Boehm-system oboe, finally evolving an elaborate design of his own ('old spider-keys', now preserved in the Bate Collection), yet in spite of all his efforts, his tone was remembered as having been coarser than everybody cared for.

4. Though he continued to manufacture the Boehm-system oboe, Triébert must have accepted its shortcomings, for only six years after the Klosé patent, he brought out his own *thumb-plate system*, sometimes confusingly named *système Boehm* in tutors of the time (and by French second-hand dealers even today) on account of its rings. In this system, the right hand preserves the simple-system arrangement while the left hand utilizes Boehm rings in a new manner for bringing the C and B♭ fingerings into one neat scheme (Chapter IV). It will be noticed that the former note is fingered as it is on the Boehm-system (by lifting the left thumb), though the mechanical principle involved is entirely different.

5. Now Barret re-enters the story, this time as an inventor. In the preceding system, Triébert supplied a side key to avoid having to trill with the thumb-plate. Shortly afterwards, towards 1860, Barret substituted for this key his right hand action, in which putting down any of the four right hand fingers could make C and B♭ as an alternative to lifting the left thumb from the thumb-plate. In England this system was widely used for a number of years, as the number of surviving instruments bears witness, but its complicated mechanism (which includes automatic octave keys) too easily goes out of adjustment; players gradually found that one could do very well with thumb-plate *or* right-hand action, but not with both on one instrument.

MECHANIZATION

6. Towards 1880, Triébert, in his last model, turned over to the second of these alternatives, substituting right hand C and B♭ action (actuated by ring IV only, however) for the thumb-plate: the Conservatoire system, to which Lorée and Gillet subsequently added perforated finger-plates (Chapter IV).

Returning to players in England, Barret died in 1875 and was succeeded by more brilliant foreigners—Frenchmen and Belgians—playing on one or other of the Triébert models: Dubrucq, Lalande and de Buscher, all remembered for their exquisite playing, with pure, steady tone; Lalande's pathetic sweetness of tone was said to draw tears from the violinists tuning to his A. Continuing this distinguished line is our leading contemporary figure, Leon Goossens. By contrast, Malsch, the first German oboist of note in England since Griesbach, is recalled as a player of the more bagpipish kind. He was one of the four original woodwind principals of the London Symphony Orchestra in 1904, the others having been Daniel Wood (flute), Manuel Gomez (clarinet) and E. F. James (bassoon).

Again we may quote Lafleur's catalogue of the early 1870s for a general picture of the oboe in Victorian England. Thumb-plate, Barret, Boehm and half-Boehm (i.e. with Boehm right hand) will all be noticed:

The Oboe, the most delicate of all the Musical Instruments, has been greatly improved of late years, owing to the constant labours and ability of the world-renowned maker Mons. Triébert, who may be called the Stradivarius of Oboe makers. . . . The instruments are all most carefully tested by the celebrated Oboe player Mons. Barret, now retired from the leading situations he occupied at the Opera and societies in London.

Triébert's Oboe, rosewood, 12 keys, German silver or real silver mounted.
   15 keys, with metal-lined joints.
   The same with plate for top D and double use of E flat.
   17 keys, with C plate and B♭ for left thumb.
   The same, with shake for C♯, down to low B♭.
Triébert's Oboe with octave keys at double employ.
   The same with Barret celebrated system.
   The same with Boehm system for the right hand.
   Ditto, down to A. [The dearest: £45].
   etc.

Pastoral Oboe in G or A♭ acute, maple, 4 brass keys.
   „   „   Boehm system, in G, rosewood.
   „   „   10 keys, rosewood Military Oboe. N.B. This is a very powerful instrument for marching out, the usual Oboe in C being lost in the heavy quick-march music.

Our own make Oboes.
   Boehm system, cocoa; 15 keys; 12 keys (etc.).
   13 keys and two rings, ordinary make (capital for beginners), boxwood, brass keys (£3. 15. 0).
   etc.

Corno Inglese, Triébert's make.
Baritone Oboe, rosewood, G.S. mounts, Triébert's make.
   etc.
Superior Morton's English make Cor Anglais, 13 keys, down to B♭.

Musette (reed included)—Pastoral Instrument to imitate the Swiss Pipe.
   Triébert's make, cocoa, 8 keys (etc.).
      Boxwood, brass-mounted.

The 'Pastoral Oboe' was rather like a musette but more finely constructed, with F sharp brille and two octave keys, and wider bore (fig. 77). The firm of Millereau, in their catalogue of 1874, expressed 'much pleasure in introducing to the notice of gentlemen artists and bandmasters this charming little instrument, which, by its novelty and most striking qualities must soon become a general favourite. . . . A broad reed is used, therefore there is nothing distressing in the blowing. . . . Solos upon Highland bagpipe melodies are very effective on this instrument and they can be made quite a feature of. Pretty and elegant in appearance, easy to blow, the pastoral oboe recommends itself particularly to gentlemen amateurs.' But there is no evidence that gentlemen amateurs showed much interest in it, while bandmasters certainly showed none.

Clarinet systems

It is usually a simple matter to identify the best-loved professional wind instrument of any given epoch: it is the one which was especially likened to the human voice. At the end of the sixteenth century this was said of the cornett; at the beginning of the eighteenth, of the oboe; and now, in the early part of the nineteenth century, the distinction has passed to the clarinet. The clarinet, wrote William Gardiner in 1832, 'approaches the tone of the female voice nearer than any other instrument, and as a principal in the orchestra it now sustains a distinguished part. ... In the hands of Willman and Baermann the clarinet is brought under complete subjection. In quality of tone it is warm and powerful; partaking somewhat of the oboe and the trumpet combined, and the lustre of its tones adds great refulgency to the orchestra.'

Baermann was acknowledged the greatest player of the time. Weber wrote the concertos for him (1811) and he introduced them on a Griessling & Schlott instrument with ten keys. Willman was the greatest player in England and, in the estimation of visiting critics, an artist second only to the celebrated German. From the 1820s onwards he played on thirteen-keyed instruments of the typical English type as made by Key and others, still with the plain C hole for the right little finger (Plate XXXI). Having as yet no brille, there was an F♯ key for finger VI running up the right-hand side of the bottom joint for use in conjunction with the . . . / . o o fingering. A cross-key for finger V duplicated this and was, in fact, the key that Willman normally used, reserving the side key for arpeggios and ascending slurs. In the lack of rollers or other aids to sliding the little fingers, many German makers fitted Muller's two very useful branches to the C♯ key and the E♭ key. These curved round behind the joint for operation by the right thumb, greatly facilitating B–C♯ and so on. The C♯ branch is just visible in Plate XXXI. Outside Germany the branches were little known though Willman had one fitted to his B key. The rest of the fingering, both in England and on the Continent, was plain simple-system. Muller gives the fullest analysis of it in his tutor.

Germans played with the reed downwards as we do today. Willman played with it uppermost; English players began to change over in the next generation—a few years after the French, who changed in the 1830s when Berr, a German, became professor at the Conservatoire. Berr advocated reed-downwards mainly on the grounds that it thus took less effort to blow; (for tone, Muller wrote that neither method had any advantage over the other). In Italy, however, some were still playing with the reed upwards quite recently.

Like his flutist colleague Nicholson, Willman was not only the leading orchestral principal in London, but also an indispensable soloist all over the country; these were the last great days of the woodwind soloist, and these two artists were the public's favourites. No series of concerts in London, or festival in the provinces, was complete without a solo or concerto from one of them. Of the two, Willman's taste was perhaps the closer to our own, for besides the inevitable fantasias (Baermann's was a favourite) he performed his instrument's classics, including Mozart's concerto. He must have been a beautiful player; musical journals are filled with praise for the soothing quality of his tone. Moreover, individual artistry apart, these old thirteen-keyed boxwood clarinets are almost unbeatable for tone, so long as the correct mouthpiece and small, hard reed are used with them. There are no details of Willman's reeds, but Muller gives about the same dimensions as those of a present-day German reed (except in overall length) while the mouthpiece described in his tutor has a narrow, tapered slot and a very long, open lay (quite 30 millimetres long). English mouthpieces were similar, though even more pointed. The modern big mouthpiece came in with the reformed simple-system clarinet first brought out in the 1840s by the Belgian makers Sax and Albert (Chapter V).

No front-rank foreign clarinettist came over to settle in England until the close of the century. Willman was succeeded by another great English player, Lazarus, and Mr Rendall has told us what his instruments were: until 1855, instruments by Key, of the old type but with a brille added (a twelve-keyed B♭ and a ten-keyed A); then, after five years with an ingenious design by Fieldhouse, he adopted the Albert instruments (fitted with the B♮ side key), which he played for the rest of his life. He retained the long lay (one inch) though using a reed of medium strength on the large Albert mouthpiece. Bernard Shaw, who knew about wind instruments from his early days in Dublin, wrote an interesting comparison between English and German players during the latter days of Lazarus (the early 1890s). German clarinettists, he said, 'use reeds which give a more strident, powerful, appealing tone than in England; and the result is that certain passages (in *Der Freischütz*, for example) come out with a passion and urgency that surprises the tourist used to Egerton, Lazarus and Clinton. But in the *Parsifal* Prelude, or the second movement of Beethoven's Fourth Symphony, one misses the fine tone and dignified continence of the English fashion'. The same comparison is often heard in England today.

The Boehm-system clarinet (1843) was beginning to interest Belgian, Italian and American players in the 1870s. In England, Lazarus recommended it, but did not change to it himself, and nor did any important player until the arrival of Gomez, from Spain, who brilliantly held principal positions in the London orchestras from about 1890, playing all parts on a B♭ full Boehm. Outstanding among his converts to the Boehm-system was Charles Draper, who brings us up to modern times and well-known players, many of whom were his pupils. Especially beautiful in Draper's playing was a wonderful unity of tone, technique and musical feeling. His chamber-music recordings, made towards the end of his life, remain a rare delight and a memorial to a very great period of English wind-playing (e.g. Beethoven's *Septet* and Schubert's *Octet*, with E. W. Hinchliffe on Buffet bassoon, and Aubrey Brain on French horn).

Details of other nineteenth-century clarinet systems are given in Rendall, e.g. of the Romero clarinet formerly used to some extent in Spain. Several living British players started on the *Pupeschi system*: a simple-system clarinet with articulated G♯ key actuated by the B key touch; it lacked the usual G♯ touch.

From Lafleur's catalogue of about 1870:

CLARINETS:

Boehm System. The *Alliance Musicale* celebrated Boehm system clarinet (ne plus ultra) with two mouthpieces; Brazilian ebony or cocoa, silver mounted (£22).

Set of three clarinets, A, B♭ and C (£65).

etc.

Genuine Celebrated Belgian Clarinet, by J. B. Albert. Superior to any yet introduced to the Profession and Public.

A, B♭, C or E♭ Clarinets, 13 keys, two rings, cocoa.

A, B♭, C or E♭ with new patent C♯ key.

Sets of three, A, B♭ and C (£25 to £55).

Alliance Musicale perfect Albert Model, 14 keys, 2 rings, the new patent
C♯, etc., cocoa.
etc.

Cheap Clarinets, suitable for beginners:
  Boehm system, boxwood, brass-mounted (£6. 16. 0).
  Albert model, stained boxwood, brass-mounted, 13 keys, 2 rings (45/-).
  Ordinary 13-key.
  10-key ditto.
  6-key ditto (£1).
Military Metal Clarinets.

Tenor, Alto, E♭ or F Clarinets:
  Boehm system, Buffet's make, cocoa.
    Ditto, boxwood and brass.
etc.
B♭ Bass Clarinets, Boehm system [as above, etc.]:
Saxophones (Very Best Make). These modern instruments are easily
mastered by any clarinet player and are a powerful addition to the Reed
Instruments in a Military Band. Made of Brass. B♭ Soprano, E♭ Alto
Tenor, B♭ Tenor Baritone, and E♭ Baritone Bass (9 to 12 gns.; silver
plated extra).

Bassoon systems

The London woodwind in the time of Beethoven demanded
fine, rich bassoon-playing to support Nicholson, Griesbach and
Willman, and it was splendidly provided by the last two great
players of the old English school. The elder was Holmes,
mentioned in the last chapter, and from about 1820 he was
succeeded by Mackintosh. No details are preserved of their
actual instruments, nor did either leave a tutor to record the
fine points of the technique. But they certainly used London-
made instruments (very likely by Milhouse), which had become
more assertive in tone than formerly, partly through opening
out the bell (which took on a vase or funnel shape in the outside) and partly through enlarging certain low-note holes,
particularly the right thumb-hole. Added to the eight keys of *c.*
1800 was a middle C♯ key (usually for right thumb) and sometimes a B♭ key for VI. Mackintosh was admired for his full,
round sound; 'it struck me', noted an English visitor to Germany quoted by Adam Carse, 'that the bassoons used on the
Continent generally have not the same roundness of tone as
those of English manufacture' (though he added that the

Continental instruments were very sweet, and were loud enough to balance the other woodwind). Early nineteenth-century English bassoons by Milhouse, Key, etc., have a distinctive quality of their own especially clear and sweet in the tenor register. The model was one with great possibilities for the future, and had it survived to be improved and developed as the foreign models were, we might have come to possess a very remarkable instrument today. But the same thing happened as with the oboe. Hard upon the heels of Barret and the French oboe, came Baumann, a Paris-trained Belgian, with the French bassoon. With this (almost certainly a Savary instrument), Baumann set a new and long-lasting fashion in England.

Again, the French idea of playing was quite different from the English. An English writer, in the *Harmonicon* in 1830, makes the recommendation, very likely quoted from Mackintosh himself, 'to play a strong reed down'. The consequence, according to Barr (bassoon tutor, Paris, 1832), was that the English players were quite unable to play *piano* since their coarse reeds need excessive force in tonguing. However the same writer in the *Harmonicon* alludes to 'foreigners whose fuzzy tone and meaningless execution' recall a turkey-cock sweeping its wings along the ground in a farmyard. It is not difficult to imagine the kind of bassoon-sound that gave this impression.

If, however, the allusion is to Baumann, the writer may have heard him on an off day, for he was clearly a fine player, and he reigned in London for close on twenty-five years. 'If he does not possess the full round tone of other performers on this delicious instrument, he has the greater power of delicate inflection, and 'a breathingness of sound that might "create a soul under the ribs of death".' Nothing could sum up the traditional French woodwind playing better.

The celebrated maker Savary *jeune* (Paris) finished work in 1850, but his instruments were passed down from generation to generation of bassoon-players like old violins, and several remained in use until the end of orchestral sharp pitch in the 1920s. William Wotton, the greatly-admired player who succeeded Baumann, and his brother Tom, both played the Savary (with the old brass keys). Wotton's successor, E. F. James, played a Morton flat-pitch bassoon but a Savary sharp-pitch. At the time of Baumann's arrival the Savary had been an eleven-keyed instrument with a pin-hole in the crook. By about 1850 there was a crook key operated only by the high A and C keys; also middle C♯ and E♭ keys on the tenor joint, and—though for many years omitted from cheaper or army instruments—a low B key.

Besides those of Savary (which were in due course closely copied in London by Key), bassoons by Buffet and Triébert were becoming well-known by the mid-century. These often incorporated rings mentioned in Chapter VI, for tuning certain fingerings, and suggested mainly by Jancourt, the mid-century professor at the Conservatoire. Jancourt is now remembered chiefly for his fine tutor, in which he insists on the importance of *vibration*—a fingered vibrato akin to Nicholson's on the flute, though done rather differently, namely by a *tremblement* of the fingers above the holes (*au dessus des trous*). He describes it only for certain notes, thus: shaking with idle fingers of the right hand for $f'\sharp$, g', c'' and above, and for the middle C's, C♯'s and B's; and with idle left hand fingers for the E's and D's. The vibration, he stresses, must be used only to express real feeling; when it sounds calculated, its effect is merely ridiculous. Such a means for vibrato may appear quaint today, but it is interesting to find it prescribed by one of the leading Parisian woodwind players only a century ago.

Another Triébert experiment was the Boehm-system bassoon devised by the Paris player Marzoli (fig. 77). Its holes were all placed at acoustically logical positions, sarrusophone-wise. An instrument of unbelievable complexity and utter poverty of tone, fortunately it never caught on. The ingenious Haseneier, in Germany, devised a far better design of bassoon with holes laid out logically—very much as on his better-remembered contrabassoon (the contrabassophone)—and with Boehm-like fingering, but few instruments seem to have been made.

From Lafleur's catalogue of about 1870:

BASSOONS:

Triébert's make, Boehm system, maple, G.S. mounted.
Triébert's make, 19 keys, mounted on needles.

Triébert's make, 17 keys, long crook key, top F key, maple, metal-lined joints (£24).

Our own make, improved ordinary system, 19 keys, 3 rings, maple, G.S. mounted.
>The following notes are perfectly free: C♯, D and E♭, 3rd octave, without the A♭ key. B natural of 2nd and 3rd octaves, without the B♭ key.

Ditto, brass-mounted (£14).

Ditto, 15-key, maple, Ordinary Bassoon [crook key worked only by the thumb keys, i.e. not 'long crook key'].

Ditto, 12 keys [no low B natural].

Morton's perfect English make Bassoon, brass mounted (£25). G.S. mounted 4 gns. extra; real silver 16 gns.
>The tenor joints and all finger holes are lined and bushed with ebony (a great improvement to the tone).

Tenor Bassoons. Morton's Superior English Make.

Brass keys on pillars.

With extra keys; G.S. or silver mounts extra.

The New Contra-Fagotto or Double Bassoon in C.
>A want greatly felt and a magnificent addition in a Military Band [Morton Contrabassophone, see Chap. VI].

Best English make a perfect instrument, with all the latest improvements, brass mounted (£70).

G.S. mounted, 8 gns. extra (etc.).

Sarrusophones. These newly invented and Patented Reed Instruments are of great value in bands where Oboes and Bassoons are absent. Being beautiful in tone and possessing great sonority, they are destined before long to take up an important position in the Military Band, in which the soft powers of the Oboe and the Bassoon are lost. The fingering is very much as the Clarinet and it would be very little trouble for Clarinet players to learn it.
>E♭ soprano; B♭ soprano; E♭ alto; B♭ tenor; E♭ baritone; B♭ bass; E♭ contrabass; and Double Bass or Contra Bassoon in B♭ or C (£17).

The 'Tenor Bassoon', better known as *tenoroon*, was in F, a fourth above the bassoon. Such small bassoons, already noticed in Chapter XI, continued to be built by Savary and others for obscure purposes. Jancourt used to play solos on one, and so did E. F. James, using a rosewood instrument by Morton with brass keys. The only recorded nineteenth-century instances of its use in the orchestra are two: (1) At Bordeaux, where the two cor anglais parts in Halévy's *La Juive* used to be played on oboe and tenoroon; and (2) in London about 1870, when Dr

Stone had a theory that Bach's oboe da caccia parts were intended for small bassoons, and resolutely performed them so in festival performances, using two Savary tenoroons with an unnamed accomplice.

THE HECKEL. The first twenty-five years of the twentieth century was for London and most English woodwind playing a period of golden maturity. Boehm flute, French oboe and bassoon, and the Franco-Belgian clarinets had been in regular use for upwards of fifty years and become thoroughly assimilated into the country's own feeling of woodwind-playing—'the fine tone and dignified continence of the English fashion', as Shaw put it so well. But late in the 1920s, fresh movements were brewing. A few young flutists (Geoffrey Gilbert and Frank Butterworth were the first) went to study at Paris. The Lancashire schools of sensational oboe-playing were gaining the upper hand through the influence of Leon Goossens and his many pupils, and of Alec Whittaker, who came down from Manchester to be principal oboe in the newly-formed B.B.C. Symphony Orchestra, 1930. And at this same time—just a hundred years after the arrival of Barret and Baumann with the first French instruments—the Heckel invasion began.

The story of the Heckel bassoon begins about 1825, when Carl Almenraeder, a bandmaster and contemporary of the Savarys, set out to cure certain faults of the classical bassoon. The worst trouble lay in the sharpness and wobbliness of the A's in the middle two octaves. Of course, a proficient player overcame this with practice, as he still does today with those French-system bassoons that preserve traces of the same fault, but nevertheless it must have proved a great stumbling-block to the less apt pupils and a great nuisance to bandmasters like Almenraeder who had to train them. He located the cause of the trouble in the position of hole VI, and the remedy in moving this hole some 9 inches down the butt, where finger VI closed it by a long key. To equalize the octave, he bored a vent in the adjacent large bore of the butt, this vent being closed by a second key mounted on the same lever (nowadays the main hole and its vent are both covered by a single pad). He also readjusted the position and size of other holes and keys (Carse has quoted the details in *Musical Wind Instruments*, p. 196) and added the open low B key and alternative F♯ and A♭ keys still characteristic of the German bassoon.

Thus far, Almenraeder was entirely successful, producing an instrument on which the notes came out as steadily and evenly as they do on the small woodwind. But the tone-quality suffered. Heckel has written, 'the clear, hard tone and greater volume of the new bassoon was less pleasing than the delicate, soft tone-colour of the old'—'the old' being the nine-keyed models by Grenser of Dresden and others, in which the bassoon had reached its orchestral zenith in the scores of Beethoven. (The hard, cutting quality of the reformed design lingers on in many fairly modern-looking German instruments by lesser makers dating from around fifty and sixty years ago; some of these are still in circulation and are to be avoided.) It has been the achievement of the firm of Heckel to undo the damage to the tone while yet preserving the technical benefits. The work included patient attention to the bore (working gradually towards a true cone, as Triébert did with the oboe) and refinement of the manufacture by every possible means. During one period, Wagner himself was in and out of the workshop watching progress with keen interest. Of the perfected model, said to have made its Bayreuth début in 1879, Heckel justly wrote that 'the old singing quality was restored without loss of volume, clarity and uniform strength of the notes'. Further gradual improvements since then have led to the instrument as we now know it.

During the time of the growing-pains of the Almenraeder-Heckel remodelling in Germany, Austria had its own bassoon, the old '*Wiener Fagott*' of Ziegler and others. This formed a distinct type of its own. Like the Heckel it retained the eighteenth-century German position of the low E♭ key—for left little finger (the low C♯ key being added next to it in both cases). Also it had duplicate F♯ and G♯ keys on the butt. But like the French bassoon it had a partly-cylindrical bell, and the low B was made by opening a closed key (preserving the classical venting of long joint and bell, instead of having an open key, as on the Heckel). The upper part of the tenor joint was usually made extendable with rack and pinion as a tuning slide. From about the 1870s, however, Vienna adopted the perfected Heckel and has used it ever since.

The story next takes us to Manchester, where Richter, having taken over the Hallé in 1899, considered that the local bassoonists were inadequate, and sent to Vienna for a principal bassoon. Schieder therefore arrived, with his Heckel, followed a few years later by a second player also from Vienna. At the same time, to train local men in the use of the new instrument, a scholarship was endowed at the Manchester College with Schieder as professor (his son is now assistant principal to Oehlberger in the Vienna Philharmonic) and Archie Camden, today one of the leading British players of the German bassoon, as the first scholar.

Gradually, interest in the German bassoon began to develop in London; first through recordings of orchestras such as the Berlin and Vienna Philharmonics and the Philadelphia Symphony (emigrants from Central Europe had already established the Heckel in America); and also through Camden's well-known recording of Mozart's Concerto with the Hallé, in which he was then principal. However, the actual shock that brought about the mass change-over was, as already mentioned, the 1930 visit of the New York Philharmonic. The Heckel has its faults, as we have since discovered; but the effect of the two Americans upon those who had never heard the instrument in the flesh before was unforgettable. The strange novelty of their tone at once appealed to some, though not to others, who said that it sounded too much like a horn; but what struck everybody was how everything they played seemed to come out so effortlessly and so clearly, and during the next few years the question whether or not to change over was in every London bassoon-player's mind. Richard Newton was among the first to change, shortly followed by John Alexandra, who successfully brought off a hair-raising change from the Buffet in the space of ten days before recording Beethoven's Fifth Symphony with Koussevitsky. Next, Archie Camden came south to become principal in the B.B.C. Symphony, and that was that.

It was all so unexpected that one wonders what might happen next, especially with our more frequent contact with players of other countries. Nearly every leading British woodwind player at present has at least one close friend amongst the star performers on the Continent and in America. The number of young players who go to study in Paris, Brussels, Amsterdam, Vienna and Geneva grows yearly (while conversely, two established British artists, Reginald Kell and Arthur Gleghorn, have become well known as clarinet and flute teachers in America). And on top of these things there is the unending stream of recordings of foreign artists and orchestras. However, the signs are that instrument-design is now drifting towards a world-standard. With the continual refining of orchestral performance, players prefer the instruments that give them the feeling of the most secure control, and America has already picked these out: metal Boehm flute, Conservatoire-system oboe, Boehm clarinet, and Heckel bassoon (and likewise German horns for the same reason).

It is a possibility that more and more countries will settle on this particular quartet of models, partly for the reason just given and partly through the present production trends towards world uniformity. In the long run, this would be a pity, because none of the four are perfect, and the co-existence of other models (which also have faults, but different ones) keeps criticism alive. Disappearance of the German clarinet or the French bassoon, for instance, would on these grounds be a very great loss.

Another stimulating thing is the growing interest in the 'antiques'—the classical models of a hundred and fifty years ago and more. So recently mere prizes for museum curators or toys for the musician at home, they have now already become, in several instances in England and on the Continent, professional instruments on which players have performed publicly and broadcast. How far this can be taken remains to be seen. It is no joke, after playing for six days of the week on one's modern instrument, to perform on the seventh upon one's antique, probably having already done six hours' recording on that day itself on the modern instrument. Nor does this make for displaying the antique at its best. How it could be managed is certainly a problem; but it would make a logical and desirable continuation of the practical research started by Mahillon and Dolmetsch years ago. One feels sorry for the poor *fortepiano*—the classical piano now returning to fashion—struggling in one of its own concertos against our modern woodwind. The players can and will play as *softly* as they are asked to; but it is a question not of loudness but of the *character* of resonance and tone. But surely, somebody always remarks when the subject of the antiques comes up, Mozart would have been thrilled could he have heard our modern instruments! Perhaps he would have been. On the other hand, perhaps he wouldn't; and to suggest so implies no disparagement of the genius and devoted labours of Boehm, Buffet, Triébert and Heckel, who have kept the woodwind player abreast with the demands of composer and conductor, and have placed him so well on top of his work today.

List of the Old London Makers and Suppliers

The following list is extracted from the far larger list of particulars of English wind-instrument makers and dealers that R. Morley Pegge has compiled and has generously placed at the author's disposal. It enables one to date one's 'finds' from the name, and often also the address, stamped on the instrument.[1]

Astor, *maker*:
Geo. Astor, 26 Wych St., 1778–97.
Astor (& Co.), 79 Cornhill, 1798–1826.
Astor & Horwood, *same address*, 1815–22.
Astor & Co., 3 Anne St., 1821–30.

Bilton, *maker; ex-foreman to Cramer*:
Richard Bilton, 14 Mount Row, c. 1824–26.
  „ „ 93 Westminster Bridge Rd., 1826–56.

Bland, *dealer and piano-maker*:
A. Bland & Weller, c. 1790 to c. 1818.

Boosey, *publisher; made woodwind from* 1818:
Thos. Boosey, 28 Holles St., 1850–56.
T. Boosey & Sons, 24 Holles St., 1856–74.
Boosey & Co., 295 Regent St., 1874–1930.
Boosey & Hawkes, *same address*, 1930– .

Bressan, *maker (especially flutes and recorders)*:
Late seventeenth century to middle of eighteenth century.

Broderip & Wilkinson, *publisher, dealer*: 1798–1808.

[1] Note to second edition: With the appearance of Lyndesay G. Langwill's *Index of Musical Wind-Instrument Makers* (1960) this list is now superseded for anyone desiring full information. In the present edition, corrections, from Langwill, are incorporated.

Cahusac, *maker*:

    Thos. Cahusac, Strand, *c.* 1755–94.

        ,,   ,,   Gt. Newport St., 1784–94.

        ,,   ,,   & Sons, 196 Strand, (1794)–1798.

        ,,   ,,   senior, 41 Haymarket, 1800–05.

        ,,   ,,   ,,   114 New Bond St., 1805–08.

    W. M. Cahusac, 196 Strand, 1800–11.

        ,,   79 Holborn, 1811–16.

Clementi, *dealer and maker*:

    Clementi & Co., 26 Cheapside, 1802–21; *also*—195 Tottenham Court Rd., 1805–21.

    Clementi, Collard & Collard, 26 Cheapside, 1822–30.

    Collard & Collard, *same address, c.* 1767– .

Collier, *? maker*: Thos. Collier, working in 1770; no other dates known.

Cotton, *? maker*: Wm. Cotton, working during 1760s; *also*— John Cotton, Fleet St., –1794– .

Cramer, *maker; successor to Miller (though not to his premises)*:

    J. B. Cramer, 30 Charing Cross, 1799–1805.

    Cramer & Key, 2 Pall Mall, 1805–07 (*see* Key).

    Cramer & Son, 20 Pall Mall, 1807–24.

    J. B. Cramer & Co., 201 Regent St., 1824–93.

D'Almaine, *see* Goulding.

Florio, *flute-maker*: from *c.* 1757; died, 1795.

Garrett, *maker*:

    Richard Garrett, 2 King St., 1826–33.

        ,,   ,,   65 (later 64) King St., 1833–62.

    Garrett & Davis, 23 Princes St., 1862–68.

    Garrett & Co., 5 Gt. Smith St., 1869–93.

Gedney, *maker, successor to Stanesby*:

    Caleb Gedney, from *c.* 1754; died, 1769.

Gerock, *maker*:

    C. Gerock, 76 Bishopsgate within, *c.* 1804–20; *also*—1 Gracechurch St., 1816–21.

    Gerock & Co., 79 Cornhill, 1821–38.

    Gerock, Astor & Co., *the same* 1821–31.

    Gerock & Wolf, *same address*, 1831–32.

    Wolf, *same address*, 1837–45.

Wolf, 45 Moorgate St., 1840–43.

,, 20 St Martins le Grand, 1843–45.

Wolf & Figg, *same address*, 1845–53.

Goodlad, *see* Willis.

Goulding, *publisher; maker from* 1799:

Geo. Goulding, 25 James St., *c.* 1784–87; *also*—6 James St., 1787–98.

Goulding & Co., *also* Goulding, Wood & Co., *also*—Goulding, Phipps & D'Almaine—

45 Pall Mall, 1799–1804,

117 New Bond St., 1804–08,

124 New Bond St., 1808–11.

Goulding, D'Almaine & Co., 20 Soho Sq., 1810–12 and 1819–1829.

Goulding, D'Almaine & Potter, *same address*, 1811–23.

Goulding & D'Almaine, 20 Soho Sq., 1823–34.

D'Almaine & Co., *same address*, 1834–58.

,, 104 New Bond St., 1858–66.

Hale, *flute-maker*:

John Hale, 20 Chandos St., 1784–1804.

Key, *maker*:

Thos. Key, 2 Pall Mall, 1808–13.

,, 20 Charing Cross, *c.* 1815–56– .

Fredk. Key, *same address*, 1854–58, *also*—

Key, Rudall, Rose & Carte, 1856–58.

Kusder, *maker*: working in 1799.

Lawson, *makers*:

H. Lawson, 29 John St., before 1800.

,, 5 Nassau St., before 1814 to 1818.

J. Lawson, 198 Tottenham Court Rd., 1818–45.

Longman, *publisher and dealer*:

Longman & Co., 26 Cheapside, 1769–71.

Longman & Lukey, *same address*, 1771–77.

Longman & Broderip, *same address*, 1777–98.

Longman & Clementi, *same address*, 1798–1800.

Metzler, *maker*:

Metzler, 343 Oxford St., *c.* 1800.

V. Metzler, 105 Wardour St., 1812–16.

Metzler & Son, *or* Geo. Metzler & Co., *same address*, 1816–42. *The same*, Gt. Marlborough St., 1842–1920.

Milhouse, *maker*:

(Milhouse, Newark, Notts., from *c*. 1763 to 1788.)
W. Milhouse, 100 Wardour St., 1788–98.
    „   337 Oxford St., 1799–1828.
W. Milhouse & Son, *same address*, 1828–36.
Richard Milhouse, *same address*, 1836–40.

Miller, *maker; subsequently made for Clementi*:

G. Miller, 79 Cornhill, *c*. 1775–99.

Monzani, *flute-maker*:

T. Monzani, 2 Pall Mall, 1799–1804.
    „   3 Old Bond St., 1804–07.
Monzani & Co., *same address and others*, 1807–20.
Monzani & Hill, 28 Regent St., 1820–29.
Hill, late Monzani, *same address*, 1829–39.

Morton, *oboe and bassoon maker*:

Alfred Morton (*various addresses*), from 1847 to 1898.

Parker, *maker*:

John Parker, 52 Long Lane, *c*. 1770–*c*. 1815.

Payne, *? makers*: G. C. Payne, 1808–35; *also*—Richard and Geo. Payne, 13 Little Newport St., 1835–41.

Potter, *flute-maker, etc.*:

Richard Potter, Green Dragon Lane, 1745–64.
    „   „   5 Pemberton Row, 1764–*c*. 1787.
    „   „   5 Johnson's Court, *c*. 1787–1800.
R. Potter & Son, *same address*, *c*. 1801–1808.
W. H. Potter, *same address*, 1809–1817.
S. Potter, 20 King St., *c*. 1817–*c*. 1836.
    „   37 Marsham St., 1837–39.
H. Potter, *same address*, 1839–41.
    „   2 Bridge St., 1841–57.
    „   30 Charing Cross, 1858–1904.
H. Potter & Co., 36 West St., from after 1904.

Proser, *maker*: 1777–1795.

Prowse, *maker, especially of flutes; previously with Clementi*:

T. Prowse, 3 Wenlock St., 1816–33.

,, 3 Old Jewry, 1833–34.

,, 13 Hanway St., 1834–68.

Rudall, *flute-makers*:

Geo. Rudall, 5 Clement's Inn, *c.* 1820–21.

Rudall & Rose, 7 Tavistock St., *c.* 1821–27.

,, ,, 15 Piazza, Covent Gdn., *c.* 1827–37.

,, ,, 1 Tavistock St., 1837–47.

,, ,, 38 Southampton St., 1847–54.

Rudall Rose & Carte & Co., 100 New Bond St., 1854–57.

,, ,, ,, ,, 20 Charing Cross, 1856–78.

(*See also* Key, Rudall, Rose & Carte.)

Rudall Carte & Co., 23 Berners St., 1878–1955; etc.

Schuchart, *maker*: died, 1765.

Stanesby, *makers*:

T. Stanesby, senior, died 1734.

T. Stanesby, junior, died 1754.

Ward, *maker; sometime foreman to Monzani & Hill*:

Cornelius Ward, 36 Gt. Titchfield St., 1836–60.

,, ,, 172 Gt. Portland St., 1860–70.

Whitaker, *dealer*:

Whitaker & Co., 24 Travies Inn, etc., *c.* 1820–30.

Willis, *maker*:

John Willis, 3 Angel Court, *c.* 1808–25.

Willis & Goodlad, 25 Villiers St., 1825–29.

Goodlad & Co., *same address*, 1829–37.

Wood, *maker*:

Jas. Wood, 22 Hart St., before 1799, *then* 76 James St. until 1804, *and* Stangate St. until 1808.

Jas. Wood & Son, 50 New Compton St., before 1817 to 1829.

Geo. Wood, *same address*, 1829–36.

Wood & Ivy, *same address*, 1836–47.

APPENDIX 2

Parlour Pipes

These are the perfect instruments for anyone who likes to make wind music, but is obliged to make it all alone. Parlour pipes are mellow-toned bagpipes suitable for playing indoors as well as outdoors. They are bellows-blown, so that the performer can smoke and converse if he wishes to, just as fiddlers and pianists can. One type is mentioned in Chapter XI: the old French musette. The chief species today are both from the British Isles: the Northumbrian small-pipe, and the Irish union pipe.

The Northumbrian Small-pipe, first heard of in the seventeenth century, is thought to be derived from the French musette. Once the favourite popular instrument of Tyneside, it was rapidly falling out of use in the nineteenth century, and would probably have disappeared altogether but for the work of Northumbrian Piper's Societies in Newcastle-upon-Tyne, through whose efforts the instrument is now restored to much of its former popularity.

The *bellows*, of leather nailed between two boards, are like a household bellows but with two leather straps instead of handles. The strap attached to the inner board is buckled round the waist; the other, attached to the outer board (which has the air inlet valve), is buckled round the right arm above the elbow. The nozzle is a leather or mackintosh tube with a lapped wooden end which is pushed into the socket of a similar tube leading from the bag. The bag is kept filled with full, firm strokes of the right arm (avoiding the tendency to do this in time with the music) while the left arm presses the bag and controls the feed to the pipes in the usual way.

The *chanter* has a double reed but a *cylindrical* bore, with the usual seven holes plus thumb-hole, and, today, at least five closed keys. Its unique feature is that the lower end is permanently stopped, so that if all holes are closed there can be no sound. Hence by closing all holes between the notes of a melody, the pipe can be played in every sort of detached manner (just as a woodwind instrument is through tonguing) and gracing is used little. To make the most of this faculty, the chanter is played entirely with strictly closed fingering; only one hole is uncovered for each note, thus—*g'*: . / . . . / . . . / o; *a'*: . / . . . / . . o / .; *b'*: . / . . . / . o . / . and so on up to o / . . . / . . . / . (*g''*). The tone is soft and attractive, and a good performace is pleasantly varied with contrasts of smooth legato with a pure staccato. All kinds of tune can be played on it with excellent effect. The basic keys are those by which the compass is extended three notes downwards (*f'♯*, *e'*, *d'*) and two upwards (*a''*, *b''*), any other keys being for semitones. As on other bagpipes with keys, the keys are operated by the digits not employed in the normal fingering, i.e. right thumb and left little finger. When making a note with a key, all finger-holes are closed in order to preserve the closed fingering.

The *drones* are held in a common stock. They are closed at the bottom, the note issuing from a small hole in the side, and a drone can be silenced by pushing in the bead projecting from the bottom. Of the usual four drones, three are used at a time, thus:

g'	–
d'	*d'*
g	*a*
–	*d*

the left-hand column showing the drones set for playing in G, and the right hand for D (the third drone then being retuned to *a* by its tuning slides, or in some cases by bringing into operation an exit higher up by a special valve actuated by turning the bead). On some pipes the other drones can also be raised a tone to secure tunings suitable for minor tunes, as a', e', a for example.

A modern instruction book for the Northumbrian small-pipe is Fenwick's published for the Northumbrian Pipers' Society, Newcastle-upon-Tyne, 1931, and including valuable reed-making instructions by W. A. Cocks.

Union Pipe. This is the national bagpipe of Ireland, dating back in its present form to the eighteenth century. (There is much doubt as to the authenticity of the name 'uillean pipe' which was put forward as the correct name by Grattan Flood and others. Leo Rowsome, to whose untiring labours the present popularity of the instrument is largely due, calls it 'union pipe', though he really prefers its other name, the 'Irish organ' or 'organ pipes', which his father, also a famous player, used to use.)

The *bellows* are as described above. The *chanter* has a comparatively narrow conical bore (which some of the old makers used to bore with army bayonets), with the usual holes and optional chromatic keys.

A movement that plays an important part in performance is stopping the lower end of the chanter against the right knee, and to ensure airtight stopping, players either tie a square of soft leather—the 'piper's apron'—round the thigh just above the knee, or else they have fitted to the base of the chanter a hinged valve which hangs open until the chanter is lowered on the knee. There are different ways of playing the union pipe according to whether or not the chanter is kept down on the knee (except that it always has to be lifted for the lowest note, d', made with all finger-holes covered). *Playing off the knee:* the little finger is kept on its hole except for low d'. For e', finger VI is lifted, and so on up to d'' (all off). Now comes the great beauty of the union pipe—full availability of the upper register, with its sweet, singing tone. To reach it, the chanter is momentarily lowered on the knee and all holes are closed. This silences the reed. In this same instant the wind pressure is increased by a slight jerk of the left arm on the bag, with the effect that upon resuming the fingering, the reed suddenly vibrates faster and the chanter overblows the octave cleanly. An undue amount of jumping from one register to the other is avoided thanks to the prevailing contour of Irish tunes (e.g. reels, jigs and hornpipes) in which phrases on the whole rise and stay high for several notes before dropping again. In slow tunes, vibrato is extensively made on long notes by trilling on the hole next below the note-hole for the note in question.

Playing with the chanter on the knee brings in that same faculty for making detached notes through closed fingering noticed above on the Northumbrian small-pipe.

The accompanying pipes are all held in one large stock, and lie in a bunch across the right thigh. They number six: three drones and three regulators. Of the *drones* (*d'*, *d* and *D*) the deepest ends with a turned-up brass tube—the 'trumpet'—terminating in a round brass or ivory box with exit hole at the side. This is to assist tuning the drones. To silence one drone while tuning another, a finger is placed across its end and gently removed. To restart it, the finger is again placed across the end, but now suddenly removed, which jerks the reed into action. On the longest drone the 'trumpet' brings the lower end within reach for this operation.

The *regulators* are three harmony pipes of different lengths, each with conical bore and double reed like the chanter reed (but graded in size), and the lower end is closed by a stopper. Each carries a series of large, heavily-sprung closed keys and will sound no note until one of these keys is pressed. The keys on the three regulators are so laid out that any three keys in a row give a simple chord when pressed simultaneously (fig. 78) and they are struck in this manner by the lower edge of the right hand while the chanter is being played. They are struck staccatissimo to give accompanying chords to a reel or jig, usually four in a bar, though now and then the second and third beats and the fourth and first, are tied, introducing a syncopated effect. As the diagram shows, they are but simple chords, and they make their greatest effect if they are introduced only now and then during a piece, and not all the time. The lift that they then suddenly give to the music is marvellous, and at the end of the piece the appropriate chord on the regulators is sustained, to produce a blaze of harmony under the chanter's last note.

In slow airs the regulators are often employed in a different way. During moments when only the left hand is occupied fingering the chanter (i.e. from *g'* to *d''*), the right hand is moved from the chanter to play upon the regulator keys with the fingers, giving not only a wider choice of chord, but also the freedom to work in contrapuntal figures of accompaniment on the individual keys. Rowsome and others devise very beautiful accompaniments to slow tunes like 'Londonderry Air' in this way. Some older pipes have one or two extra regulators for

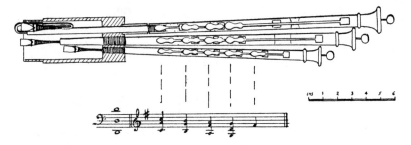

Fig. 78. *Diagram of Union-pipe regulators. (To the left, the regulator stock is drawn in section, with the three drones omitted.)*

supplying bass notes (e.g., *G*, *A*, *B*, *c*) when playing on the regulators with the fingers in this manner.

Each regulator can be tuned by means of a length of rush that runs some distance up the bore from the bottom, where it is held on a brass pin which passes out through the stopper to a tuning bead. To flatten a regulator the rush is pushed further in, and vice versa.

The Scottish *Lowland Pipe* is no longer regularly played. There are two forms, both with bellows, and with three drones in a common stock. The ordinary form has a chanter like that of the Highland pipe, but with narrower conical bore. Its drones are tuned in the Highland way, *a, a, A*. The *miniature* form has a short cylindrical chanter (though it may be tapered on the outside), and this, unlike the cylindrical chanter of the Northumbrian small-pipe, is open-ended and fingered in the ordinary way.

APPENDIX 2

Thanks to this bore, the Highland pitch and scale are obtained with a shorter chanter, and there has been talk of a revival of the Scottish miniature pipe in the form of a mouth-blown pipe with two or three separate drones, for young persons whose hands are too small to manage the full-sized Highland chanter.

APPENDIX 3

Notes on Maintenance

Wiping out after playing. The object of this is not to dry the bore completely, but merely to remove the worst and to avoid leaving one side of the bore always wetter than the other. Therefore the wiper, whether pull-through or mop (or for the oboe, a feather is suitable), should not fit too tightly, as this can harm the bore and eventually send the instrument out of tune.

Joints. If *too tight,* apply grease. Goose-grease used to be preferred, but manufacturers now supply various substitutes. If *too loose,* apply a few turns of lapping thread over the cork. This is thread impregnated with a mixture of beeswax and tallow. Manufacturers supply it in reels. The loose joint can then be re-corked next time the instrument goes to the repairer.

Stiff axle. Occasionally a stiff axle can be cured by oiling, but more often it is due to a knock which has bent the outer sleeve or caused a pillar to press against it. If it is too stiff to be temporarily cured by an elastic band, the only thing is to remove the axle and gently try to straighten things (unless the repairer can be visited at once).

Sticking pad. A key sticks down although it can turn freely and its spring is acting properly. Clean the pad and its seating with spirits on a handkerchief; or dry the pad with French chalk, or even with a soft lead pencil.

Leaking key. This may be due simply to a lever having got bent so as to foul another lever; or to the cork-bearing surface having fallen off a connecting heel in the mechanism. But more often a *pad* has fallen out, or become worn or mis-seated; or else a *spring* has failed. If the leak is difficult to locate, perform the smoke test. Stop up the lower end with a handkerchief, blow in cigarette smoke while covering all the holes and watch where the smoke comes out, preferably with an accomplice also watching. If it is obvious that the leaking key has simply become bent, it can usually be carefully bent back. In other cases the key must be removed in order to replace the pad (or the spring—see below). Makers supply sets of spare pads for every instrument. They are of kid, or of goldbeater's skin or similar tissue. (If necessary, one can make a home-made pad from an old kid glove, or from a sausage skin, cutting out a circle a little bigger than the key and sewing it into a bag; a disc of felt or cotton-wool is put in the bag, and on top of it a disc of thin card; the threads of the bag are then pulled tight and knotted.)

To mount a pad, melt into the cup of the key a little sealing wax (or a glue of shellac dissolved in spirits; or, as professional repairers often use with skin pads, French cement). Place a pad of the right size centrally and level in the cup while the adhesive is warm. Replace the key on the instrument, warm again (e.g. with the point of a match flame), and press down lightly to seat the pad. Occasionally a pad needs to be seated *not* level in the cup, in which case it can be packed where necessary by extra quantities of adhesive.

Flute pads are perforated, being secured with a screw washer (which prevents them bulging), and their height can be adjusted with paper washers placed in the cup. But on flutes with perforated finger-plates, the pads are glued in. Like oboe pads, flute pads are difficult to replace oneself owing to the complex interlinkage of the mechanism; and indeed with every instrument, pad trouble is far best dealt with by a professional repairer. Re-padding really accurately, so that the instrument blows smoothly and easily right through its compass, is a very skilled job.

Spring failure. A few elastic bands are best carried in the instrument case as first aid for this. Sets of spare springs are obtainable, while a needle spring can also be made from steel spring wire, or from a sewing needle of the right gauge, cutting it to length, hammering the thick end flat so that it will grip fast in the hole in the pillar, and tempering the rest blue. Having inserted it, it is given a bias to the desired side with pliers. A flat spring can be cut from sheet brass, drilling a hole for the attaching-screw, and hardening by hammering.

First treatment for an antique woodwind instrument. Remove keys. Scrub joints. When quite dry, oil with linseed, especially the bore, which may absorb a lot. Wipe excess oil off the outside and polish, and when dry, re-lap all joints. Re-pad the keys for which scrap pieces of soft leather may be obtained from a piano repairer or from an engineering factory. Springs may have to be replaced, cutting from brass sheet and tempering by hammering.

Bibliography

A short list of material for further reading. It might have been handy to confine the list to works written in English, were it not that so many of the finest studies of musical instruments have been in French, German, etc., and at least some of these must be included. Among current periodicals, the American magazines *Woodwind* and *The Clarinet*, now *Woodwind World*, always contain something interesting.

The tutors are mainly selected for their historical interest. Several of the old ones are still being reprinted, whole or in part, and remain as useful as ever.

'Grove' denotes *Grove's Dictionary of Music and Musicians*, Fifth Edition, 1954; 'Lavignac' denotes *Encyclopédie de la Musique et Dictionnaire du Conservatoire*, by Lavignac and de la Laurencie, Paris, 1913 and onwards.

GENERAL

Brand, J., *Band Instrument Repairing Manual*, Selmer, Elkhart, U.S.A.

Carse, A., *Musical Wind Instruments*, London, 1939, New York, 1964.

Forsyth, C., *Orchestration*, 1914, etc. (Still unbeatable.)

Goldman, R. Franko, *The Concert Band*, New York, 1946.

Langwill, L. G., *Index of Musical Wind-Instrument Makers*, Edinburgh, 1960 (published by the author, 9 Melville St., Edinburgh, 3).

MacGillivray, J. A., 'The Woodwind', in *Musical Instruments through the Ages*, ed. A. Baines, London, Penguin Books, 1961.

Marcuse, S., *Musical Instruments, A Comprehensive Dictionary*, New York, 1964.

Miller, G., *The Military Band*, Novello, 1912. (The best introduction to band scoring.)

Wagner, Joseph, *Band Scoring*, New York, 1960.

BIBLIOGRAPHY

ACOUSTICS

Culver, C. A., *Musical Acoustics*, Philadelphia, 1947.

Hague, B., 'Tonal Spectra of wind instruments', *Proceedings of the Royal Musical Association*, 1947.

Helmholtz, *On the Sensations of Tone* (English translation by Ellis, 1875. The classic treatise on musical acoustics.)

Lloyd, Ll. S., *Music and Sound*, 1937, 1951.

Wood, Alexander, *The Physics of Music*, 1944.

FLUTE

Bate, P., *The Flute*, London, 1969.

Boehm, T., *Essay on the Construction of Flutes*, 1882.

—, *The Flute and Flute-playing*, transl. Dayton Miller, 1922, 1964.

Chapman, F. B., *Flute Technique*, 1936. (With lists of flute music.)

Fitzgibbon, H. M., *The Story of the Flute*, 1914.

Gilliam, L. E., and Lichtenwanger, W., *The Dayton C. Miller Flute Collection, A Checklist of the Instruments*, Washington, 1961.

James, W. N., *A Word or Two on the Flute*, 1826.

Lavignac: 'La flûte', by Taffanel and Fleury.

Lorenzo, L. de, *My Complete Story of the Flute*, New York, 1951.

Miller, Dayton C., *A Bibliography of the Flute*, Cleveland, 1935.

Quantz, *Versuch einer Anweisung die Flöte Traversiere zu spielen*, Berlin, 1752; facsimile reprint by Bärenreiter, 1953.

Rockstro, R. S., *A Treatise on the Flute*, 1890, 1928.

Ventzke, K., *Die Boehmflöte*, Frankfurt-am-Main, 1966.

Welch, C., *History of the Boehm Flute*, 1883, etc.

Tutors

Complete Tutor for the German Flute, various editions from 1746 onwards.

Drouet, *Méthode*, 1830?

Gunn, *Art of Playing the German Flute*, 1793.

Hotteterre le Romain, *Principes*, 1707 (the first tutor for the one-keyed flute); facsimile reprint of 1728 edition, Berlin, 1941.

BIBLIOGRAPHY

Langey, *Tutor for the Flute* (many editions, with charts for nearly every system).

Lorenzoni, *Saggio per ben sonare il flauto traverso*, 1779.

Moyse, *Enseignement complet de la flûte*, 1921. (The authoritative work on the modern French style.)

Nicholson, C., *Complete Preceptor*, c. 1816; *A School for the Flute*, 1836.

Potter, H., & Co., *Flute Tutor for B flat Flute, F Flute, etc.* (modern tutor for the band flutes).

Radcliff, *Nicholson's School for the Flute*, 1872. (An enlarged edition, with description of the Radcliff model.)

Schwedler, *Methode*, 1893. (The last great tutor for the simple-system flute.)

Tromlitz, *Ueber die Flöten mit mehrern Klappen*, 1800. (Dealing with the addition of keys to the one-keyed flute.)

Tulou, *Méthode*, 1845?

Wragg, *Improved Flute preceptor*, 1806.

OBOE

Bate, P., *The Oboe*, London, 1956.

Grove: 'Oboe', by E. Halfpenny and P. A. T. Bate.

Halfpenny, E., many historical articles in *Galpin Society Journal*, II, etc.

Lavignac: 'Hautbois', by Bleuzet.

Marx, J., 'The Tone of the Baroque Oboe', *Galpin Society Journal*, IV, 1951

Rothwell, E., *Oboe Technique*, 1953. (With full list of music for oboe and cor anglais.)

Sprenkle, R., and Ledet, D., *The art of oboe playing*, Evanston, Illinois, 1961.

Tutors

[Bannister], *The Sprightly Companion*, 1695. (The first known oboe tutor.)

Barret, *Complete Method*, 1850.

Brod, *Méthode*, 1832.

Complete Tutor for the Hoboy, 1750, etc. Also *New and Complete Instructions*, 1790, etc.

Freillon-Poncein, *La véritable manière . . .*, 1700.

BIBLIOGRAPHY

Froelich, *Vollständige theorisch-practische Musiklehre*, 1811.

Garnier, *Méthode*, 1797? (The first official tutor for the Paris Conservatoire.)

Gillet, F. *Méthode pour le début du hautbois*, 1940 (in French and English together).

Langey, *Tutor* (with charts).

Sellner, *Oboeschule*, 1825. (Reprinted later in Italian, etc.)

CLARINET

Grove: 'Clarinet', by F. G. Rendall.

Kroll, O., *Die Klarinette*, Kassel, 1965. Engl. transl. 1968.

Lavignac: 'La clarinette', by Mimart.

MacGillivray, J. A., 'Recent Advances in Woodwind Fingering Systems', *Galpin Society Journal*, XII, 1959.

Rendall, F. G., *The Clarinet*, 1954.

Thurston, F., *Clarinet Technique*, London, 1955.

Weston, P., *Clarinet Virtuosi of the Past*, London, 1971.

Tutors

Backofen, *Anweisung zur Klarinette*, 1803.

Baermann, C., *Vollständige Clarinettenschule*, 1864, etc.

Complete Instructions for the Clarinet, 1785?, etc.

Froelich (*see above under* OBOE).

Jettl, *Klarinettenschule*, 1949. (For Oehler system.)

Klosé, *Méthode*, 1843. (The original tutor for the Boehm-system.)

Langey, *Tutor* (with charts for both systems).

Lazarus, *New and Modern Method*, 1881.

Lefèvre, *Méthode*, 1802.

Mahon, *New and Complete Preceptor*, 1803.

Muller, *Méthode*, c. 1825.

Thurston and Frank, *The Clarinet*, 1945.

BASSOON

Camden, A., *Bassoon Technique*, London, 1962. (With 'A List of music for the bassoon' compiled by William Waterhouse.)

Grove: 'Bassoon', by L. G. Langwill.

Heckel, W., *Der Fagott*, Leipzig, 1931.

Laborde, *Essai sur la Musique*, 1780, with a long article on the bassoon by Cugnier.

BIBLIOGRAPHY

Langwill, L. G., *The Bassoon and Double Bassoon*, Hinrichsen's Miniature Surveys, 1948.

——, *The Bassoon and Contrabassoon*, London, 1965.

——, 'The Double bassoon', *Proceedings of the Royal Musical Association*, 1942.

——, 'The Curtal', *Musical Times*, April 1937.

Lavignac: 'Le basson', by Letellier and Flament.

Tutors

Almenraeder, *Fagottschule*, 1841.

Berr, *Méthode complète de Basson*, 1836?

Complete Instructions for the Bassoon, 1790?, etc.

Eley, *Tutor*, *c.* 1810.

Froelich (*see under* OBOE).

Jancourt, *Grande méthode*, 1880, etc.

Langey, *Tutor*.

Oubradous, *Enseignement complet du basson*, 1938.

Ozi, *Méthode*, 1797?, 1803. (For the Paris Conservatoire.)

Piard, *Enseignement du Contrebasson* (modern).

Weissenborn, *Praktische Fagott-schule*, 1887.

OTHER INSTRUMENTS

Bagpipes

Baines, A., *Bagpipes*, Oxford, Pitt Rivers Museum, 1960.

Borjon, *Traité de la musette*, Lyons, 1672.

Cocks, W. A., & Bryan, J. F., *The Northumbrian Bagpipes*, Newcastle upon Tyne, 1967. (Manual for making.)

Fenwick, *Instruction Book for the Northumbrian Small-pipes*, 1931.

Logan, *Tutor for the Highland Bagpipe*, 1923, etc.

O'Neill, F., *Irish Folk Music*, Chicago, 1910.

Rowsome, L., *Tutor for the Uillean Pipes*, Dublin, 1936.

Recorder

Bannister, *The Most Pleasant Companion*, 1681.

Complete Flute master, 1690, etc. *New Flute master*, 1706, etc.

Ganassi, *Opera intitulata Fontegara*, 1535. (facsimile reprint, Milan, 1934).

Giesbert, *Method for the Recorder Flute*, 1936.

Hunt, E., *The Recorder and its Music*, London, 1962.

BIBLIOGRAPHY

———, *Concise Tutor*, 1935.

Peter, H., *The Recorder, its Traditions and its Tasks* (Transl. from the German by S. Godman), London and New York, 1958.

Rowland-Jones, *Recorder Technique*, London, 1959.

Welch, C., *Six Lectures on the Recorder*, 1911.

Virdung, *Musica getutscht*, 1511 (facsimile reprint, Cassel, 1931).

Sarrusophone

Lavignac: 'Le Sarrusophone', by Leruste.

Saxophone

Davis, B., *The Saxophone*, 1932.

Grove: 'Saxophone', by P. A. T. Bate.

Kool, J., *Das Saxophon*, Leipzig, 1931.

Serpent

Hermenge, *Méthode élémentaire*, 1820?

Morley-Pegge, R., 'Serpent', in *Grove*.

Shawm

Baines, A. C., 'Shawms of the sardana coblas', *Galpin Society Journal*, V.

Coll, J., *Método de tiple y tenora*, Barcelona, 1950.

PRIMITIVE, ORIENTAL, FOLK, ANTIQUITY

(This is a difficult list to draw up, since much of the best material is in short articles scattered in anthropological, archaeological and other journals and magazines. The following are among the most valuable works.)

Alexandru, T., *Instrumentele muzicale ale poporului Romín*, Bucharest, 1956.

Ankermann, B., *Die afrikanischen Musikinstrumente*, Berlin, (Museum für Völkerkunde), 1894.

Broemse, P., *Flöten, Schalmeien, Sackpfeifen . . .*, Prague, 1937. (A very full account of Yugoslav folk instruments.)

Closson, H., in *Studien zur Musikgeschichte* (*Festschrift für Guido Adler*), Vienna, 1930. (Description and photographs of ancient Egyptian pipes and reeds.)

BIBLIOGRAPHY

Crane, F., *Extant Medieval Instruments*, Iowa, 1972.

Day, C. R., *The Musical Instruments of Southern India*, 1891.

Densmore, F., numerous studies on North American Indian music and instruments in Bulletins of the *Bureau of American Ethnology*, Washington, 1910, etc.

Donostia and Tomas, 'Instrumentos de música popular española', in *Anuario Musical*, Barcelona, II, 1947.

Erlanger, R. de, *La Musique Arabe*, Paris, 1930, etc. (Translation of the important medieval Arabic works on music and instruments.)

Farmer, H. G., *Studies in Oriental Musical Instruments*, 1931, 2.

Galpin, F. W., *The Music of the Sumerians*, 1937.

Gand, H. in der, *Volkstümliche Musikinstrumente in der Schweitz*, 1937. (An interesting account of primitive survivors in Switzerland.)

Harcourt, R. and M. de, *La musique des Incas et ses survivances*, Paris, 1925.

Harich Schneider, E., a full description of the Japanese Court Music, with flute, *hichiriki* and mouth-organ *sho*, with music examples, in *Musical Quarterly*, Jan. 1953.

Hickmann, H., *Catalogue général des antiquités égyptiennes du Musée du Caire: Instruments de musique*, 1952.

Howard, A. A., 'The aulos or tibia', *Harvard studies of Philology*, 1893. (Propounds a 'speaker hole' theory for the overblowing.)

Izikowitz, K. G., *Musical and other Sound Instruments of the South American Indians*, Göteborg, 1935.

Kaudern, W. T., *Musical Instruments of the Celebes*, Göteborg, 1927.

Khin Saw, 'Burmese Music', *Journal of the Burma Research Society*, 1940. (With an account of the Burmese wind instruments.)

Kirby, P. R., *The Musical Instruments of the Native Races of South Africa*, 1934. (A splendid first-hand study.)

Klier, K. M., *Volkstümliche Musikinstrumente in den Alpen*, Kassel, 1956.

BIBLIOGRAPHY

Kodály, Z., *Folk Music of Hungary*, London, 1960.

Kunst, J., *Music in Flores*, Leiden, 1942. (Very interesting on bamboo flageolets, etc.)

——, *Music in Java*, The Hague, 1949. (But beware of the theory of 'blown fifths'.)

Lavignac:
    'Chine-Corée', by M. Courant.
    'Egypte' (ancient), by V. Loret.
    'Grèce' (ancient), by M. Emmanuel.
    'Inde', by J. Grosset.
    'La Musique Arabe', by J. Rouanet.
    'La Musique Turque', by R. Yekta Bey.
    'La Musique Persane', by C. Huart.
    'La Musique dans la Birmanie', by G. Knosp.

Mahillon, V., *Catalogue descriptif et analytique du Musée instrumental du Conservatoire Royal de Musique, Bruxelles*, Ghent, 1893, etc., 5 vols. (A great pioneer work, especially on folk and non-European instruments.)

Malm, W. P., *Japanese Music and Musical Instruments*, Rutland, Vermont, and Tokyo, 1959.

Matos, M. Garcia, 'Instrumentos musicales folklóricos de España', *Anuario Musical*, Barcelona, XI, 1956 (Hornpipes).

Moule, A. C., 'List of the Musical Instruments of the Chinese', *Journal of the North China Branch of the Royal Asiatic Society*, 1908.

Reinach, Th., article *Tibia* in Daremberg and Saglio, *Dictionnaire des antiquités greques et romaines*, Paris, 1877–1919. (The fullest existing study of the aulos.)

Sachs, C., *Geist und Werden der Musikinstrumente*, Berlin, 1929. (This work is already a classic—a master work that holds a place in ethno-musicology comparable to that held by Helmholz's celebrated work in the field of musical acoustics. One waits hopefully for a second Alexander Ellis to translate *Geist und Werden* into English. Its central topic is the evolution of types and their diffusion over the world.)

——, *The History of Musical Instruments*, New York, 1940.

——, (Many other works, listed in the ample bibliography of the last-mentioned well-known book.)

Schaeffner, A., *Origine des instruments de musique*, Paris, 1936. (A stimulating general study.)

Schlesinger, K., *The Greek Aulos*, 1939. (A volume of interesting conjectures based on practical research with pipes.)

Seewald, O., *Beiträge zu Kenntniss der steinzeitlichen Musik-instrumente Europas*, Vienna, 1934. (Details and drawings of stone-age flutes, etc.)

Stainer, Sir J., *The Music of the Bible*, ed. Galpin, 1914.

Vega, C., *Los Instrumentos musicales aborigenes y criollos de la Argentina*, Buenos Aires, 1946.

Vertkov, K., Blagodatov, G., and Yazovitskaya, E., *Atlas Muzykalnykh Instrumentov Narodov SSSR*, Moscow, 1963.

Vidal, *Lou Tambourin*, 1862. (The classic work on the Provençal pipe and tabor.)

Villoteau, G. A., Vols. 13, 14 of *Description de l'Egypte*, Paris, 1812, etc.

WOODWIND HISTORY (from Middle Ages onwards)

Agricola, M., *Musica Instrumentalis Deutsch*, Wittemberg, 1528, 1545. (Reprint, Leipzig, 1896.)

Arbeau, T., *Orchésographie*, Lengres, 1588. (English translation by C. W. Beaumont, 1925.)

Benoit, M., *Musiques de Cour (1661-1733)*, Paris, 1971.

Bessaraboff, N., *Ancient European Musical Instruments*, Boston, 1941. (Collection of the Boston Museum of Fine Arts.)

Bonanni, F., *Gabinetto armonico*, Rome, 1722.

Buchner, A., *Musical Instruments through the Ages*, London, n.d.

Carse, A., *The Orchestra in the XVIIIth century*, 1940.

——, *The Orchestra from Beethoven to Berlioz*, 1948.

Dahlqvist, R., 'Taille, Oboe da Caccia and Corno Inglese', *Galpin Society Journal*, XXVI, 1973.

Day, C. R., *Descriptive Catalogue of Musical Instruments at the Royal Military Exhibition, London, 1890*, London, 1891. (With notes on many important early instruments loaned by the Brussels Conservatoire Museum.)

BIBLIOGRAPHY

Diderot et D'Alembert, *Encyclopédie*, Paris, 1767, etc. (With plates showing the construction of instruments, and instrument-makers' tools.)

Eisel, J. P., *Musicus autodidaktos*, Erfurt, 1738.

Galpin, F. W., *Old English Instruments of Music*, 1910, 1965.

Gehot, *Complete Instructor of every instrument*, 1790?

Harrison, F., and Rimmer, J., *European Musical Instruments*, London, 1964.

Karstadt, 'Der Zink' (Cornett), *Archiv für Musikforschung*, 2.

Kastner, G., *Manuel général de musique militaire*, Paris, 1848.

Kinsky, G., *History of Music in Pictures*, Leipzig, 1929

Kinsky, 'Doppelrohrblattinstrumente mit Windkapsel' ('Double-reed instruments with reed cap'), *Archiv für Musikwissenschaft*, 7. (With a discussion of the dolzaina problem.)

Kroll, 'Das Chalumeau', *Zeitschrift für Musikwissenschaft*, 15.

Inventories

    Baines, 'Two Cassel inventories', *Galpin Society Journal*, IV (with a list of further early inventories).

    Augsburg (Fugger), 1566, in *Archiv für Musikwissenschaft*, 1964.

    Cöthen, 1706, in *Bach Jahrbuch*, 1905.

    Detmold, 1790, in *Freiburger Studien für Musikgeschichte*, 1934.

    Krems, 1739, in *Monatshefte für Musikgeschichte*, XX, 1888.

    Ossegg, in *Z. für Musikwissenschaft*, 4.

Laborde, *Essai sur la musique*, Paris, 1780.

Lesure, F., 'La facture instrumentale à Paris au 16me siècle', *Galpin Society Journal*, VII.

MacDermott, K. H., *The Old Church Gallery Minstrels*, 1948.

Majer, J. F. B. C., *Museum Musicum*, 1732, reprint Kassel, 1954.

Mahillon, V., *Catalogue descriptif* (*see above*).

Marix, J., *Histoire de la musique et des musiciens de la cour de Bourgogne*, 1420–1467, Strasbourg, 1939.

Marvin, B., 'Recorders and English Flutes in European Collections', *Galpin Society Journal*, XXV, 1972.

Mersenne, M., *Harmonie universelle*, Paris, 1936, reprint, Paris, 1964. (In Latin, 1648.)

BIBLIOGRAPHY

Nickel, E., *Der Holzblasinstrumentenbau in der freien Reichsstadt Nürnberg*, Munich, 1971.

Philibert Jambe-de-Fer, *Epitome musical*, Lyons, 1556.

Pierre, C., *La facture instrumentale*, Paris, 1889.

Praetorius, M., *Syntagma musicum*, Wolfenbüttel, 1618–19.

Sachs, C., *Sammlung alter Musikinstrumente bei der Staatliche Hochschule*, Berlin, 1922. (Catalogue of the Berlin collection.)

Schlosser, J. von, *Alte Musikinstrumente*, Vienna, 1920. (Catalogue of the Vienna Kunsthistorisches Museum collection.)

Speer, D., *Grundrichtiger Unterricht*, Ulm, 1687.

Stephens, G. A., 'The Waits of the City of Norwich', *Norfolk Archaeology*, 1933.

Straeten, E. van de, *La Musique aux Pays-Bas*, Brussels, 1867–1888 (especially Vols. IV and VII).

Talbot, J., Manuscript notes on music and instruments, *c.* 1696 (Christ Church, Oxford, Music MS. 1187). See Baines, 'The Talbot MS', *Galpin Society Journal*, I.

Terry, C. S., *Bach's Orchestra*, 1932.

Thoinan, E., *Les Hotteterre et les Chédeville*, Paris, 1894.

Trichet, P., *Traité des Instruments de Musique*, *c.* 1640, ed. F. Lesure, Neuilly-sur-Seine, 1957.

Trojano, M., *Dialoghi*, Venice, 1569. (Account of the music at Munich in 1568.)

Turrini, G., 'L'Accademia filarmonica di Verona . . . e il suo patrimonio musicale antico', *Acti e memorie della Accademia di agricoltura, scienze e lettere di Verona*, 1941.

Warner, T. E., *An Annotated Bibliography of Woodwind Instruction Books, 1600-1830*, Detroit, 1967.

Weber, R., 'Some Researches into Pitch in the 16th Century . . . Instruments in the Accademia Filarmonica of Verona', *Galpin Society Journal*, XXVIII, 1975.

Weigel, J. C., *Musicalisches Theatrum*, ed. A. Berner, Kassel, 1961.

Wright, R., *Dictionnaire des instruments de musique*, London, 1941. (Useful references for medieval instrument-names.)

Zedler, *Universal-Lexicon*, Halle, 1732–54. Articles 'Jagt-Hautbois', 'Schallmey', 'Regimentspfeiffer', 'Zinck', etc.

Glossary of Terms

ARTICULATION. Detaching the notes on a wind instrument, normally by tonguing.

ATTACK. The clean start to a note or phrase.

BARREL. The short joint of a clarinet into which the mouthpiece is inserted. (But in woodwind manufacture, the axle on which a key turns.)

BELL. The flared bottom end of many wind instruments.

BRILLE. The F♯ correcting device on oboes and non-Boehm clarinets; basically embodying two rings and a small vent key.

CANTABILE. Playing in a singing manner.

CHANTER. The melody pipe of a bagpipe.

CLOSED KEY. A key that rests normally closed by its spring.

CONICAL BORE. A tapered bore, sometimes a true truncated cone. With flutes, generally understood to mean a taper inwards towards the bottom end (*contracting bore*); with reed instruments, a taper outwards towards the bottom end (*expanding bore*).

CROOK. Any curved metal tube leading from the player's mouth to the top end of the instrument.

CROSS-KEY. Any small closed key that lies across the body of the instrument between two finger-holes.

CYLINDRICAL BORE. A parallel-sided bore, sometimes ending with an expansion in a bell.

DOUBLE HOLE. *See* HALF-HOLING.

DOUBLE REED. A twin-bladed vibrating reed, made in various ways.

EDGE. The mouth-hole edge or voicing edge of instruments of the Flute Class. *Edge-frequency:* the sound-generating principle of these instruments.

EMBOUCHURE. The manner in which the player holds his lips, jaws, etc., while playing. (Also sometimes, though not in this book, the mouth-hole of a flute.)

FLAGEOLET. (1) Strictly, a small European 'whistle-flute' with six holes (two of them at the back in the French species). (2) A general term for all instruments of the Flute Class that have an artificial air-slit.

FLUTE. Besides its precise meaning of a transverse flute, the general class-name for all instruments of the edge-vibrated kind.

FOOT-KEYS. Open keys for the right little finger on a flute.

FREQUENCY. Vibrations per second. Or loosely, any regular, sustained, vibration.

FUNDAMENTAL. The full-length vibration of an air-column, reckoned in the harmonic series as the first harmonic.

GRACING. Bagpipe articulation by means of grace-notes.

HALF-HOLING. Half uncovering a hole with the finger. Usually, if the hole concerned is for finger I, it is the upper half that is uncovered, but if it is for any other finger, the lower half. (Very often the amount of uncovering required is actually less than half.) *Also:* (1) uncovering one of the pair of small holes (*double hole*) sometimes provided for a single finger on recorders and old oboes; and (2) uncovering the small perforation in the *half-hole plate* of the oboe.

JOINT. (1) Each of the sections that fit together when an instrument is assembled. (2) The tenon and socket junction by which these sections fit into one another.

KEY. In woodwind mechanism, a sprung lever bearing a padded cup or plate, for covering a hole that otherwise lies out of reach of the fingers.

LAPPING. Waxed thread or thin sheet cork, by which the ends of joints are kept air-tight.

LEGATO. Slurred, i.e. not tongued.

MOUTH-HOLE. The hole across which a flute is blown, sometimes called the embouchure hole.

NOTE-HOLE. The opened hole through which any given note speaks.

GLOSSARY OF TERMS

OCTAVE KEY. A key opened to give the upper register on certain instruments.

OPEN KEY. A key that rests normally open under its spring.

OVERBLOWING. Sounding the upper and high registers on a woodwind instrument. Also occasionally used in the sense of 'to blow too hard' or 'to force the tone' (but not in this book).

PIROUETTE. The wooden lip-rest carried on the staple of European band shawms.

REED INSTRUMENT. An instrument whose sound is generated by the vibration of a reed.

REGISTERS. The various parts of a woodwind instrument's compass, each being based on certain harmonics, thus:

low register: fundamentals;

upper register: 2nd harmonics (sometimes running into 3rd harmonics near the top); on the clarinet, 3rd harmonics throughout;

high register: 3rd, 4th, 5th, etc., harmonics; on the clarinet, 5th, 7th, 9th, etc., harmonics.

RING (RING KEY). A metal ring hinged on an axle, surrounding a finger hole and pressed down by the finger.

SHAKE KEY. The same as trill key.

SHARP PITCH. A former English playing pitch, nearly half a semitone above present standard pitch and still used in brass bands. *See* Chapter I.

SIDE KEY. A key (there may be as many as four of them) on the right hand side of an instrument and actuated by the middle joint of the right forefinger. The saxophone also has three left hand side keys.

SIMPLE SYSTEM. A term applied to the following types of instrument (and their variants): eight-keyed flute; oboes without thumb-plate or Conservatoire action; plain non-Boehm-system clarinets; French-system bassoons without additional keywork.

SINGLE REED. A single-bladed vibrating reed, made either separately (as for the clarinet) or by cutting a tongue in a tube of cane (as for a bagpipe drone).

SPEAKER KEY (REGISTER KEY). The left thumb key on a clarinet.

STAPLE. The short, tapered metal tube on which a double reed is made (or placed after making) in expanding-bore reed instruments, e.g. the oboe. If curved, it is called a crook.

STOCK. The wooden holders lashed into the openings of a bagpipe bag, to hold the pipes.

STOPPED (with instruments of the flute class). Complete closure—permanent or momentary—of the bottom end.
Stopped pipe: a flute tube so closed; or a reed instrument that reproduces similar accoustical phenomena.

TENON. The end of a joint that fits into a corresponding socket in the next joint.

TONGUING. Articulation by the tongue.

TOUCH (key touch). The end of a key upon which the finger is applied.

TRILL KEY. A key intended solely or mainly for making a particular trill.

TUBE-LENGTH (for a given note on an instrument). The sounding-length of the instrument from the blowing end to the note hole (but in fact a little beyond it, the amount depending upon the size of the hole, the diameter of the bore, etc.).

VENT. (1) Generally, any aperture in the tube of a wind instrument. (2) *Vent, vent-hole* or *vent key*: an extra hole or key added for tuning a note.
Venting: the efficiency of an opened hole (aided in many cases by the open holes further down) in establishing communication between air-column and outer air.

VIBRATO. A common adornment of the tone, consisting of a gentle, continuous rise and fall in either the strength or the pitch of the notes, made unconsciously or consciously by the breathing or by the embouchure.

VOICING, VOICING HOLE. The aperture that provides the *edge* in instruments of the flageolet kind.

Index

INDEX

Bainbridge, 208
Bal musette, 115–6
Balfour, 193
Bands
  cobla, 114, 228
  flute, 59–62
  medieval, 232
  military
    eighteenth century, 283–5, 308
    modern, 60, 96, 100, 115, 142, 166–8, 219–30
    oriental, 231–2
    renaissance, 232–3
    sixteenth-century, 240, 268–72
    waits, 272
Bannister, 279
Baritone oboe, 98, 327
Barret, 96, 316, 325–9
Barret action: oboe, 101; clarinet, 138, XIII
Bartók, 66, 180
Bas instruments, 234
Bass clarinet, 125, 127–9, XI, XIV, XXXI
Bass flute
  ancient, 250
  band, 60–2, IV
  orchestral, 57–9, II
Bass horn, 308
Bass oboe, 98–9
Bass pommer, 268, 271, Fig. 63
Bassanelli, 265, Fig. 62
Basse danse, 233
Basse de musette, 286
Basset horn, 125–7, 306–7, 313, XI, XXVIII
Basson = bassoon (Fr.), 286
Bassonetti, 290
Bassoon
  acoustics, 34, 36, 38, 149
  Boehm-system, 327, 336
  construction, 150
  crooks, 49, 51, 152
  eighteenth-century and classical period, 26, 286–9, 312–4, XXV, XXIX, XXX
  keywork, 286–7, 312
  later English model, 334–5

Bassoon—*continued*
  reeds, 287
  fingering, general points, 152
  French system, 153, 274, XV
    fingering, 158–9
    history, 153, 335–6
    rings, 159, 336
  German system, 153–4, XV
    compared with French, 154–7
    fingering, 159–62
    history, 338–40
    low A, 163
    use of left thumb, 160–2
    with French fingering, 159*n.*
  mutes, 163
  origins, 263
  pitch adjustments, 49, 51
  price, 153
  producing the sound, 151–2
  reed, VI
    adjustment, 86
    cane, 77
    construction, 77–9, 83–6, 155
    French/German, 86
    history, 263, 287, 335
    single reed, 87
  sixteenth-century, *see* Curtal
  sling, 150
  small bassoons, 264, 289, 337
  tonguing, 39–42
  vibrato, 14, 155, 336
  Viennese old system, 339
Bate, Philip, 59, 305, 328
Baumann, 316, 335
Bechet, 146
Beer, 299
Beethoven, 95, 100, 123, 164, 290, 312, 333, 339–40
Bell, woodwind
  bulbous, 96, 213, 235, 283, 304–305, VIII, XXVIII, XXX
  origin, 196
Berlin
  Hochschule Museum, 238, 258, 265
  Hofkapelle, 241, 258
  Philharmonic Orchestra, 128, 163
Berlioz, 57, 60, 97, 123, 143, 146
Berr, 331, 335

INDEX

INDEX

INDEX

INDEX

INDEX

INDEX

INDEX

INDEX

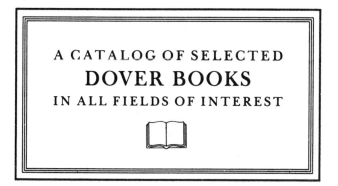

A CATALOG OF SELECTED
DOVER BOOKS
IN ALL FIELDS OF INTEREST

A CATALOG OF SELECTED DOVER
BOOKS IN ALL FIELDS OF INTEREST

CONCERNING THE SPIRITUAL IN ART, Wassily Kandinsky. Pioneering work by father of abstract art. Thoughts on color theory, nature of art. Analysis of earlier masters. 12 illustrations. 80pp. of text. 5⅜ × 8½. 23411-8 Pa. $3.95

ANIMALS: 1,419 Copyright-Free Illustrations of Mammals, Birds, Fish, Insects, etc., Jim Harter (ed.). Clear wood engravings present, in extremely lifelike poses, over 1,000 species of animals. One of the most extensive pictorial sourcebooks of its kind. Captions. Index. 284pp. 9 × 12. 23766-4 Pa. $12.95

CELTIC ART: The Methods of Construction, George Bain. Simple geometric techniques for making Celtic interlacements, spirals, Kells-type initials, animals, humans, etc. Over 500 illustrations. 160pp. 9 × 12. (USO) 22923-8 Pa. $9.95

AN ATLAS OF ANATOMY FOR ARTISTS, Fritz Schider. Most thorough reference work on art anatomy in the world. Hundreds of illustrations, including selections from works by Vesalius, Leonardo, Goya, Ingres, Michelangelo, others. 593 illustrations. 192pp. 7⅛ × 10¼. 20241-0 Pa. $9.95

CELTIC HAND STROKE-BY-STROKE (Irish Half-Uncial from "The Book of Kells"): An Arthur Baker Calligraphy Manual, Arthur Baker. Complete guide to creating each letter of the alphabet in distinctive Celtic manner. Covers hand position, strokes, pens, inks, paper, more. Illustrated. 48pp. 8¼ × 11. 24336-2 Pa. $3.95

EASY ORIGAMI, John Montroll. Charming collection of 32 projects (hat, cup, pelican, piano, swan, many more) specially designed for the novice origami hobbyist. Clearly illustrated easy-to-follow instructions insure that even beginning papercrafters will achieve successful results. 48pp. 8¼ × 11. 27298-2 Pa. $2.95

THE COMPLETE BOOK OF BIRDHOUSE CONSTRUCTION FOR WOOD-WORKERS, Scott D. Campbell. Detailed instructions, illustrations, tables. Also data on bird habitat and instinct patterns. Bibliography. 3 tables. 63 illustrations in 15 figures. 48pp. 5¼ × 8½. 24407-5 Pa. $1.95

BLOOMINGDALE'S ILLUSTRATED 1886 CATALOG: Fashions, Dry Goods and Housewares, Bloomingdale Brothers. Famed merchants' extremely rare catalog depicting about 1,700 products: clothing, housewares, firearms, dry goods, jewelry, more. Invaluable for dating, identifying vintage items. Also, copyright-free graphics for artists, designers. Co-published with Henry Ford Museum & Greenfield Village. 160pp. 8¼ × 11. 25780-0 Pa. $9.95

HISTORIC COSTUME IN PICTURES, Braun & Schneider. Over 1,450 costumed figures in clearly detailed engravings—from dawn of civilization to end of 19th century. Captions. Many folk costumes. 256pp. 8⅜ × 11¼. 23150-X Pa. $11.95

STICKLEY CRAFTSMAN FURNITURE CATALOGS, Gustav Stickley and L. & J. G. Stickley. Beautiful, functional furniture in two authentic catalogs from 1910. 594 illustrations, including 277 photos, show settles, rockers, armchairs, reclining chairs, bookcases, desks, tables. 183pp. 6½ × 9¼.   23838-5 Pa. $9.95

AMERICAN LOCOMOTIVES IN HISTORIC PHOTOGRAPHS: 1858 to 1949, Ron Ziel (ed.). A rare collection of 126 meticulously detailed official photographs, called "builder portraits," of American locomotives that majestically chronicle the rise of steam locomotive power in America. Introduction. Detailed captions. xi + 129pp. 9 × 12.   27393-8 Pa. $12.95

AMERICA'S LIGHTHOUSES: An Illustrated History, Francis Ross Holland, Jr. Delightfully written, profusely illustrated fact-filled survey of over 200 American lighthouses since 1716. History, anecdotes, technological advances, more. 240pp. 8 × 10¾.   25576-X Pa. $11.95

TOWARDS A NEW ARCHITECTURE, Le Corbusier. Pioneering manifesto by founder of "International School." Technical and aesthetic theories, views of industry, economics, relation of form to function, "mass-production split" and much more. Profusely illustrated. 320pp. 6⅛ × 9¼. (USO)   25023-7 Pa. $9.95

HOW THE OTHER HALF LIVES, Jacob Riis. Famous journalistic record, exposing poverty and degradation of New York slums around 1900, by major social reformer. 100 striking and influential photographs. 233pp. 10 × 7⅞.
22012-5 Pa $10.95

FRUIT KEY AND TWIG KEY TO TREES AND SHRUBS, William M. Harlow. One of the handiest and most widely used identification aids. Fruit key covers 120 deciduous and evergreen species; twig key 160 deciduous species. Easily used. Over 300 photographs. 126pp. 5⅜ × 8½.   20511-8 Pa. $3.95

COMMON BIRD SONGS, Dr. Donald J. Borror. Songs of 60 most common U.S. birds: robins, sparrows, cardinals, bluejays, finches, more—arranged in order of increasing complexity. Up to 9 variations of songs of each species.
Cassette and manual 99911-4 $8.95

ORCHIDS AS HOUSE PLANTS, Rebecca Tyson Northen. Grow cattleyas and many other kinds of orchids—in a window, in a case, or under artificial light. 63 illustrations. 148pp. 5⅜ × 8½.   23261-1 Pa. $4.95

MONSTER MAZES, Dave Phillips. Masterful mazes at four levels of difficulty. Avoid deadly perils and evil creatures to find magical treasures. Solutions for all 32 exciting illustrated puzzles. 48pp. 8¼ × 11.   26005-4 Pa. $2.95

MOZART'S DON GIOVANNI (DOVER OPERA LIBRETTO SERIES), Wolfgang Amadeus Mozart. Introduced and translated by Ellen H. Bleiler. Standard Italian libretto, with complete English translation. Convenient and thoroughly portable—an ideal companion for reading along with a recording or the performance itself. Introduction. List of characters. Plot summary. 121pp. 5¼ × 8½.
24944-1 Pa. $2.95

TECHNICAL MANUAL AND DICTIONARY OF CLASSICAL BALLET, Gail Grant. Defines, explains, comments on steps, movements, poses and concepts. 15-page pictorial section. Basic book for student, viewer. 127pp. 5⅜ × 8½.
21843-0 Pa. $4.95

BRASS INSTRUMENTS: Their History and Development, Anthony Baines. Authoritative, updated survey of the evolution of trumpets, trombones, bugles, cornets, French horns, tubas and other brass wind instruments. Over 140 illustrations and 48 music examples. Corrected and updated by author. New preface. Bibliography. 320pp. 5⅜ × 8½. 27574-4 Pa. $9.95

HOLLYWOOD GLAMOR PORTRAITS, John Kobal (ed.). 145 photos from 1926–49. Harlow, Gable, Bogart, Bacall; 94 stars in all. Full background on photographers, technical aspects. 160pp. 8⅜ × 11¼. 23352-9 Pa. $11.95

MAX AND MORITZ, Wilhelm Busch. Great humor classic in both German and English. Also 10 other works: "Cat and Mouse," "Plisch and Plumm," etc. 216pp. 5⅜ × 8½. 20181-3 Pa. $5.95

THE RAVEN AND OTHER FAVORITE POEMS, Edgar Allan Poe. Over 40 of the author's most memorable poems: "The Bells," "Ulalume," "Israfel," "To Helen," "The Conqueror Worm," "Eldorado," "Annabel Lee," many more. Alphabetic lists of titles and first lines. 64pp. 5³⁄₁₆ × 8¼. 26685-0 Pa. $1.00

SEVEN SCIENCE FICTION NOVELS, H. G. Wells. The standard collection of the great novels. Complete, unabridged. First Men in the Moon, Island of Dr. Moreau, War of the Worlds, Food of the Gods, Invisible Man, Time Machine, In the Days of the Comet. Total of 1,015pp. 5⅜ × 8½. (USO) 20264-X Clothbd. $29.95

AMULETS AND SUPERSTITIONS, E. A. Wallis Budge. Comprehensive discourse on origin, powers of amulets in many ancient cultures: Arab, Persian, Babylonian, Assyrian, Egyptian, Gnostic, Hebrew, Phoenician, Syriac, etc. Covers cross, swastika, crucifix, seals, rings, stones, etc. 584pp. 5⅜ × 8½. 23573-4 Pa. $12.95

RUSSIAN STORIES/PYCCKNE PACCKA3bl: A Dual-Language Book, edited by Gleb Struve. Twelve tales by such masters as Chekhov, Tolstoy, Dostoevsky, Pushkin, others. Excellent word-for-word English translations on facing pages, plus teaching and study aids, Russian/English vocabulary, biographical/critical introductions, more. 416pp. 5⅜ × 8½. 26244-8 Pa. $8.95

PHILADELPHIA THEN AND NOW: 60 Sites Photographed in the Past and Present, Kenneth Finkel and Susan Oyama. Rare photographs of City Hall, Logan Square, Independence Hall, Betsy Ross House, other landmarks juxtaposed with contemporary views. Captures changing face of historic city. Introduction. Captions. 128pp. 8¼ × 11. 25790-8 Pa. $9.95

AIA ARCHITECTURAL GUIDE TO NASSAU AND SUFFOLK COUNTIES, LONG ISLAND, The American Institute of Architects, Long Island Chapter, and the Society for the Preservation of Long Island Antiquities. Comprehensive, well-researched and generously illustrated volume brings to life over three centuries of Long Island's great architectural heritage. More than 240 photographs with authoritative, extensively detailed captions. 176pp. 8¼ × 11. 26946-9 Pa. $14.95

NORTH AMERICAN INDIAN LIFE: Customs and Traditions of 23 Tribes, Elsie Clews Parsons (ed.). 27 fictionalized essays by noted anthropologists examine religion, customs, government, additional facets of life among the Winnebago, Crow, Zuni, Eskimo, other tribes. 480pp. 6⅛ × 9¼. 27377-6 Pa. $10.95

FRANK LLOYD WRIGHT'S HOLLYHOCK HOUSE, Donald Hoffmann. Lavishly illustrated, carefully documented study of one of Wright's most controversial residential designs. Over 120 photographs, floor plans, elevations, etc. Detailed perceptive text by noted Wright scholar. Index. 128pp. 9¼ × 10¾.
27133-1 Pa. $11.95

THE MALE AND FEMALE FIGURE IN MOTION: 60 Classic Photographic Sequences, Eadweard Muybridge. 60 true-action photographs of men and women walking, running, climbing, bending, turning, etc., reproduced from rare 19th-century masterpiece. vi + 121pp. 9 × 12. 24745-7 Pa. $10.95

1001 QUESTIONS ANSWERED ABOUT THE SEASHORE, N. J. Berrill and Jacquelyn Berrill. Queries answered about dolphins, sea snails, sponges, starfish, fishes, shore birds, many others. Covers appearance, breeding, growth, feeding, much more. 305pp. 5¼ × 8¼. 23366-9 Pa. $7.95

GUIDE TO OWL WATCHING IN NORTH AMERICA, Donald S. Heintzelman. Superb guide offers complete data and descriptions of 19 species: barn owl, screech owl, snowy owl, many more. Expert coverage of owl-watching equipment, conservation, migrations and invasions, etc. Guide to observing sites. 84 illustrations. xiii + 193pp. 5⅜ × 8½. 27344-X Pa. $8.95

MEDICINAL AND OTHER USES OF NORTH AMERICAN PLANTS: A Historical Survey with Special Reference to the Eastern Indian Tribes, Charlotte Erichsen-Brown. Chronological historical citations document 500 years of usage of plants, trees, shrubs native to eastern Canada, northeastern U.S. Also complete identifying information. 343 illustrations. 544pp. 6½ × 9¼. 25951-X Pa. $12.95

STORYBOOK MAZES, Dave Phillips. 23 stories and mazes on two-page spreads: Wizard of Oz, Treasure Island, Robin Hood, etc. Solutions. 64pp. 8¼ × 11.
23628-5 Pa. $2.95

NEGRO FOLK MUSIC, U.S.A., Harold Courlander. Noted folklorist's scholarly yet readable analysis of rich and varied musical tradition. Includes authentic versions of over 40 folk songs. Valuable bibliography and discography. xi + 324pp. 5⅜ × 8½. 27350-4 Pa. $7.95

MOVIE-STAR PORTRAITS OF THE FORTIES, John Kobal (ed.). 163 glamor, studio photos of 106 stars of the 1940s: Rita Hayworth, Ava Gardner, Marlon Brando, Clark Gable, many more. 176pp. 8⅜ × 11¼. 23546-7 Pa. $11.95

BENCHLEY LOST AND FOUND, Robert Benchley. Finest humor from early 30s, about pet peeves, child psychologists, post office and others. Mostly unavailable elsewhere. 73 illustrations by Peter Arno and others. 183pp. 5⅜ × 8½.
22410-4 Pa. $5.95

YEKL and THE IMPORTED BRIDEGROOM AND OTHER STORIES OF YIDDISH NEW YORK, Abraham Cahan. Film Hester Street based on Yekl (1896). Novel, other stories among first about Jewish immigrants on N.Y.'s East Side. 240pp. 5⅜ × 8½. 22427-9 Pa. $6.95

SELECTED POEMS, Walt Whitman. Generous sampling from *Leaves of Grass*. Twenty-four poems include "I Hear America Singing," "Song of the Open Road," "I Sing the Body Electric," "When Lilacs Last in the Dooryard Bloom'd," "O Captain! My Captain!"—all reprinted from an authoritative edition. Lists of titles and first lines. 128pp. 5³⁄₁₆ × 8¼. 26878-0 Pa. $1.00

THE BEST TALES OF HOFFMANN, E. T. A. Hoffmann. 10 of Hoffmann's most important stories: "Nutcracker and the King of Mice," "The Golden Flowerpot," etc. 458pp. 5⅜ × 8½. 21793-0 Pa. $8.95

FROM FETISH TO GOD IN ANCIENT EGYPT, E. A. Wallis Budge. Rich detailed survey of Egyptian conception of "God" and gods, magic, cult of animals, Osiris, more. Also, superb English translations of hymns and legends. 240 illustrations. 545pp. 5⅜ × 8½. 25803-3 Pa. $11.95

FRENCH STORIES/CONTES FRANÇAIS: A Dual-Language Book, Wallace Fowlie. Ten stories by French masters, Voltaire to Camus: "Micromegas" by Voltaire; "The Atheist's Mass" by Balzac; "Minuet" by de Maupassant; "The Guest" by Camus, six more. Excellent English translations on facing pages. Also French-English vocabulary list, exercises, more. 352pp. 5⅜ × 8½. 26443-2 Pa. $8.95

CHICAGO AT THE TURN OF THE CENTURY IN PHOTOGRAPHS: 122 Historic Views from the Collections of the Chicago Historical Society, Larry A. Viskochil. Rare large-format prints offer detailed views of City Hall, State Street, the Loop, Hull House, Union Station, many other landmarks, circa 1904–1913. Introduction. Captions. Maps. 144pp. 9⅜ × 12¼. 24656-6 Pa. $12.95

OLD BROOKLYN IN EARLY PHOTOGRAPHS, 1865–1929, William Lee Younger. Luna Park, Gravesend race track, construction of Grand Army Plaza, moving of Hotel Brighton, etc. 157 previously unpublished photographs. 165pp. 8⅞ × 11¾. 23587-4 Pa. $13.95

THE MYTHS OF THE NORTH AMERICAN INDIANS, Lewis Spence. Rich anthology of the myths and legends of the Algonquins, Iroquois, Pawnees and Sioux, prefaced by an extensive historical and ethnological commentary. 36 illustrations. 480pp. 5⅜ × 8½. 25967-6 Pa. $8.95

AN ENCYCLOPEDIA OF BATTLES: Accounts of Over 1,560 Battles from 1479 B.C. to the Present, David Eggenberger. Essential details of every major battle in recorded history from the first battle of Megiddo in 1479 B.C. to Grenada in 1984. List of Battle Maps. New Appendix covering the years 1967–1984. Index. 99 illustrations. 544pp. 6½ × 9¼. 24913-1 Pa. $14.95

SAILING ALONE AROUND THE WORLD, Captain Joshua Slocum. First man to sail around the world, alone, in small boat. One of great feats of seamanship told in delightful manner. 67 illustrations. 294pp. 5⅜ × 8½. 20326-3 Pa. $5.95

ANARCHISM AND OTHER ESSAYS, Emma Goldman. Powerful, penetrating, prophetic essays on direct action, role of minorities, prison reform, puritan hypocrisy, violence, etc. 271pp. 5⅜ × 8½. 22484-8 Pa. $5.95

MYTHS OF THE HINDUS AND BUDDHISTS, Ananda K. Coomaraswamy and Sister Nivedita. Great stories of the epics; deeds of Krishna, Shiva, taken from puranas, Vedas, folk tales; etc. 32 illustrations. 400pp. 5⅜ × 8½. 21759-0 Pa. $9.95

BEYOND PSYCHOLOGY, Otto Rank. Fear of death, desire of immortality, nature of sexuality, social organization, creativity, according to Rankian system. 291pp. 5⅜ × 8½. 20485-5 Pa. $8.95

A THEOLOGICO-POLITICAL TREATISE, Benedict Spinoza. Also contains unfinished Political Treatise. Great classic on religious liberty, theory of government on common consent. R. Elwes translation. Total of 421pp. 5⅜ × 8½. 20249-6 Pa. $8.95

MY BONDAGE AND MY FREEDOM, Frederick Douglass. Born a slave, Douglass became outspoken force in antislavery movement. The best of Douglass' autobiographies. Graphic description of slave life. 464pp. 5⅜ × 8½. 22457-0 Pa. $8.95

FOLLOWING THE EQUATOR: A Journey Around the World, Mark Twain. Fascinating humorous account of 1897 voyage to Hawaii, Australia, India, New Zealand, etc. Ironic, bemused reports on peoples, customs, climate, flora and fauna, politics, much more. 197 illustrations. 720pp. 5⅜ × 8½. 26113-1 Pa. $15.95

THE PEOPLE CALLED SHAKERS, Edward D. Andrews. Definitive study of Shakers: origins, beliefs, practices, dances, social organization, furniture and crafts, etc. 33 illustrations. 351pp. 5⅜ × 8½. 21081-2 Pa. $8.95

THE MYTHS OF GREECE AND ROME, H. A. Guerber. A classic of mythology, generously illustrated, long prized for its simple, graphic, accurate retelling of the principal myths of Greece and Rome, and for its commentary on their origins and significance. With 64 illustrations by Michelangelo, Raphael, Titian, Rubens, Canova, Bernini and others. 480pp. 5⅜ × 8½. 27584-1 Pa. $9.95

PSYCHOLOGY OF MUSIC, Carl E. Seashore. Classic work discusses music as a medium from psychological viewpoint. Clear treatment of physical acoustics, auditory apparatus, sound perception, development of musical skills, nature of musical feeling, host of other topics. 88 figures. 408pp. 5⅜ × 8½. 21851-1 Pa. $9.95

THE PHILOSOPHY OF HISTORY, Georg W. Hegel. Great classic of Western thought develops concept that history is not chance but rational process, the evolution of freedom. 457pp. 5⅜ × 8½. 20112-0 Pa. $9.95

THE BOOK OF TEA, Kakuzo Okakura. Minor classic of the Orient: entertaining, charming explanation, interpretation of traditional Japanese culture in terms of tea ceremony. 94pp. 5⅜ × 8½. 20070-1 Pa. $3.95

LIFE IN ANCIENT EGYPT, Adolf Erman. Fullest, most thorough, detailed older account with much not in more recent books, domestic life, religion, magic, medicine, commerce, much more. Many illustrations reproduce tomb paintings, carvings, hieroglyphs, etc. 597pp. 5⅜ × 8½. 22632-8 Pa. $10.95

SUNDIALS, Their Theory and Construction, Albert Waugh. Far and away the best, most thorough coverage of ideas, mathematics concerned, types, construction, adjusting anywhere. Simple, nontechnical treatment allows even children to build several of these dials. Over 100 illustrations. 230pp. 5⅜ × 8½. 22947-5 Pa. $7.95

DYNAMICS OF FLUIDS IN POROUS MEDIA, Jacob Bear. For advanced students of ground water hydrology, soil mechanics and physics, drainage and irrigation engineering, and more. 335 illustrations. Exercises, with answers. 784pp. 6⅛ × 9¼. 65675-6 Pa. $19.95

SONGS OF EXPERIENCE: Facsimile Reproduction with 26 Plates in Full Color, William Blake. 26 full-color plates from a rare 1826 edition. Includes "The Tyger," "London," "Holy Thursday," and other poems. Printed text of poems. 48pp. 5¼ × 7. 24636-1 Pa. $4.95

OLD-TIME VIGNETTES IN FULL COLOR, Carol Belanger Grafton (ed.). Over 390 charming, often sentimental illustrations, selected from archives of Victorian graphics—pretty women posing, children playing, food, flowers, kittens and puppies, smiling cherubs, birds and butterflies, much more. All copyright-free. 48pp. 9¼ × 12¼. 27269-9 Pa. $5.95

PERSPECTIVE FOR ARTISTS, Rex Vicat Cole. Depth, perspective of sky and sea, shadows, much more, not usually covered. 391 diagrams, 81 reproductions of drawings and paintings. 279pp. 5⅜ × 8½. 22487-2 Pa. $6.95

DRAWING THE LIVING FIGURE, Joseph Sheppard. Innovative approach to artistic anatomy focuses on specifics of surface anatomy, rather than muscles and bones. Over 170 drawings of live models in front, back and side views, and in widely varying poses. Accompanying diagrams. 177 illustrations. Introduction. Index. 144pp. 8⅜ × 11¼. 26723-7 Pa. $8.95

GOTHIC AND OLD ENGLISH ALPHABETS: 100 Complete Fonts, Dan X. Solo. Add power, elegance to posters, signs, other graphics with 100 stunning copyright-free alphabets: Blackstone, Dolbey, Germania, 97 more—including many lower-case, numerals, punctuation marks. 104pp. 8⅛ × 11. 24695-7 Pa. $8.95

HOW TO DO BEADWORK, Mary White. Fundamental book on craft from simple projects to five-bead chains and woven works. 106 illustrations. 142pp. 5⅜ × 8. 20697-1 Pa. $4.95

THE BOOK OF WOOD CARVING, Charles Marshall Sayers. Finest book for beginners discusses fundamentals and offers 34 designs. "Absolutely first rate . . . well thought out and well executed."—E. J. Tangerman. 118pp. 7¾ × 10⅝. 23654-4 Pa. $5.95

ILLUSTRATED CATALOG OF CIVIL WAR MILITARY GOODS: Union Army Weapons, Insignia, Uniform Accessories, and Other Equipment, Schuyler, Hartley, and Graham. Rare, profusely illustrated 1846 catalog includes Union Army uniform and dress regulations, arms and ammunition, coats, insignia, flags, swords, rifles, etc. 226 illustrations. 160pp. 9 × 12. 24939-5 Pa. $10.95

WOMEN'S FASHIONS OF THE EARLY 1900s: An Unabridged Republication of "New York Fashions, 1909," National Cloak & Suit Co. Rare catalog of mail-order fashions documents women's and children's clothing styles shortly after the turn of the century. Captions offer full descriptions, prices. Invaluable resource for fashion, costume historians. Approximately 725 illustrations. 128pp. 8⅜ × 11¼. 27276-1 Pa. $11.95

THE 1912 AND 1915 GUSTAV STICKLEY FURNITURE CATALOGS, Gustav Stickley. With over 200 detailed illustrations and descriptions, these two catalogs are essential reading and reference materials and identification guides for Stickley furniture. Captions cite materials, dimensions and prices. 112pp. 6½ × 9¼. 26676-1 Pa. $9.95

EARLY AMERICAN LOCOMOTIVES, John H. White, Jr. Finest locomotive engravings from early 19th century: historical (1804–74), main-line (after 1870), special, foreign, etc. 147 plates. 142pp. 11⅜ × 8¼. 22772-3 Pa. $10.95

THE TALL SHIPS OF TODAY IN PHOTOGRAPHS, Frank O. Braynard. Lavishly illustrated tribute to nearly 100 majestic contemporary sailing vessels: Amerigo Vespucci, Clearwater, Constitution, Eagle, Mayflower, Sea Cloud, Victory, many more. Authoritative captions provide statistics, background on each ship. 190 black-and-white photographs and illustrations. Introduction. 128pp. 8⅞ × 11¾. 27163-3 Pa. $13.95

EARLY NINETEENTH-CENTURY CRAFTS AND TRADES, Peter Stockham (ed.). Extremely rare 1807 volume describes to youngsters the crafts and trades of the day: brickmaker, weaver, dressmaker, bookbinder, ropemaker, saddler, many more. Quaint prose, charming illustrations for each craft. 20 black-and-white line illustrations. 192pp. 4⅝ × 6. 27293-1 Pa. $4.95

VICTORIAN FASHIONS AND COSTUMES FROM HARPER'S BAZAR, 1867–1898, Stella Blum (ed.). Day costumes, evening wear, sports clothes, shoes, hats, other accessories in over 1,000 detailed engravings. 320pp. 9⅜ × 12¼.
22990-4 Pa. $13.95

GUSTAV STICKLEY, THE CRAFTSMAN, Mary Ann Smith. Superb study surveys broad scope of Stickley's achievement, especially in architecture. Design philosophy, rise and fall of the Craftsman empire, descriptions and floor plans for many Craftsman houses, more. 86 black-and-white halftones. 31 line illustrations. Introduction. 208pp. 6½ × 9¼. 27210-9 Pa. $9.95

THE LONG ISLAND RAIL ROAD IN EARLY PHOTOGRAPHS, Ron Ziel. Over 220 rare photos, informative text document origin (1844) and development of rail service on Long Island. Vintage views of early trains, locomotives, stations, passengers, crews, much more. Captions. 8⅞ × 11¾. 26301-0 Pa. $13.95

THE BOOK OF OLD SHIPS: From Egyptian Galleys to Clipper Ships, Henry B. Culver. Superb, authoritative history of sailing vessels, with 80 magnificent line illustrations. Galley, bark, caravel, longship, whaler, many more. Detailed, informative text on each vessel by noted naval historian. Introduction. 256pp. 5⅜ × 8½. 27332-6 Pa. $6.95

TEN BOOKS ON ARCHITECTURE, Vitruvius. The most important book ever written on architecture. Early Roman aesthetics, technology, classical orders, site selection, all other aspects. Morgan translation. 331pp. 5⅜ × 8½. 20645-9 Pa. $8.95

THE HUMAN FIGURE IN MOTION, Eadweard Muybridge. More than 4,500 stopped-action photos, in action series, showing undraped men, women, children jumping, lying down, throwing, sitting, wrestling, carrying, etc. 390pp. 7⅞ × 10⅝. 20204-6 Clothbd. $24.95

TREES OF THE EASTERN AND CENTRAL UNITED STATES AND CANADA, William M. Harlow. Best one-volume guide to 140 trees. Full descriptions, woodlore, range, etc. Over 600 illustrations. Handy size. 288pp. 4½ × 6⅜.
20395-6 Pa. $5.95

SONGS OF WESTERN BIRDS, Dr. Donald J. Borror. Complete song and call repertoire of 60 western species, including flycatchers, juncoes, cactus wrens, many more—includes fully illustrated booklet. Cassette and manual 99913-0 $8.95

GROWING AND USING HERBS AND SPICES, Milo Miloradovich. Versatile handbook provides all the information needed for cultivation and use of all the herbs and spices available in North America. 4 illustrations. Index. Glossary. 236pp. 5⅜ × 8½. 25058-X Pa. $6.95

BIG BOOK OF MAZES AND LABYRINTHS, Walter Shepherd. 50 mazes and labyrinths in all—classical, solid, ripple, and more—in one great volume. Perfect inexpensive puzzler for clever youngsters. Full solutions. 112pp. 8⅛ × 11.
22951-3 Pa. $4.95

PIANO TUNING, J. Cree Fischer. Clearest, best book for beginner, amateur. Simple repairs, raising dropped notes, tuning by easy method of flattened fifths. No previous skills needed. 4 illustrations. 201pp. 5⅜ × 8½. 23267-0 Pa. $5.95

A SOURCE BOOK IN THEATRICAL HISTORY, A. M. Nagler. Contemporary observers on acting, directing, make-up, costuming, stage props, machinery, scene design, from Ancient Greece to Chekhov. 611pp. 5⅜ × 8½. 20515-0 Pa. $11.95

THE COMPLETE NONSENSE OF EDWARD LEAR, Edward Lear. All nonsense limericks, zany alphabets, Owl and Pussycat, songs, nonsense botany, etc., illustrated by Lear. Total of 320pp. 5⅜ × 8½. (USO) 20167-8 Pa. $6.95

VICTORIAN PARLOUR POETRY: An Annotated Anthology, Michael R. Turner. 117 gems by Longfellow, Tennyson, Browning, many lesser-known poets. "The Village Blacksmith," "Curfew Must Not Ring Tonight," "Only a Baby Small," dozens more, often difficult to find elsewhere. Index of poets, titles, first lines. xxiii + 325pp. 5⅜ × 8¼. 27044-0 Pa. $8.95

DUBLINERS, James Joyce. Fifteen stories offer vivid, tightly focused observations of the lives of Dublin's poorer classes. At least one, "The Dead," is considered a masterpiece. Reprinted complete and unabridged from standard edition. 160pp. 5³⁄₁₆ × 8¼. 26870-5 Pa. $1.00

THE HAUNTED MONASTERY and THE CHINESE MAZE MURDERS, Robert van Gulik. Two full novels by van Gulik, set in 7th-century China, continue adventures of Judge Dee and his companions. An evil Taoist monastery, seemingly supernatural events; overgrown topiary maze hides strange crimes. 27 illustrations. 328pp. 5⅜ × 8½. 23502-5 Pa. $7.95

THE BOOK OF THE SACRED MAGIC OF ABRAMELIN THE MAGE, translated by S. MacGregor Mathers. Medieval manuscript of ceremonial magic. Basic document in Aleister Crowley, Golden Dawn groups. 268pp. 5⅜ × 8½. 23211-5 Pa. $8.95

NEW RUSSIAN-ENGLISH AND ENGLISH-RUSSIAN DICTIONARY, M. A. O'Brien. This is a remarkably handy Russian dictionary, containing a surprising amount of information, including over 70,000 entries. 366pp. 4½ × 6⅛. 20208-9 Pa. $9.95

HISTORIC HOMES OF THE AMERICAN PRESIDENTS, Second, Revised Edition, Irvin Haas. A traveler's guide to American Presidential homes, most open to the public, depicting and describing homes occupied by every American President from George Washington to George Bush. With visiting hours, admission charges, travel routes. 175 photographs. Index. 160pp. 8¼ × 11. 26751-2 Pa. $10.95

NEW YORK IN THE FORTIES, Andreas Feininger. 162 brilliant photographs by the well-known photographer, formerly with *Life* magazine. Commuters, shoppers, Times Square at night, much else from city at its peak. Captions by John von Hartz. 181pp. 9¼ × 10¾. 23585-8 Pa. $12.95

INDIAN SIGN LANGUAGE, William Tomkins. Over 525 signs developed by Sioux and other tribes. Written instructions and diagrams. Also 290 pictographs. 111pp. 6⅛ × 9¼. 22029-X Pa. $3.50

ANATOMY: A Complete Guide for Artists, Joseph Sheppard. A master of figure drawing shows artists how to render human anatomy convincingly. Over 460 illustrations. 224pp. 8⅜ × 11¼. 27279-6 Pa. $10.95

MEDIEVAL CALLIGRAPHY: Its History and Technique, Marc Drogin. Spirited history, comprehensive instruction manual covers 13 styles (ca. 4th century thru 15th). Excellent photographs; directions for duplicating medieval techniques with modern tools. 224pp. 8⅜ × 11¼. 26142-5 Pa. $11.95

DRIED FLOWERS: How to Prepare Them, Sarah Whitlock and Martha Rankin. Complete instructions on how to use silica gel, meal and borax, perlite aggregate, sand and borax, glycerine and water to create attractive permanent flower arrangements. 12 illustrations. 32pp. 5⅜ × 8½. 21802-3 Pa. $1.00

EASY-TO-MAKE BIRD FEEDERS FOR WOODWORKERS, Scott D. Campbell. Detailed, simple-to-use guide for designing, constructing, caring for and using feeders. Text, illustrations for 12 classic and contemporary designs. 96pp. 5⅜ × 8½. 25847-5 Pa. $2.95

OLD-TIME CRAFTS AND TRADES, Peter Stockham. An 1807 book created to teach children about crafts and trades open to them as future careers. It describes in detailed, nontechnical terms 24 different occupations, among them coachmaker, gardener, hairdresser, lacemaker, shoemaker, wheelwright, copper-plate printer, milliner, trunkmaker, merchant and brewer. Finely detailed engravings illustrate each occupation. 192pp. 4⅝ × 6. 27398-9 Pa. $4.95

THE HISTORY OF UNDERCLOTHES, C. Willett Cunnington and Phyllis Cunnington. Fascinating, well-documented survey covering six centuries of English undergarments, enhanced with over 100 illustrations: 12th-century laced-up bodice, footed long drawers (1795), 19th-century bustles, 19th-century corsets for men, Victorian "bust improvers," much more. 272pp. 5⅜ × 8¼. 27124-2 Pa. $9.95

ARTS AND CRAFTS FURNITURE: The Complete Brooks Catalog of 1912, Brooks Manufacturing Co. Photos and detailed descriptions of more than 150 now very collectible furniture designs from the Arts and Crafts movement depict davenports, settees, buffets, desks, tables, chairs, bedsteads, dressers and more, all built of solid, quarter-sawed oak. Invaluable for students and enthusiasts of antiques, Americana and the decorative arts. 80pp. 6½ × 9¼. 27471-3 Pa. $7.95

HOW WE INVENTED THE AIRPLANE: An Illustrated History, Orville Wright. Fascinating firsthand account covers early experiments, construction of planes and motors, first flights, much more. Introduction and commentary by Fred C. Kelly. 76 photographs. 96pp. 8¼ × 11. 25662-6 Pa. $8.95

THE ARTS OF THE SAILOR: Knotting, Splicing and Ropework, Hervey Garrett Smith. Indispensable shipboard reference covers tools, basic knots and useful hitches; handsewing and canvas work, more. Over 100 illustrations. Delightful reading for sea lovers. 256pp. 5⅜ × 8½. 26440-8 Pa. $7.95

FRANK LLOYD WRIGHT'S FALLINGWATER: The House and Its History, Second, Revised Edition, Donald Hoffmann. A total revision—both in text and illustrations—of the standard document on Fallingwater, the boldest, most personal architectural statement of Wright's mature years, updated with valuable new material from the recently opened Frank Lloyd Wright Archives. "Fascinating"—*The New York Times*. 116 illustrations. 128pp. 9¼ × 10¾. 27430-6 Pa. $10.95

PHOTOGRAPHIC SKETCHBOOK OF THE CIVIL WAR, Alexander Gardner. 100 photos taken on field during the Civil War. Famous shots of Manassas, Harper's Ferry, Lincoln, Richmond, slave pens, etc. 244pp. 10⅝ × 8¼.
22731-6 Pa. $9.95

FIVE ACRES AND INDEPENDENCE, Maurice G. Kains. Great back-to-the-land classic explains basics of self-sufficient farming. The one book to get. 95 illustrations. 397pp. 5⅜ × 8½. 20974-1 Pa. $7.95

SONGS OF EASTERN BIRDS, Dr. Donald J. Borror. Songs and calls of 60 species most common to eastern U.S.: warblers, woodpeckers, flycatchers, thrushes, larks, many more in high-quality recording. Cassette and manual 99912-2 $8.95

A MODERN HERBAL, Margaret Grieve. Much the fullest, most exact, most useful compilation of herbal material. Gigantic alphabetical encyclopedia, from aconite to zedoary, gives botanical information, medical properties, folklore, economic uses, much else. Indispensable to serious reader. 161 illustrations. 888pp. 6½ × 9¼. 2-vol. set. (USO) Vol. I: 22798-7 Pa. $9.95
Vol. II: 22799-5 Pa. $9.95

HIDDEN TREASURE MAZE BOOK, Dave Phillips. Solve 34 challenging mazes accompanied by heroic tales of adventure. Evil dragons, people-eating plants, bloodthirsty giants, many more dangerous adversaries lurk at every twist and turn. 34 mazes, stories, solutions. 48pp. 8¼ × 11. 24566-7 Pa. $2.95

LETTERS OF W. A. MOZART, Wolfgang A. Mozart. Remarkable letters show bawdy wit, humor, imagination, musical insights, contemporary musical world; includes some letters from Leopold Mozart. 276pp. 5⅜ × 8½. 22859-2 Pa. $7.95

BASIC PRINCIPLES OF CLASSICAL BALLET, Agrippina Vaganova. Great Russian theoretician, teacher explains methods for teaching classical ballet. 118 illustrations. 175pp. 5⅜ × 8½. 22036-2 Pa. $4.95

THE JUMPING FROG, Mark Twain. Revenge edition. The original story of The Celebrated Jumping Frog of Calaveras County, a hapless French translation, and Twain's hilarious "retranslation" from the French. 12 illustrations. 66pp. 5⅜ × 8½. 22686-7 Pa. $3.95

BEST REMEMBERED POEMS, Martin Gardner (ed.). The 126 poems in this superb collection of 19th- and 20th-century British and American verse range from Shelley's "To a Skylark" to the impassioned "Renascence" of Edna St. Vincent Millay and to Edward Lear's whimsical "The Owl and the Pussycat." 224pp. 5⅜ × 8½. 27165-X Pa. $4.95

COMPLETE SONNETS, William Shakespeare. Over 150 exquisite poems deal with love, friendship, the tyranny of time, beauty's evanescence, death and other themes in language of remarkable power, precision and beauty. Glossary of archaic terms. 80pp. 5³⁄₁₆ × 8¼. 26686-9 Pa. $1.00

BODIES IN A BOOKSHOP, R. T. Campbell. Challenging mystery of blackmail and murder with ingenious plot and superbly drawn characters. In the best tradition of British suspense fiction. 192pp. 5⅜ × 8½. 24720-1 Pa. $5.95

THE WIT AND HUMOR OF OSCAR WILDE, Alvin Redman (ed.). More than 1,000 ripostes, paradoxes, wisecracks: Work is the curse of the drinking classes; I can resist everything except temptation; etc. 258pp. 5⅜ × 8½.   20602-5 Pa. $5.95

SHAKESPEARE LEXICON AND QUOTATION DICTIONARY, Alexander Schmidt. Full definitions, locations, shades of meaning in every word in plays and poems. More than 50,000 exact quotations. 1,485pp. 6½ × 9¼. 2-vol. set.
Vol. I: 22726-X Pa. $16.95
Vol. 2: 22727-8 Pa. $15.95

SELECTED POEMS, Emily Dickinson. Over 100 best-known, best-loved poems by one of America's foremost poets, reprinted from authoritative early editions. No comparable edition at this price. Index of first lines. 64pp. 5³/₁₆ × 8¼.
26466-1 Pa. $1.00

CELEBRATED CASES OF JUDGE DEE (DEE GOONG AN), translated by Robert van Gulik. Authentic 18th-century Chinese detective novel; Dee and associates solve three interlocked cases. Led to van Gulik's own stories with same characters. Extensive introduction. 9 illustrations. 237pp. 5⅜ × 8½.
23337-5 Pa. $6.95

THE MALLEUS MALEFICARUM OF KRAMER AND SPRENGER, translated by Montague Summers. Full text of most important witchhunter's "bible," used by both Catholics and Protestants. 278pp. 6⅝ × 10.   22802-9 Pa. $11.95

SPANISH STORIES/CUENTOS ESPAÑOLES: A Dual-Language Book, Angel Flores (ed.). Unique format offers 13 great stories in Spanish by Cervantes, Borges, others. Faithful English translations on facing pages. 352pp. 5⅜ × 8½.
25399-6 Pa. $8.95

THE CHICAGO WORLD'S FAIR OF 1893: A Photographic Record, Stanley Appelbaum (ed.). 128 rare photos show 200 buildings, Beaux-Arts architecture, Midway, original Ferris Wheel, Edison's kinetoscope, more. Architectural emphasis; full text. 116pp. 8¼ × 11.   23990-X Pa. $9.95

OLD QUEENS, N.Y., IN EARLY PHOTOGRAPHS, Vincent F. Seyfried and William Asadorian. Over 160 rare photographs of Maspeth, Jamaica, Jackson Heights, and other areas. Vintage views of DeWitt Clinton mansion, 1939 World's Fair and more. Captions. 192pp. 8⅞ × 11.   26358-4 Pa. $12.95

CAPTURED BY THE INDIANS: 15 Firsthand Accounts, 1750–1870, Frederick Drimmer. Astounding true historical accounts of grisly torture, bloody conflicts, relentless pursuits, miraculous escapes and more, by people who lived to tell the tale. 384pp. 5⅜ × 8½.   24901-8 Pa. $8.95

THE WORLD'S GREAT SPEECHES, Lewis Copeland and Lawrence W. Lamm (eds.). Vast collection of 278 speeches of Greeks to 1970. Powerful and effective models; unique look at history. 842pp. 5⅜ × 8½.   20468-5 Pa. $14.95

THE BOOK OF THE SWORD, Sir Richard F. Burton. Great Victorian scholar/adventurer's eloquent, erudite history of the "queen of weapons"—from prehistory to early Roman Empire. Evolution and development of early swords, variations (sabre, broadsword, cutlass, scimitar, etc.), much more. 336pp. 6⅛ × 9¼. 25434-8 Pa. $8.95

AUTOBIOGRAPHY: The Story of My Experiments with Truth, Mohandas K. Gandhi. Boyhood, legal studies, purification, the growth of the Satyagraha (nonviolent protest) movement. Critical, inspiring work of the man responsible for the freedom of India. 480pp. 5⅜ × 8½. (USO)   24593-4 Pa. $8.95

CELTIC MYTHS AND LEGENDS, T. W. Rolleston. Masterful retelling of Irish and Welsh stories and tales. Cuchulain, King Arthur, Deirdre, the Grail, many more. First paperback edition. 58 full-page illustrations. 512pp. 5⅜ × 8½.
26507-2 Pa. $9.95

THE PRINCIPLES OF PSYCHOLOGY, William James. Famous long course complete, unabridged. Stream of thought, time perception, memory, experimental methods; great work decades ahead of its time. 94 figures. 1,391pp. 5⅜ × 8½. 2-vol. set.
Vol. I: 20381-6 Pa. $12.95
Vol. II: 20382-4 Pa. $12.95

THE WORLD AS WILL AND REPRESENTATION, Arthur Schopenhauer. Definitive English translation of Schopenhauer's life work, correcting more than 1,000 errors, omissions in earlier translations. Translated by E. F. J. Payne. Total of 1,269pp. 5⅜ × 8½. 2-vol. set.   Vol. 1: 21761-2 Pa. $11.95
Vol. 2: 21762-0 Pa. $11.95

MAGIC AND MYSTERY IN TIBET, Madame Alexandra David-Neel. Experiences among lamas, magicians, sages, sorcerers, Bonpa wizards. A true psychic discovery. 32 illustrations. 321pp. 5⅜ × 8½. (USO)   22682-4 Pa. $8.95

THE EGYPTIAN BOOK OF THE DEAD, E. A. Wallis Budge. Complete reproduction of Ani's papyrus, finest ever found. Full hieroglyphic text, interlinear transliteration, word-for-word translation, smooth translation. 533pp. 6½ × 9¼.
21866-X Pa. $9.95

MATHEMATICS FOR THE NONMATHEMATICIAN, Morris Kline. Detailed, college-level treatment of mathematics in cultural and historical context, with numerous exercises. Recommended Reading Lists. Tables. Numerous figures. 641pp. 5⅜ × 8½.   24823-2 Pa. $11.95

THEORY OF WING SECTIONS: Including a Summary of Airfoil Data, Ira H. Abbott and A. E. von Doenhoff. Concise compilation of subsonic aerodynamic characteristics of NACA wing sections, plus description of theory. 350pp. of tables. 693pp. 5⅜ × 8½.   60586-8 Pa. $14.95

THE RIME OF THE ANCIENT MARINER, Gustave Doré, S. T. Coleridge. Doré's finest work; 34 plates capture moods, subtleties of poem. Flawless full-size reproductions printed on facing pages with authoritative text of poem. "Beautiful. Simply beautiful."—*Publisher's Weekly*. 77pp. 9¼ × 12.   22305-1 Pa. $6.95

NORTH AMERICAN INDIAN DESIGNS FOR ARTISTS AND CRAFTS-PEOPLE, Eva Wilson. Over 360 authentic copyright-free designs adapted from Navajo blankets, Hopi pottery, Sioux buffalo hides, more. Geometrics, symbolic figures, plant and animal motifs, etc. 128pp. 8⅜ × 11. (EUK)   25341-4 Pa. $7.95

SCULPTURE: Principles and Practice, Louis Slobodkin. Step-by-step approach to clay, plaster, metals, stone; classical and modern. 253 drawings, photos. 255pp. 8⅛ × 11.   22960-2 Pa. $10.95

THE INFLUENCE OF SEA POWER UPON HISTORY, 1660–1783, A. T. Mahan. Influential classic of naval history and tactics still used as text in war colleges. First paperback edition. 4 maps. 24 battle plans. 640pp. 5⅜ × 8½.
25509-3 Pa. $12.95

THE STORY OF THE TITANIC AS TOLD BY ITS SURVIVORS, Jack Winocour (ed.). What it was really like. Panic, despair, shocking inefficiency, and a little heroism. More thrilling than any fictional account. 26 illustrations. 320pp. 5⅜ × 8½.
20610-6 Pa. $8.95

FAIRY AND FOLK TALES OF THE IRISH PEASANTRY, William Butler Yeats (ed.). Treasury of 64 tales from the twilight world of Celtic myth and legend: "The Soul Cages," "The Kildare Pooka," "King O'Toole and his Goose," many more. Introduction and Notes by W. B. Yeats. 352pp. 5⅜ × 8½.
26941-8 Pa. $8.95

BUDDHIST MAHAYANA TEXTS, E. B. Cowell and Others (eds.). Superb, accurate translations of basic documents in Mahayana Buddhism, highly important in history of religions. The Buddha-karita of Asvaghosha, Larger Sukhavativyuha, more. 448pp. 5⅜ × 8½. ,
25552-2 Pa. $9.95

ONE TWO THREE . . . INFINITY: Facts and Speculations of Science, George Gamow. Great physicist's fascinating, readable overview of contemporary science: number theory, relativity, fourth dimension, entropy, genes, atomic structure, much more. 128 illustrations. Index. 352pp. 5⅜ × 8½.
25664-2 Pa. $8.95

ENGINEERING IN HISTORY, Richard Shelton Kirby, et al. Broad, nontechnical survey of history's major technological advances: birth of Greek science, industrial revolution, electricity and applied science, 20th-century automation, much more. 181 illustrations. ". . . excellent . . ."—Isis. Bibliography. vii + 530pp. 5⅜ × 8¼.
26412-2 Pa. $14.95

ᴧ ᵣₑₑₑs subject to change without notice.

Available at your book dealer or write for free catalog to Dept. GI, Dover Publications, Inc., 31 East 2nd St., Mineola, N.Y. 11501. Dover publishes more than 500 books each year on science, elementary and advanced mathematics, biology, music, art, literary history, social sciences and other areas.

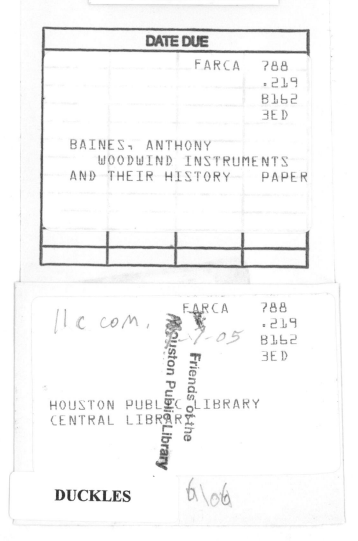